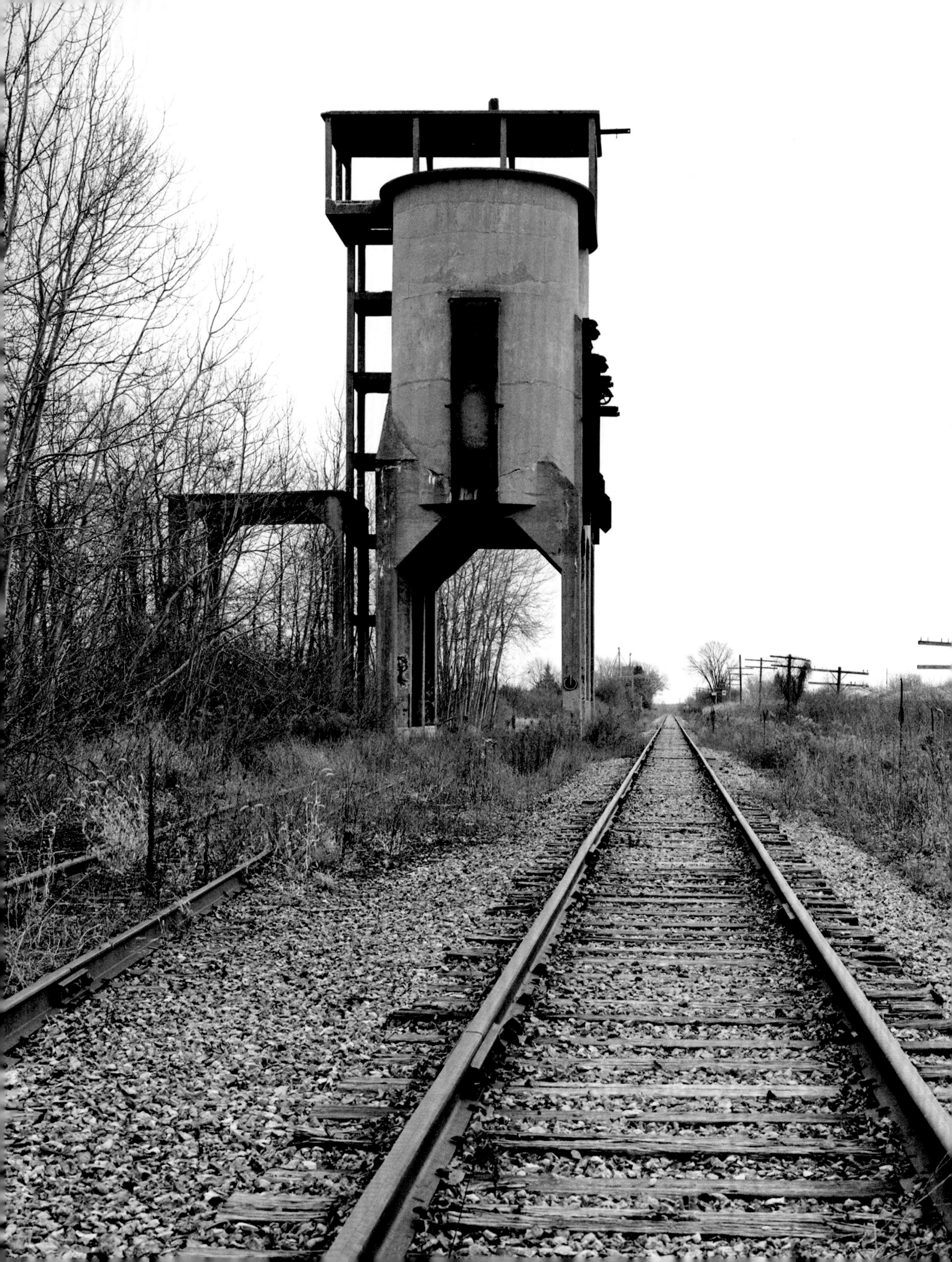

SILENT MONOLITHS
THE COALING TOWER PROJECT

PHOTOGRAPHS
BY JEFF BROUWS

FOREWORD
BY MARCELLA HACKBARDT

INTRODUCTION
BY JOHN P. HANKEY

The MIT Press
Cambridge, Massachusetts
London, England

Silent Monoliths
The Coaling Tower Project

The MIT Press would like to thank the anonymous peer reviewers who provided comments on drafts of this book. The generous work of academic experts is essential for establishing the authority and quality of our publications. We acknowledge with gratitude the contributions of these otherwise uncredited readers.

This book was set in Garamond Premier Pro and Trade Gothic by Jeff Brouws

Design and Production: Jeff Brouws

Senior Editor: Victoria Hindley,
Art, Architecture, and Design,
The MIT Press

Pre-press: Jared Stevens /
Prepare. Print. Produce.

Map: Bob Bull

Copy-editing and proofreading:
Kathi Kube and Oren Helbok

Print broker: Jeff Spoelker,
Martin Book Management, LLC

Printed and bound in China
by Reliance

Library of Congress Control Number:
2025938924

ISBN: 978-0-262-05175-0

Front Cover: Gilman, Illinois

Back Cover:
Clyman Junction, Wisconsin (left)
Great Bend, Kansas (right)

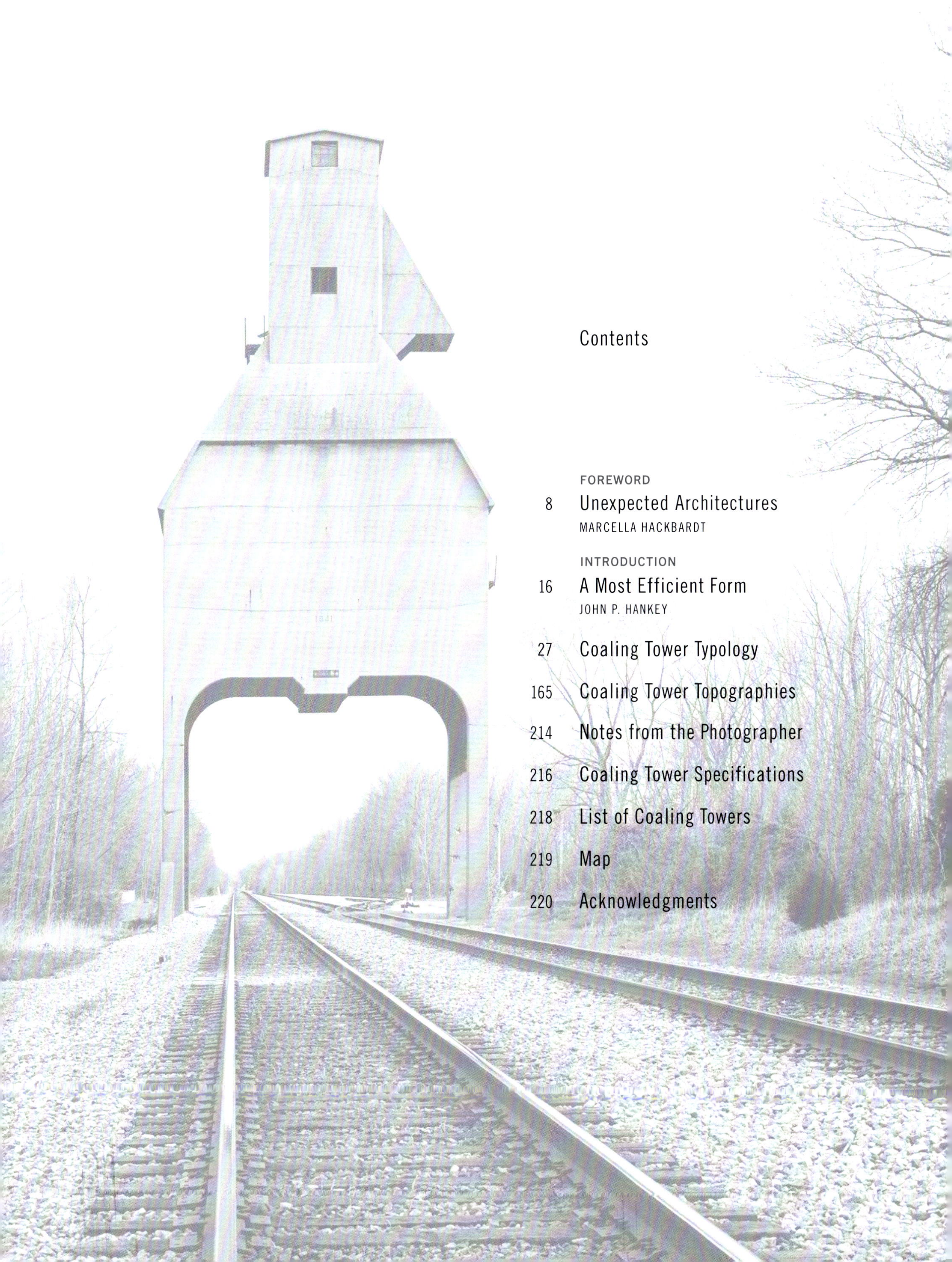

Contents

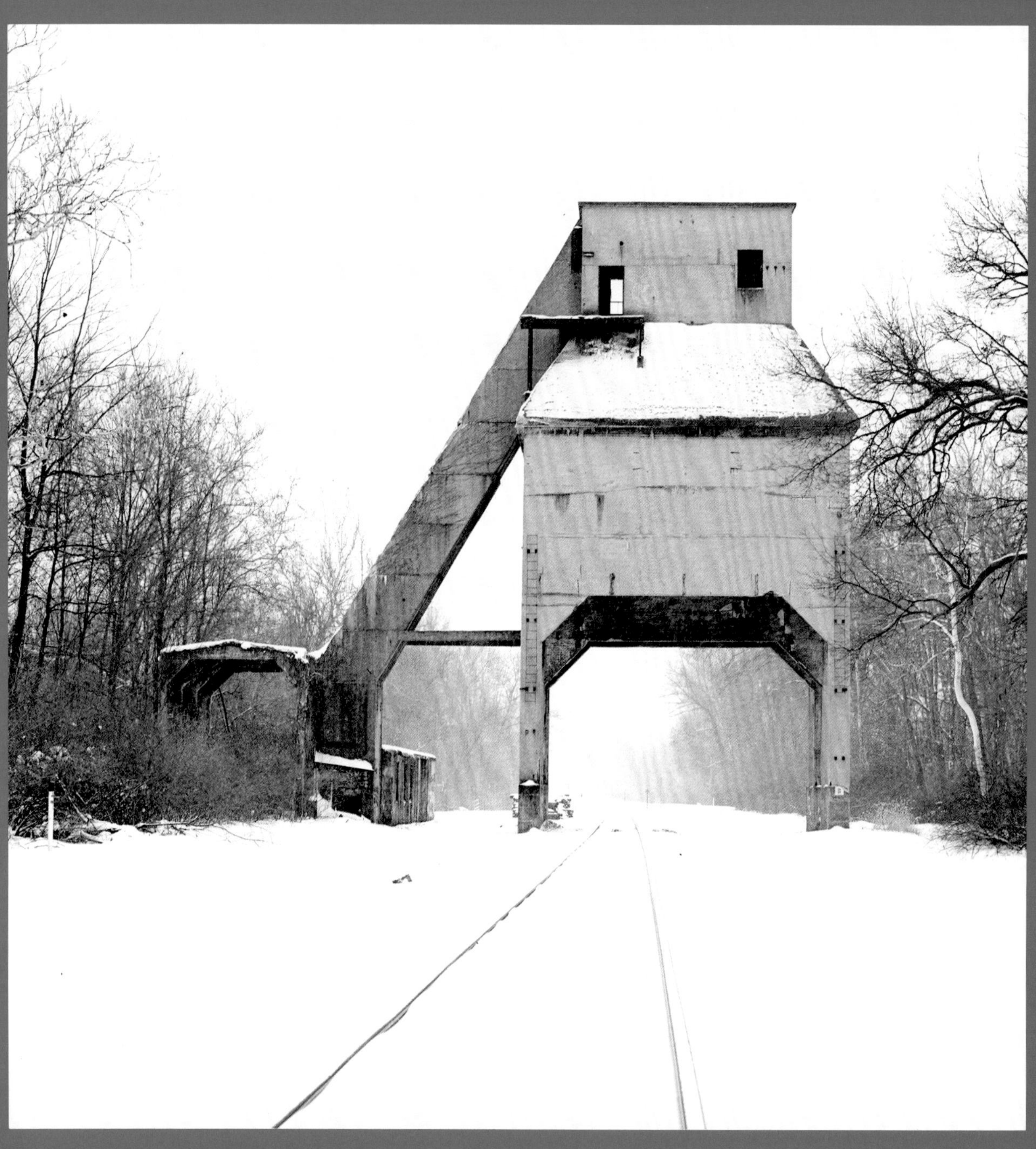

For Ed Delvers

Dear friend, road buddy extraordinaire, gentlest of human beings, MIT graduate, Class of 1972. He would have marvelled in the presence of the coaling towers, and been thrilled to partcipate in the adventure of seeking them out.

Unexpected Architectures

MARCELLA HACKBARDT

JEFF BROUWS'S EXCEPTIONAL DOCUMENTARY project reveals beautifully unexpected architectures. The forms in his work rise with vitality over present and absent rail lines, locating a landscape of transformation. These monumental and monolithic structures, known as coaling towers, stand strong on their four or more incongruously lithe legs. As masterworks of design, engineering, and functionality, they evoke edifices reminiscent of classical architecture.

Most contemporary viewers will not likely recognize the original use of these structures because the mythic figural shapes hovering over the railroad tracks provide few clues to their former function. This initial unfamiliarity leads to an aesthetic appreciation for the synthesis of physicality, materiality, and imaginative design language. The towers were built out of a raw construction material, reinforced concrete, and served one unified purpose: to store and deliver coal to steam locomotives. Given these limited variables, and the lack of any need for superfluous details, it is even more visually powerful to see their surprising mutations as expressed in the variety of their differently scaled windows, shaped roofs, cutaways, and graceful arches—occasionally encircled by vines and dense foliage.

Set alongside tracks where few humans would rest eyes on them, these statuesque behemoths are rooted in industrial design sensibilities, yet suggestive of science fiction and medieval lore. While architecture is frequently set to a human scale, these spanned openings and elongated stilts accommodate the morphology of both the locomotive and the massive chamber held above that was sized to hold tons of coal. Steel ladders that climb the towers' sides and windows near the apex—that once provided illumination for workmen—attest to a man/machine dichotomy. The resulting forms balance human and train-centered design requirements, while affirming links between technology, the creative process, and civil engineering's remarkable aptitude for performative problem solving.

Brouws practices an evidentiary form of photography, striving for objectivity and formal neutrality. *Silent Monoliths: The Coaling Tower Project* is organized into two sections, Coaling Tower Typology and Coaling Tower Topographies. Brouws carefully considered and rigorously constructed the framing of the towers for typological relationships to include the physical structure and some of the environment, providing a historical record and a meditative sense of place, and to subtly evoke the photographer's presence. The topographies are more sweeping landscapes, often seen as diptychs, that richly depict the sites' relationships between

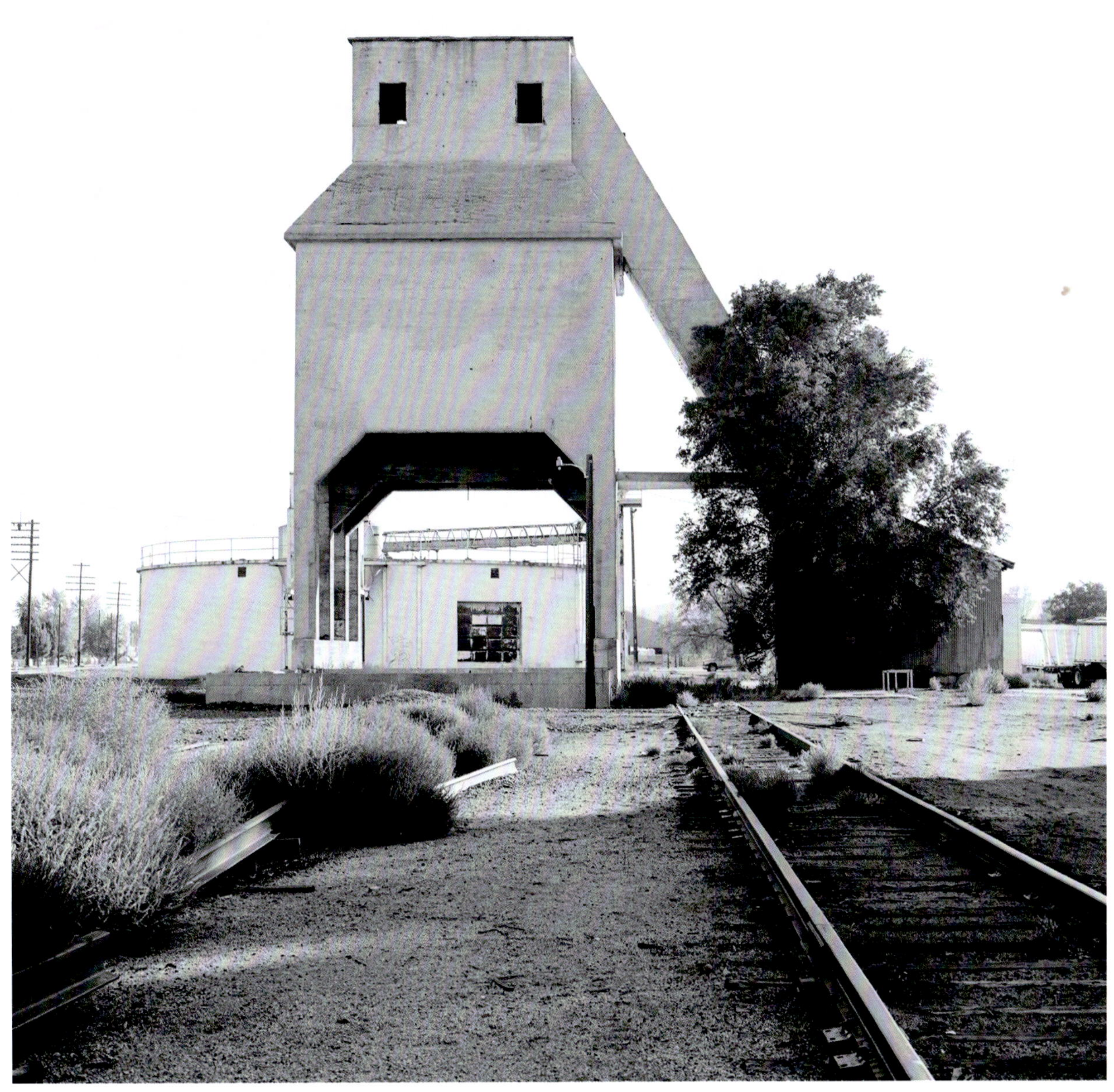

9 **GLENNS FERRY, IDAHO** Union Pacific 42°57'09.8"N 115°18'01.9"W

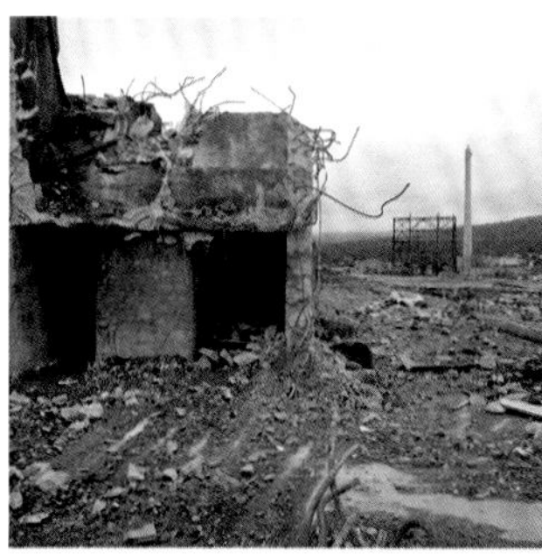
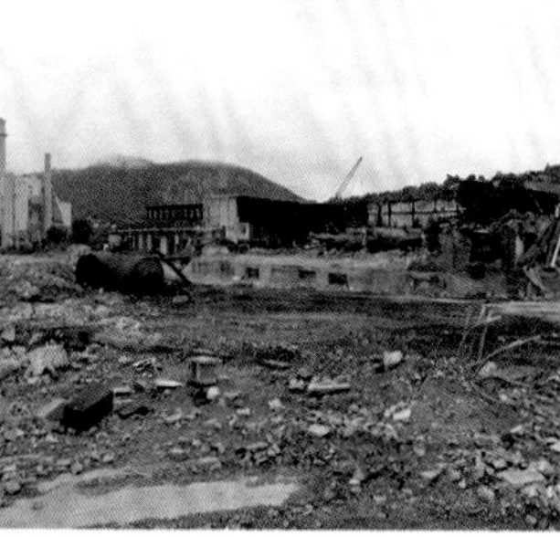

Demolition of paper mill, Berlin, New Hampshire, 2007

the man-made and the natural world. Their vacant aspects tacitly describe the still-lingering economic forces that transformed many parts of the country in the latter half of the twentieth century as America's manufacturing and industrial base declined. Conceptually these images connect with Brouws's *Discarded Landscape* series, made between 1998 and 2010, in which he documented the hollowed-out, inner-city factory districts of the Midwest and Northeast—photographic work of environments shaped by social change that emphasized a material heritage on the verge of disappearance.

PHOTOGRAPHY IS A PROCESS OF CURIOSITY and collection, and typologies serve to focus the collection with systematic attention given to common traits of like objects. Brouws's typologies share a dialogue with other practitioners of this important genre. They use comparison and clarity to examine sameness and variations on a theme. Many of the earliest photographers were themselves collectors who photographed their personal collections, such as Louis Daguerre's *Arrangement of Fossil Shells*, and William Henry Fox Talbot's *Articles of China, Articles of Glass, Objects of Crystal*, all typological expressions. Talbot's additional pioneering work with botanical specimens, a dozen still lifes of tables set for breakfast (utilizing his household prop department), and multiple studies of lace, all speak to photography's early and persistent typological drive. Photography's ability to automatically preserve detailed characteristics of its subjects spurred its speedy incorporation into all aspects of modern life after its invention, serving the classification and ordering desires of science, medicine, history, law, the domestic, and more. Modern and contemporary photographers have continued to utilize typological strategies, dedicated to documenting what seriality, repetition, and presence can reveal.

This collection makes the coaling towers, primarily built with intention away from public viewership, admirable visible. The photographs speak to and about history, engaging in archeological and cultural dialogues that span the past, present, and future. They insist that the structures are works of art worthy of careful study, and that knowledge can be gained through close observation of these uniquely modern ruins. Whether shot from straight on, or from a variety of angles, perspective dominates the pictorial space. The towers are caught between the winding, crisscrossing, and perspectival lines of train tracks and rutted roads, as much as they are caught between the order and disorder of an American cultural geography: our environmental stewardship, the history of capitalism, and the ideals of individualism and nationhood.

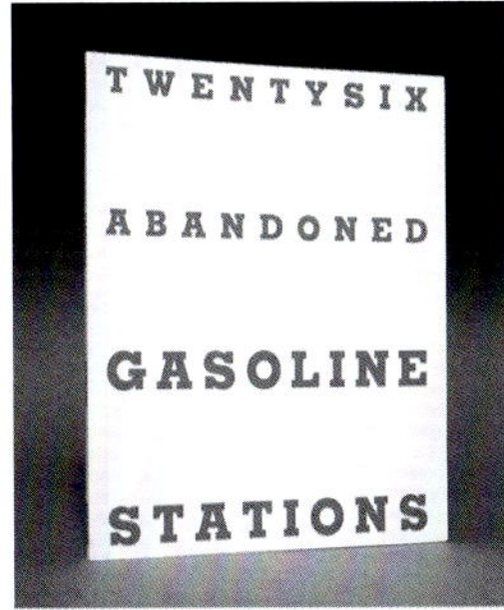

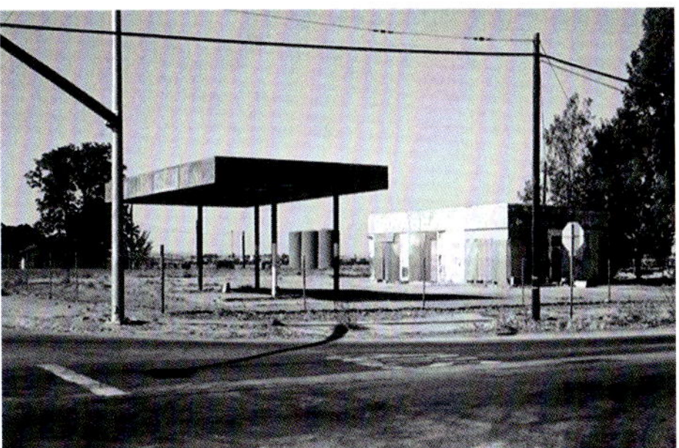

Twentysix Abandoned Gasoline Stations, 1992

Self-Serve, Bakersfield, California, 1988 from Twentysix Abandoned Gasoline Stations, 1992

BROUWS FIRST ENCOUNTERED the work of Hilla and Bernd Becher at the Newport Harbor Art Museum in 1991, at an exhibition that also featured typologies by nine contemporary artists including Ed Ruscha, Judy Fiskin, Roger Mertin, and Thomas Ruff. Especially struck by the architectural studies of blast furnaces in shadowless light made by the Bechers, and gasoline stations by Ruscha, Brouws began integrating this methodology into his work and self-published *Twentysix Abandoned Gasoline Stations* in homage to Ruscha's first book in 1992. Thus began his introduction to twentieth and twenty-first century photographers who chose to document everyday architecture, transitional industrial landscapes, or vernacular culture using typologies. Over the past twenty years he has written about his artistic indebtedness to, and admiration for, Walker Evans, New Topographics photographers like Robert Adams, Lewis Baltz, and Joe Deal, and contemporaries such as Camilo José Vergara and Mark Ruwedel. All have conceived of and organized their various photographic series into typologies at one time or another.

Contemporary typological photography is distinguished by its connection to historical content and cultural encounter, renewing the language of the genre. While conjuring visual relationships with an objective gaze, the purpose of their collections is to summon an interpretive gaze. As noted by Geoffrey Batchen, "Collecting does things to the items collected. Meanings are implied, sometimes even insisted on. And the meanings are often produced by showing things side by side, or under the same thematic heading."[1] For instance, artist Amber N. Ford's typology *Mistaken Identity* focuses on the mundane items—such as candy bars, keys, a small toy—that were mistaken for weapons, and have led to the deaths of people of color at the hands of law enforcement officers. Jonathan Vega's *A Historical Process: Unchanged Representation*, consists of a grid of 24 tintype portraits of his brother, who was incarcerated multiple times. With each arrest a mugshot was taken as a component of the process. For this series, Vega accessed the mugshots online and used each digital file to create a cropped tintype version, imbricating the standardization and impersonalization of the mugshot with a personal narrative. In another example, Magda Biernat's *Adrift* project compares polar-opposite photographs of Antarctic icebergs and empty Iñupiat Eskimo hunting cabins, as commentary on global climate change. Brouws's comprehensive survey is in part a restrained reminder of society's

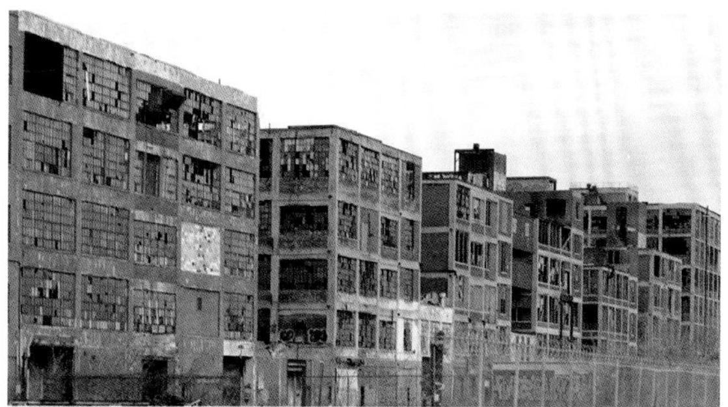

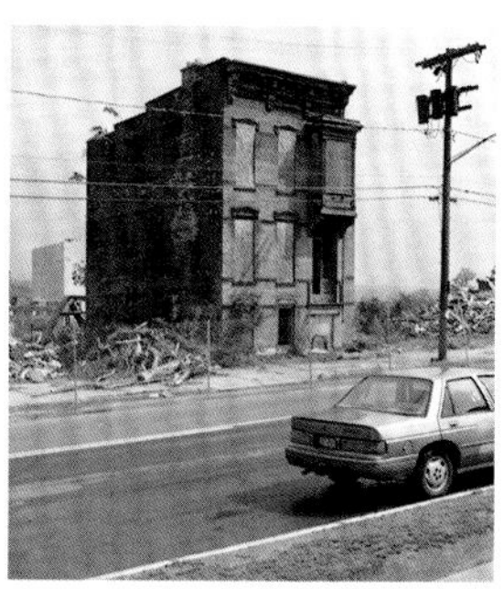

Abandoned factory, Detroit, Michigan, 2007

House in the path of redevelopment, Albany, New York, 2004

responsibilities for the changing technologies that continue to proliferate in our era, as brute concrete or fragile, now microscopic silicon chips. These and many other photographers use the conventions of taxonomy to amplify social consciousness, furthermore supported by their subjective agency and humanity.

Drawing upon strategies of sharp focus, rich detail, a collector's eye for his subjects, and an adventurous appetite for seeing and sharing the world, Brouws has persistently, throughout his photographic work, produced a coherent visual archive. Over time he has revisited several emblematic architectural forms found in the contemporary man-made landscape (gas stations, storage units, strip malls, big box stores) recording them as they commercially ebb and flow, fracture and fail, and eventually fall into a functionless state. An important aspect of his oeuvre is chronicling this "creative destruction"—the supplanting of one technology, one business, one type of building for another—as manifested within our material world, a notion first put forth by economist Joseph Schumpeter in 1942. This allows him to bear witness to evolving technological or socio-economic histories as they play out upon the landscape, while cataloging a transformation of place. That kind of documentation puts him in kinship with the New Topographics photographers who made images in the American West, ostensibly about rampant suburbanization and man's incursion on the landscape. However, Brouws and other second-generation New Topographics-inspired photographers inverted that premise, focusing instead on derelict sites that express narratives of disinvestment, abandonment, and capital flight from urban cores in the Eastern half of the United States.

The coaling tower project fits seamlessly into this context as a logical extension of the exploration of abandonment and industrial transformation. The towers themselves are remnants of a major industrial shift that occurred when America's railroads transitioned from steam locomotives to diesel power. The tracks invite consideration of the railroad system as a whole, and the profound and sometimes disquieting social and environmental consequences of nineteenth-century development. Railroads spread European settlers and goods across the nation, sparking ever-increasing economic growth and westward migration. That mobility then became associated with concepts of nationalism, pioneer spirit, free enterprise, and personal freedoms. Other historical events during this period of immigration and land grabs reveal patterns of exploitation ranging from Native American dispossession, expansion of chattel slavery, widespread discrimination among, and between, immigrant populations, and corporate graft. In the end, images of train tracks and buildings precipitate a range of positive and negative emotions intensified by the nearly mystical imprint of the railroad on the American psyche as a symbol of achievement, hope, and escape.

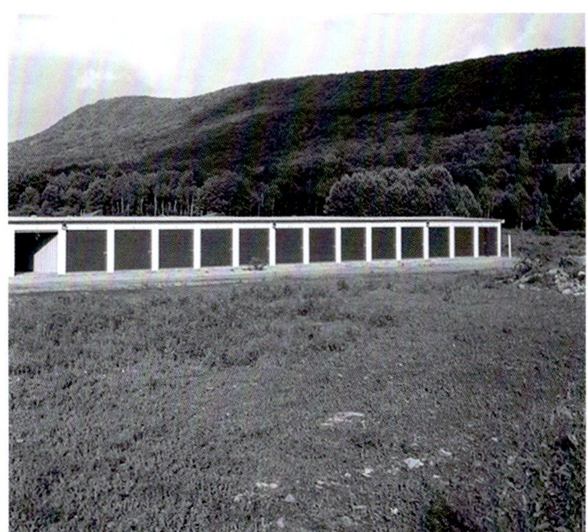
Storage Unit #15, Pennsylvania, 2001

IN 2013, BROUWS BEGAN the coaling tower project with intensive Google Earth research, followed by a two-week, 4,000-mile expedition to locate some of the towers in New York, Ohio, Indiana, Michigan, Illinois, Kentucky, and West Virginia. Since then he has driven over 20,000 miles, locating and revisiting towers, and photographing almost every known example still extant in North America from Flomaton, Alabama, on the Gulf Coast; to Hornpayne in northern Ontario, Canada; west to Glenns Ferry, Idaho; and back to the southern edge of Connecticut at New Haven.

Although much of his earlier work was done in color, for this anthology Brouws decided to shoot exclusively in black and white, and he hand-processed each roll of film. The extended silvery gray scale of the photographs further fuses the coaling towers into their environments, using abstraction to heighten a perception of form and typological rigor. His recent renewed interest in the history of nineteenth century photography extends to the inherent way a black and white photo challenges the viewer to discover

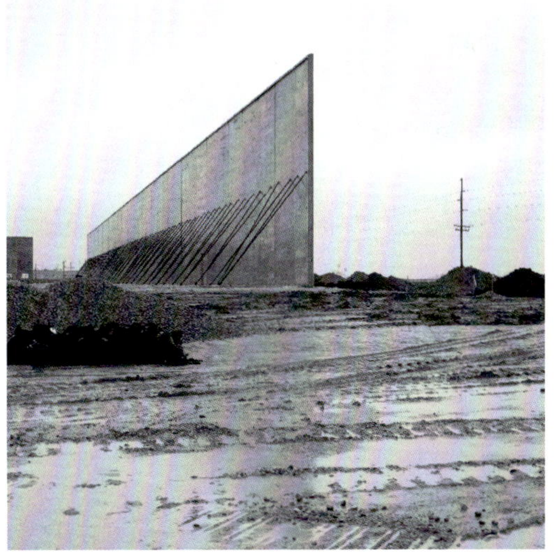
Superstore under construction on former farmland, Indiana, 2004

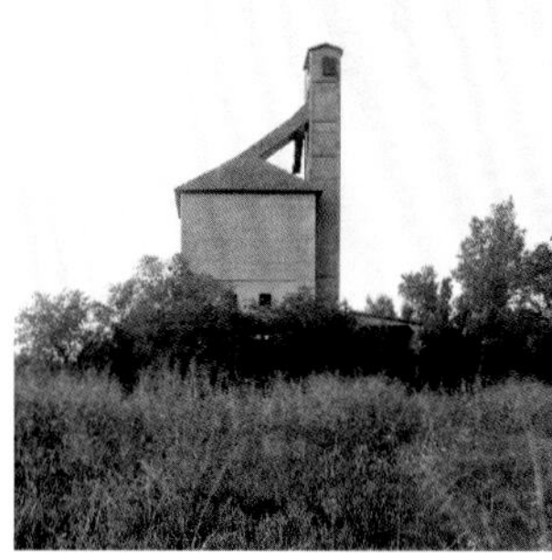

Coaling tower in unmowed field, Cushing, Oklahoma, 2013

Coaling tower in newly mowed field, Cushing, Oklahoma, 2015

more about the time frame of the photograph's production, establishing a dialogue between contemporary and historical photographs. Because the coaling towers are both not of this time, but in this time, their monochromatic presentation compellingly underscores their curious position on a continuum of past and present.

Like other photographers who work to record the evolving cultural landscape—such as William Christenberry with his photographs of rural architecture in Hale County, Alabama—Brouws returned to many coaling tower sites repeatedly allowing him to detail both the nuanced and obvious variations. They include shifts in light, seasonal changes (he favors shooting the towers in winter when trees are bare), physical alterations occurring within the landscapes surrounding the structures, and the towers' actual material condition. For example, the coaling tower at Cushing, Oklahoma, went from being somewhat obscured in an overgrown field when first visited in late autumn, to standing out like a freshly unveiled sculpture in a newly mowed area upon a second arrival in early summer, to being marooned behind a padlocked gate, inaccessible when last seen in October 2018. Several of the other towers have suffered incremental deterioration or outright demolition over the course of the five-year project (see pages 92-93), and Brouws has faithfully recorded these evolutions.

MAGNIFIED SYMBOLS OF HUMAN VISION, invention, and conquest, there is wonder to be had in the sculptural beauty of these enigmatic, hardened structures. Through Brouws, we stand diminutively as partners in inquiry before these monoliths. We encounter an in-between psychological space where we pause at an intersection on the path leading forward and the path left behind. The towers are silent, and the stillness of the almost-forgotten industrial terrain belies their testimony to the rise and fall of technology and the progression of history. In this inimitable human landscape, the past and the present meet, discretely, as demonstrated by the gradual creep of a forest's edge, or the defunct train yard turning to brownfield. Oftentimes too costly and too difficult to dismantle, the concrete towers represent architectural expressions of near-permanence. Built to withstand the weight of the coal, they are now poised to withstand the weight of time.

1 Geoffrey Batchen, "Ordering Things," in Brian Wallis ed., "The Order of Things: Photography from The Walther Collection" (Steidl, 2015) 335.

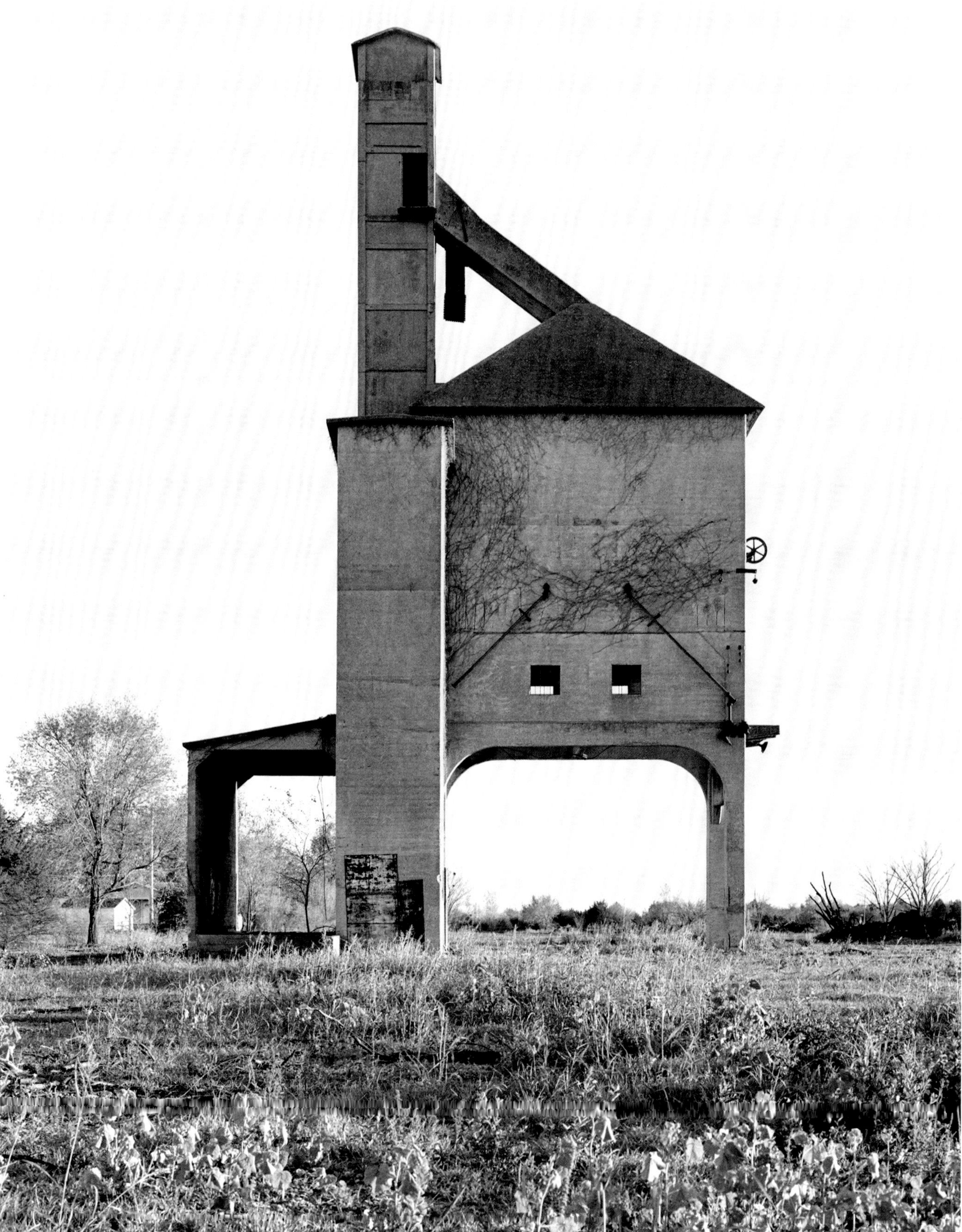

A Most Efficient Form

JOHN P. HANKEY

FEW STRUCTURES EMBODY PARADOX, irony, and anomaly like concrete railroad coaling towers. In their half-century of use—roughly 1905 through 1960—they were essential to the efficient operation of the continent's 300,000-mile railroad network. No one knows how many were built, but a reasonable estimate is between 1,500 and 2,000 throughout the United States. Surpringly, over 100 have survived into the twenty-first century as "retired-in-place" ruins, with several intentionally preserved. There is little scholarship and even less appreciation for these remarkable structures. Despite their cultural significance and impressive monumentality, they remain hidden in plain sight.

These monolithic structures occupy a kind of liminal space between architecture and engineering. By the time of their creation, the two disciplines had diverged. Great works of architecture obviously required competent engineering. Likewise, great engineering works could be positively lyrical or artistic in their form or expression. But despite the fact that coaling towers were clearly architectural and visually striking—sometimes reaching two hundred feet into the air and exhibiting a substantial presence in whatever landscape they inhabited—they have largely gone unexamined. Even as sophisticated works of engineering, they have not received the attention clearly due. That is perhaps the fundamental paradox inherent in any engagement with these once ubiquitous, now arcane, structures.

Concrete coaling towers helped revolutionize the operation of steam locomotive fleets. They were a most efficient and durable form, yet ironically what I refer to as "ephemeral architecture." Most railroads understood their physical plants to be largely consumable in the same ways locomotives and cars were scrapped as they wore out or became functionally obsolete. However, no concrete coaling tower ever wore out from use, and they tended to be so well built that it was time-consuming and expensive to demolish them. That is why so many survive today as relics in the railroad landscape.

Coaling stations evolved continually, from piles of fuel on the ground delivered to waiting locomotive tenders in buckets through a half-dozen ever-more-elaborate forms; they delivered impressive labor savings and materially increased the speed at which locomotives could replenish fuel. But few railroad managers anticipated the rapidity with which diesel locomotives would replace steam power in the mid-twentieth century and how quickly these massive concrete structures would become functionally obsolete. Some towers saw only a decade or less of use.

From about 1880 through the early twentieth century, railroads built increasingly large coaling towers. Civil engineers and practical railroaders worked out the general dimensions for tall

A rationally designed structure may not necessarily be beautiful but no building can be beautiful that does not have a rationally designed structure.

—Eugène Viollet-le-Duc
French Archtect (1814-1879)

bunkers straddling the tracks and perfected crude forms of bucket conveyors to elevate the coal. But one critical limitation remained: These sometimes immense structures were made almost entirely of wood, with all of the disadvantages that entailed. Dimensional timber of the sizes and species required was becoming increasingly hard to get and costly. Engineering such large structures with complex stresses was challenging. By their nature they were "stick built" and almost always individually designed, requiring a great deal of skilled labor and time. Wood also wears out, isn't fireproof, and rots if not treated.

Between 1900 and 1910 engineers and architects rapidly gained experience with concrete reinforced with steel rods. The evolution of these seemingly simple, but actually complex, engineering works is an example of the intersection of advancing technological prowess, pressure to reduce costs and increase efficiency, and the general cultural embrace of an industrial ethos. Smokestacks, steel mills, immense factories, and landscape features such as coaling towers represented progress. The benefits they provided seemed to mute criticism of the visual and environmental havoc they wrought on urban and rural landscapes alike.

By the mid-1920s, the coaling station had reached its most evolved form. Three Chicago-based construction firms—Ogle Construction, Fairbanks-Morse, and Roberts and Schaefer—dominated the market for concrete coaling towers in classic oligopolistic fashion. They offered turnkey construction, project financing, and a deep well of experience. The preferred form was a tall monolithic cast concrete tower in which coal was stored to be unloaded by gravity as needed. A system of bucket or similar conveyors, powered by steam, gasoline, electricity, or diesel fuel, moved the coal from ground level to an elevated bunker, from which it was dropped via steel chutes into locomotive tenders below. It is difficult to imagine how that system could be improved. The concrete coaling tower was a fine example of technological determinism—the ultimate, most efficient way to accomplish a task.

Concrete coaling towers also offered a series of mild paradoxes. The raw materials were cheap and readily available: portland cement, sand, aggregate of some kind, and water. The engineering, however, could be complex, requiring a great deal of thought as to the thickness of the walls and placement of the reinforcing steel. Building them could be challenging. Everyone—from the design engineers to the casual workers hired by the day or job—had to learn to think in terms of voids and negative space rather than the solids and positive spaces most people were accustomed to. In essence, the builders had to create a massive hollow mold. Inside was a complex web of reinforcing rods, acting like a skeleton holding the

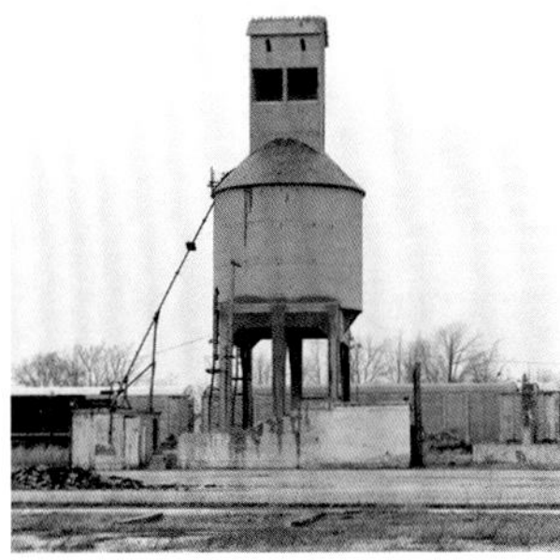

entire structure together. The strength of the steel buried and interlocked within the concrete made the structures exceptionally stable, strong, and incredibly durable.

A major railroad might have 75 to 100 coaling stations of different types along its lines. Small railroads might have but one. A substantial medium-sized railroad typically maintained thirty to sixty facilities for fuel and dispensed tens of thousands of tons of coal each day to keep its locomotives hot and working productively. They ended up in every landscape, from dense urban centers to the proverbial middle of nowhere. Sometimes coaling stations could be at locations convenient to population centers or places of railroad work. More often, coaling stations were remotely situated, as were so many railroad facilities like water stations, telegraph offices, and construction or maintenance camps. One might be called a coaling platform, coal trestle, coal wharf, coal pocket, coal dock, coal chute, or coaling tower. Their forms and names varied. Their function always remained the same.

There is also mild paradox in the ways coaling towers visually presented. From the outside, and especially devoid of their machinery and supporting facilities, they appear to be simple (although very large) containers. Some are cylindrical, some are rectangular, and most offer few clues as to what is inside. Sometimes, windows suggest that humans might actually inhabit the structures, or that light and air, however feeble, were appropriate. A person might surmise that the interiors of coaling towers were in fact places of work and still have no idea what that entailed.

The insides always featured large bins with sharply sloping sides to direct the flow of coal to narrow openings above the tracks. Each tower housed elaborate machinery to direct the coal being elevated by bucket conveyors to the appropriate bunkers. Perilous catwalks, stairs, and ladders provided access to all parts of the interiors. The machinery required routine servicing and repair. There were no gauges to determine the quantity of coal present or needed—the coaling station crew had to climb to the tops of the bunkers inside and visually estimate how many tons were on hand and how many to add.

In service, most towers alternated between periods of intense activity and stretches of utter quiet. At times, a half-dozen men might be busy inside and outside the structure, operating the machinery or doing routine maintenance. When trains arrived needing fuel (and sometimes sand for traction or water from nearby water tanks), the importance and efficiency of coaling towers was on full display. When the bins were full and the coaling tower crew had departed, and between trains, the place would seem abandoned. That was especially true at night or in bad weather.

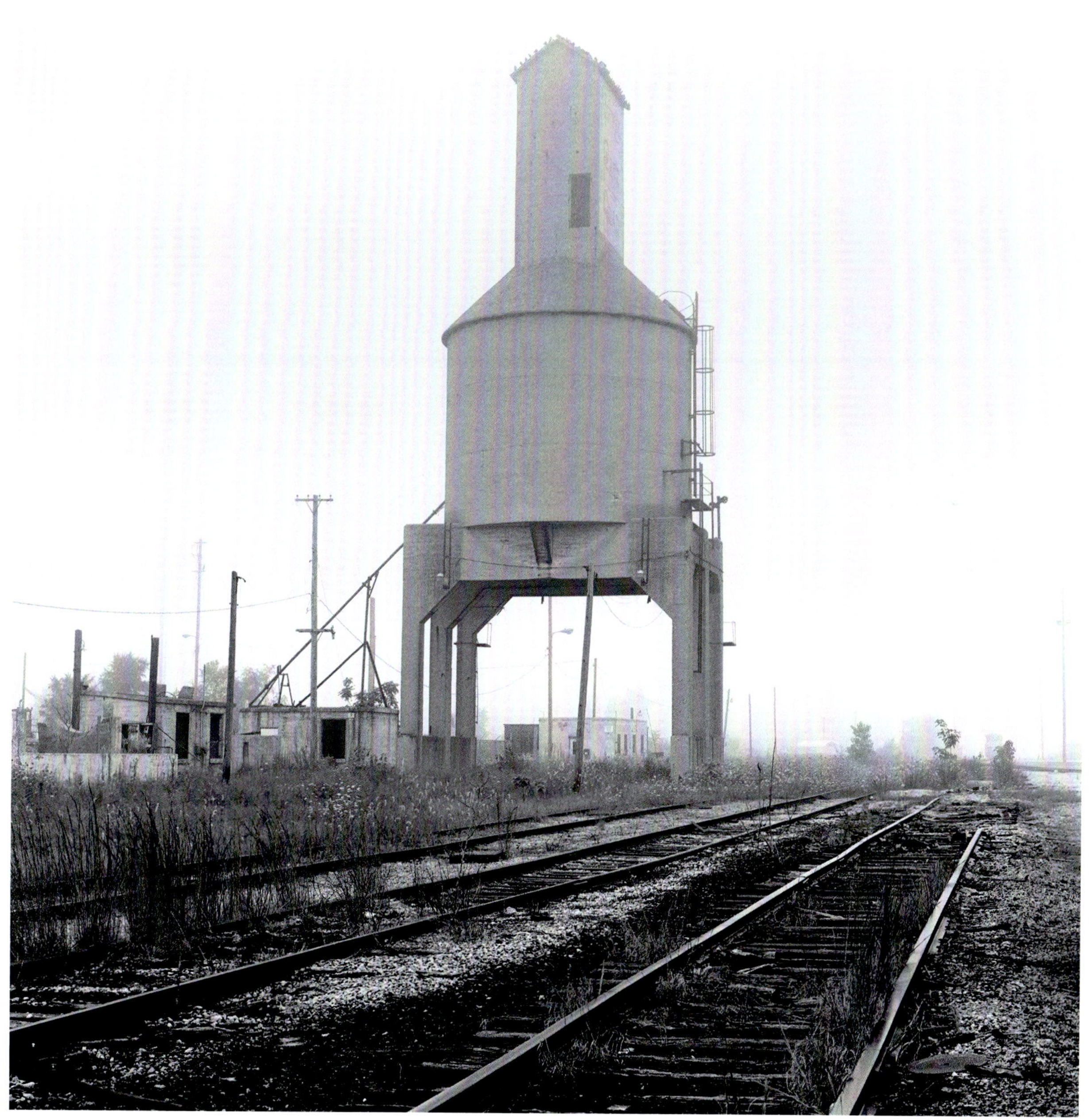

19 **FRANKFORT, INDIANA** New York, Chicago & St. Louis 40°16'55.7"N 86°31'30.1"W

COALING TOWERS DERIVED THEIR MEANING and significance from three rather abstract ideas: energy, efficiency, and independence. I doubt that their designers, or the dozens of railroad companies that invested in them, held any such notions. In their times and at their places, they were merely the best available delivery option and the logical endpoint of technological progress.

Energy—lots of it—was a tower's very essence. A full 500-ton capacity coaling tower represented millions of BTUs or the equivalent, in whatever measure or form you choose. It concentrated the output of a small mine or tens of thousands of trees in what was almost a point source. You could think of it as a massive bomb, but a very safe and slow-acting one. The potential energy it stored could power a city for days or a small town for a year, all in a footprint of a few hundred square feet. Coaling towers were contemporaneous with the development of the urban skyscraper, and noteworthy for the very same reasons: an expression of verticality, density, and the mechanical means to conquer gravity.

Efficiency was the proximate cause for the perfection of concrete coaling towers, but what made them possible was a kind of technological convergence. Since the Middle Ages, what we understand as progress has been characterized by the integration of ideas, techniques, and objectives in increasingly complex and creative combinations. The American inventor Oliver Evans worked out practical schemes to elevate grains, partially automate the flour milling process, and use external power and gravity in the 1790s. The basic principles of coaling towers were not new.

Independence is a bit trickier to define as a critical element. Coaling towers were essentially autonomous elements in a railroad's increasingly complex "system of systems." They could be erected wherever the need for locomotive fuel dictated, at busy servicing points or out in the middle of a lonely stretch of main line. They functioned within a web of relationships and management structures, but in the end the unvarying need of locomotives for reliable fuel supplies at critical locations defined both the problem and its solution. The ability to locate a stable, reliable source of that fuel wherever needed, and to have it operate independently of almost anything else going on, made twentieth-century railroad mobility possible.

World War II distorted the progress of railroad technology and delayed by a decade the rapid drive to supplant the steam locomotive with the vastly more fuel-efficient diesel locomotive. Following the war, steam would be replaced as quickly as possible. It was still a technological revolution of unprecedented scale and speed, but of entirely ordinary form, much as the telephone

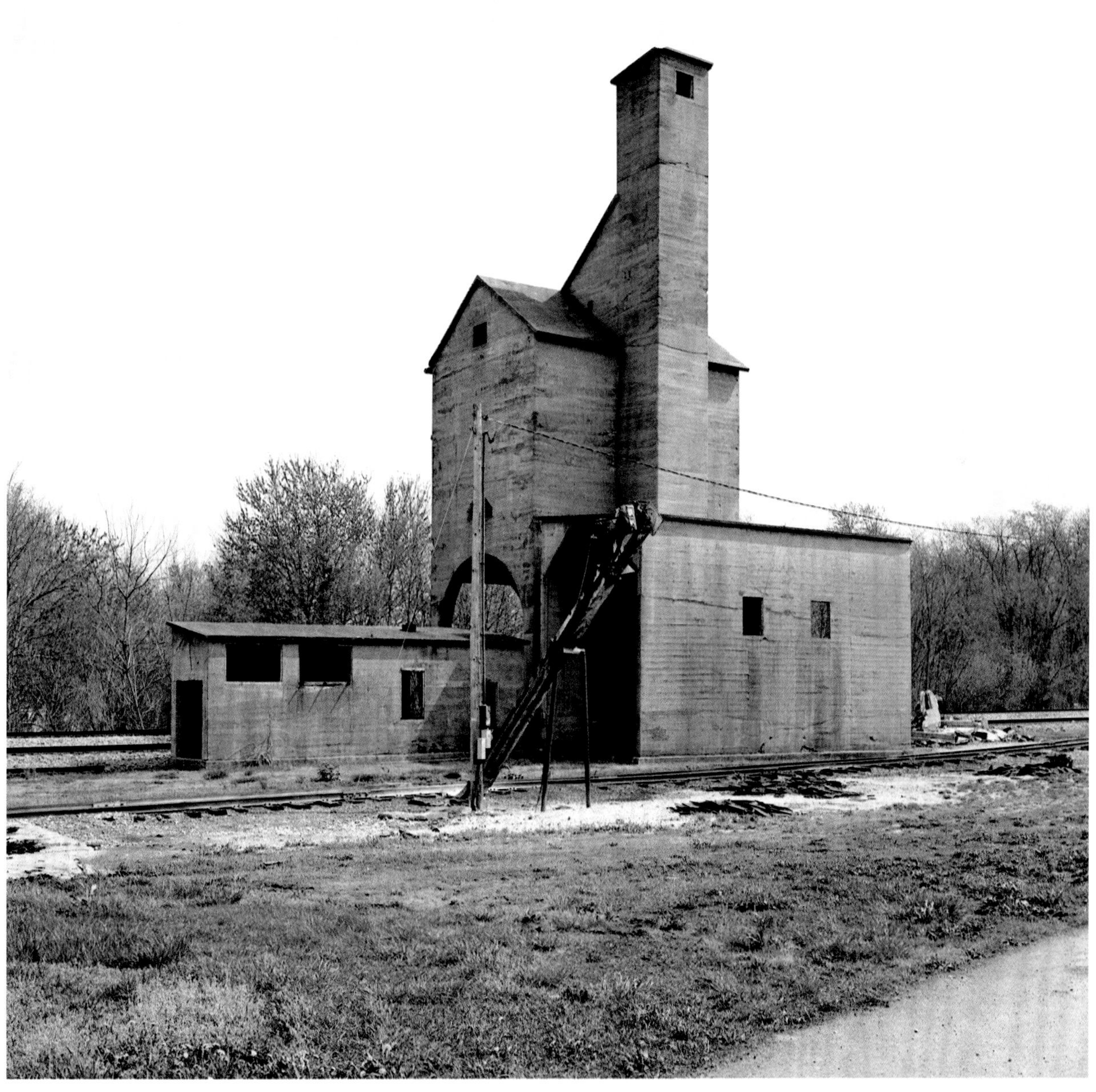

21 **IRVINGTON, KENTUCKY** Louisville & Nashville 37°52’53.9”N 86°16’53.6”W

displaced the telegraph in the early twentieth century. The steam locomotive was the primary motive power for American railroads in 1945, with perhaps a thousand diesel locomotives in service. A mere dozen years later, the figures were inverted. Around a thousand steam locomotives remained in operation, while slightly over 29,000 diesel locomotives formed the backbone of the North American railroad industry. And diesels didn't need coal.

A few railroads, however, remained commited to steam locomotives as a competitor to diesel. The Norfolk & Western Railway erected the last North American concrete coaling tower in 1956 at Iaeger, West Virginia. It was an anomalous expression of inertia and hope rather than reality and progress. By that time, railroads across the continent were tearing down even relatively new coaling towers as quickly as finances and demolition permits allowed, with the last active concrete coaling station delivering its final load of coal to a locomotive six decades ago. There is scant possibility that any surviving concrete coaling tower will ever be returned to service, little chance that any will be fully repurposed. They were specialized structures difficult to adapt for any other use.

IN 2026, THERE REMAIN THE HULKS of approximately 100 reinforced concrete coaling towers in the U.S. and Canada—perhaps 5 percent of the total built. They straddle active main lines, sit in forests near moribund rights-of-way, are subsumed in everyday landscapes, or stand tall in expansive Western deserts.

In theory, all still belong to someone. Railroads continue to demolish remaining coaling towers as part of environmental cleanup and facilities management programs. Several have met that fate over the past decade. In some cases, ownership has passed to other parties who choose to retain, remove, or reuse them as the site dictates. That was the case in Charlottesville, Virginia, recently, where a former Chesapeake & Ohio coaling tower has been integrated into a new condominium complex. A handful exist in a state of official preservation: Lake and Grand Haven, Michigan; Renovo, Pennsylvania; Sardis, Georgia; and Toronto, Ontario. Those are the exceptions. Most are truly orphans.

Therein lies another bit of irony. Except, perhaps, in the deepest recesses of the minds of the design engineers and draftsmen who reified the concept of a coaling tower into a set of detailed plans and instructions, I doubt that anyone understood their work with coaling towers as architecture or even as a creative endeavor. As time and utility changes, so also do the meanings we ascribe to even mundane, utilitarian structures such as these. They

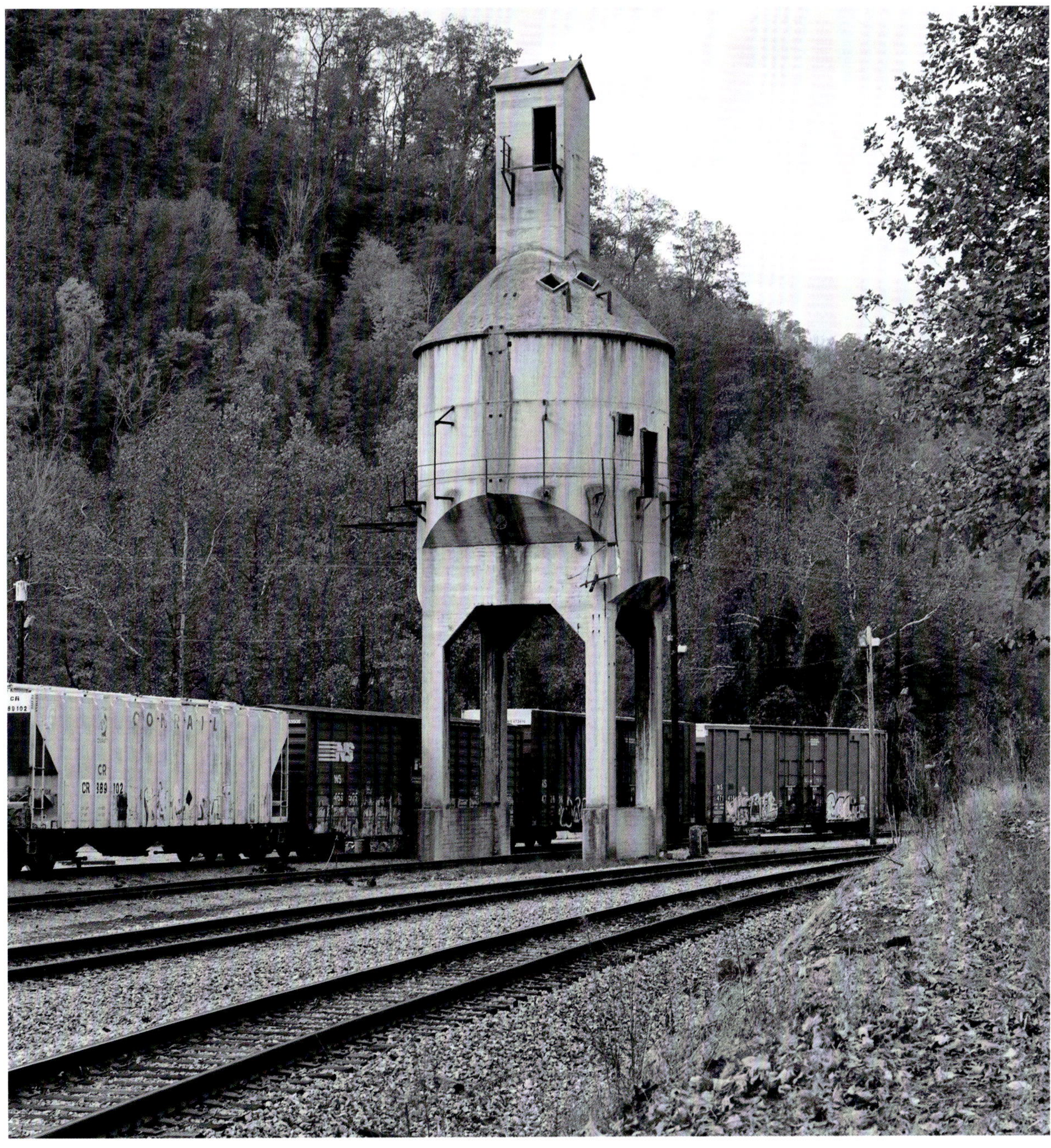

23 **IAEGER, WEST VIRGINIA** Norfolk & Western 37°27’32.8”N 81°49’03.4”W

were never intended to be, and are not now, art in any conventional sense.

Yet the images Jeff Brouws captured most certainly are art. The towers themselves are utterly deracinated, devoid of useful function, and often near-ruins. Most of their owners think of them on a continuum between mere nuisance and dangerous hazard. But art does not need to be safe or conventionally beautiful. Strife, tragedy, ugliness, and the ordinary are fertile sources for work that, in skilled hands, conveys meaning. What that might be is up to us.

In this half-decade-long project, Brouws chose to see, and record, a disparate set of industrial ruins according to simple, but profound, criteria. His work is largely done. Ours is just beginning. What do we make of these stark images? They are honest. There is no artifice, no intervention. We see what he saw at a moment in time. We are free to be curious, to like or dislike what we see, or to look away entirely. Nature will eventually have its way with these structures (with or without humans).

In the meantime, we can appreciate their form and variety. They are objects in various landscapes that invite whatever responses we contrive at first glance or patient reflection. Imagination may fill in versions of past reality or plausible future. The irresistible powers of nature to return the work of humanity to its most stable, primitive state will ultimately prevail. Steel will again be rust. Concrete will again become dissolved calcium, small rocks, and sand. They, too, may eventually become something else. The cosmos has time. We do not.

That suggests a final paradox. We at least know what they once were. Brouws caught them in the wild, as they are now. Perhaps like Neolithic henges of stone, they will stir bewilderment in future generations. What, they may wonder, were these curious structures for? Who built them—and why?

Preserved coaling tower near rail trail and former mainline of the Pere Marquette, Lake, Michigan, 2016

Coaling tower hidden in trees, Bluford, Illinois, 2014

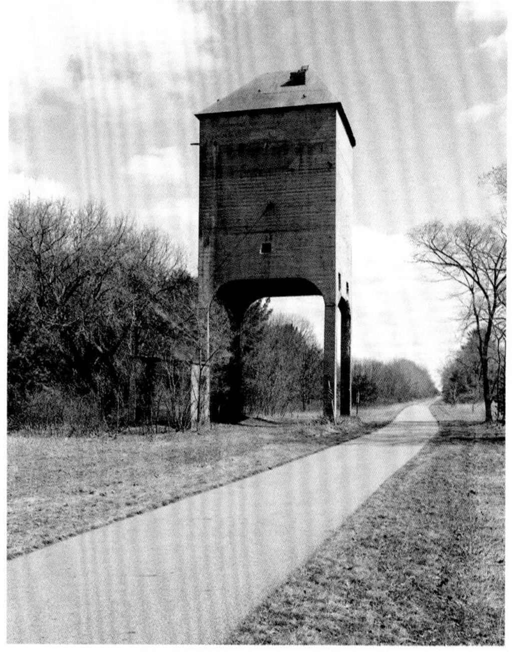

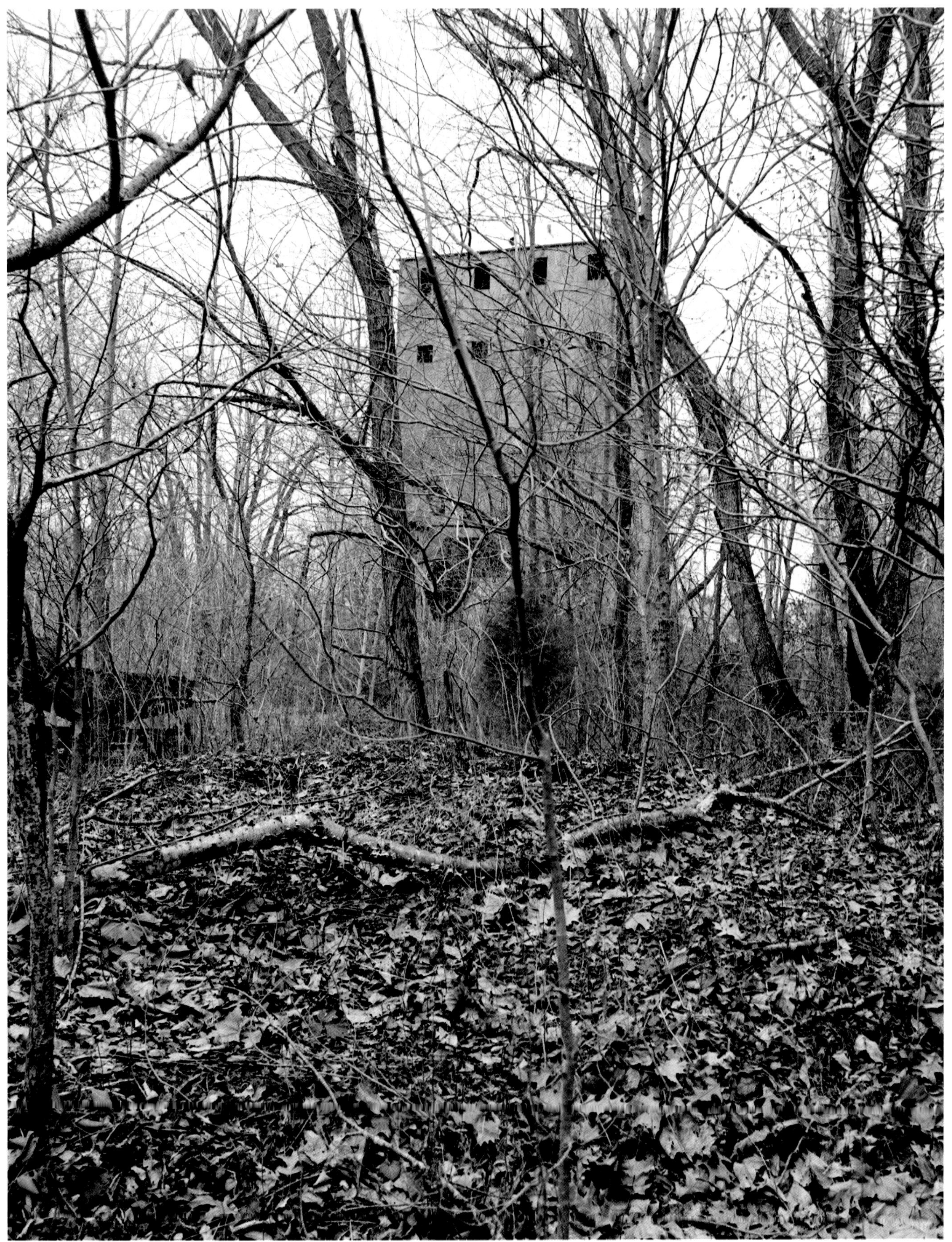

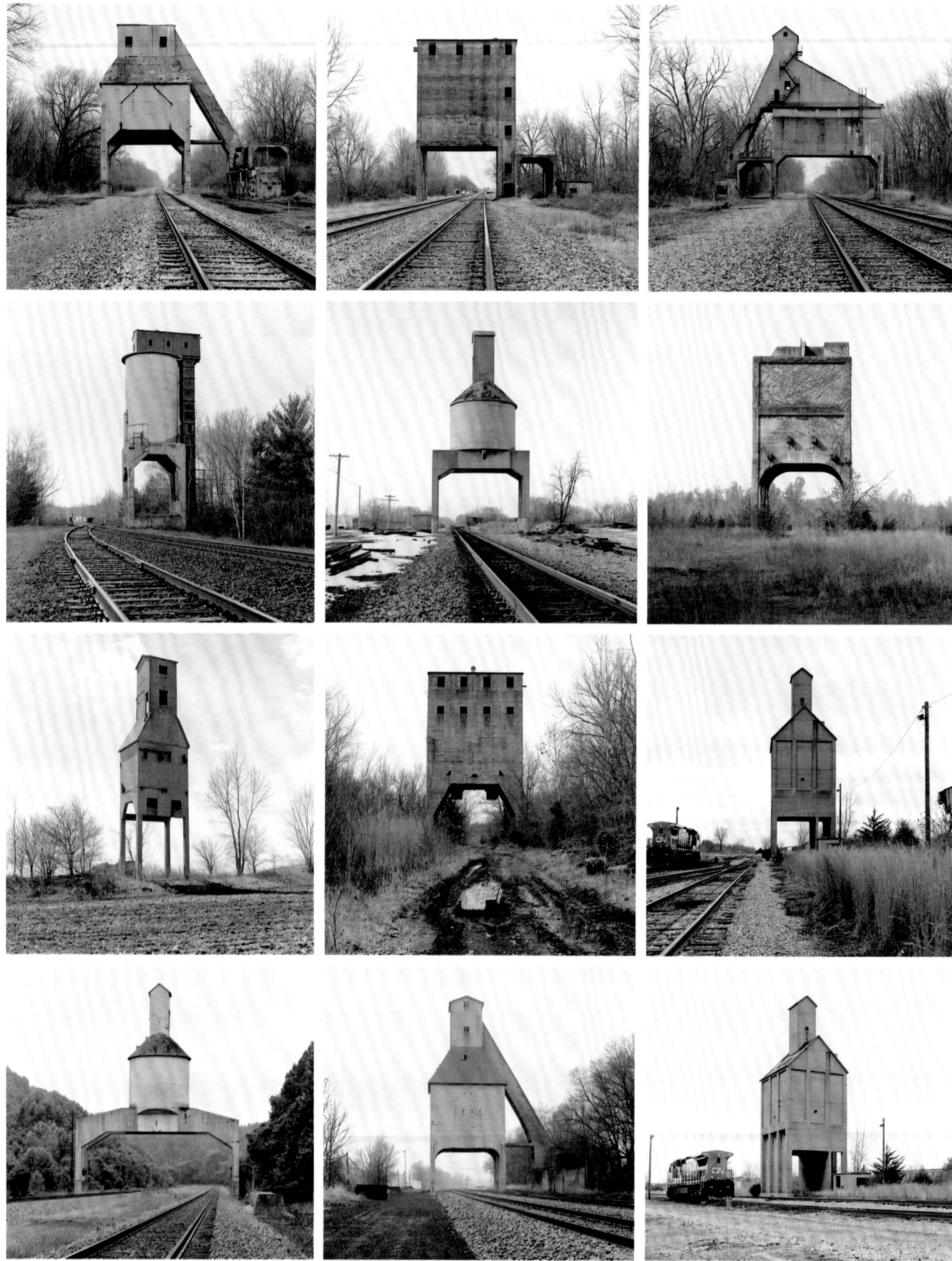
CN

TYPOLOGY

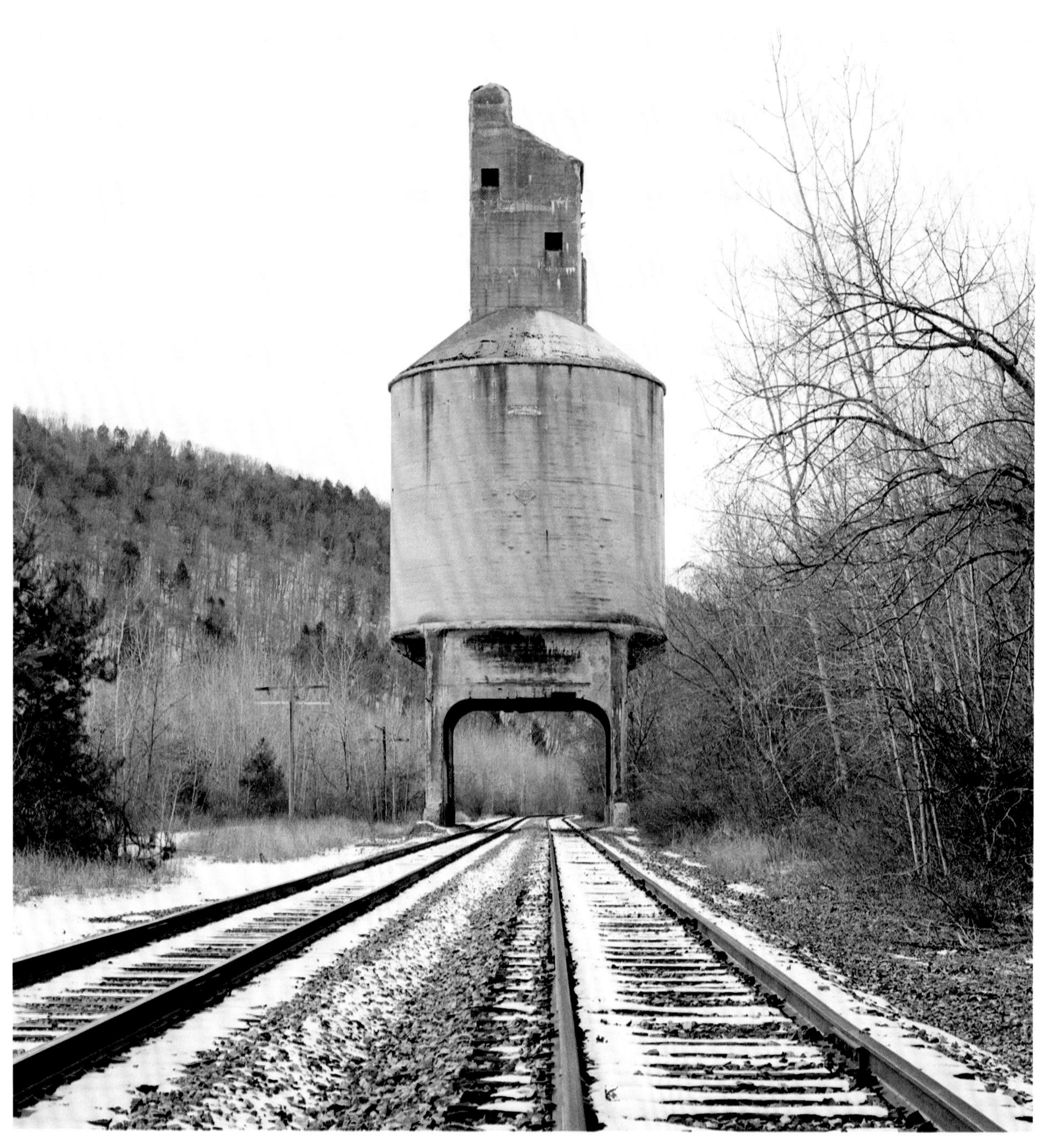

 SUSQUEHANNA, PENNSYLVANIA Erie 41°56’38.2”N 75°37’34.1”W

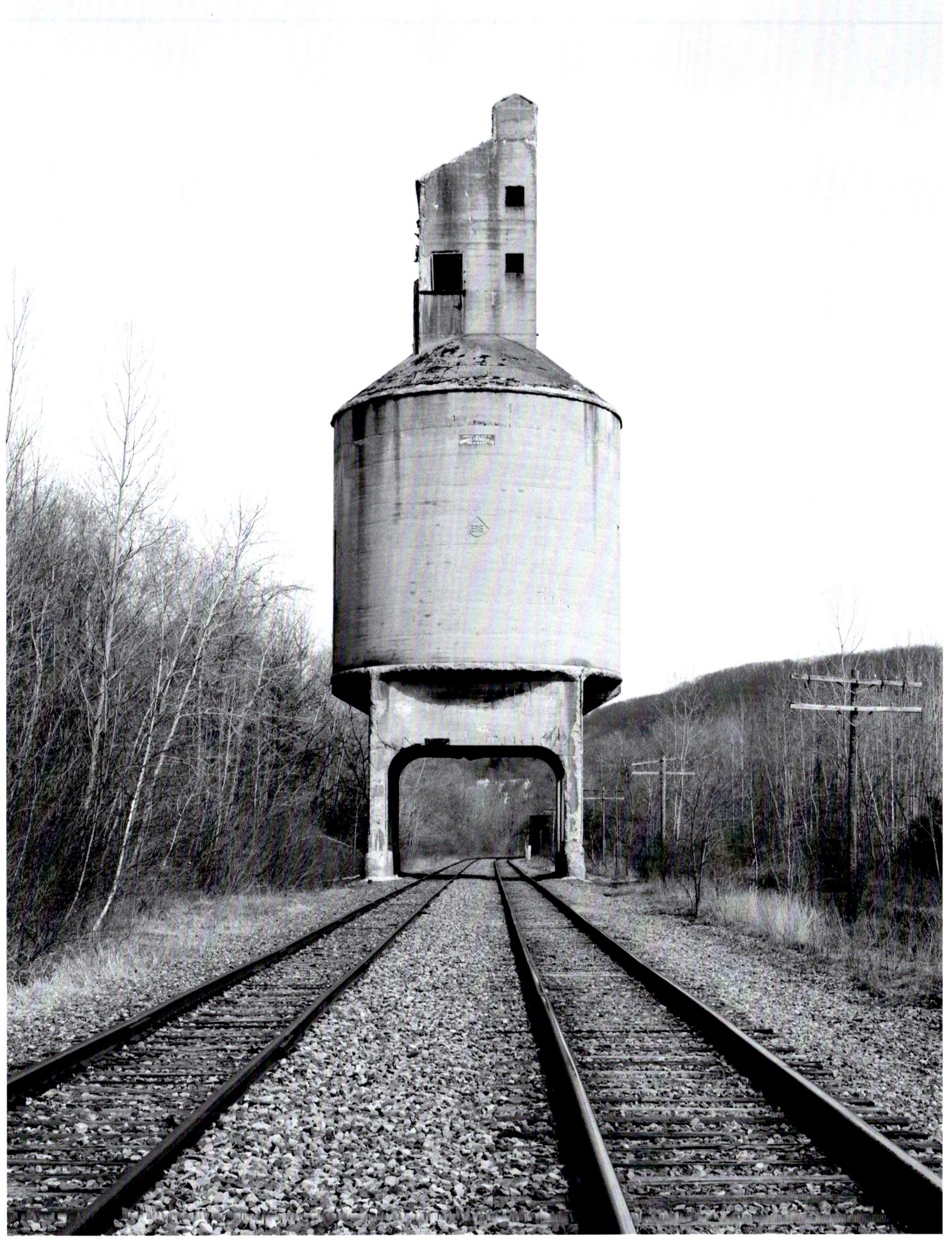
ERIE

MARION, OHIO Pennsylvania 40°38'43.5"N 83°06'16.4"W

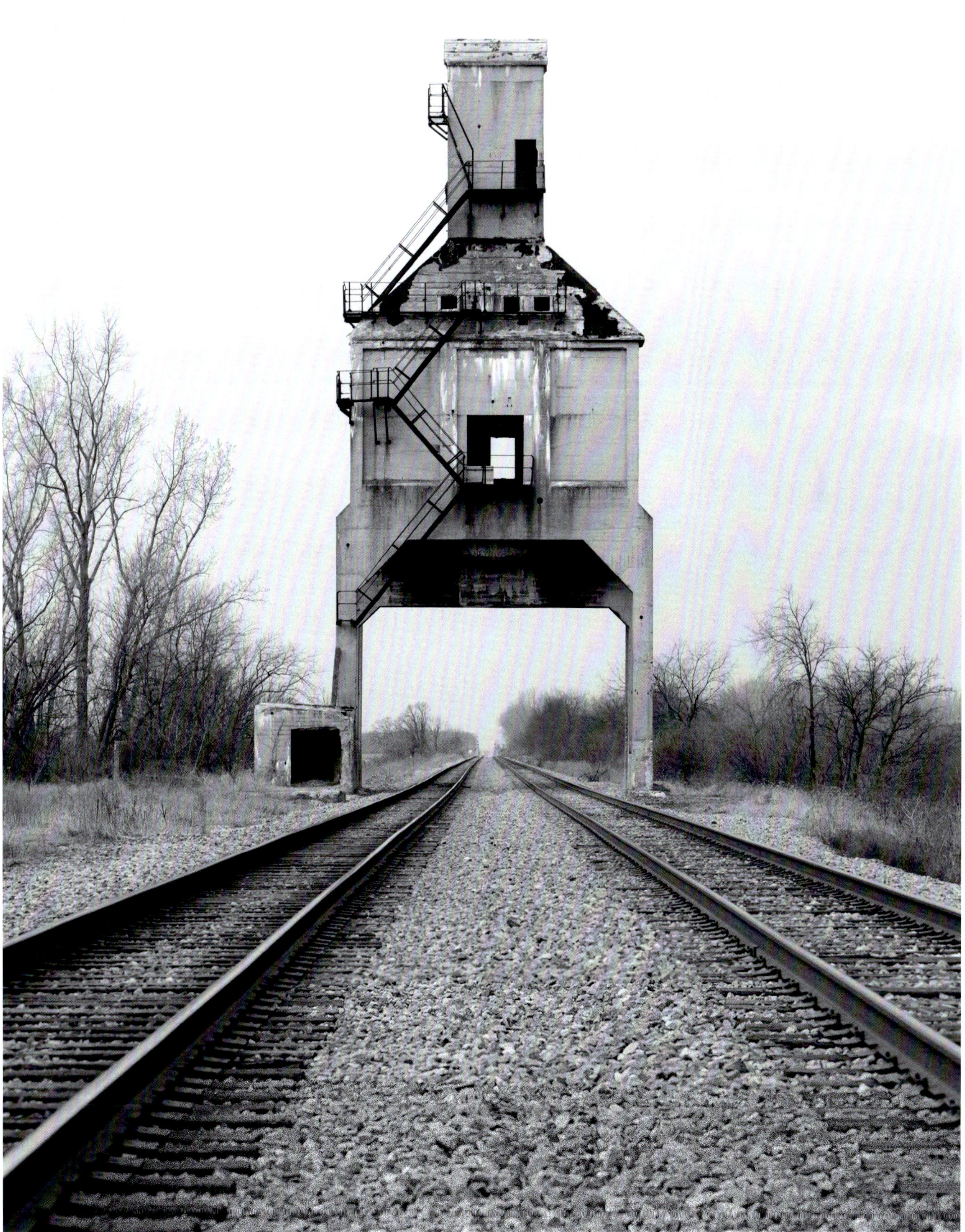

32 **BALDWIN, MICHIGAN** Pere Marquette 43°53'48.5"N 85°51'46.2"W

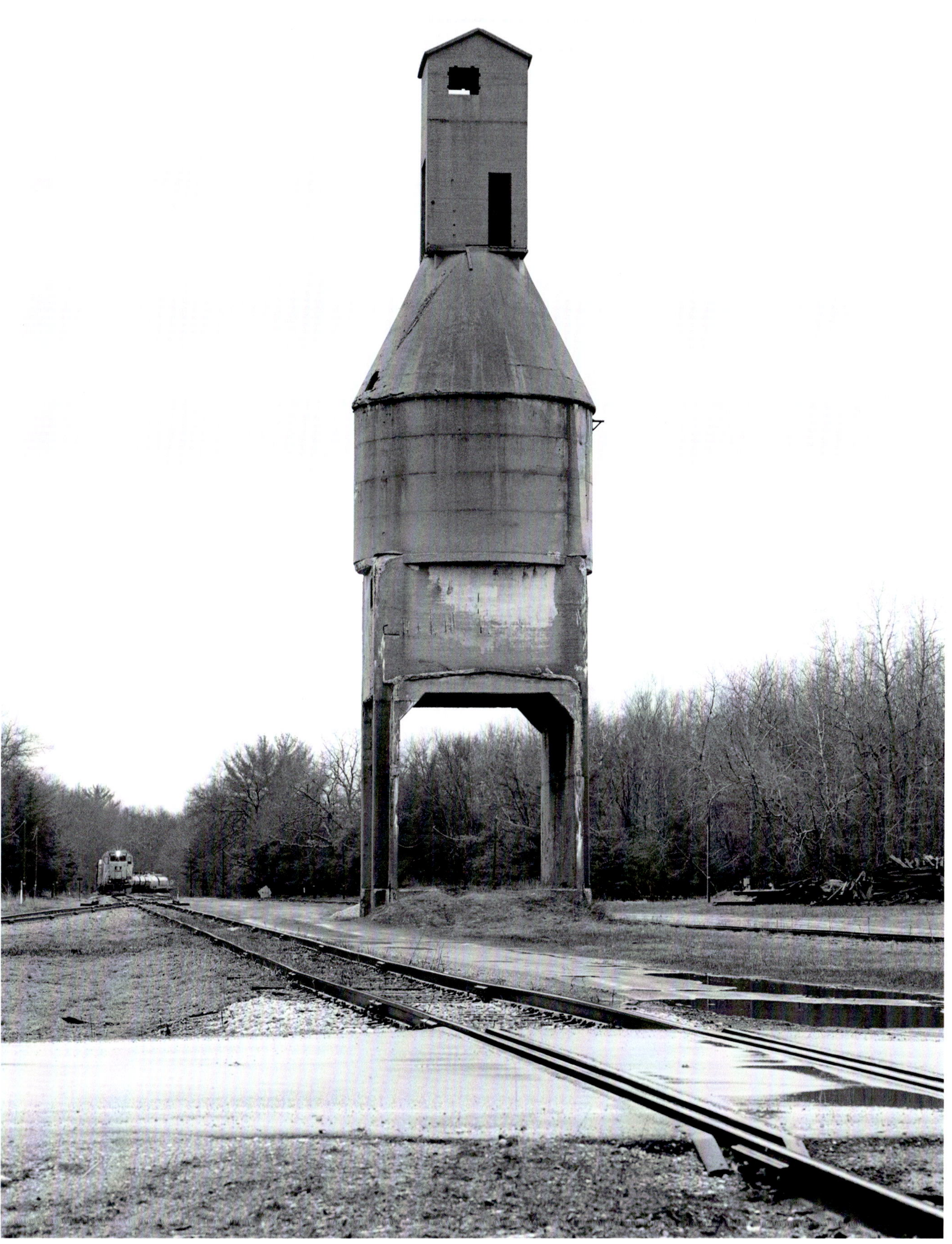

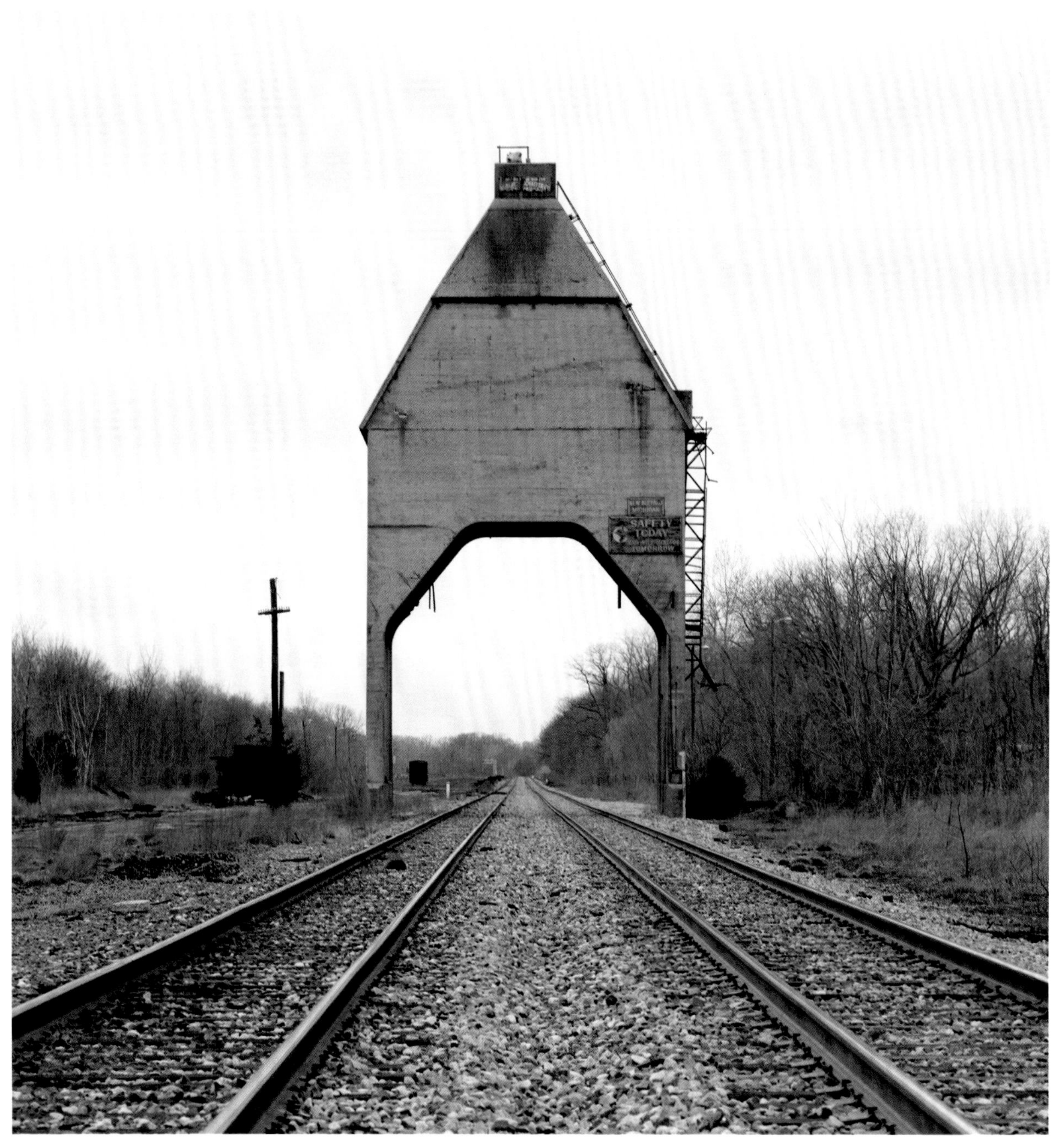

 NEW BUFFALO, MICHIGAN Pere Marquette 41°47'12.4"N 86°44'31.3"W

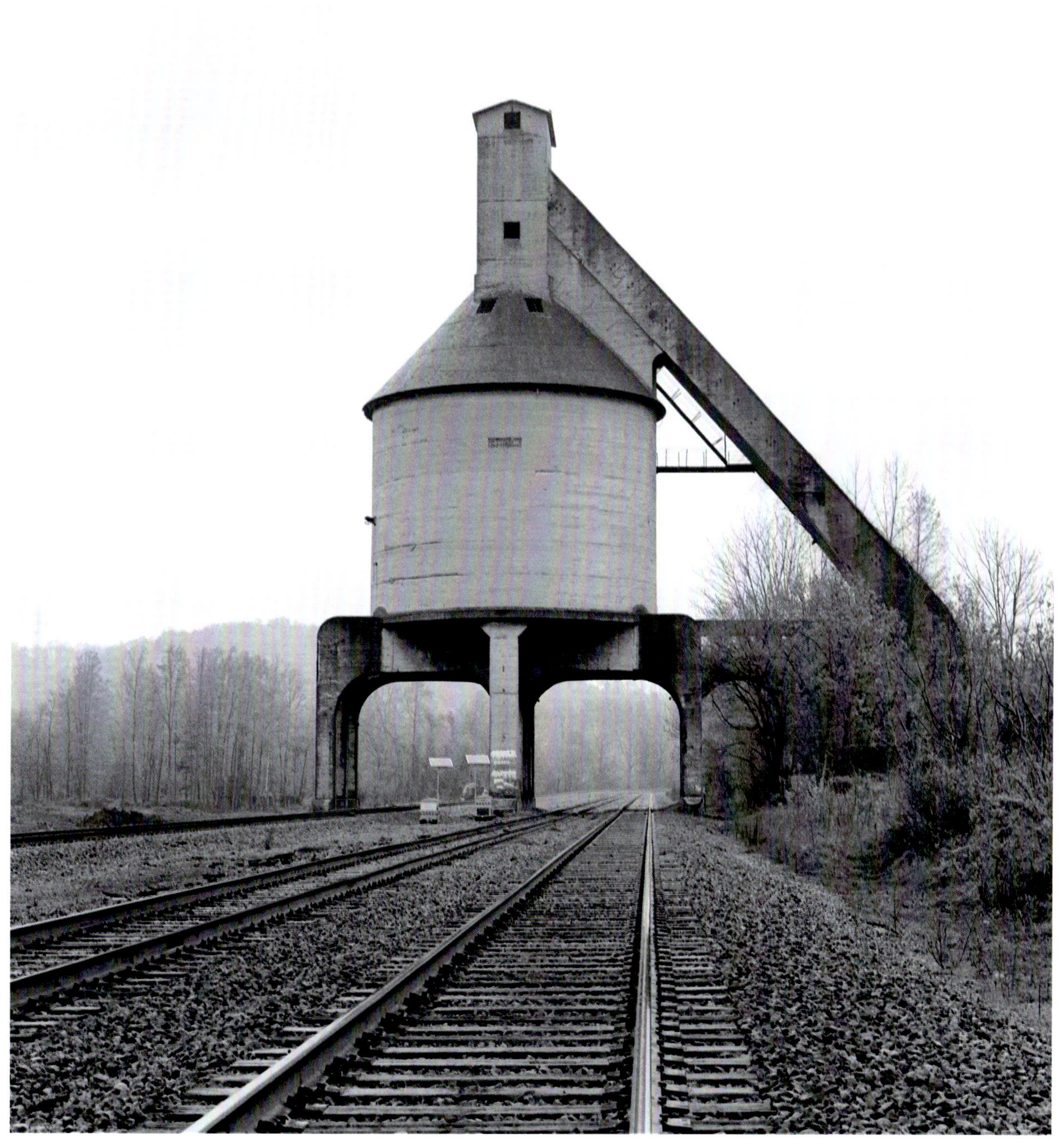

35 **PRICHARD, WEST VIRGINIA** Norfolk & Western 38°14'11.5"N 82°36'28.5"W

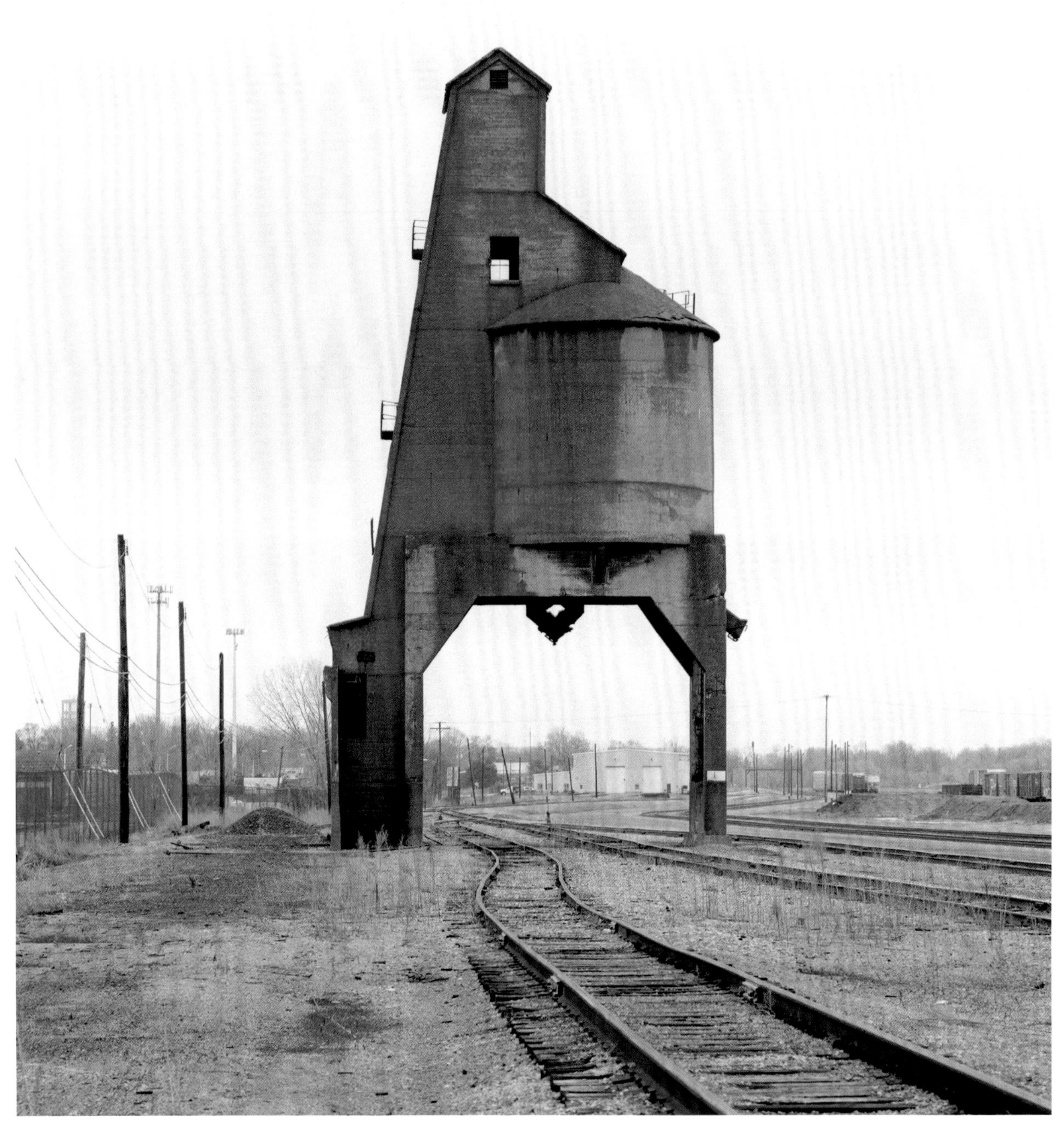

 PONTIAC, MICHIGAN Grand Trunk Western 42°39’15.7”N 83°18’57.8”W

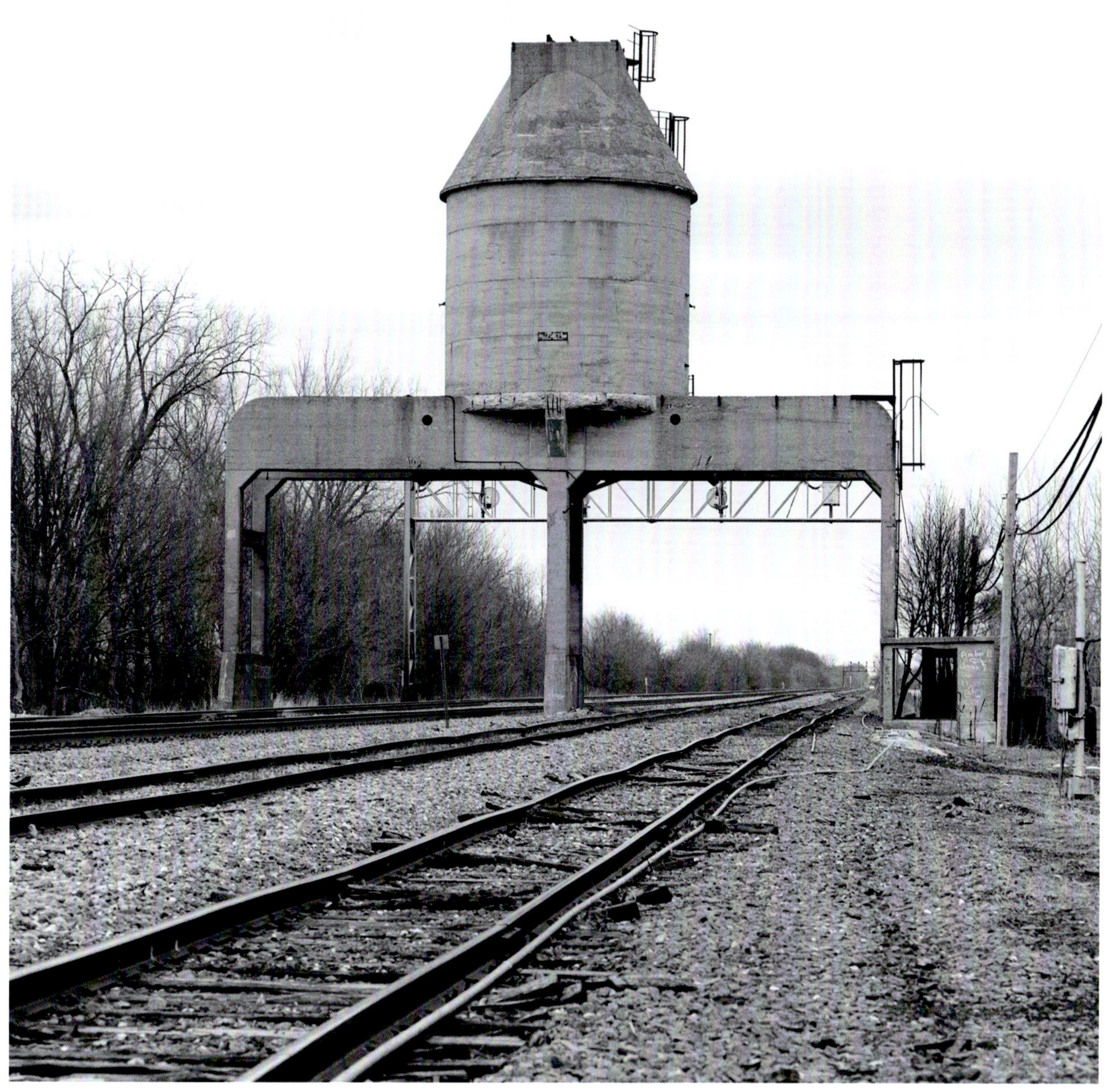

37 **NELSON, ILLINOIS** Chicago & North Western 41°47’58.6”N 89°35’48.4”W

38 **SULLIVAN, INDIANA** Chicago & Eastern Ilinois 39°06’52.7”N 87°24’19.1”W

Following Spread

CARBONDALE, ILLINOIS Illinois Central 37°44’23.5”N 89°13’03.5”W (left)

GILMAN, ILLINOIS Illinois Central 40°47’15.4”N 87°59’22.1”W (right)

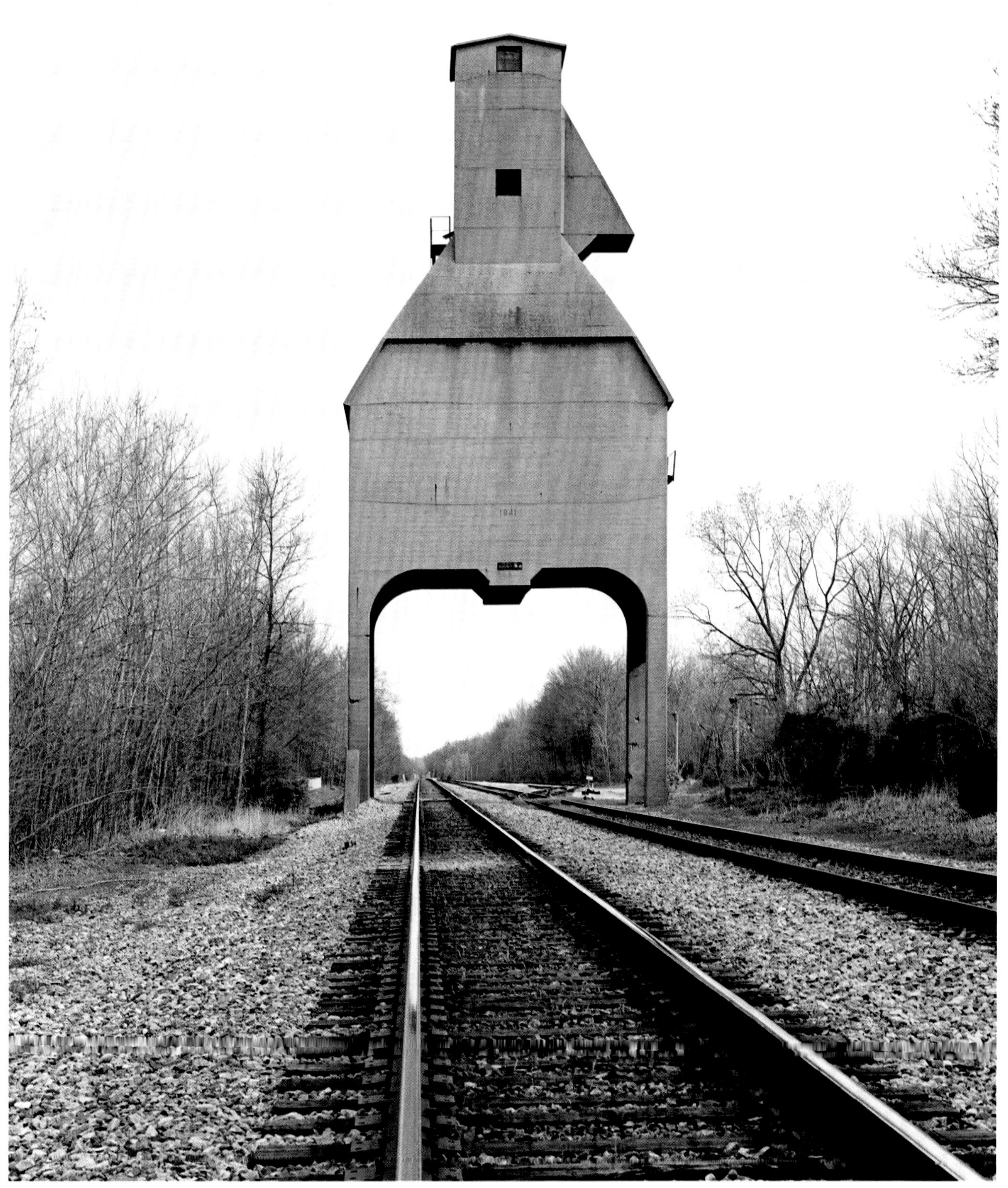

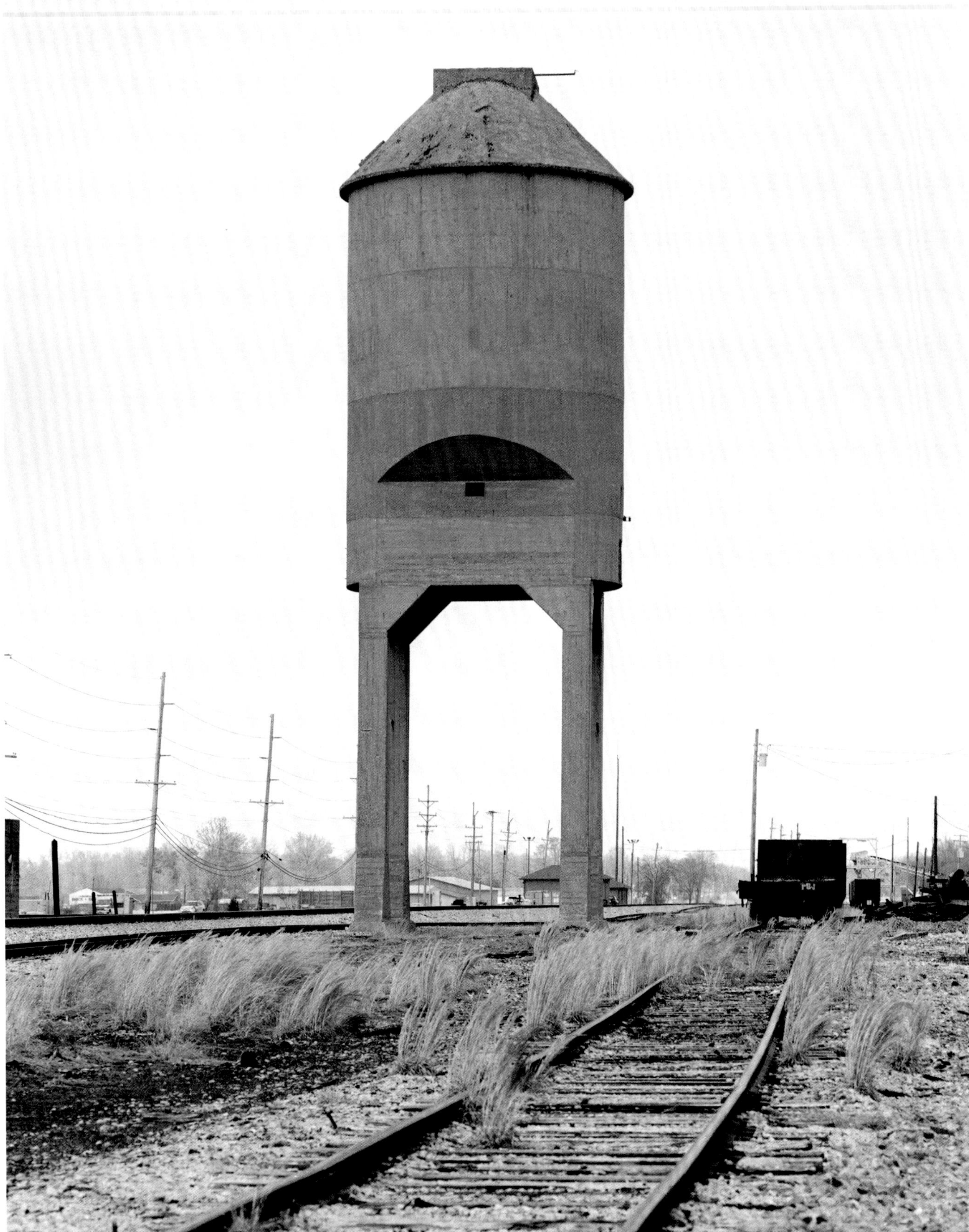

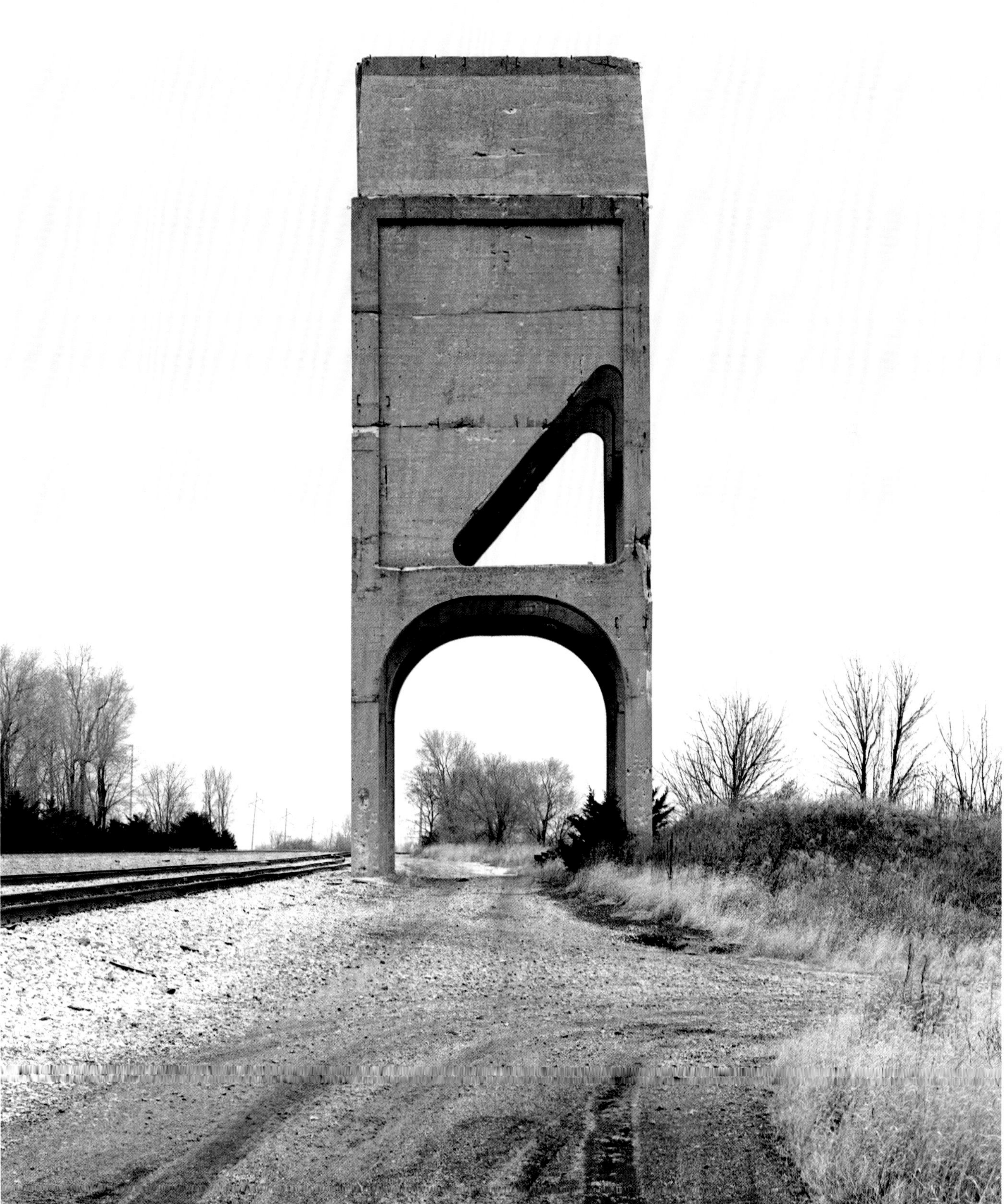

DALTON, WISCONSIN Chicago & North Western 43°39'20.0"N 89°12'30.1"W

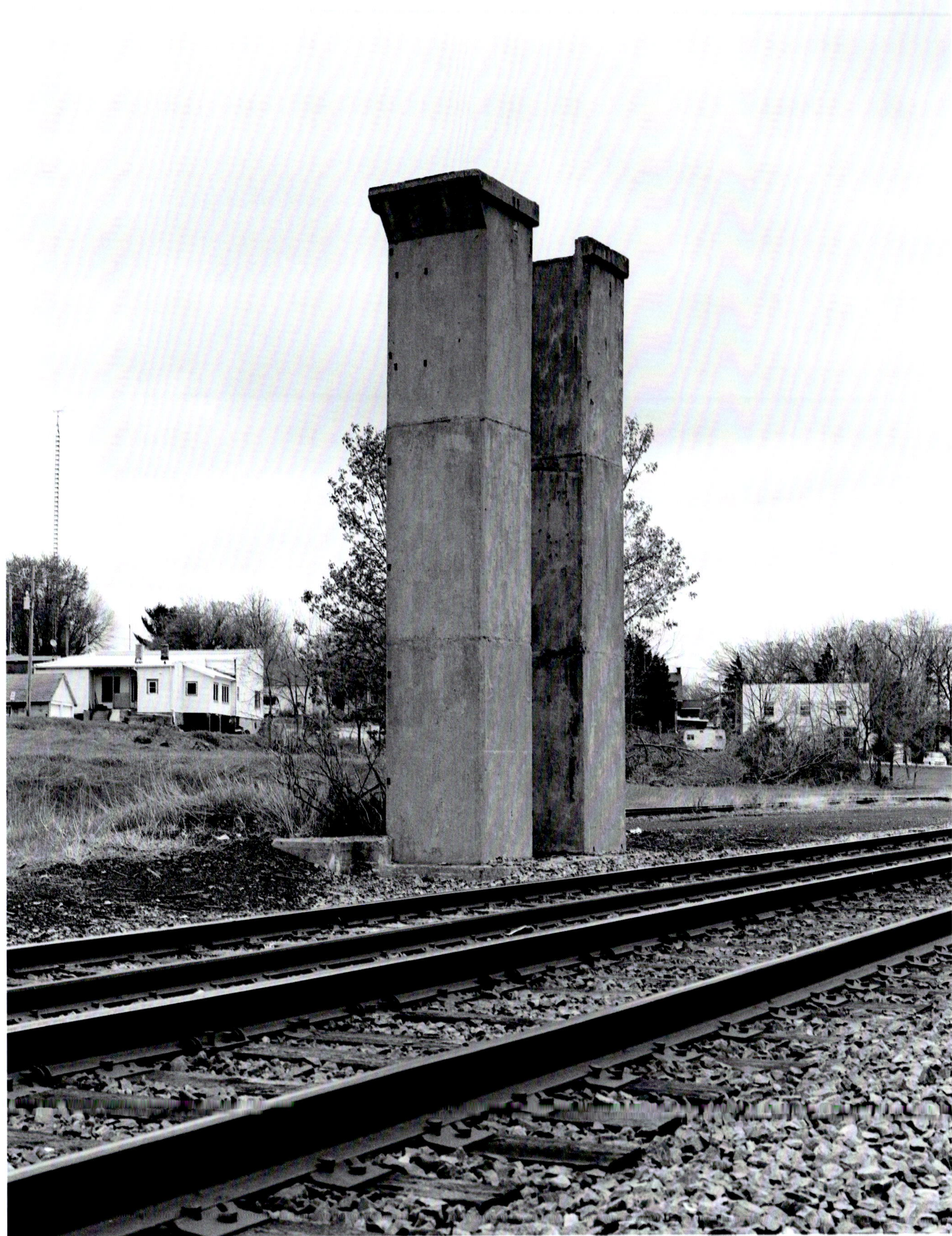

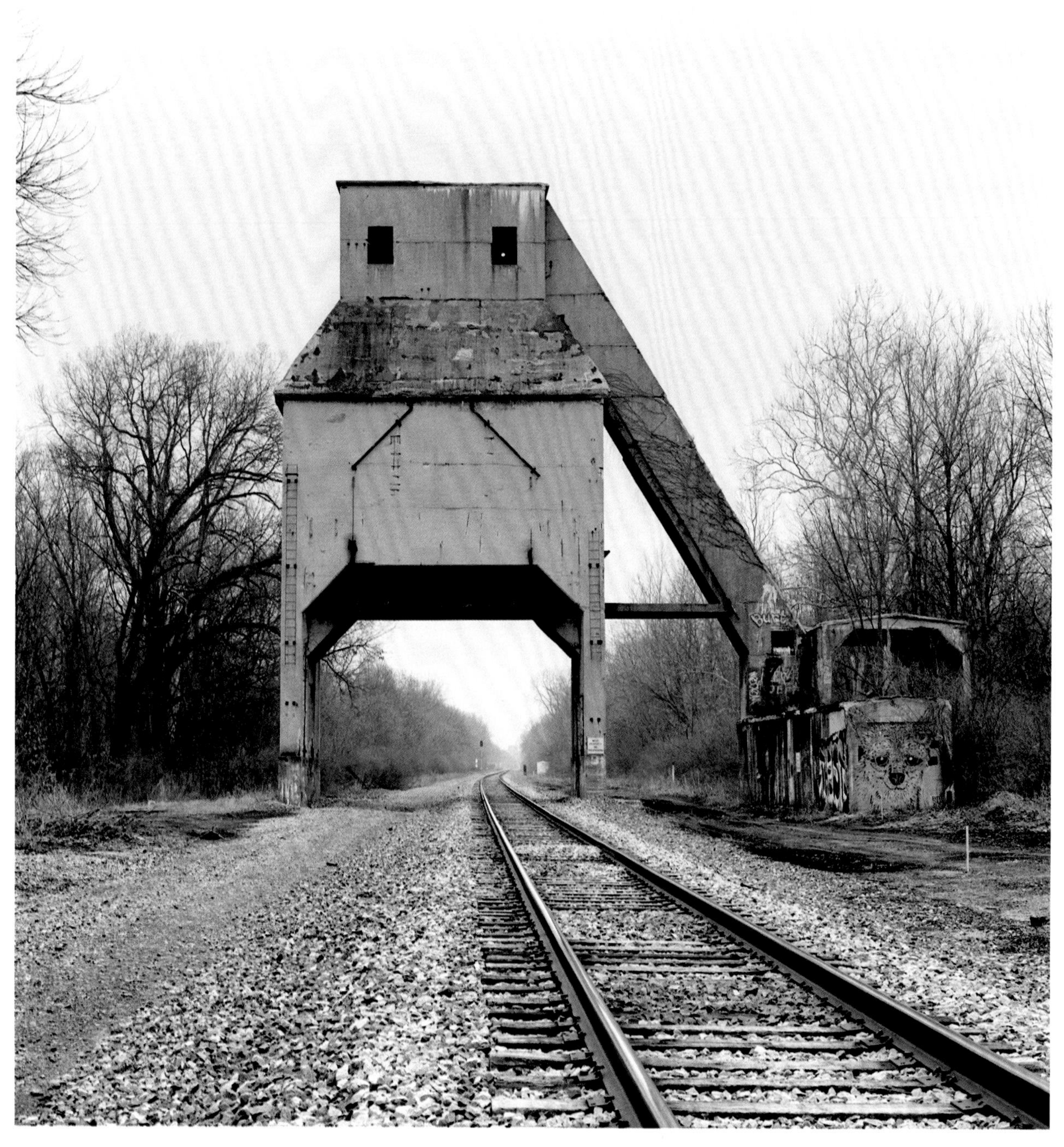

44 **AUGUSTA, MICHIGAN** Michigan Central 42°19'18.4"N 85°22'10.2"W (above)

45 **COUNCIL BLUFFS, IOWA** Illinois Central 41°16'27.5"N 95°51'50.3"W (right)

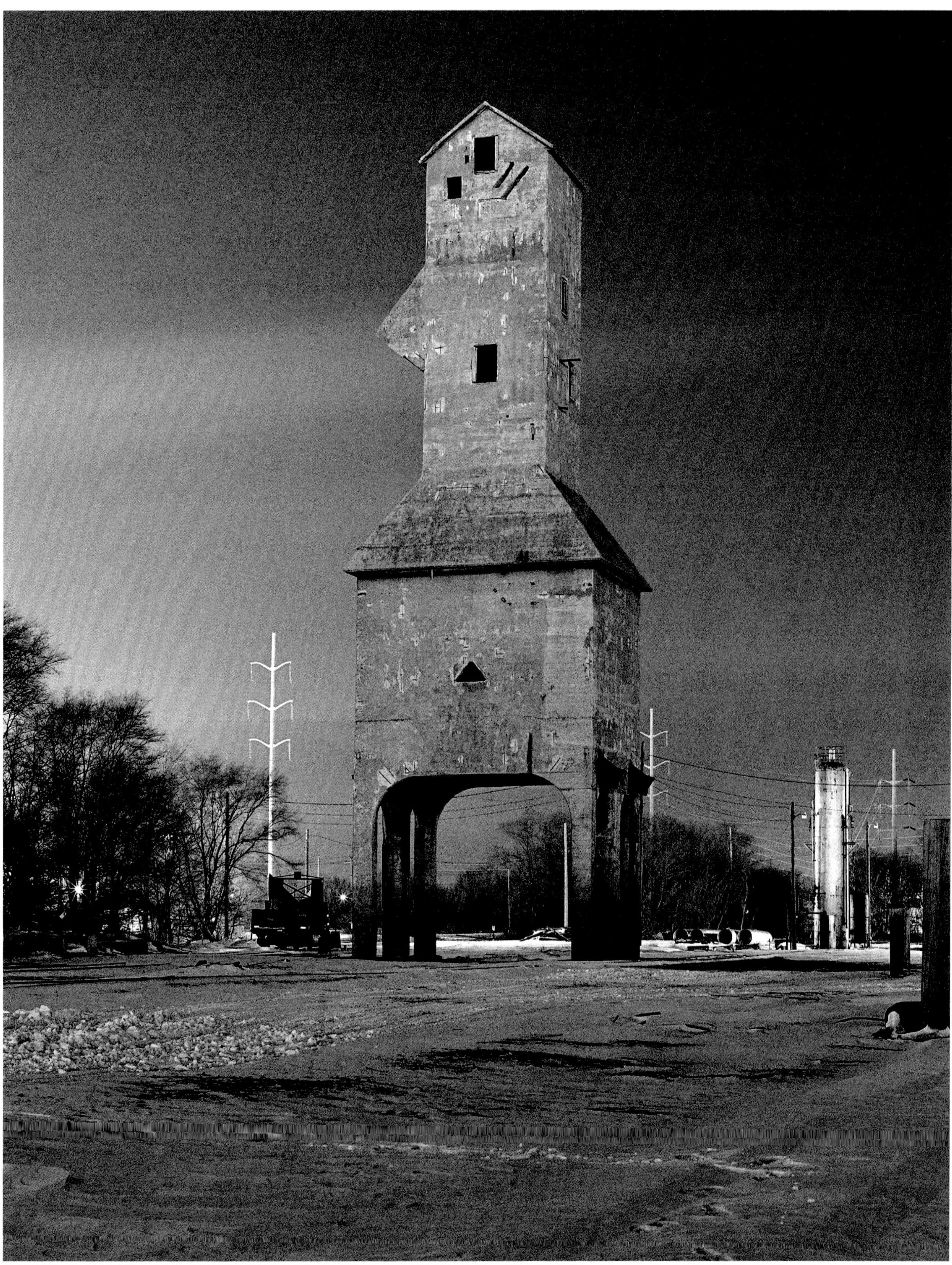

46 **LAMBERT, MISSISSIPPI** Yazoo & Mississippi Valley 34°11'53.1"N 90°16'57.1"W

Following Spread

CUSHING, OKLAHOMA Atchison, Topeka & Santa Fe 35°58'34.4"N 96°46'29.9"W (left)

IRVINGTON, KENTUCKY Louisville & Nashville 37°52'53.9"N 86°16'53.6"W (right)

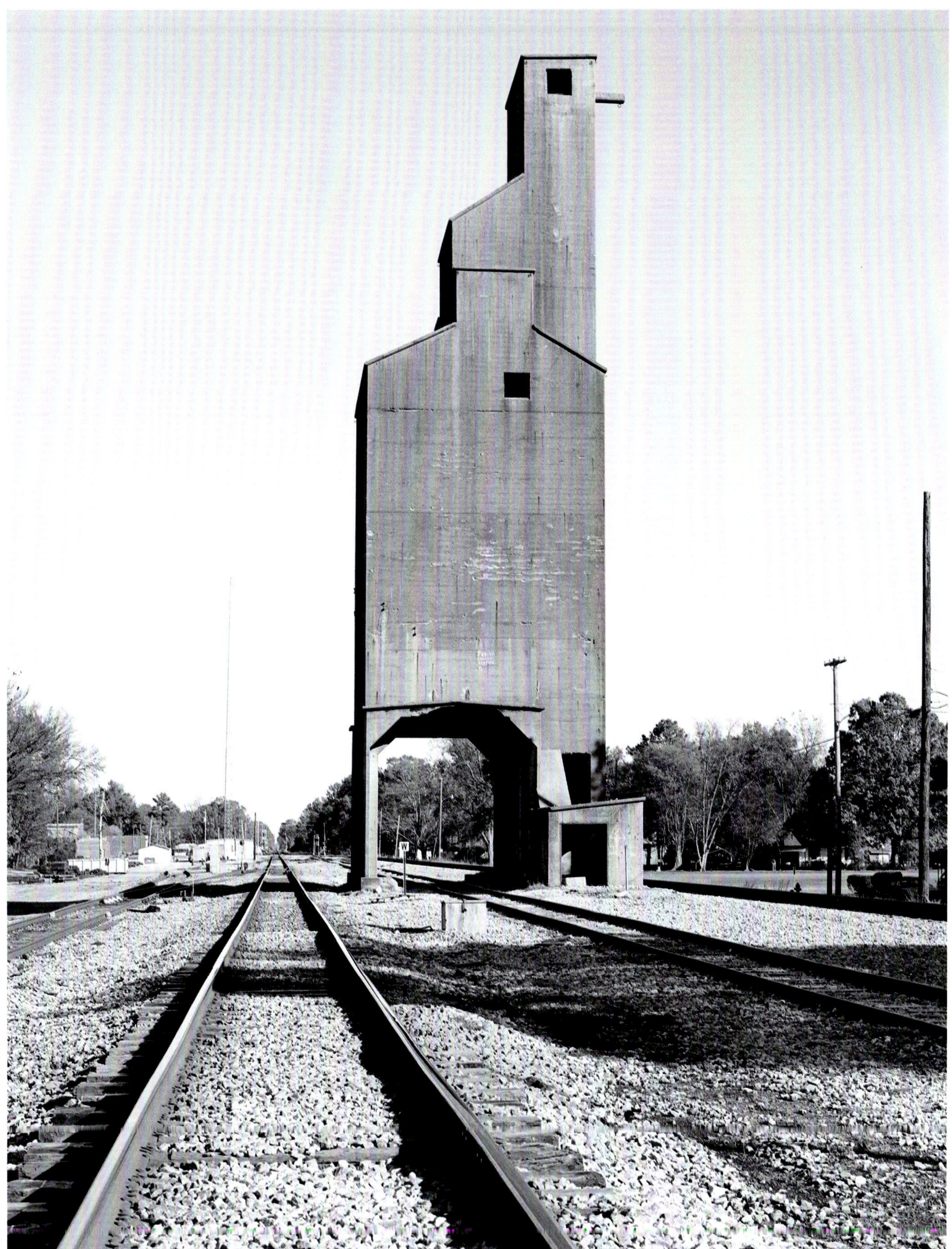

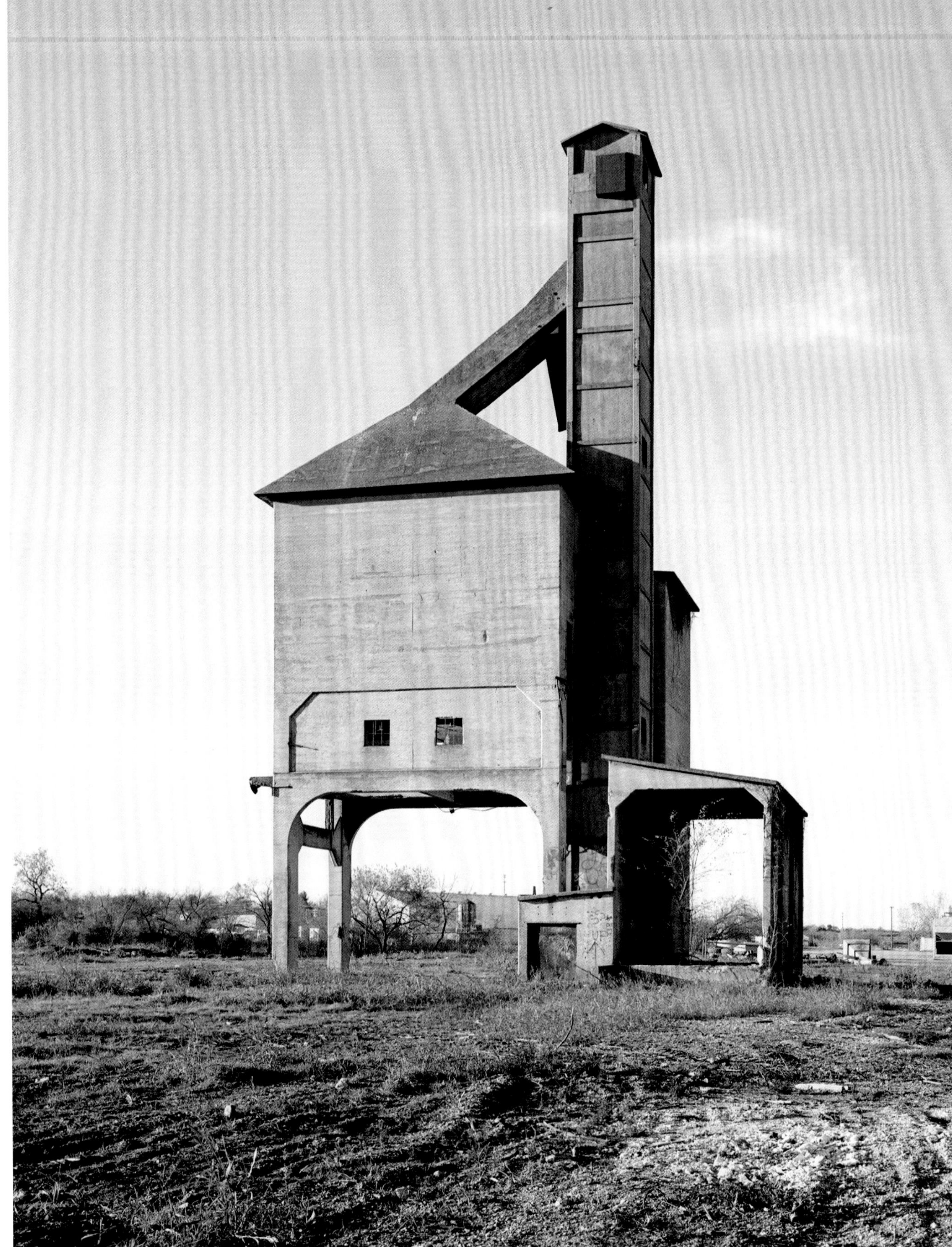

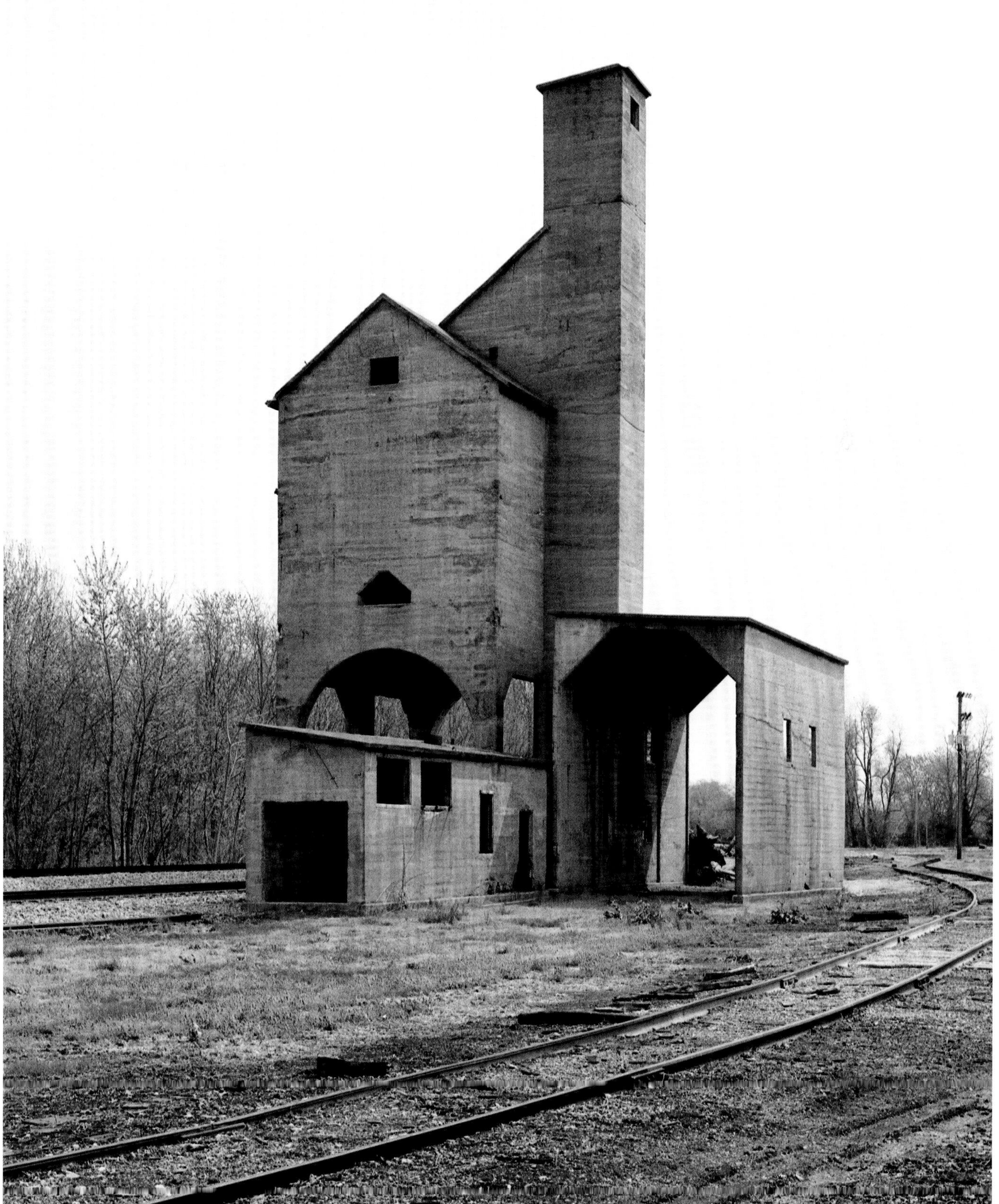

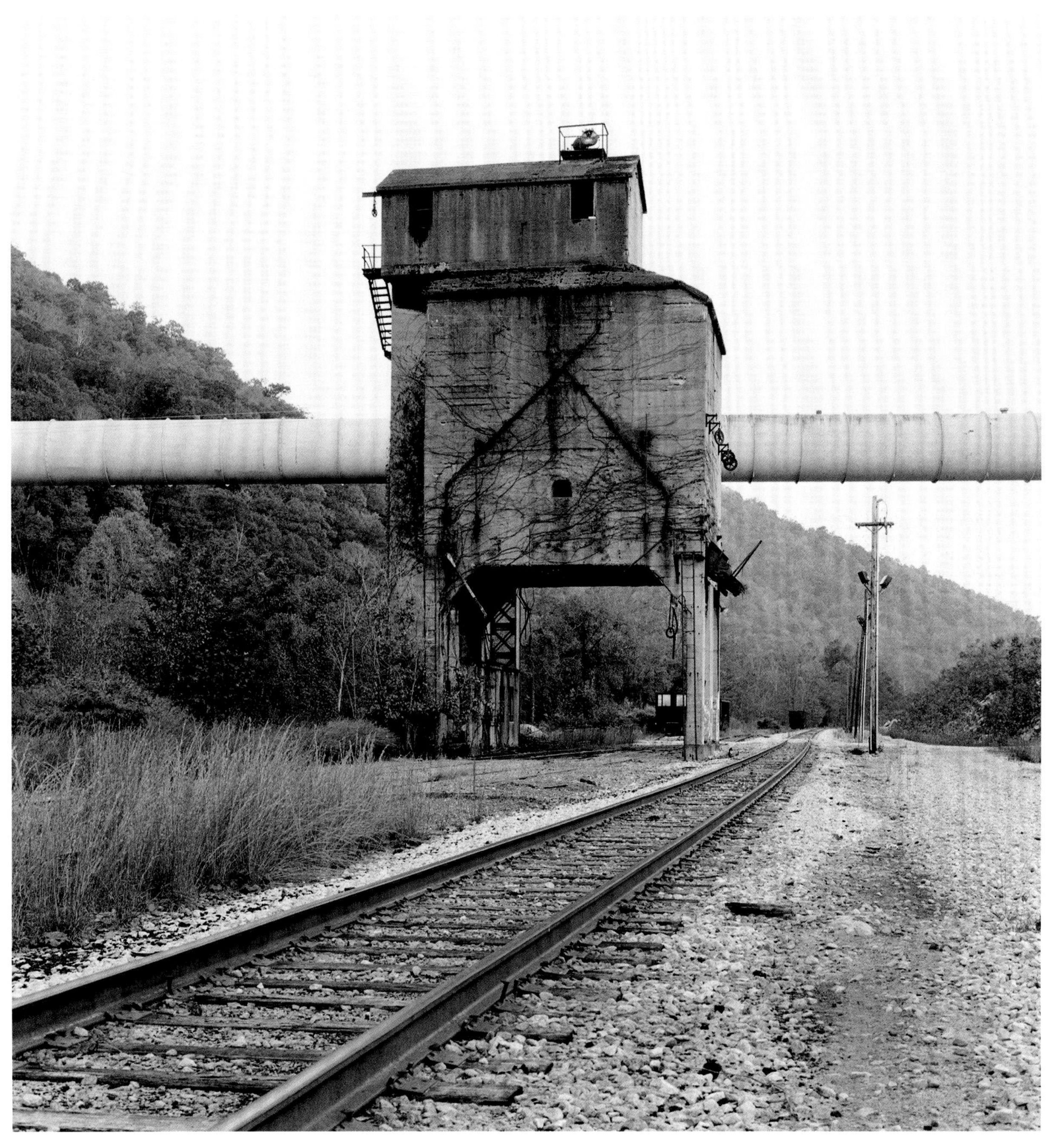

 ELK RIVER JUNCTION, WEST VIRGINIA Chesapeake & Ohio 38°00'13.8"N 81°33'05.0"W

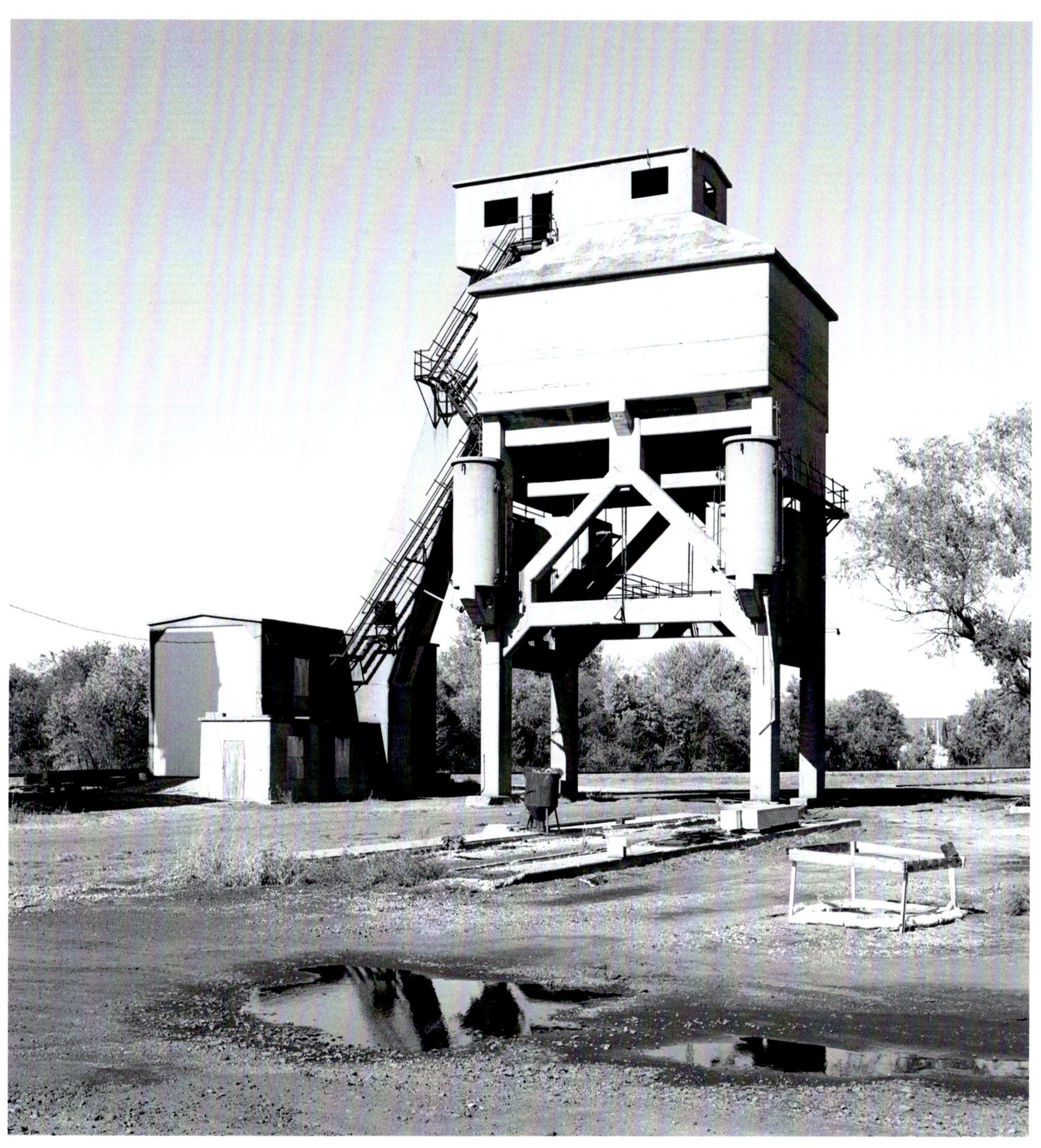

51 **MARCELINE, MISSOURI** Atchison, Topeka & Santa Fe 39°42’29.4”N 92°57’18.5”W

Following Spread

OAKFIELD, MAINE Bangor & Aroostook 46°06’14.5”N 68°08’56.4”W (left)

DERBY, MAINE Bangor & Aroostook 45°13’55.5”N 68°57’59.5”W (right)

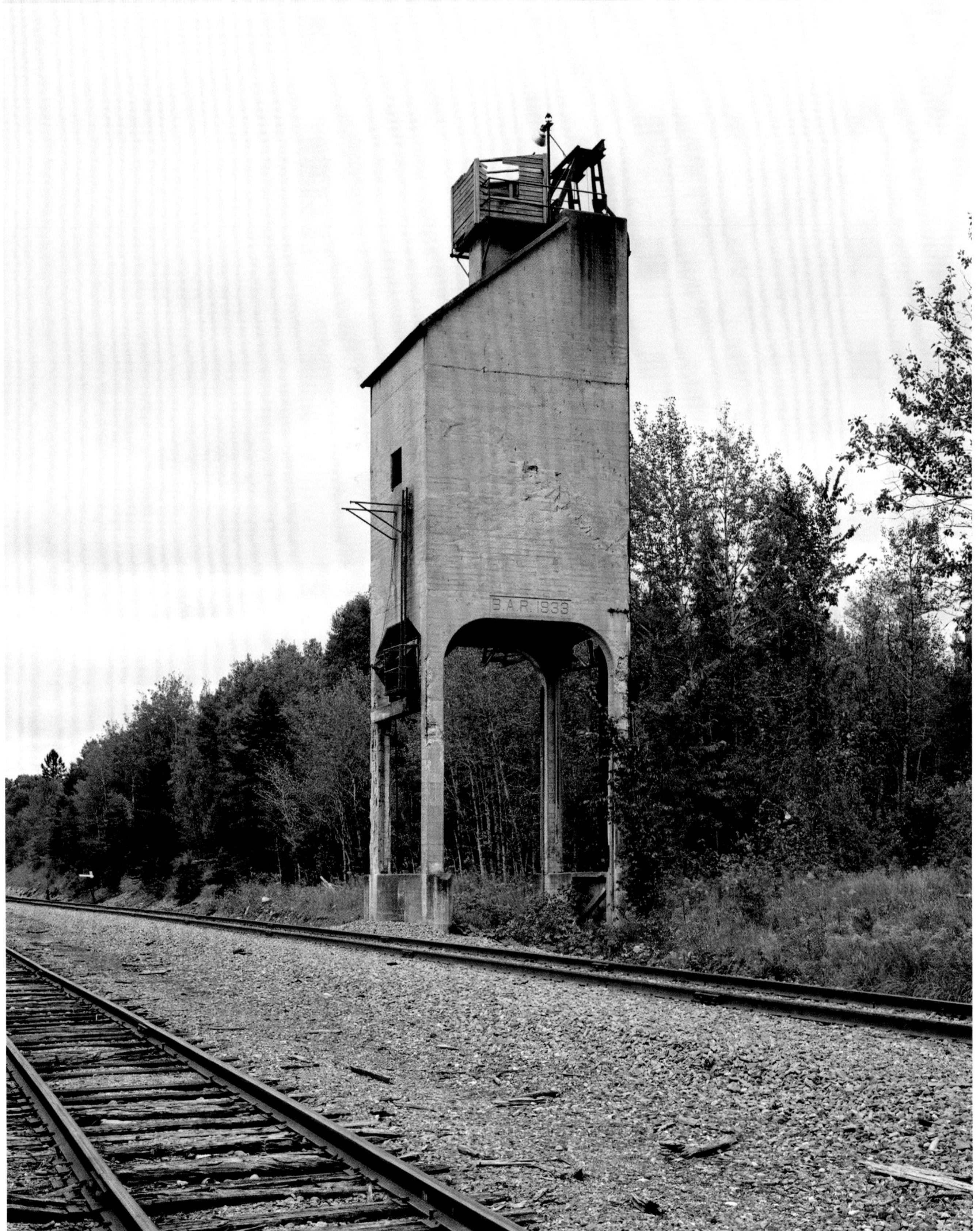
B.A.R. 1933

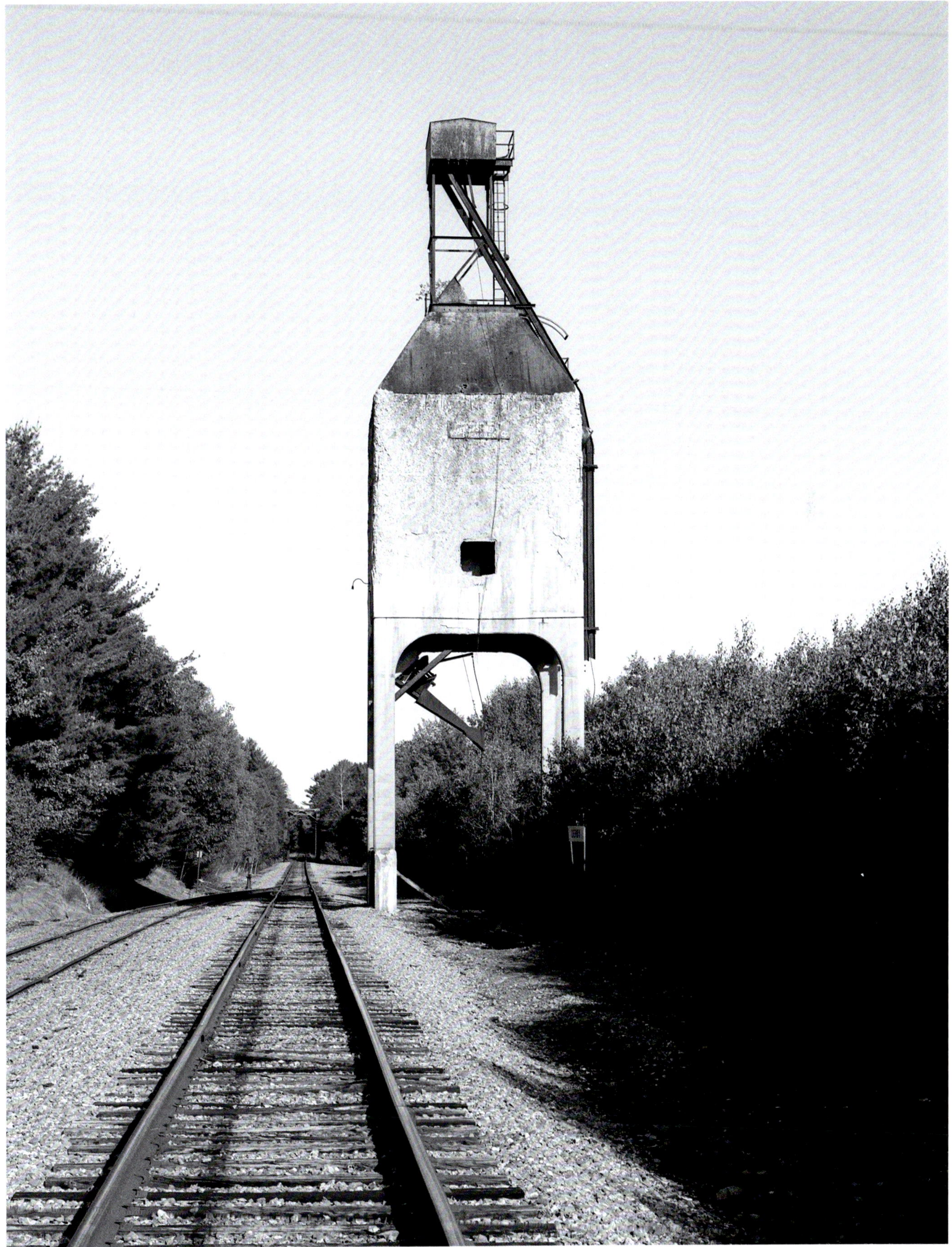

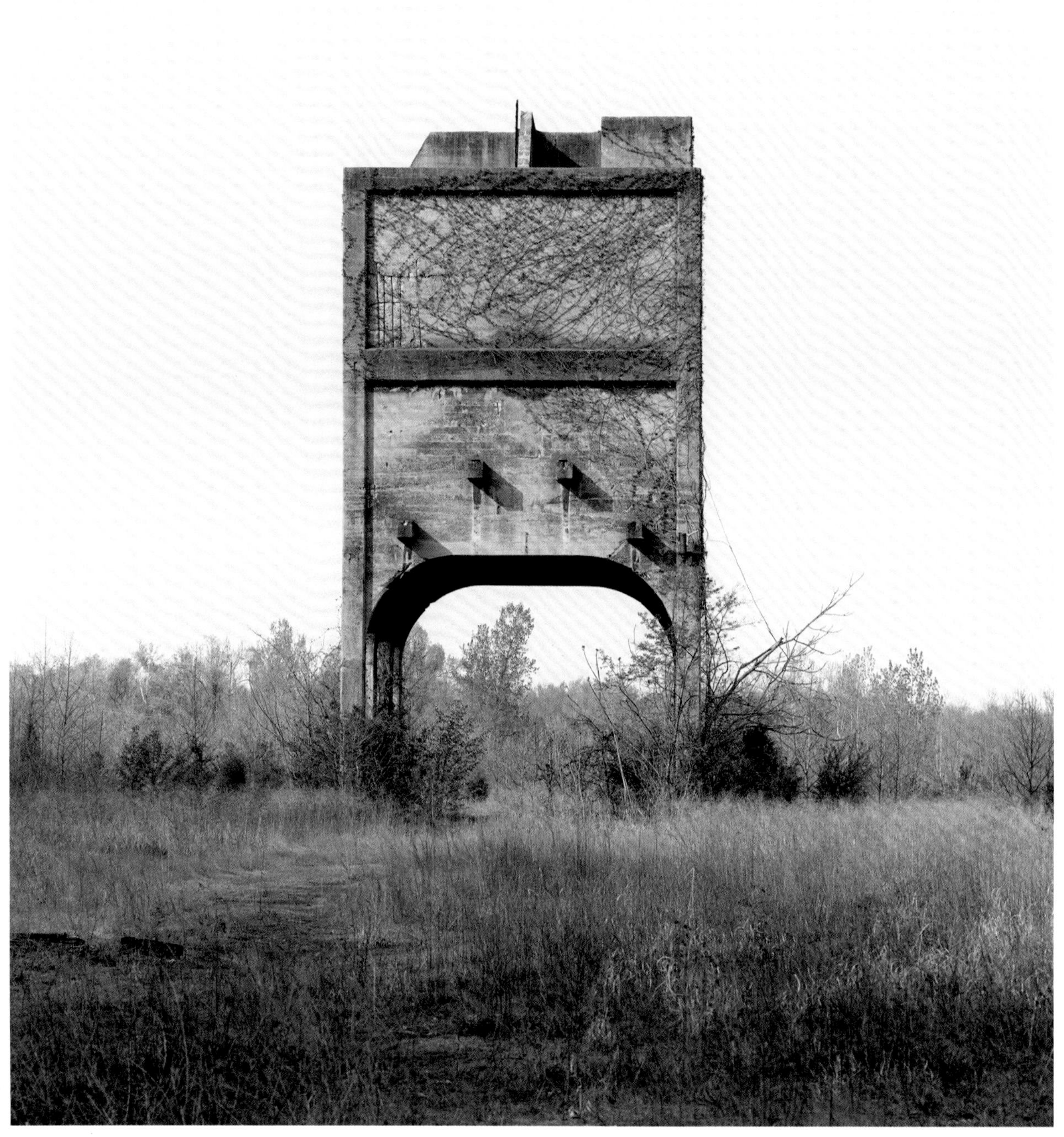

 CENTRAL CITY, KENTUCKY Illinois Central 37°17'35.4"N 87°07'06.1"W

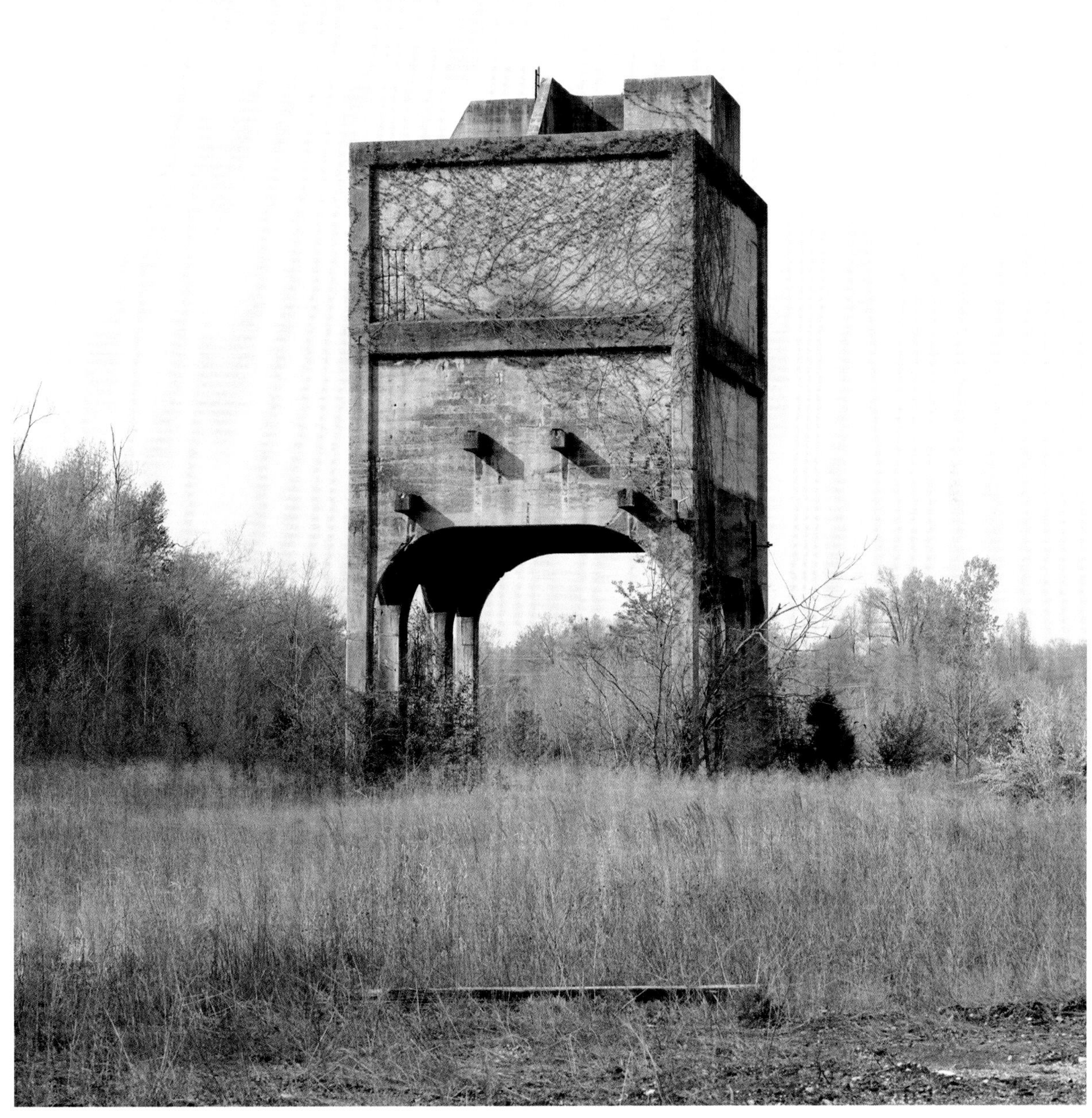

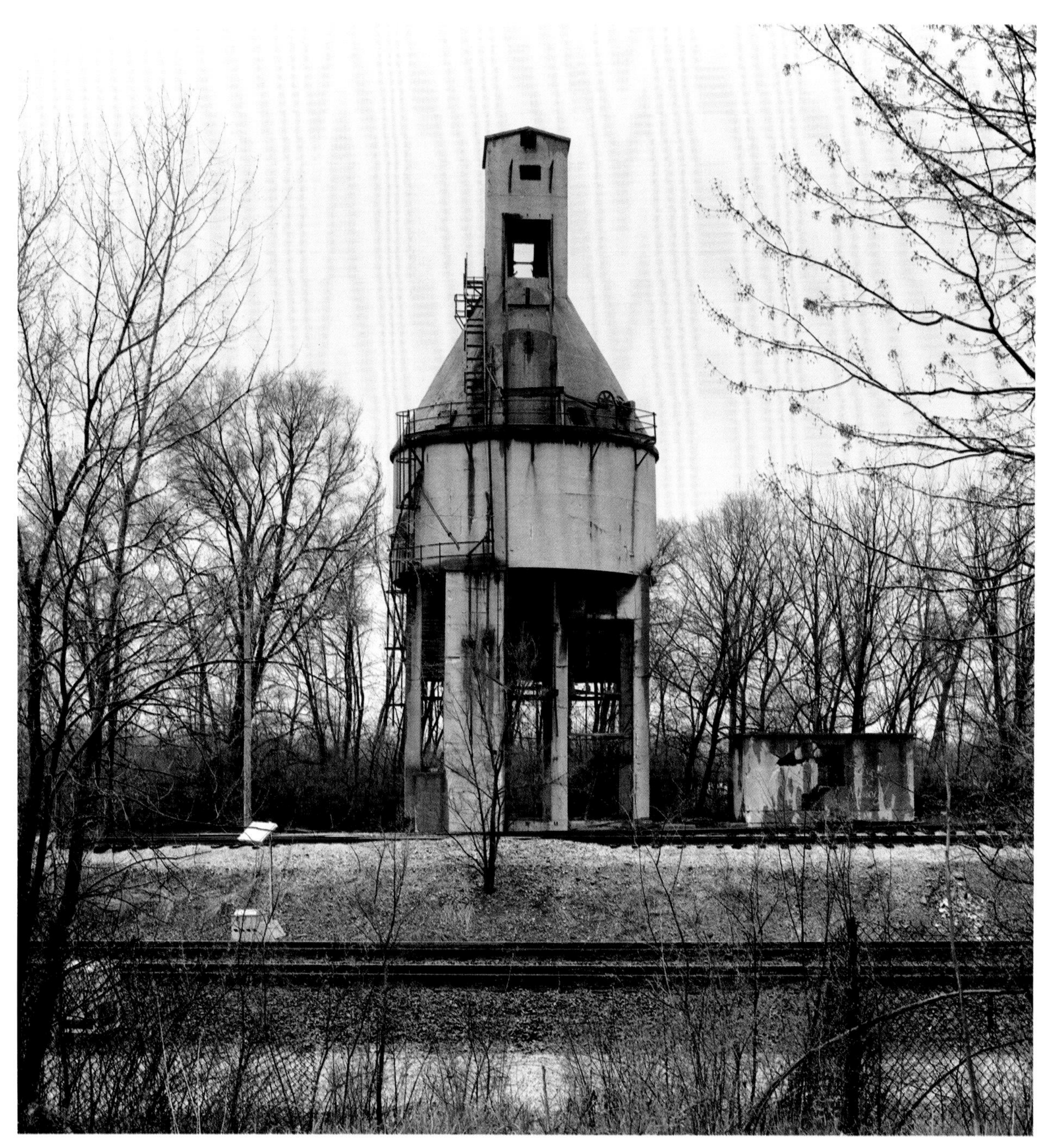

 LAFAYETTE, INDIANA Chicago, Indianapolis & Louisville 40°26'28.0"N 86°52'48.9"W

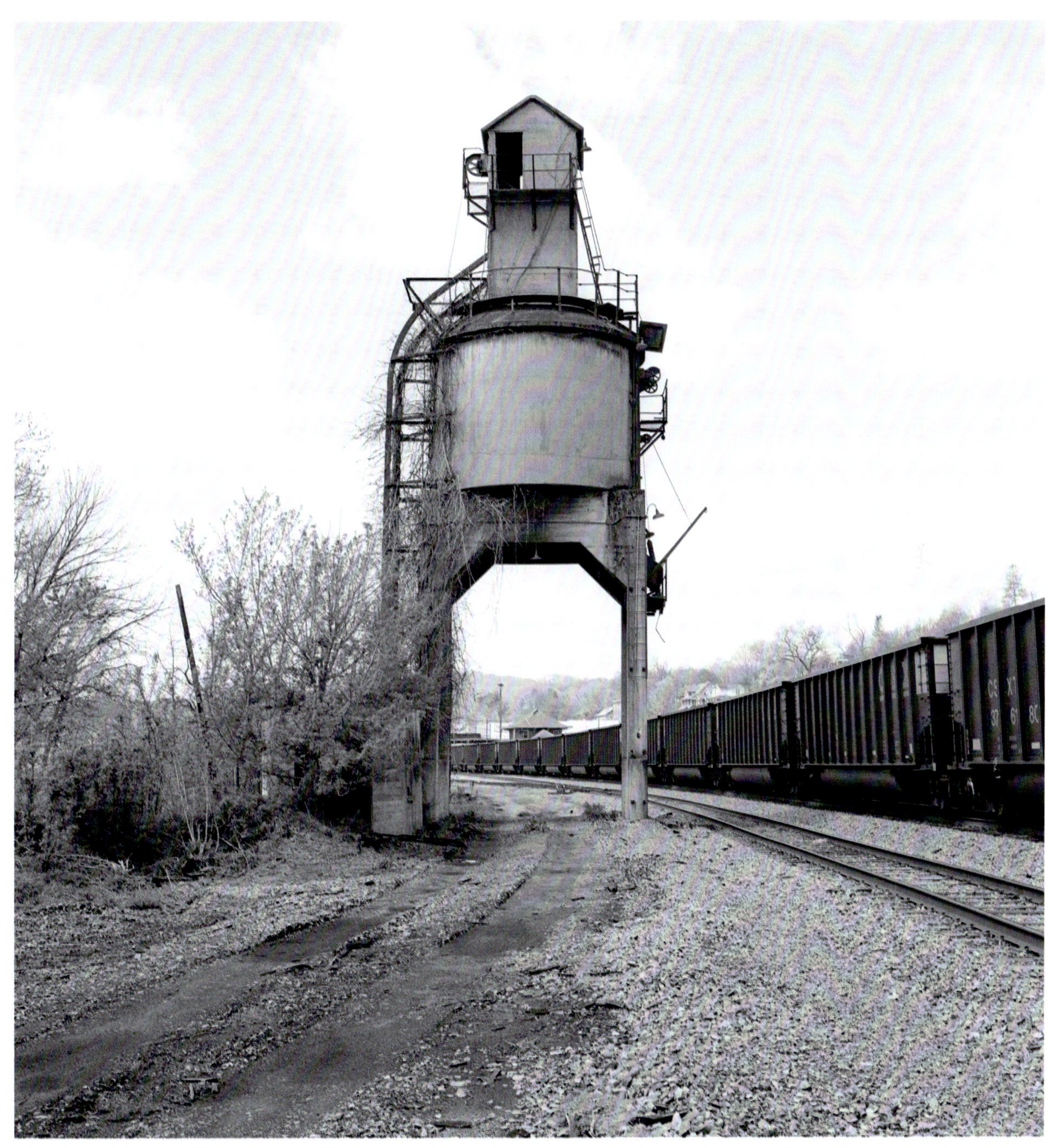

57 **RONCEVERTE, WEST VIRGINIA** Chesapeake & Ohio 37°44’56.6”N 80°27’43.2”W

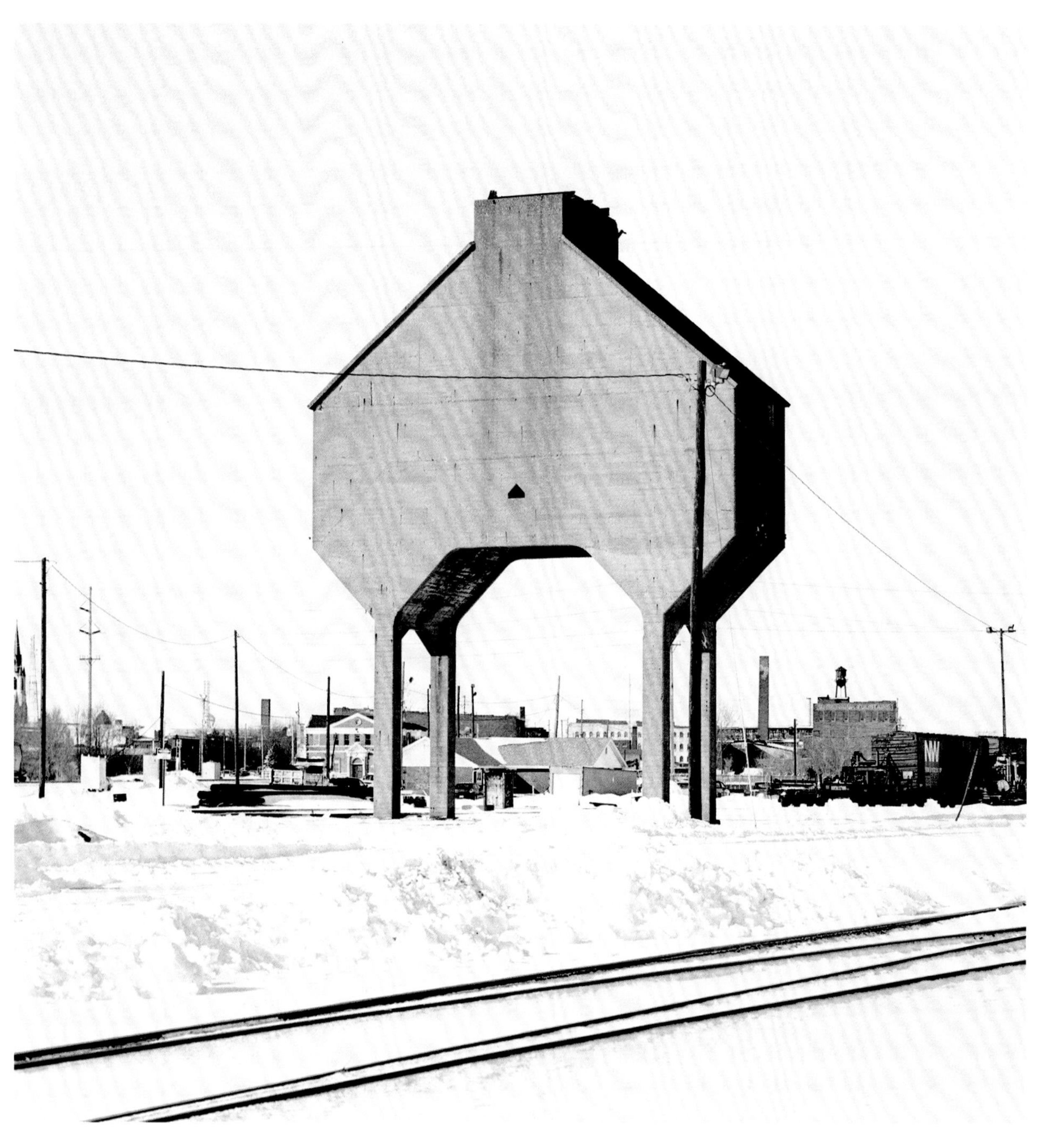

 DECATUR, ILLINOIS Wabash 39°50’53.7”N 88°56’31.0”W

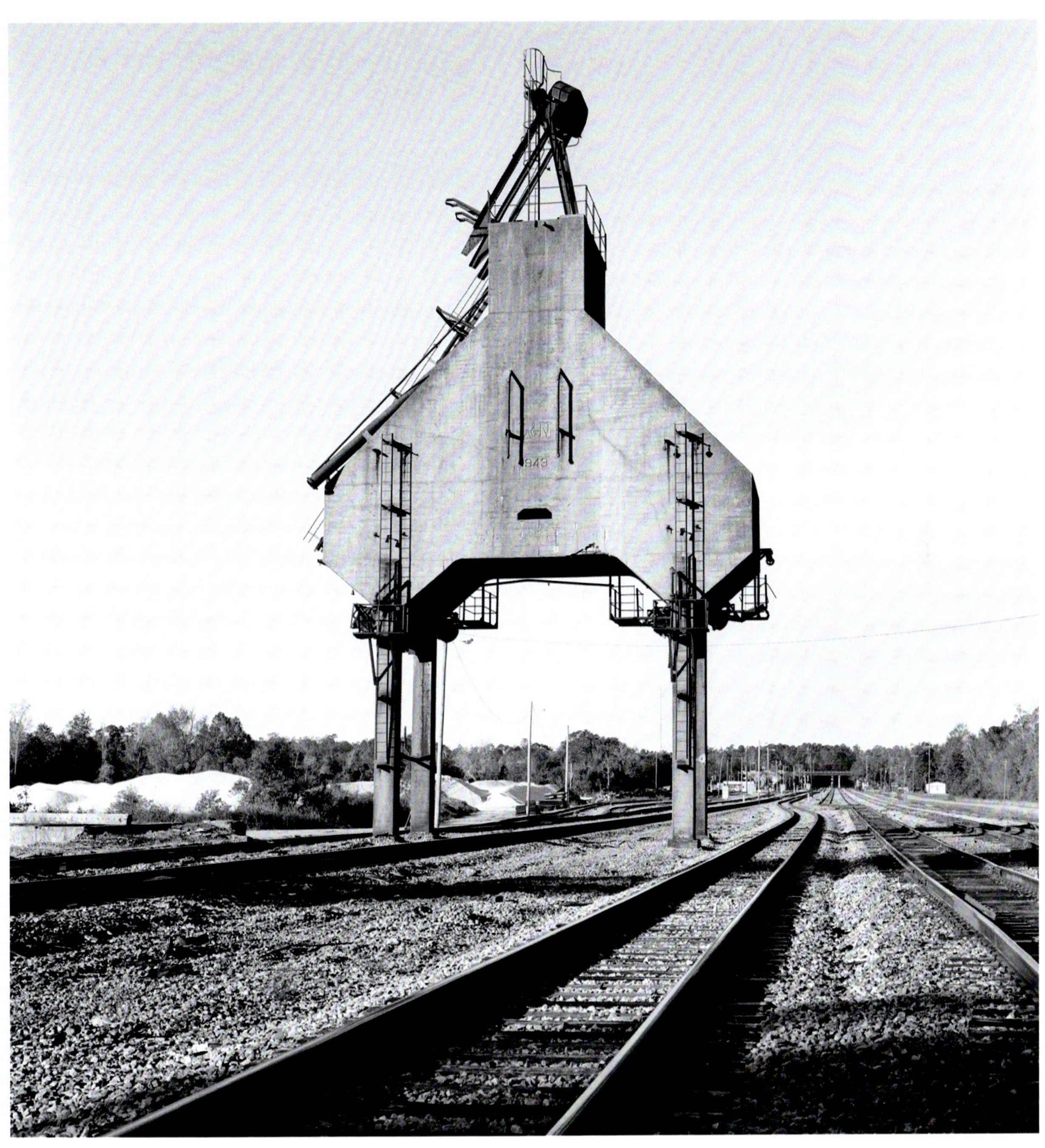

 FLOMATON, ALABAMA (demolished 2022) Louisville & Nashville 30°59’57.2”N 87°15’33.9”W

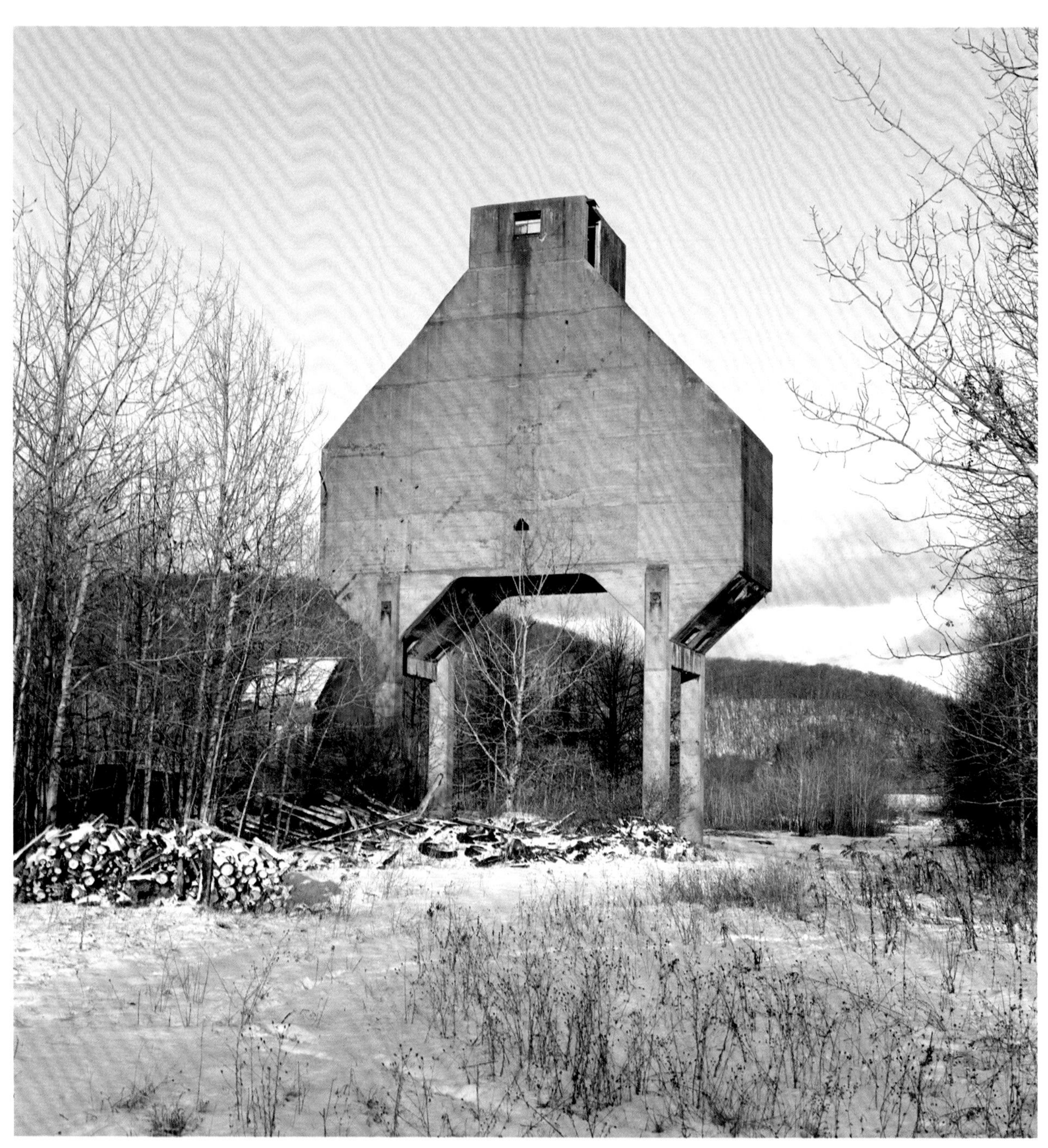

 ONEONTA, NEW YORK Delaware & Hudson 42°26’53.2”N 75°05’13.8”W

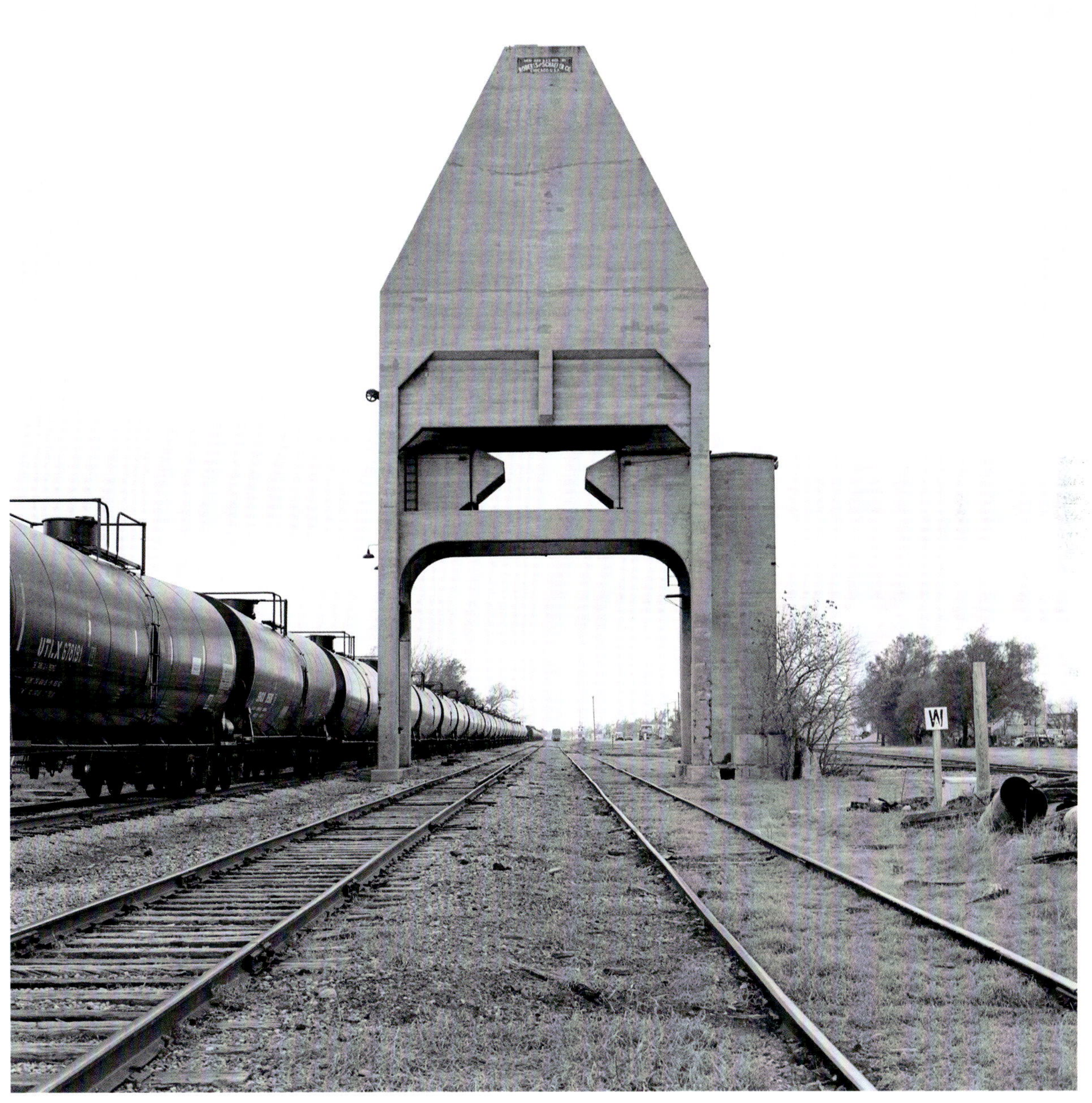

61 **GREAT BEND, KANSAS** Atchison, Topeka & Santa Fe 38°21'19.2"N 98°46'12.3"W

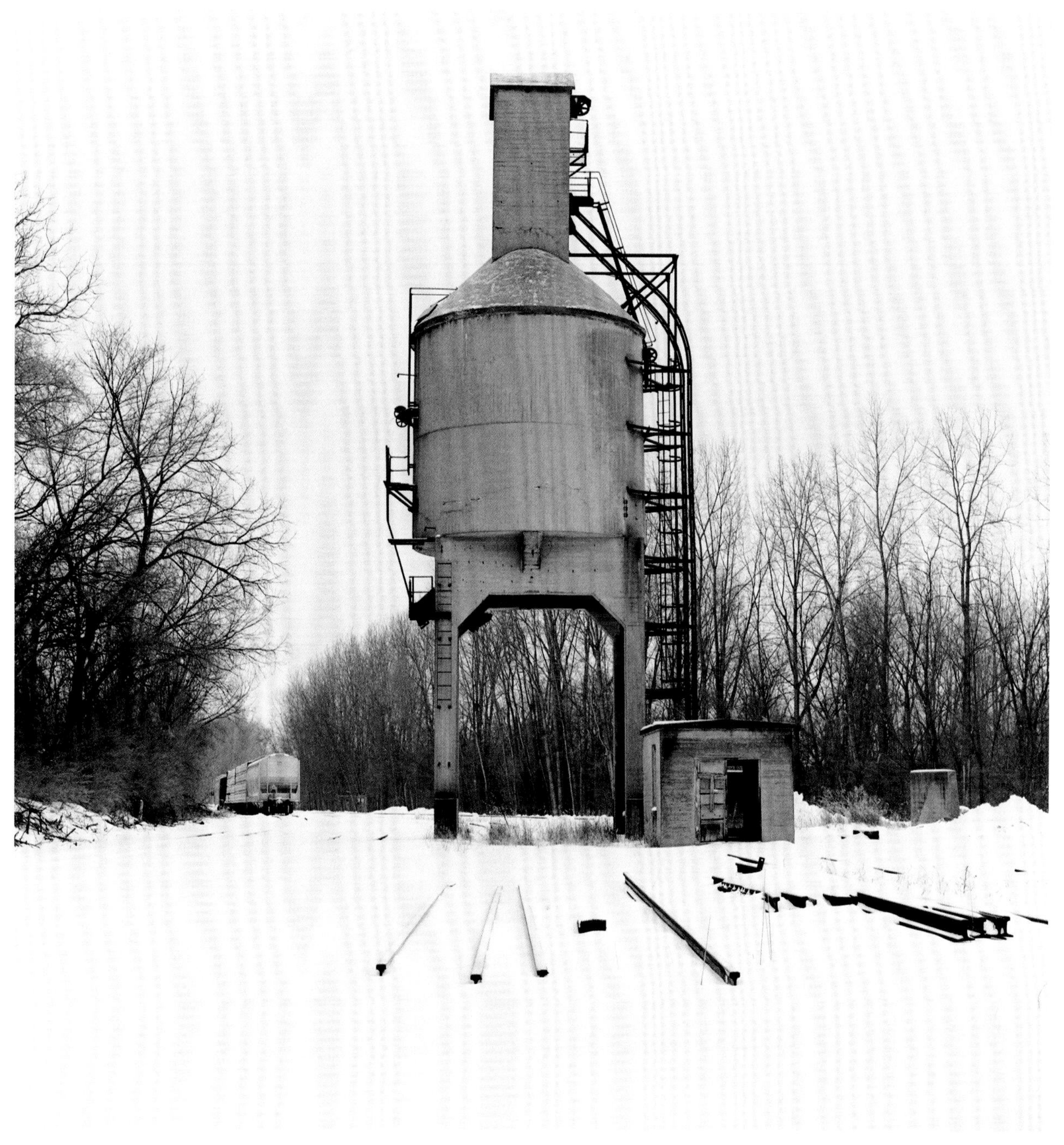

 SPRINGFIELD, OHIO Detroit, Toledo & Ironton 39°54'18.5"N 83°46'04.1"W

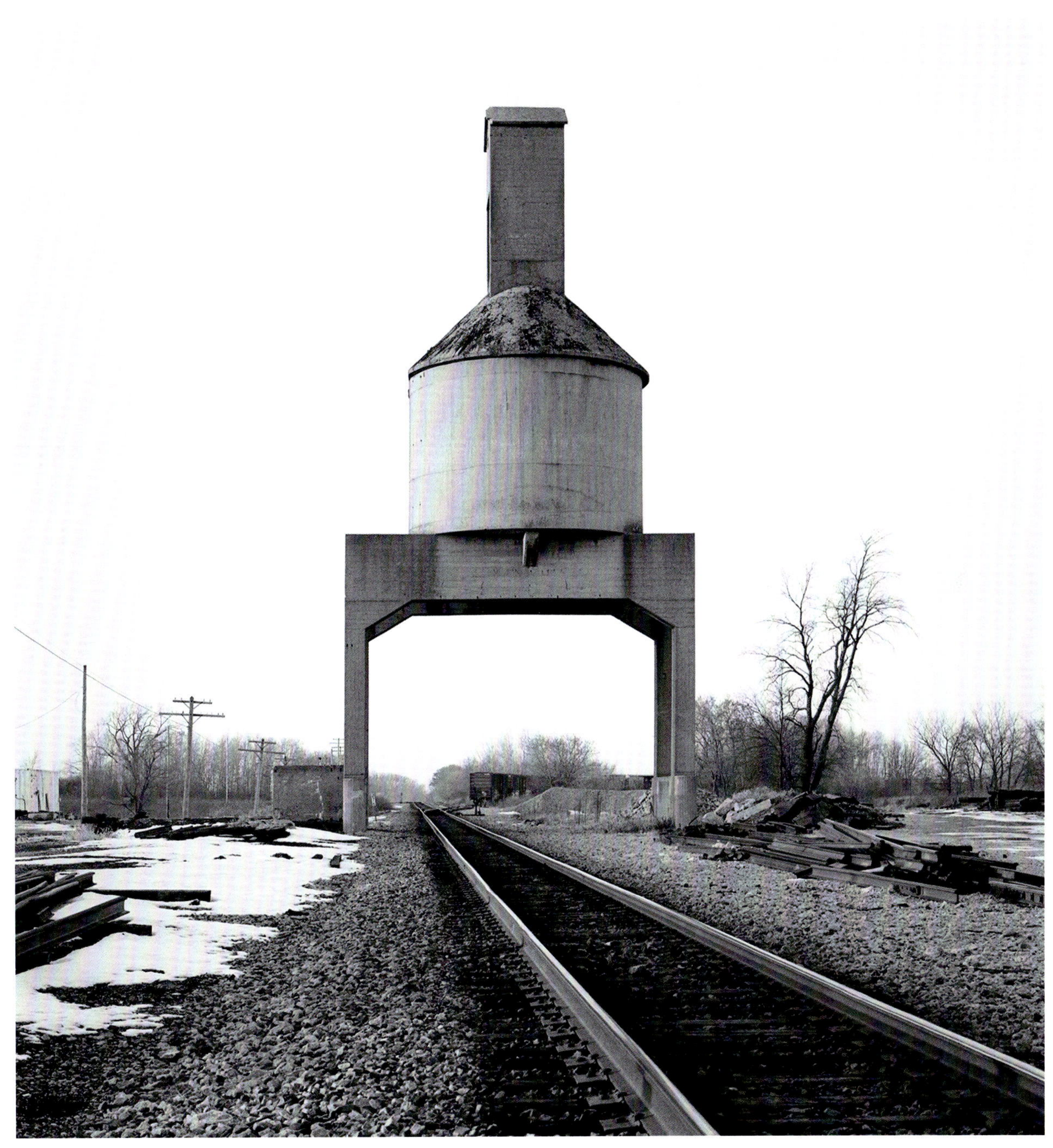

63 **CLYMAN JUNCTION, WISCONSIN** Chicago & North Western 43°19’25.0”N 88°42’55.8”W

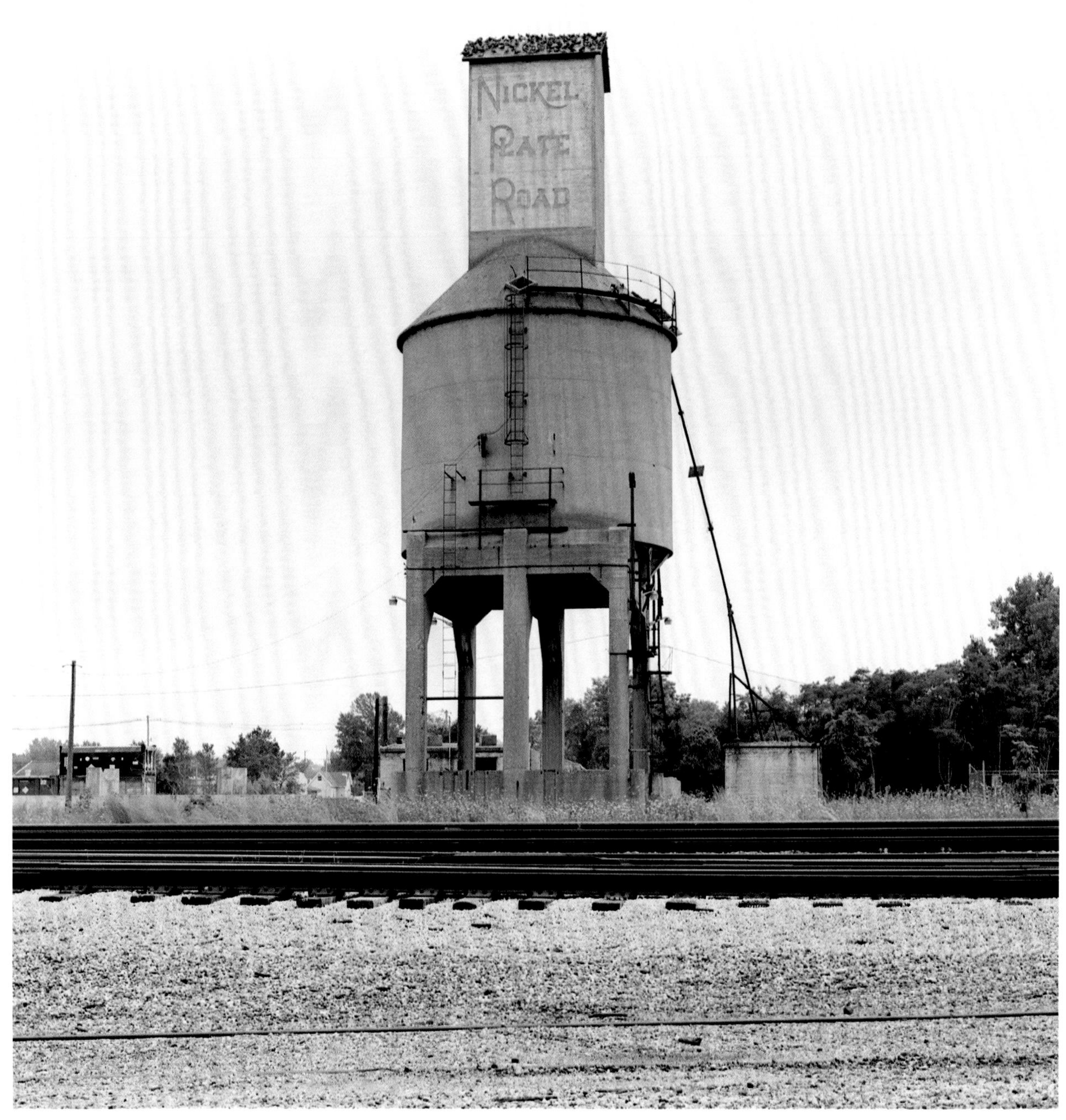

 FRANKFORT, INDIANA New York, Chicago & St. Louis 40°16’55.7”N 86°31’30.1”W

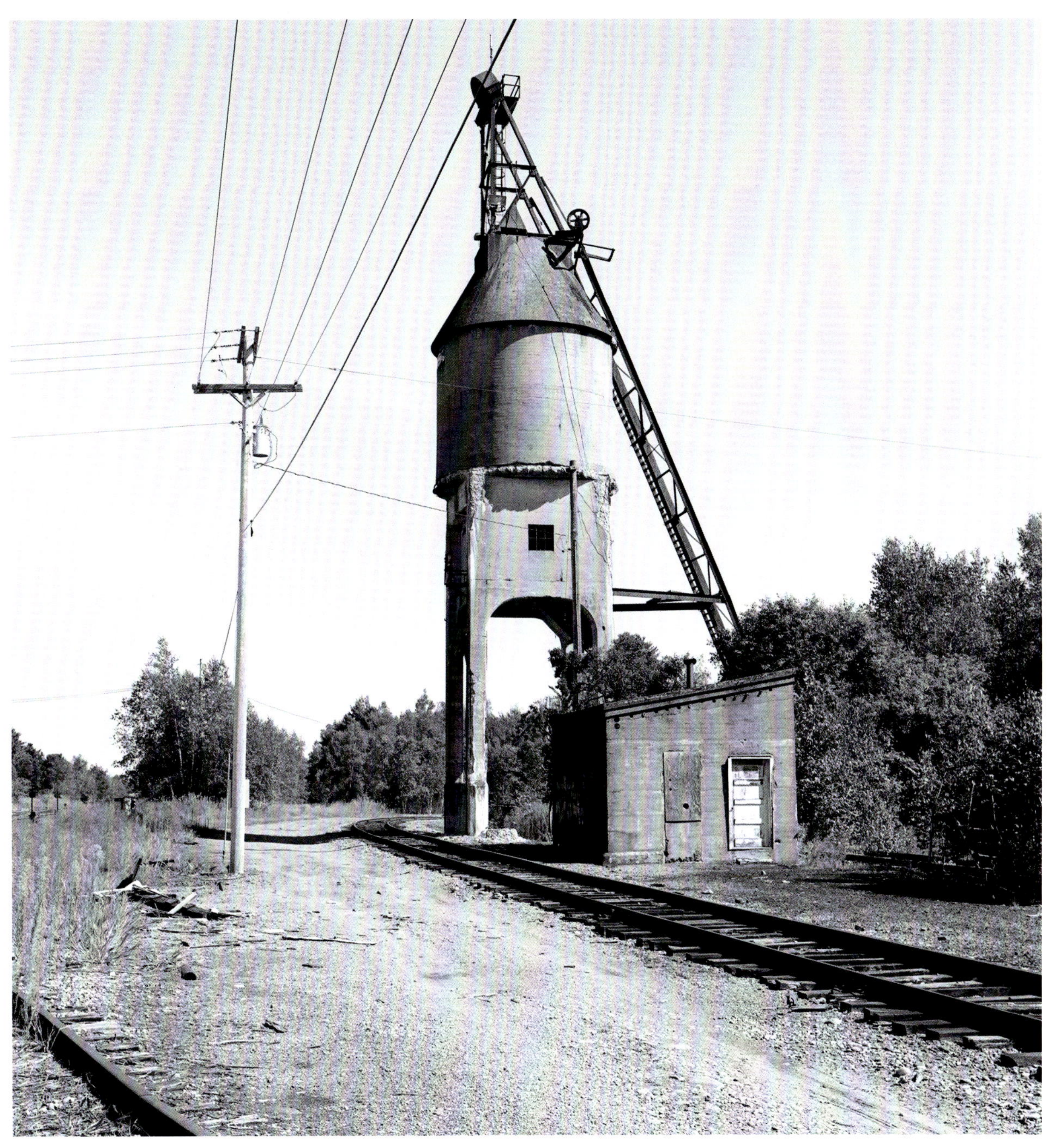

 NORTHERN MAINE JUNCTION, MAINE Bangor & Aroostook 44°47’25.7”N 68°51’39.1”W

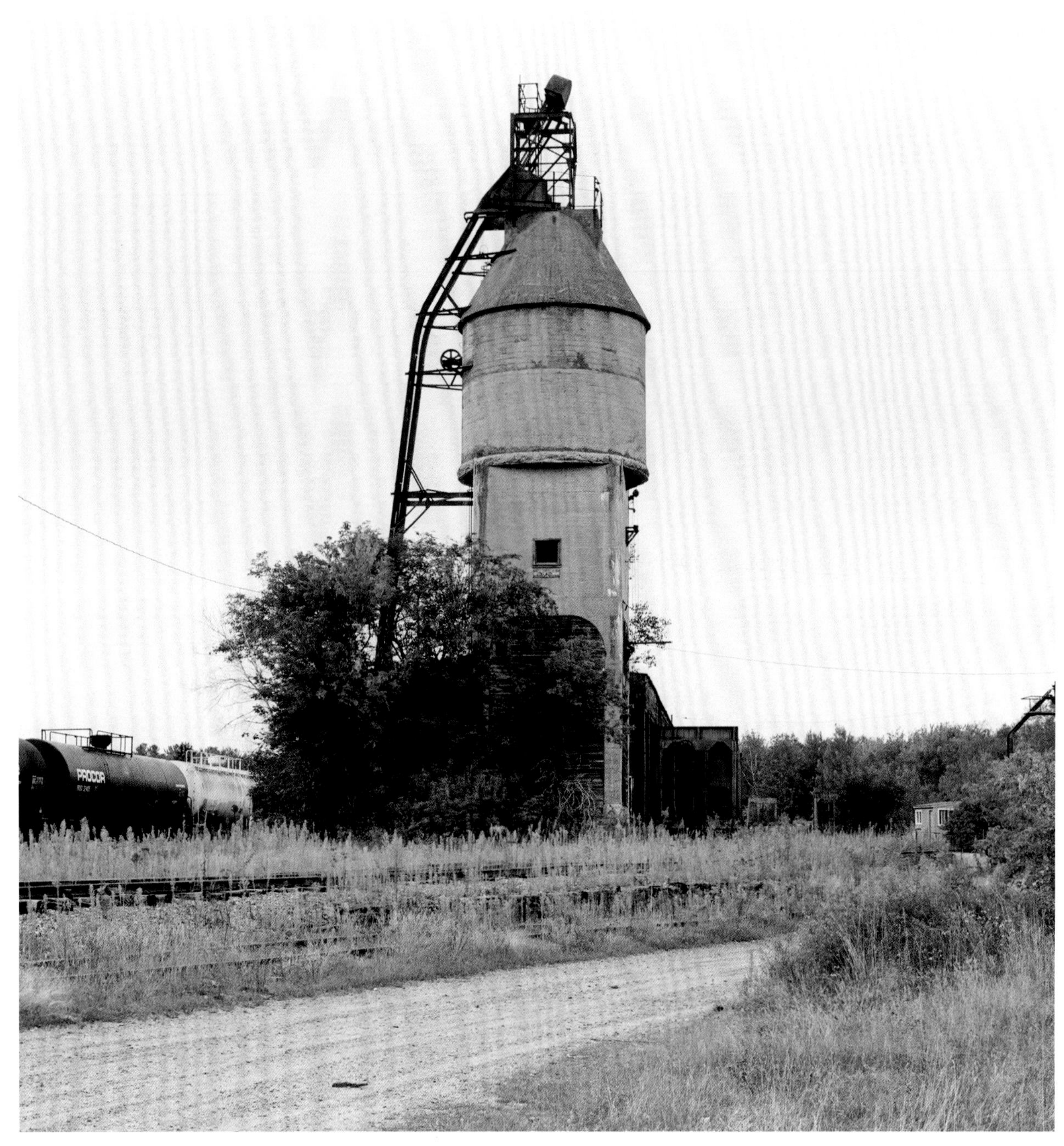

 MILLINOCKET, MAINE Bangor & Aroostook 45°40’02.7”N 68°42’45.0”W

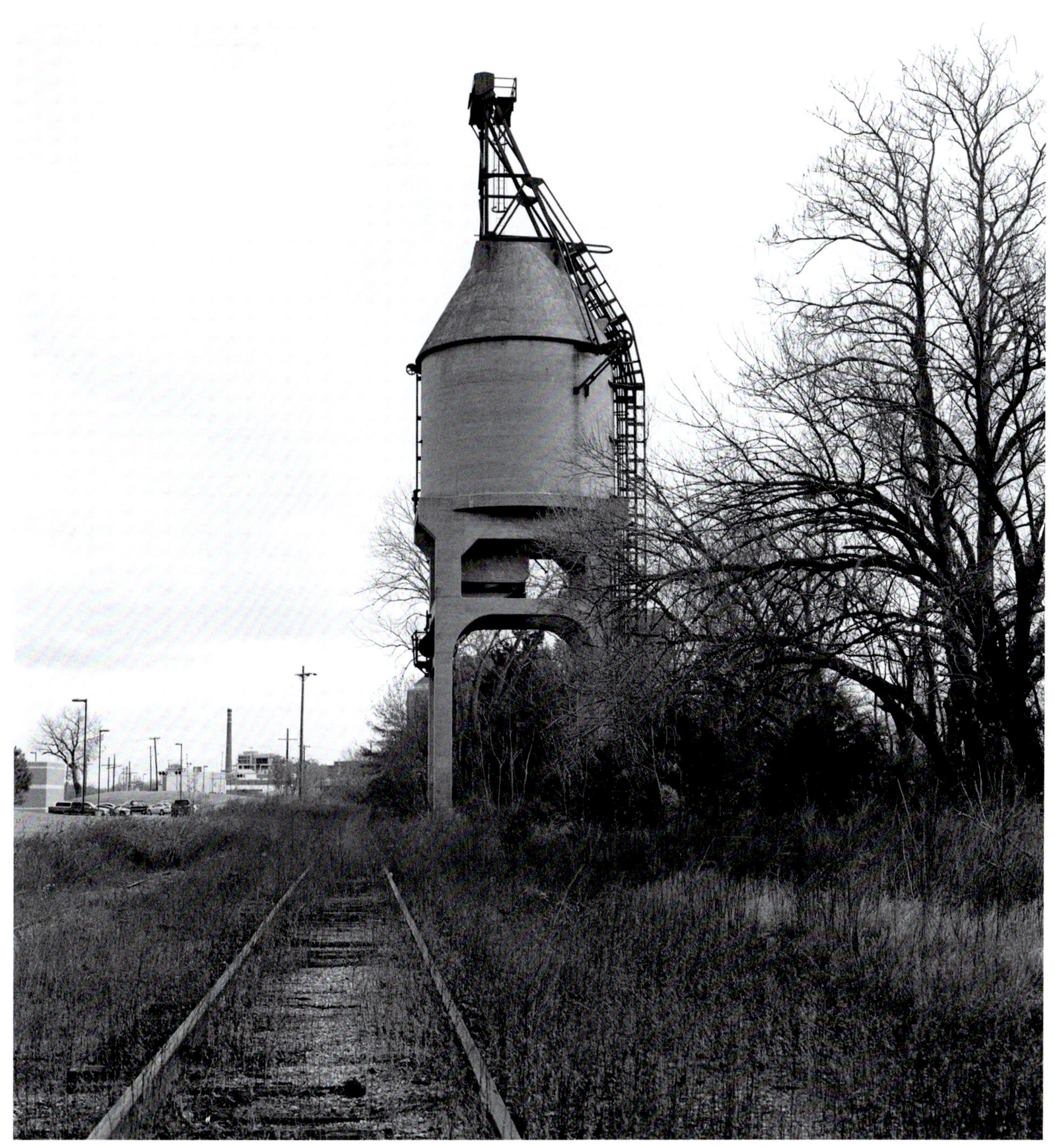

67 **BARTLESVILLE, OKLAHOMA** Missouri-Kansas-Texas 36°44’44.1”N 95°59’09.0”W

 NELSON, ILLINOIS Chicago & North Western 41°47'58.6"N 89°35'48.6"W

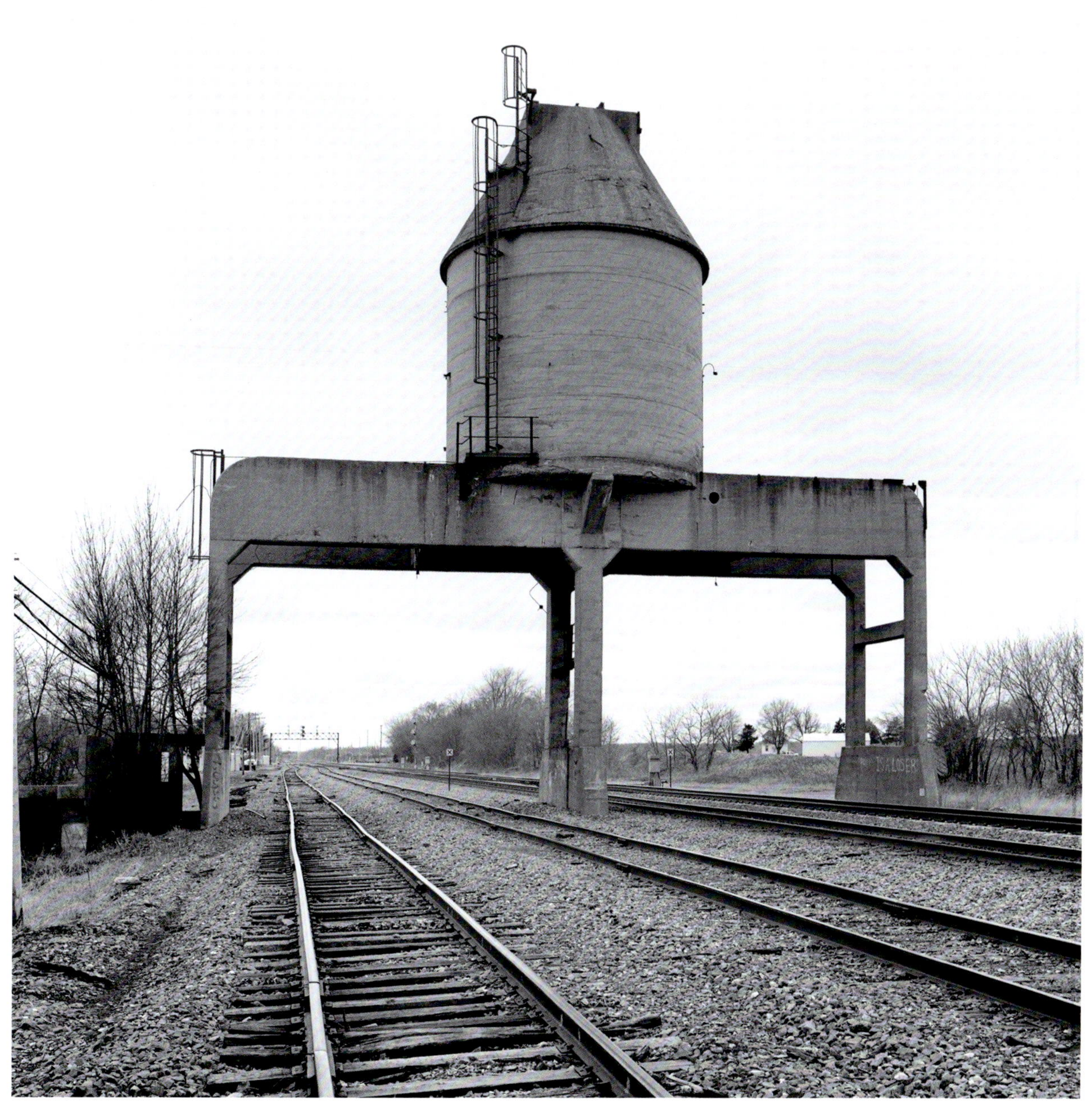

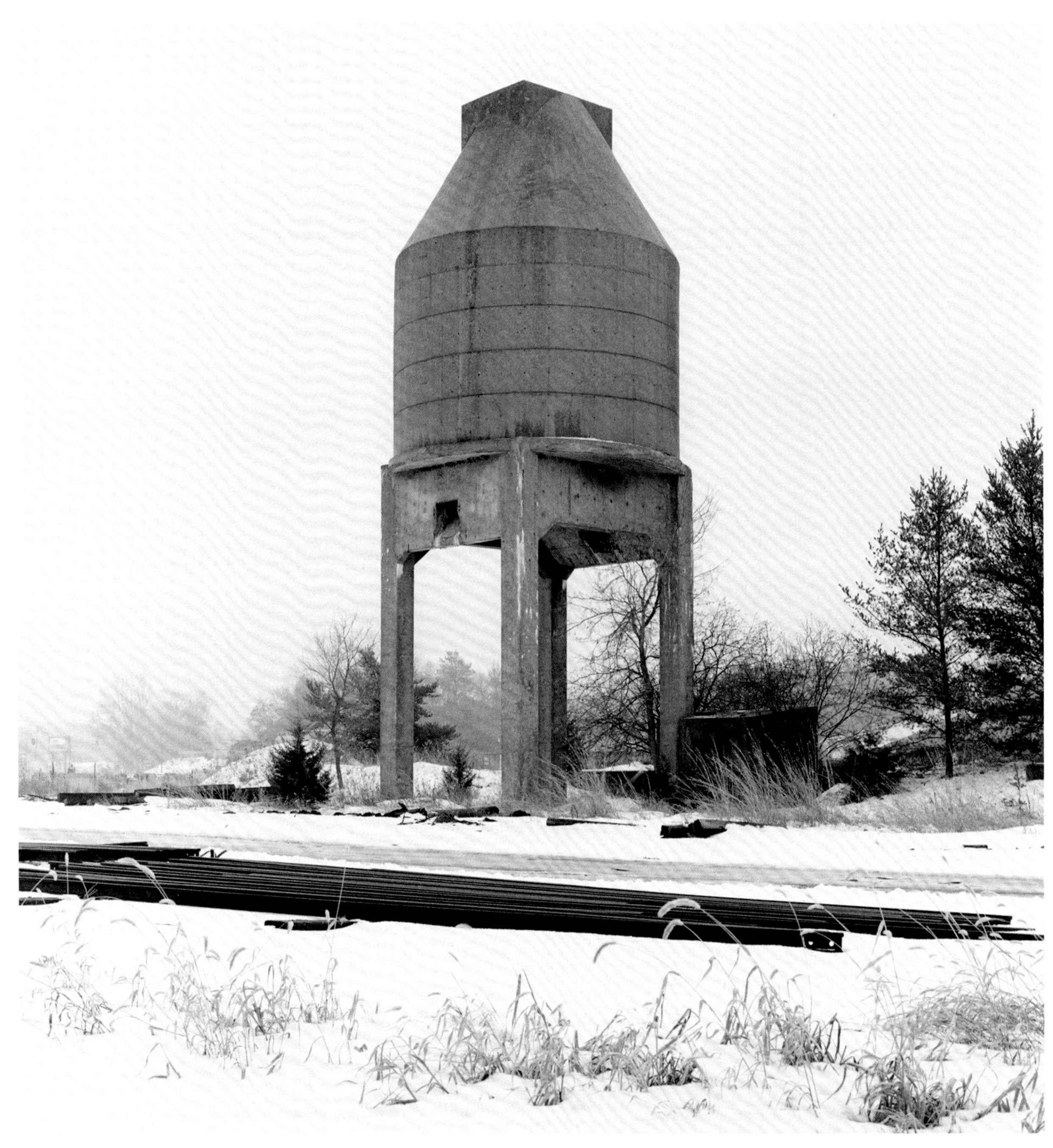

 ADAMS, WISCONSIN Chicago & North Western 43°57’10.0”N 89°49’18.0”W

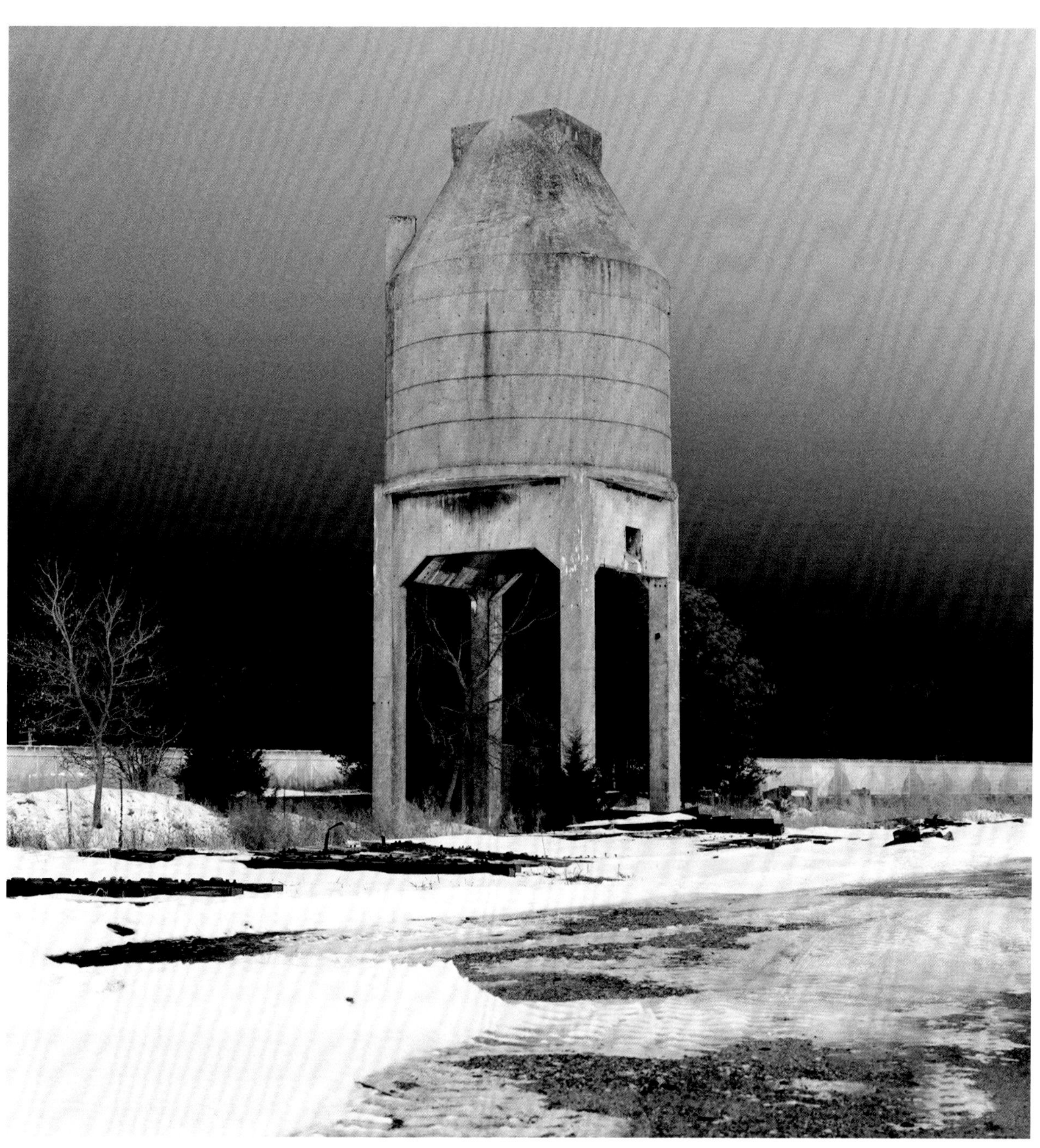

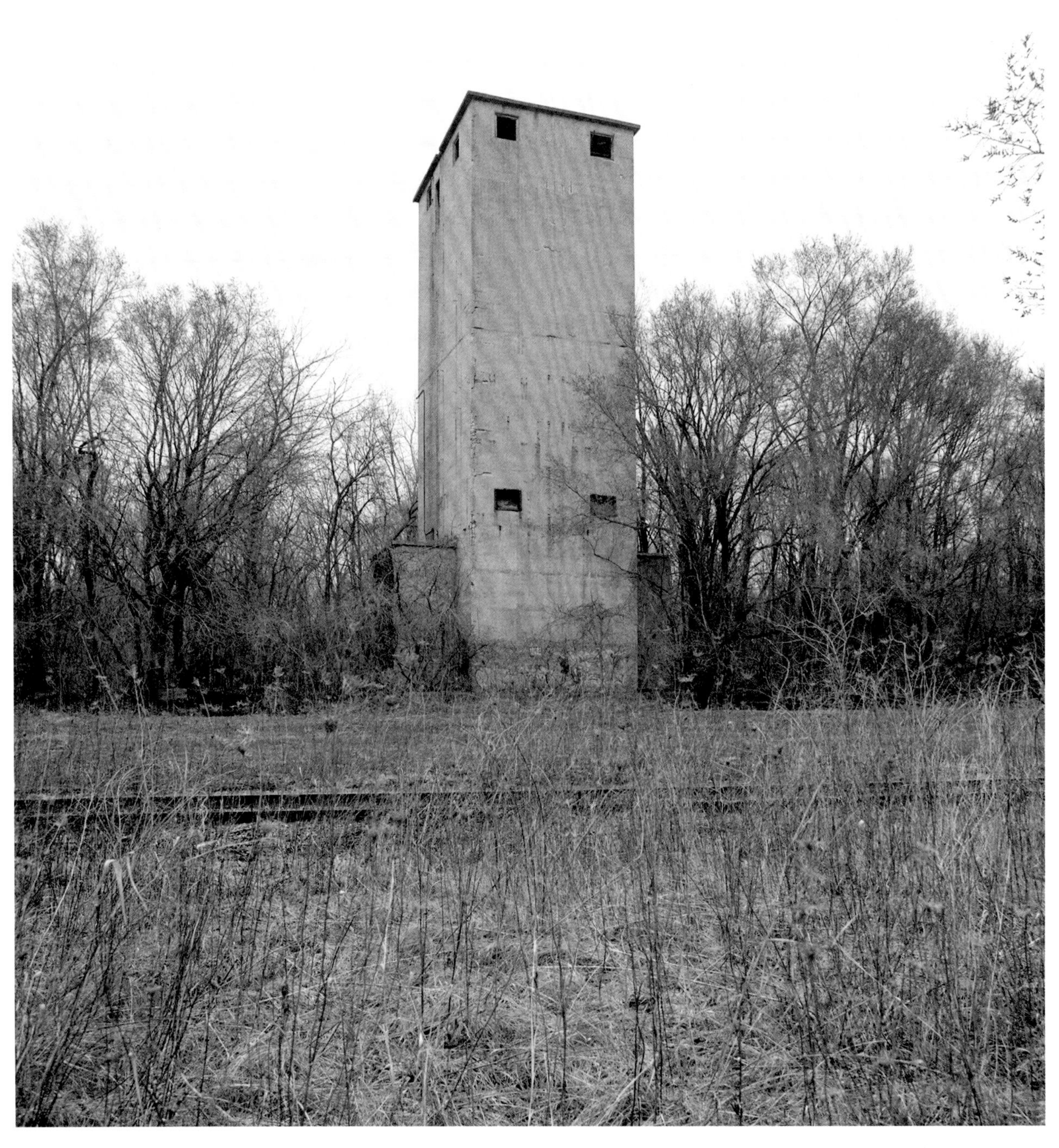

72 **FREEPORT, ILLINOIS** Illinois Central 42°17’48.2”N 89°36’31.4”W (above)

73 **MONTFORT JUNCTION, WISCONSIN** Chicago & North Western 42°57’49.6”N 90°24’31.3”W (right)

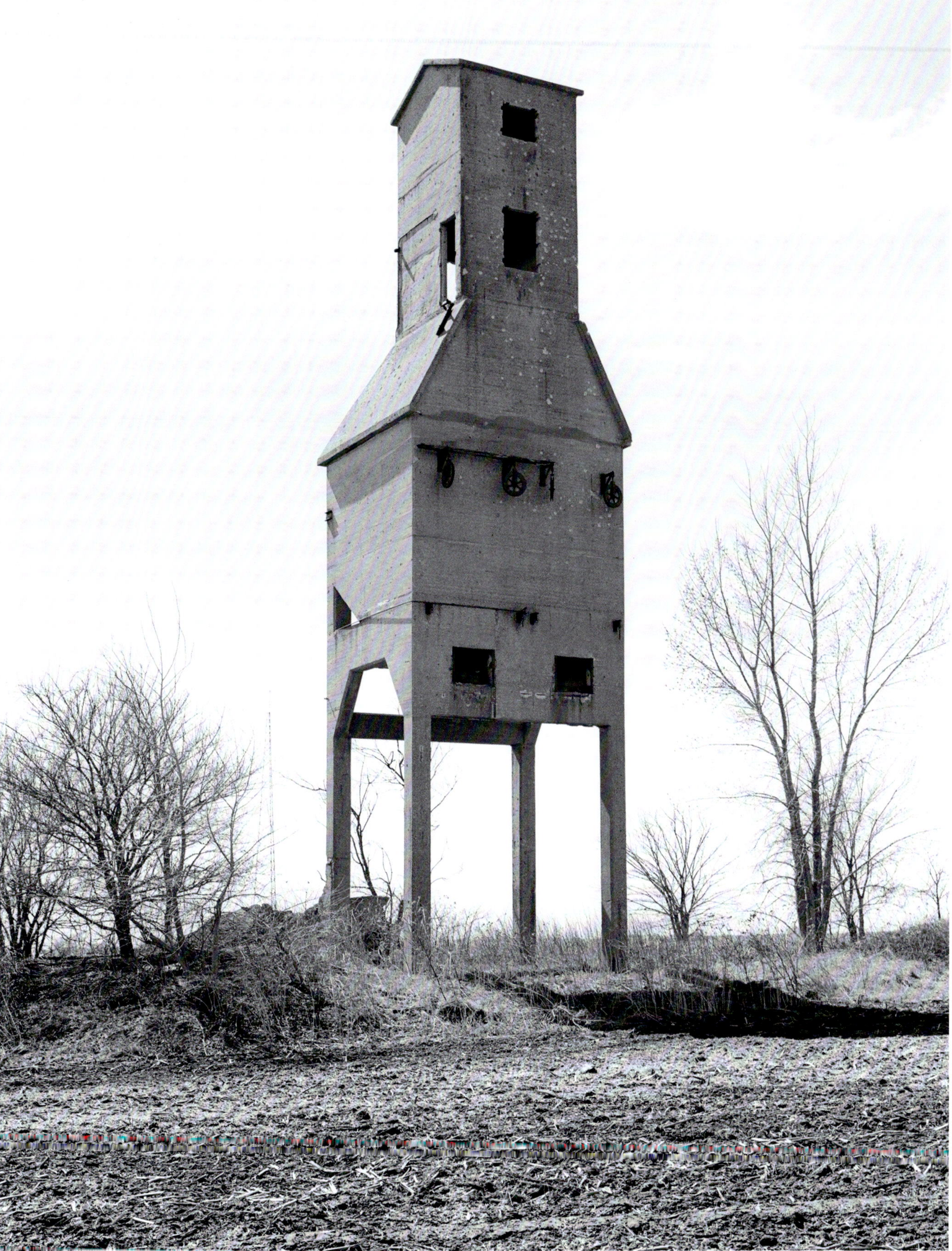

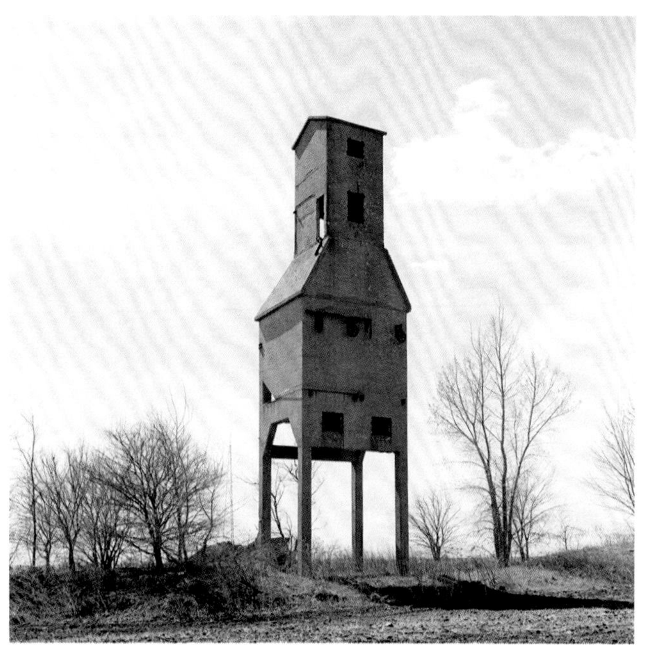

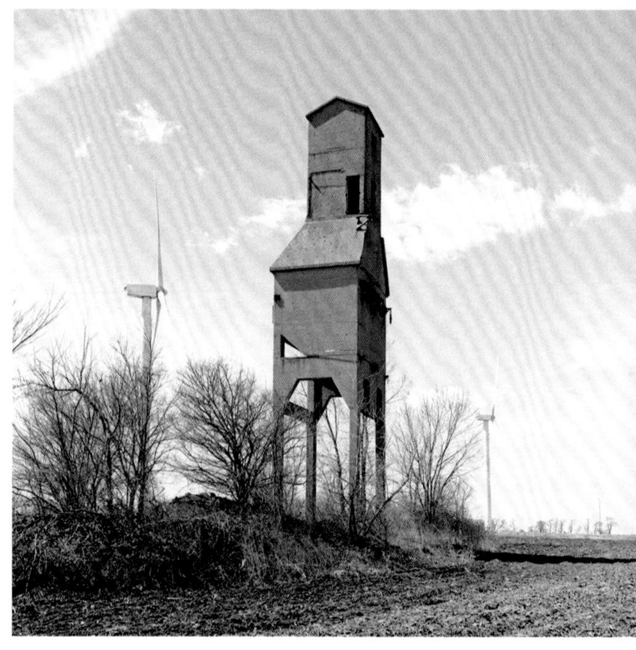

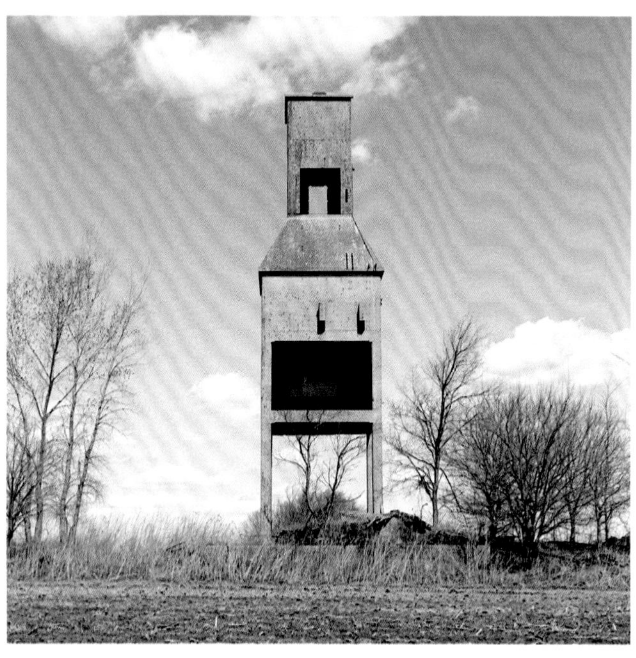

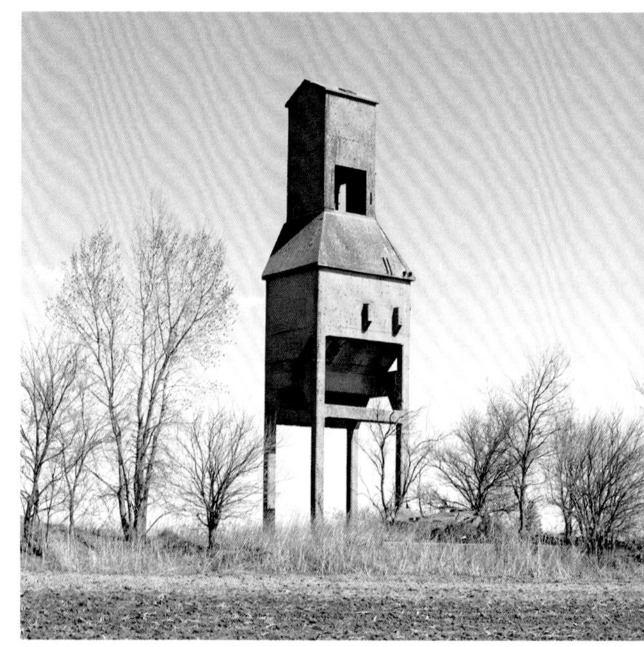

 MONTFORT JUNCTION, WISCONSIN Chicago & North Western 42°57’49.6”N 90°24’31.3”W

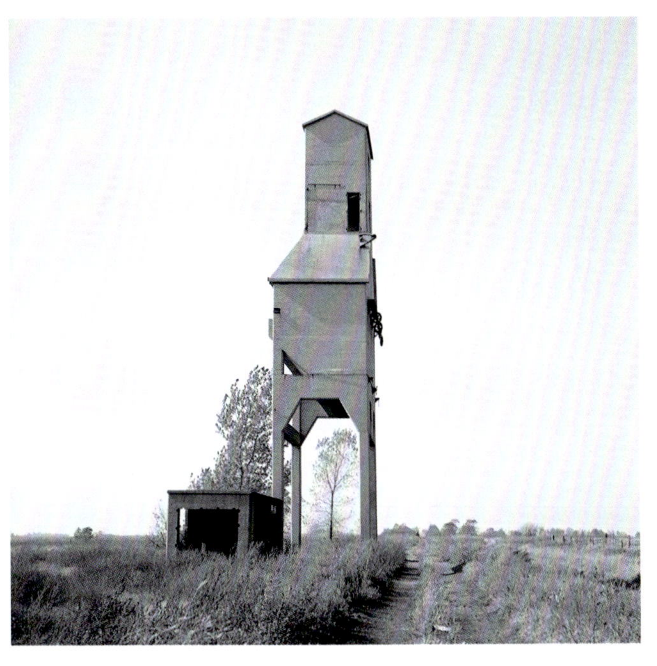

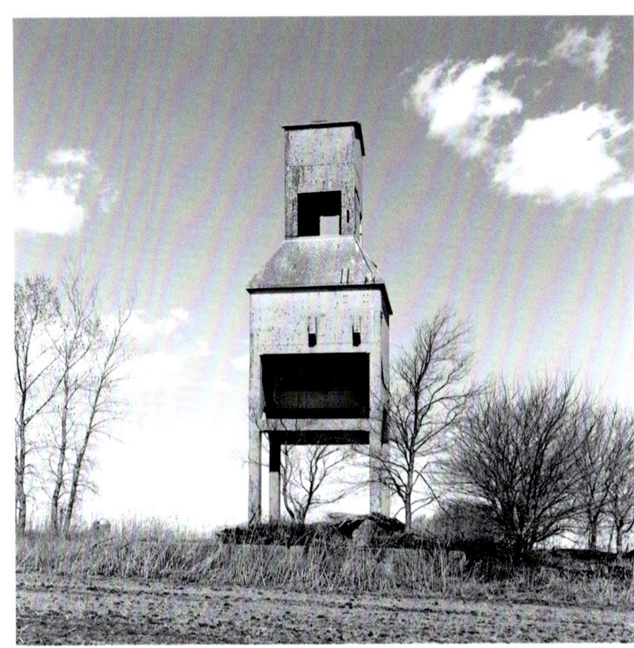

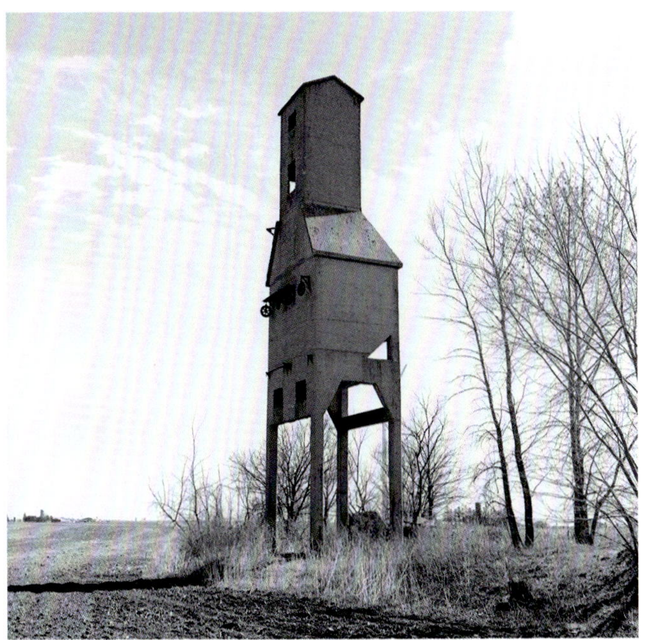

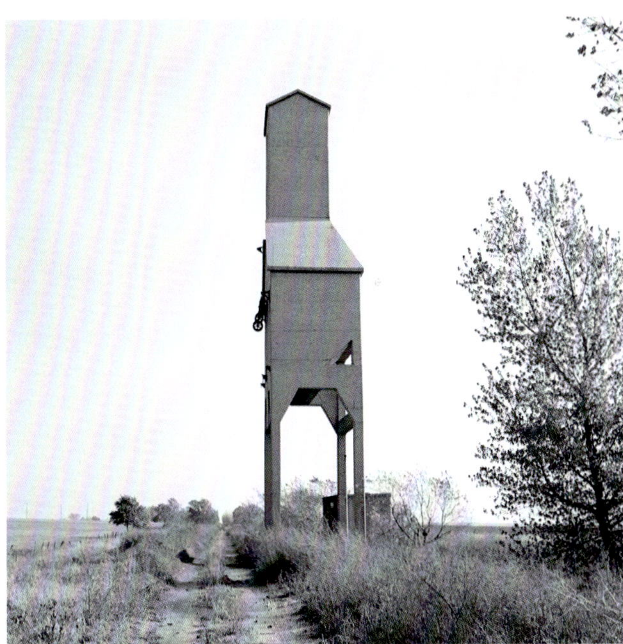

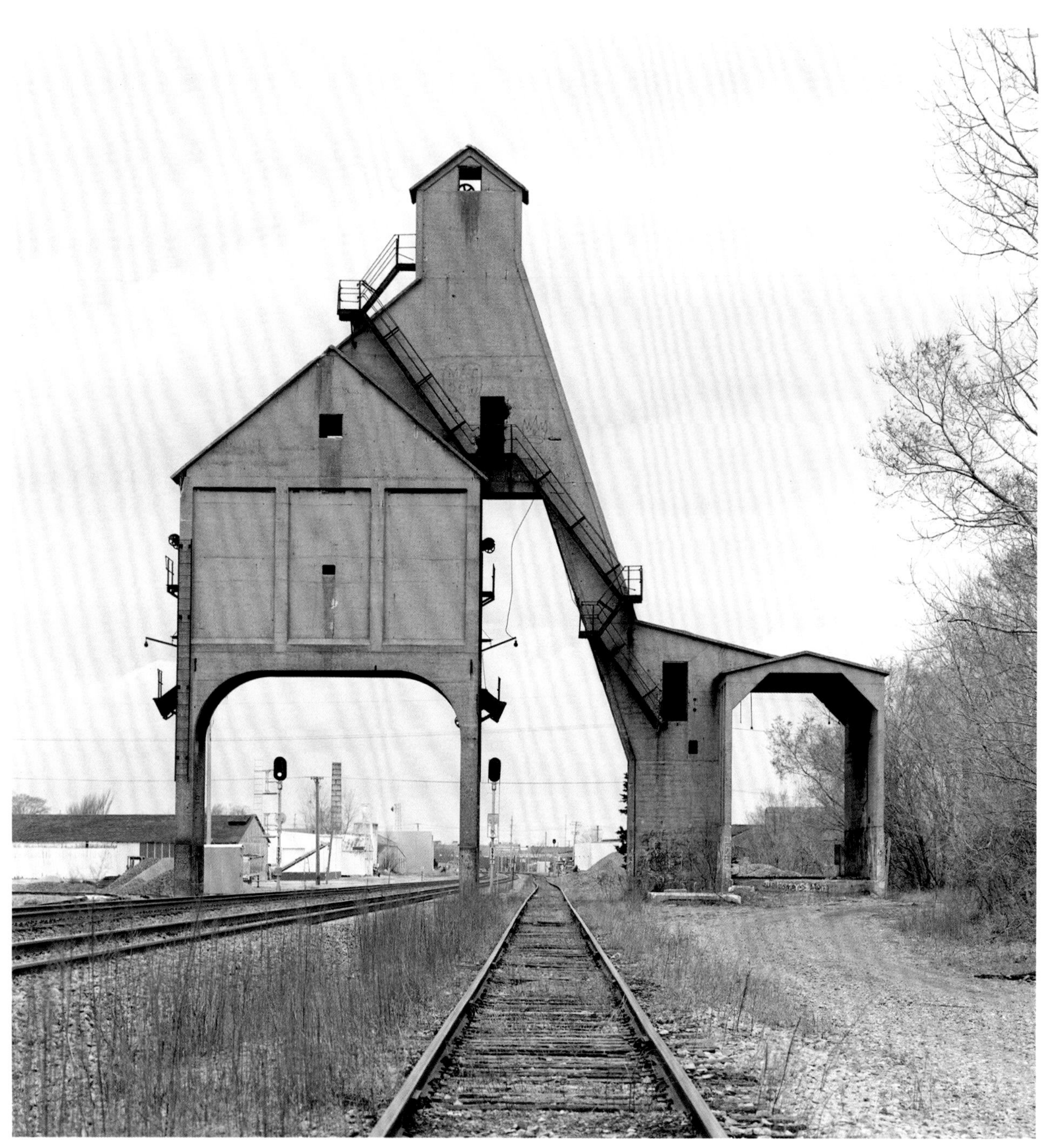

 DEKALB, ILLINOIS Chicago & North Wetern 41°55'40.1"N 88°44'00.3"W

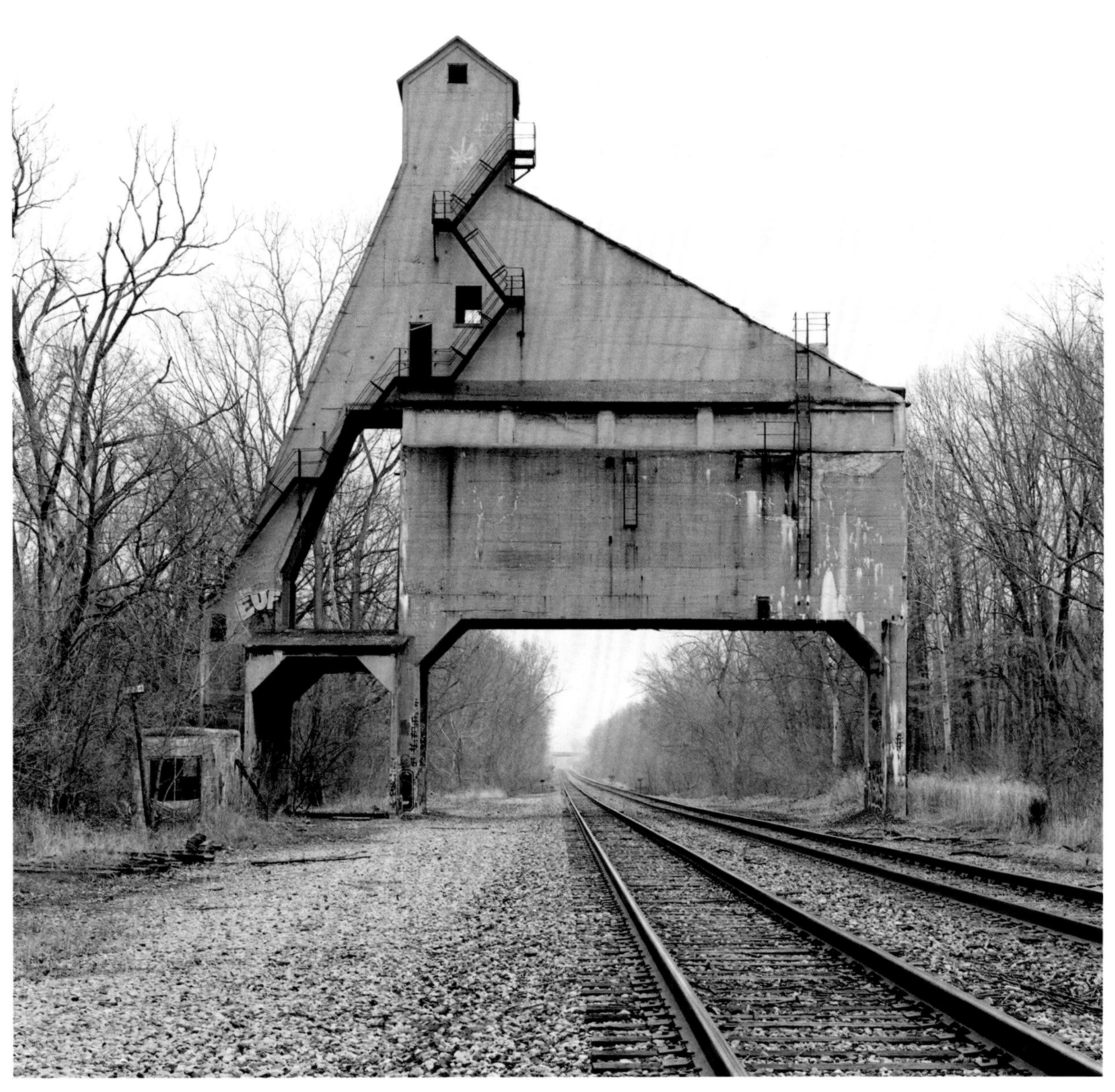

77 **LANSING, MICHIGAN** Grand Trunk Western 42°43'09.2"N 84°31'13.9"W

Following Spread

CLARENDON, MICHIGAN Michigan Central 42°07'41.1"N 84°51'51.8"W

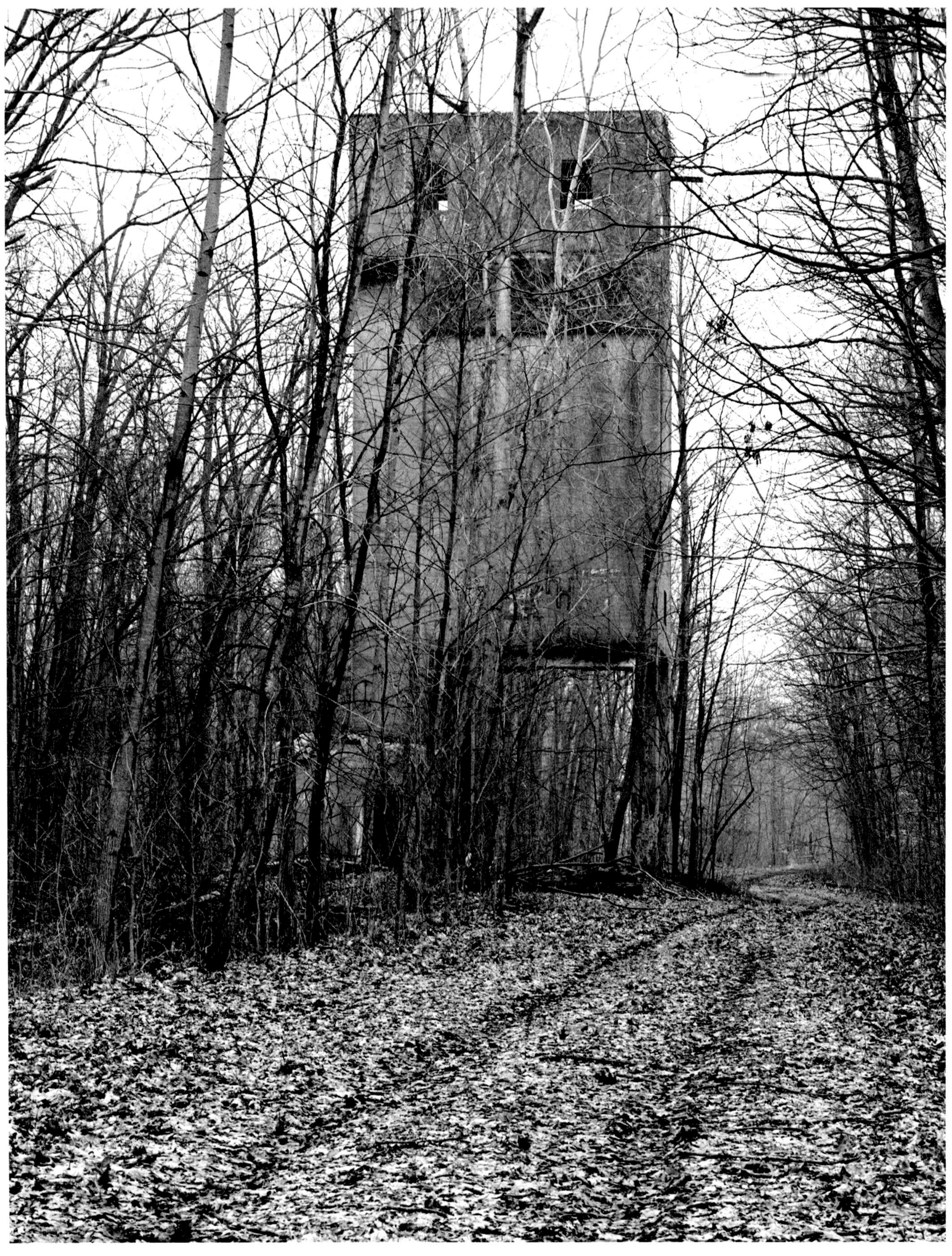

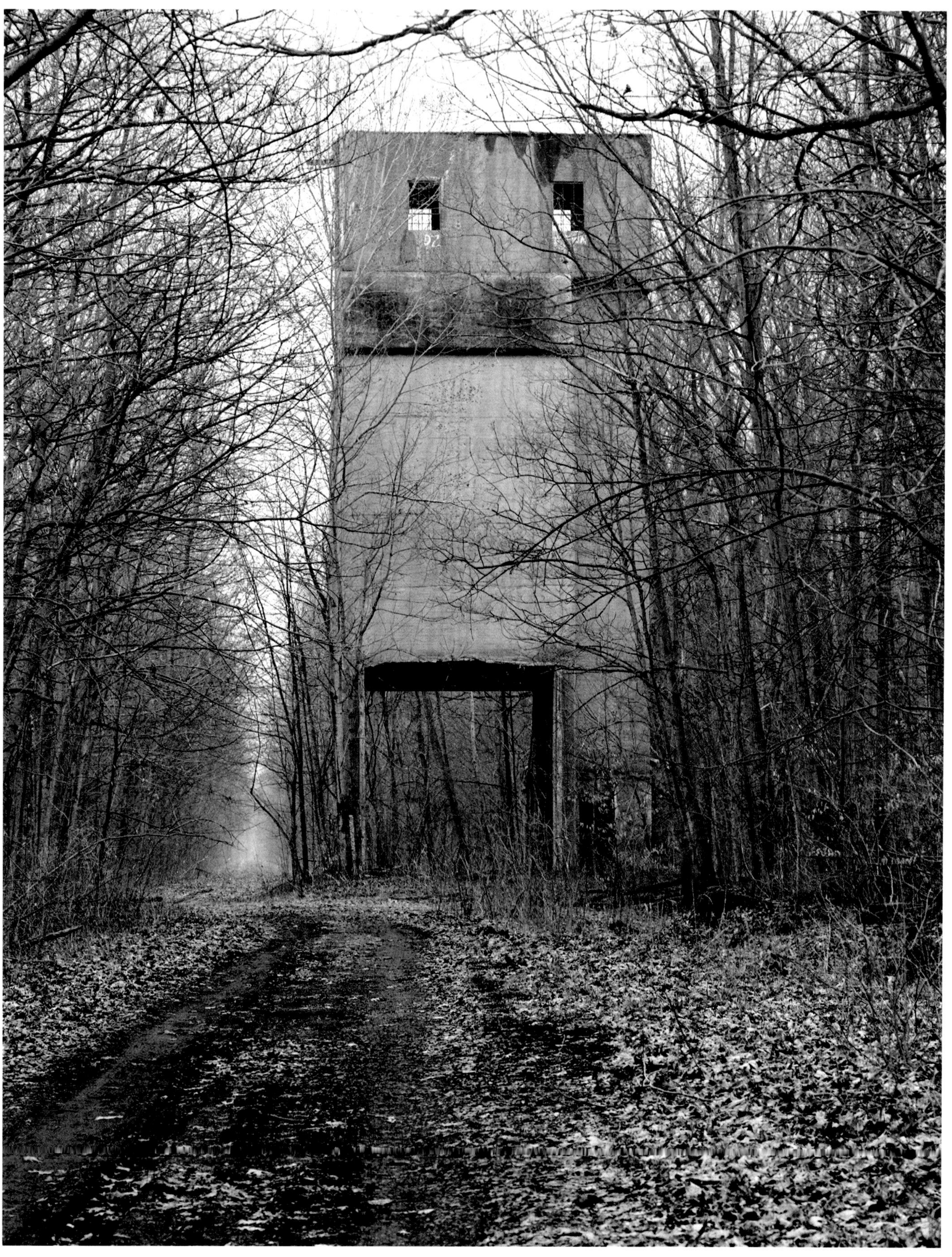

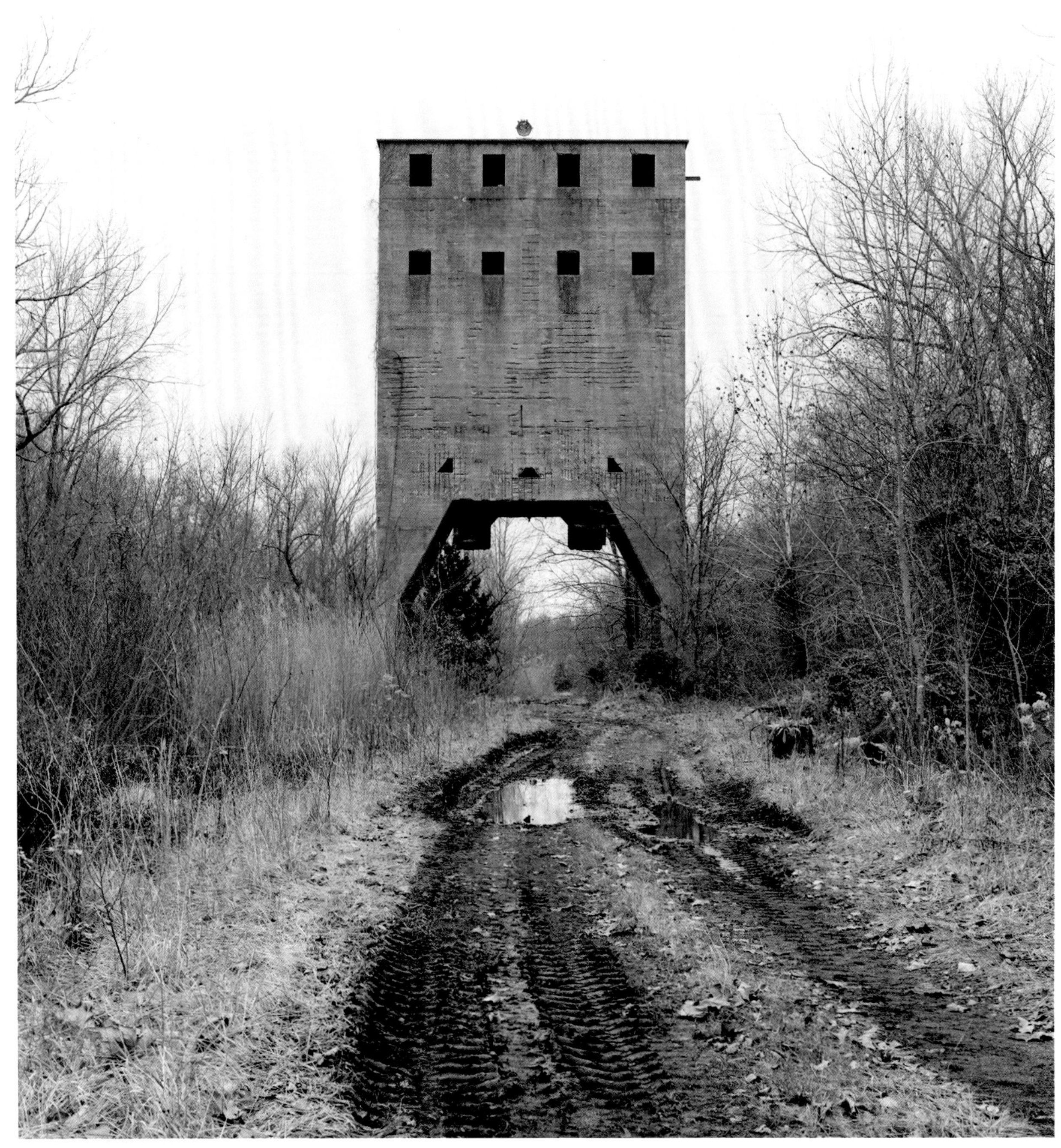

 BLUFORD, ILLIINOIS Illinois Central 38°18’57.4”N 88°43’43.0”W

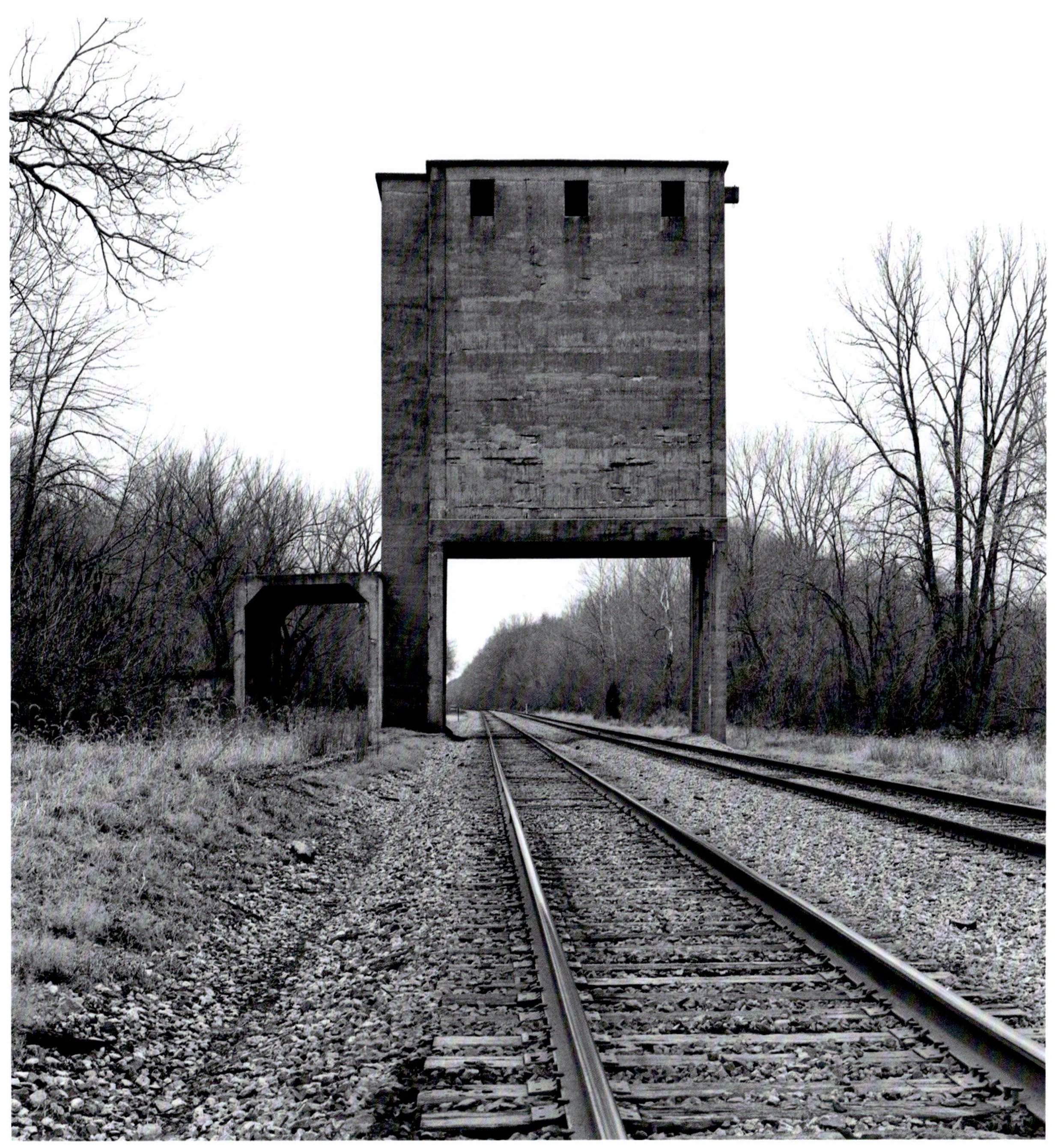

81 **REEVESVILLE, ILLINOIS** Illinois Central 37°20'45.0"N 88°43'04.3"W

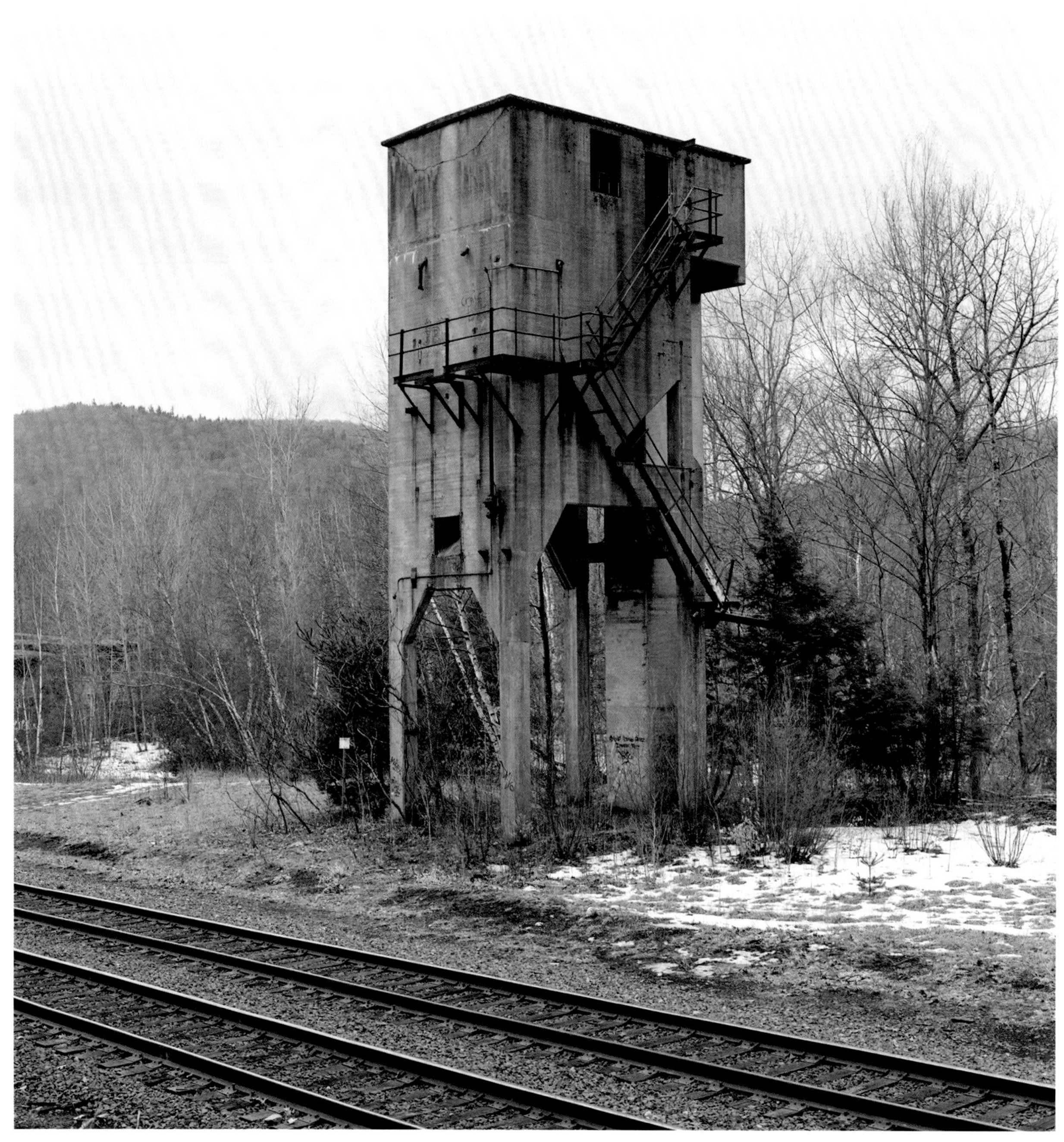

 CHESTER, MASSACHUSETTS Boston & Albany 42°17'14.5"N 72°58'56.2"W

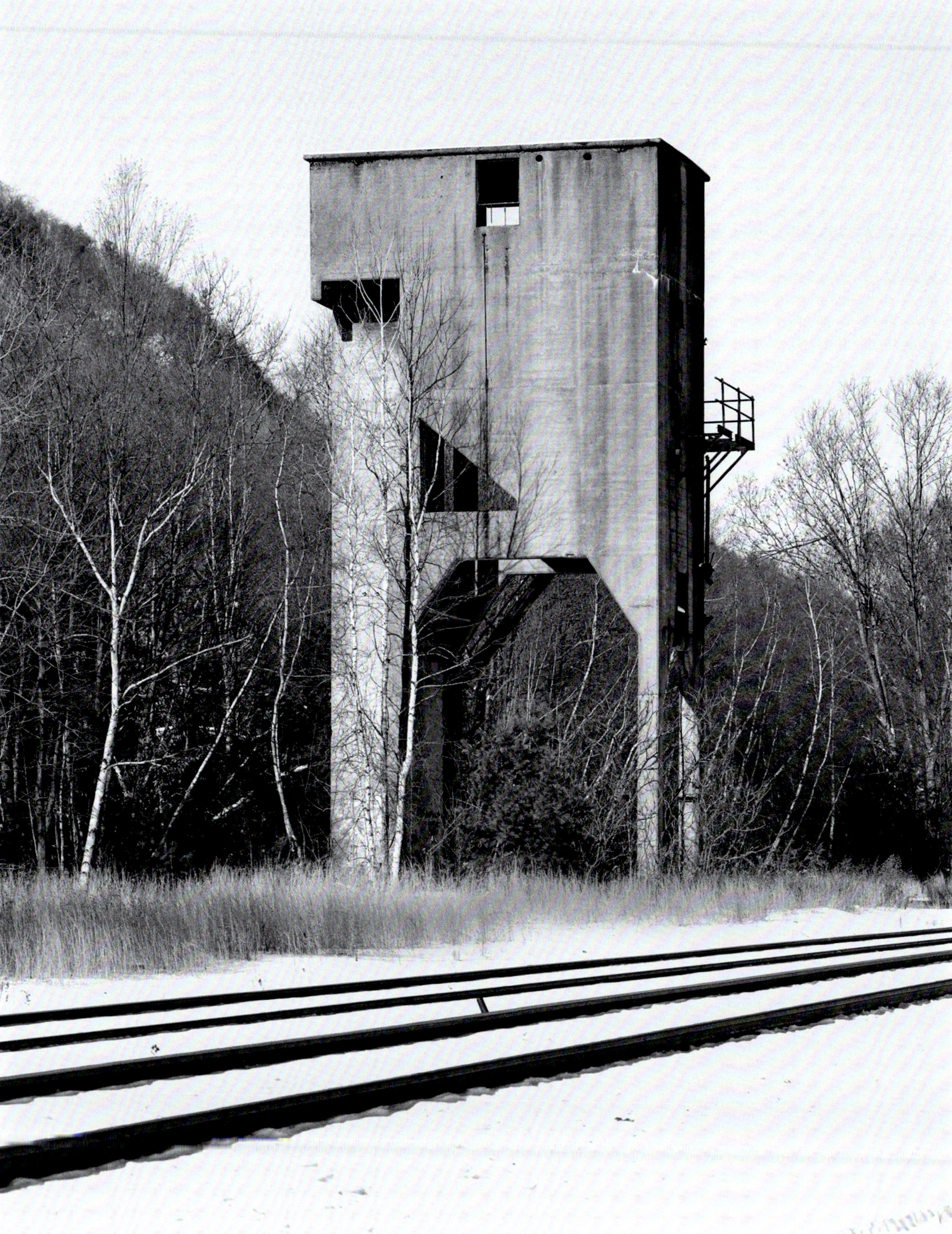

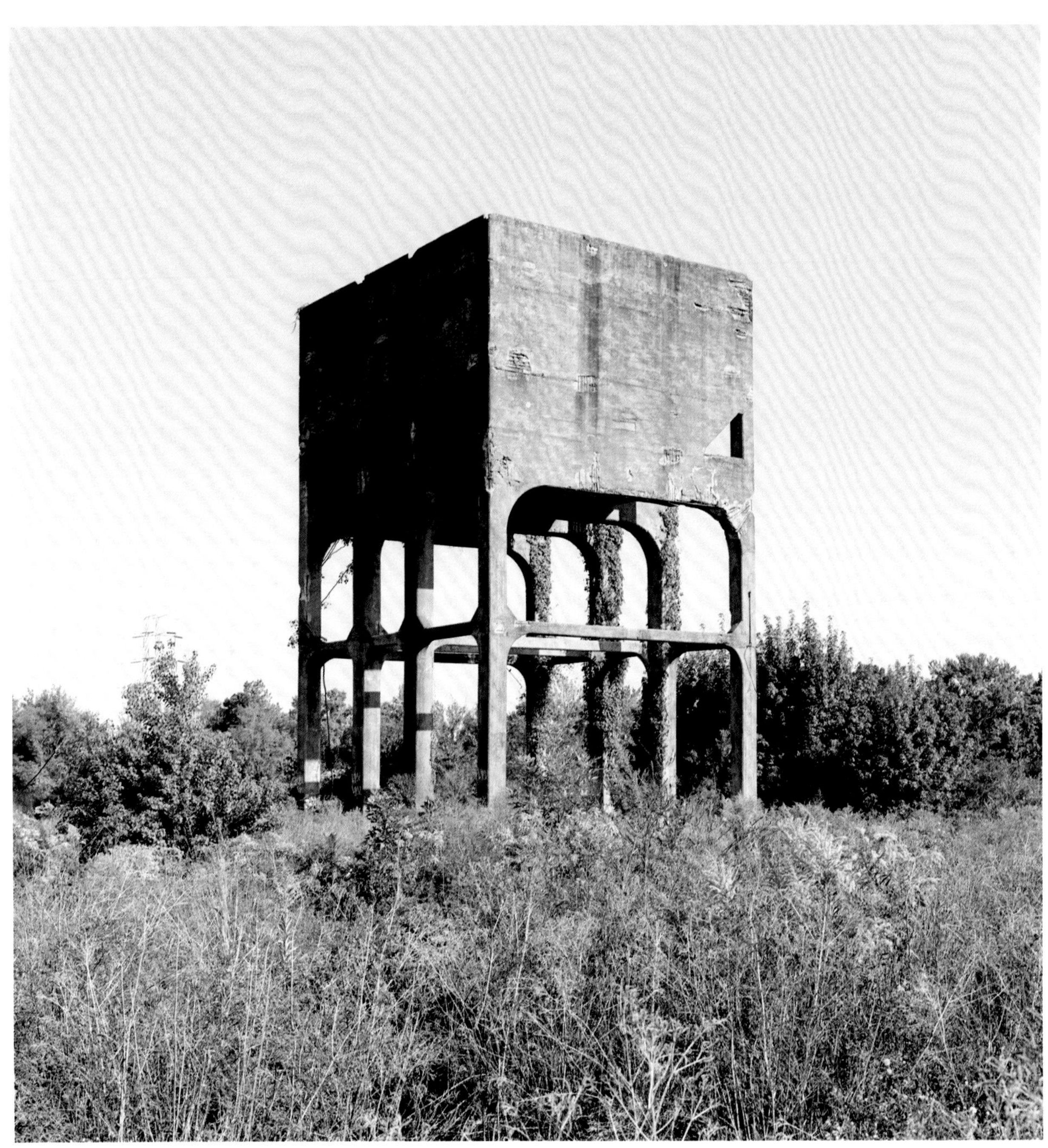

 MONTGOMERY, ALABAMA Western Railway of Alabama 32°23'30.1"N 86°18'27.3"W

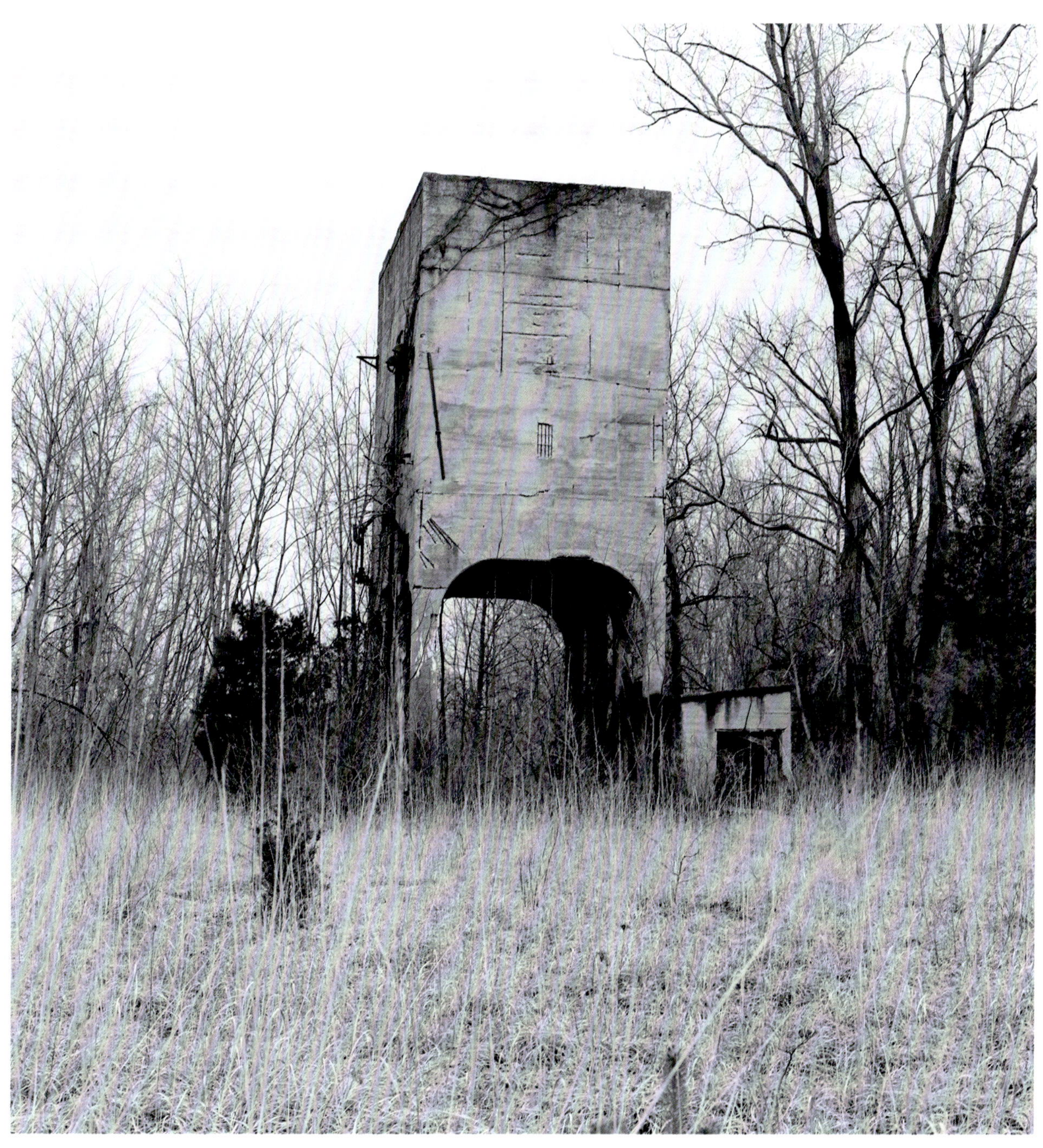

 NEW BUFFALO, MICHIGAN Pere Marquette 41°47′07.2″N 86°44′33.1″W

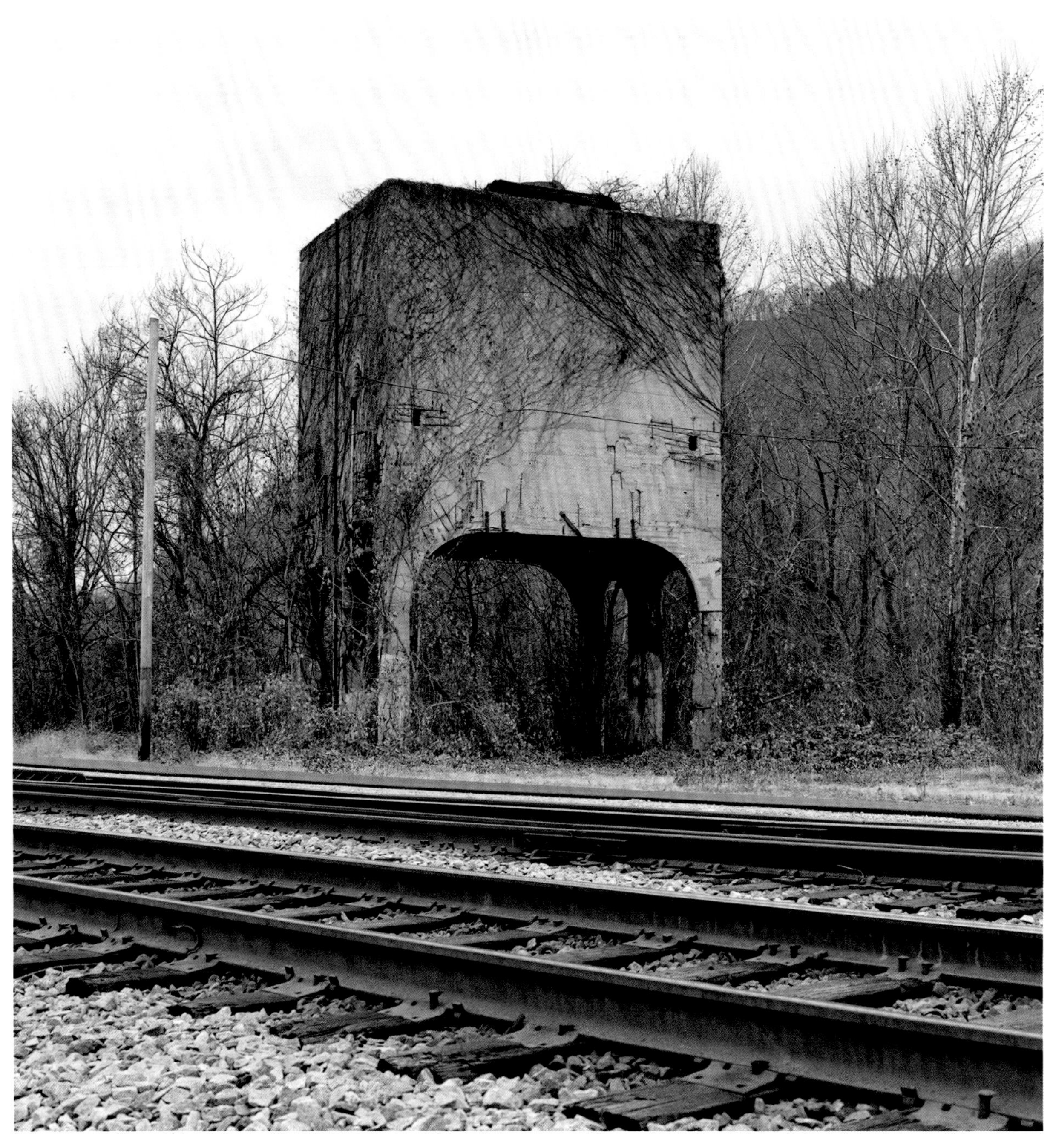

86 **HANDLEY, WEST VIRGINIA** Chesapeake & Ohio 38°11’07.4”N 81°21’25.2”W

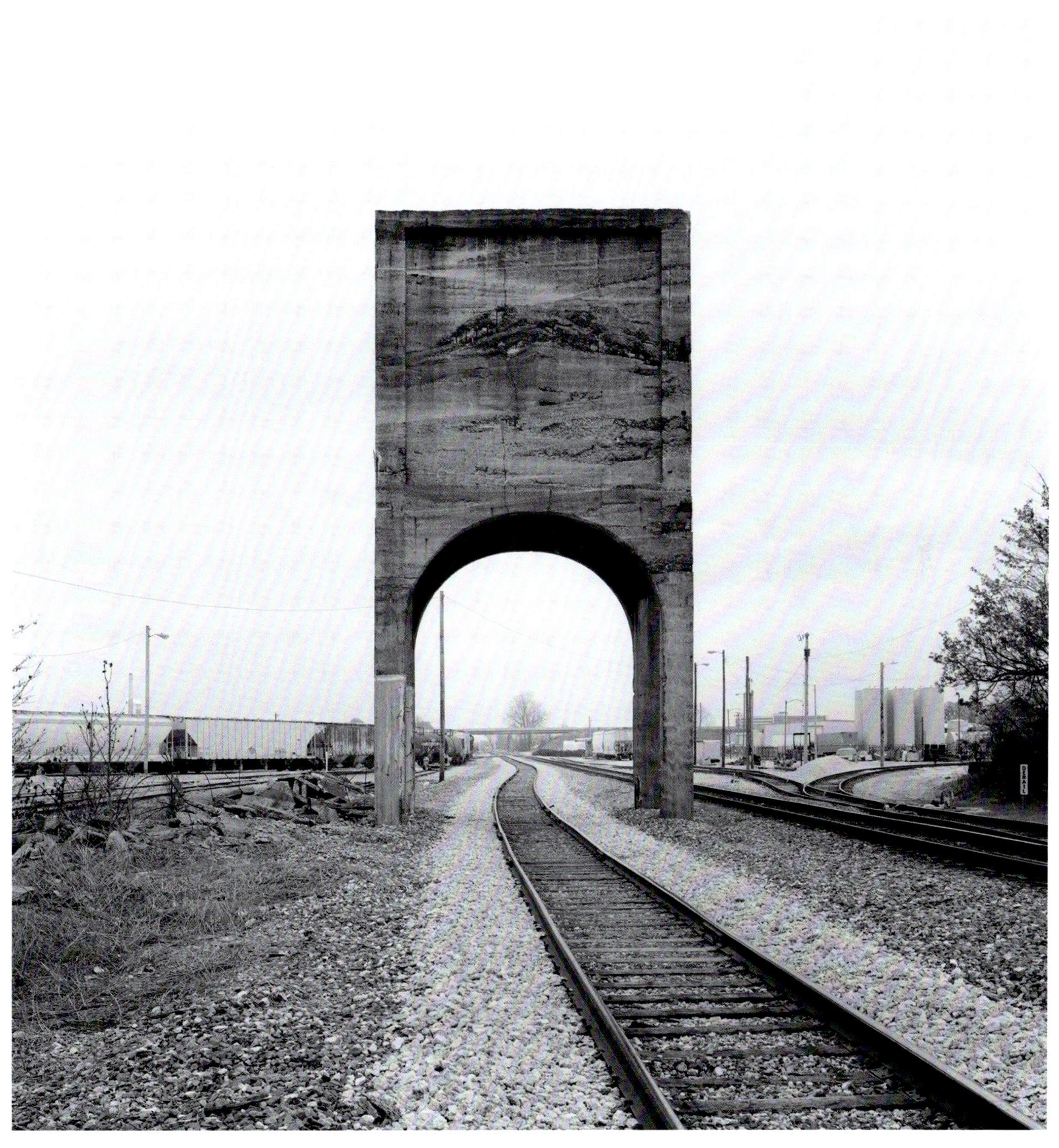

 OWENSBORO, KENTUCKY Illinois Central 37°46’18.0”N 87°05’03.0”W

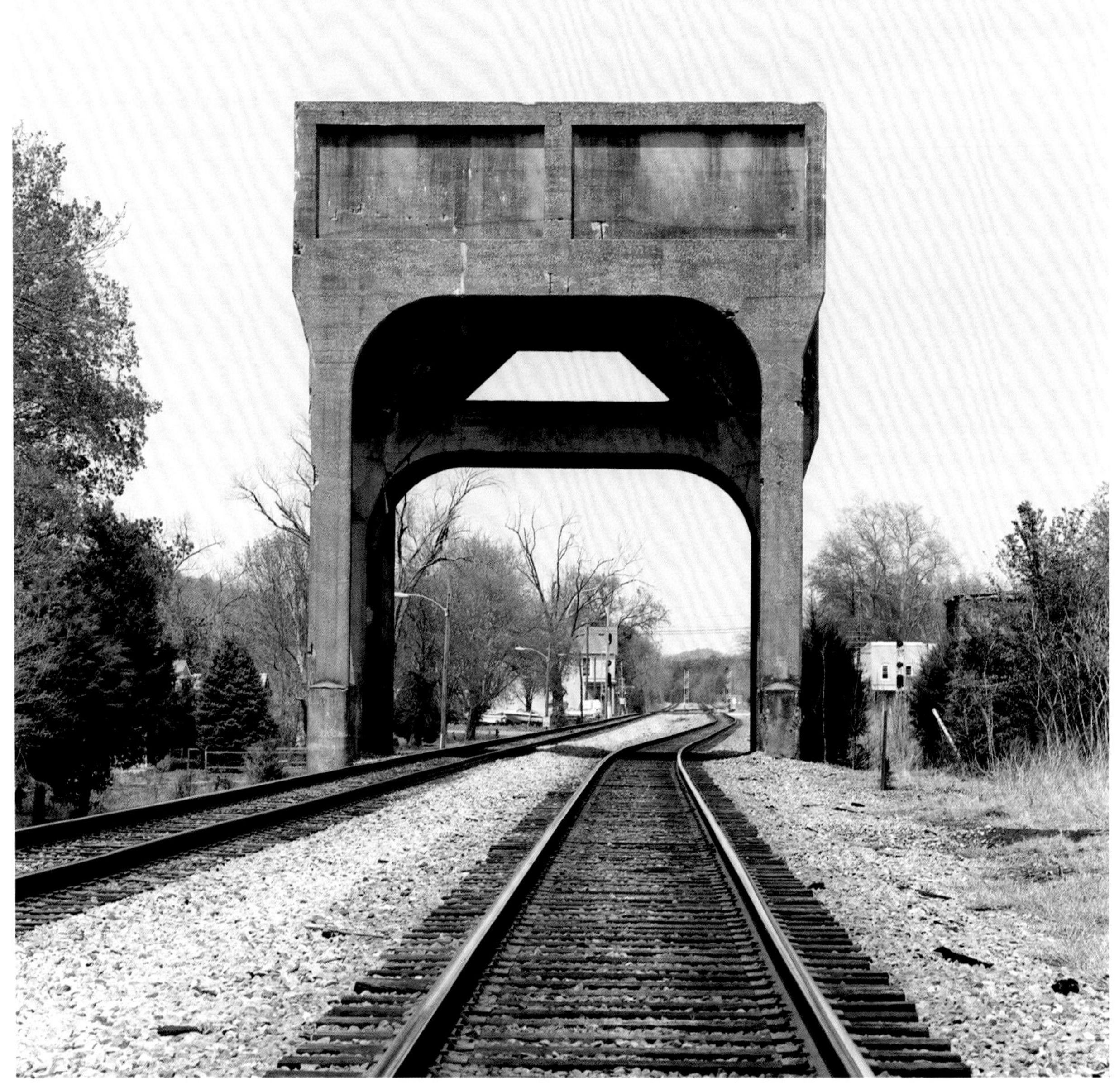

 LEBANON JUNCTION, KENTUCKY Louisville & Nashville 37°49'53.8"N 85°44'01.9"W

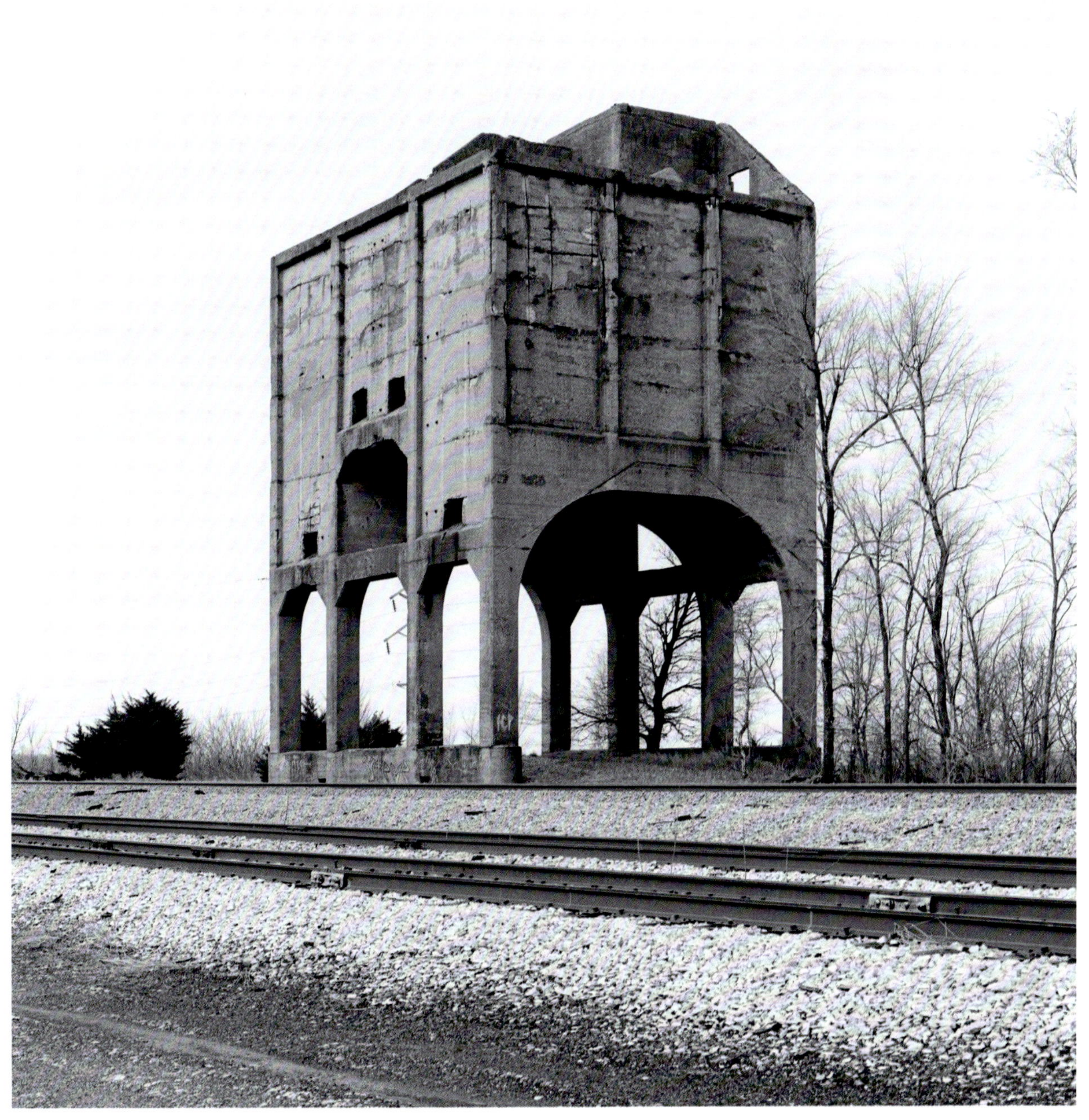

89 **GILMAN, ILLINOIS** Illinois Central 40°47'15.6"N 87°59'23.2"W

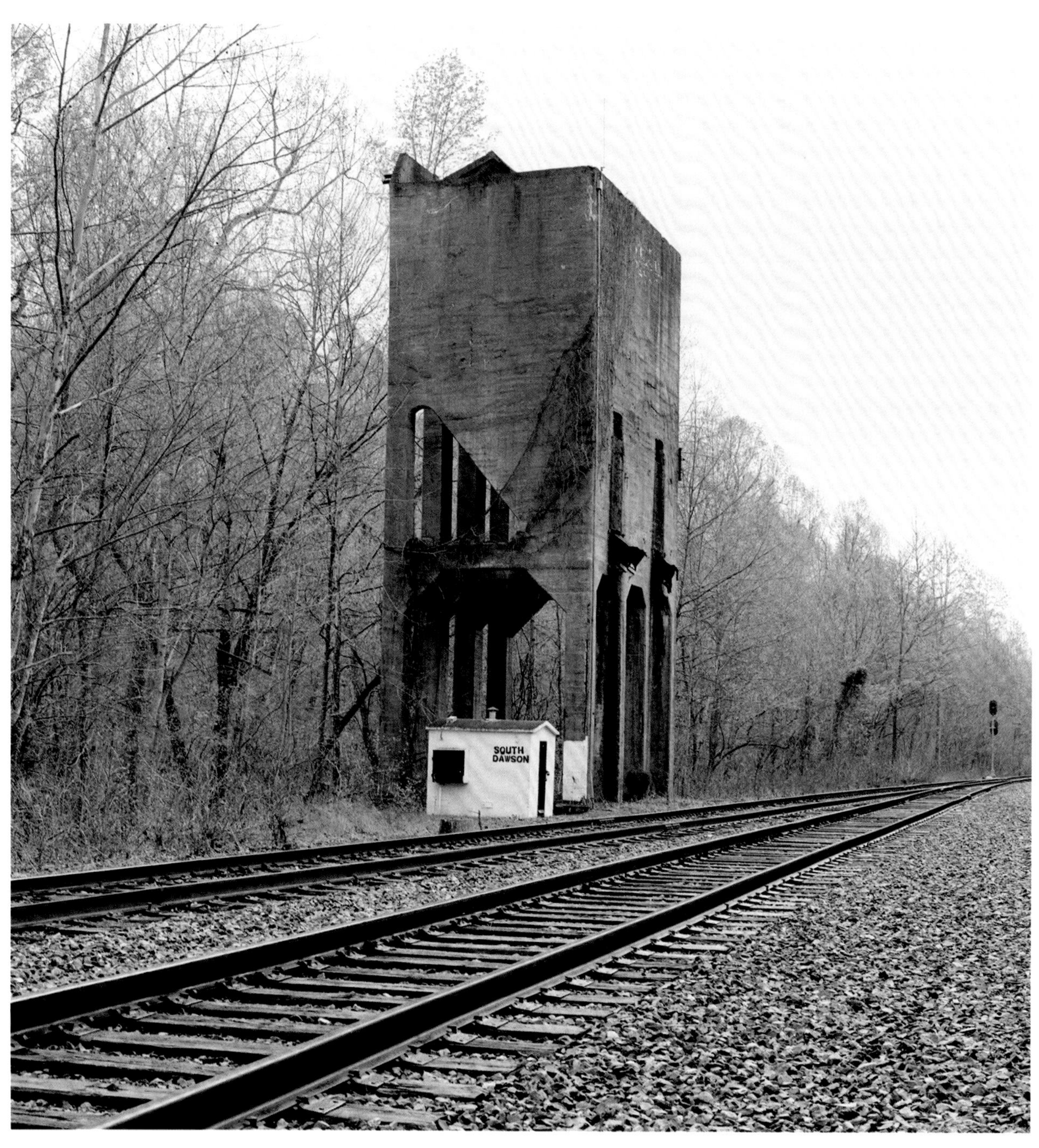

 DAWSON SPRINGS, KENTUCKY Illinois Central 37°09’53.7”N 87°40’41.2”W

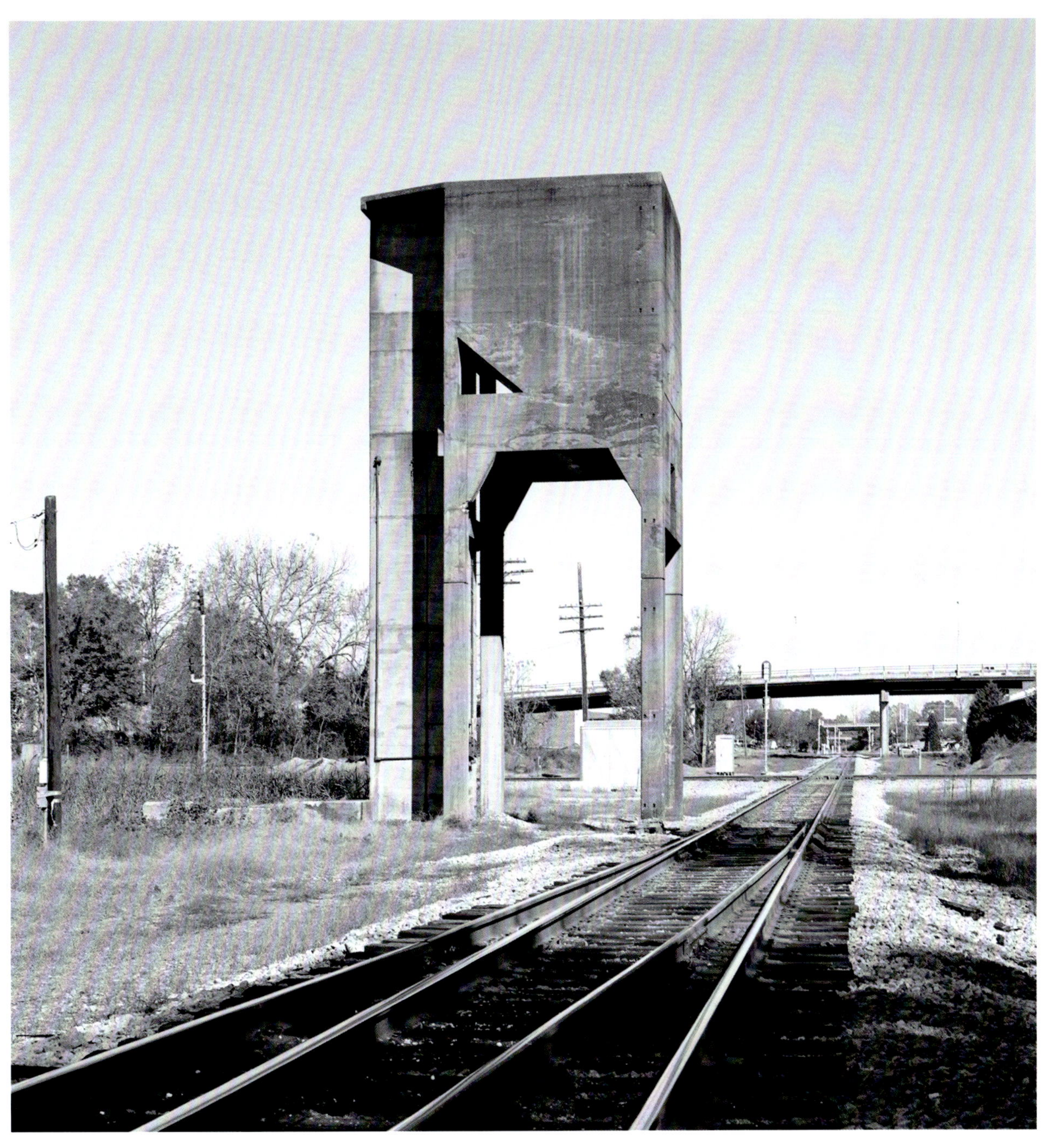

91 **OPELIKA, ALABAMA** Western Railway of Alabama 32°38’43.4”N 85°23’00.5”W

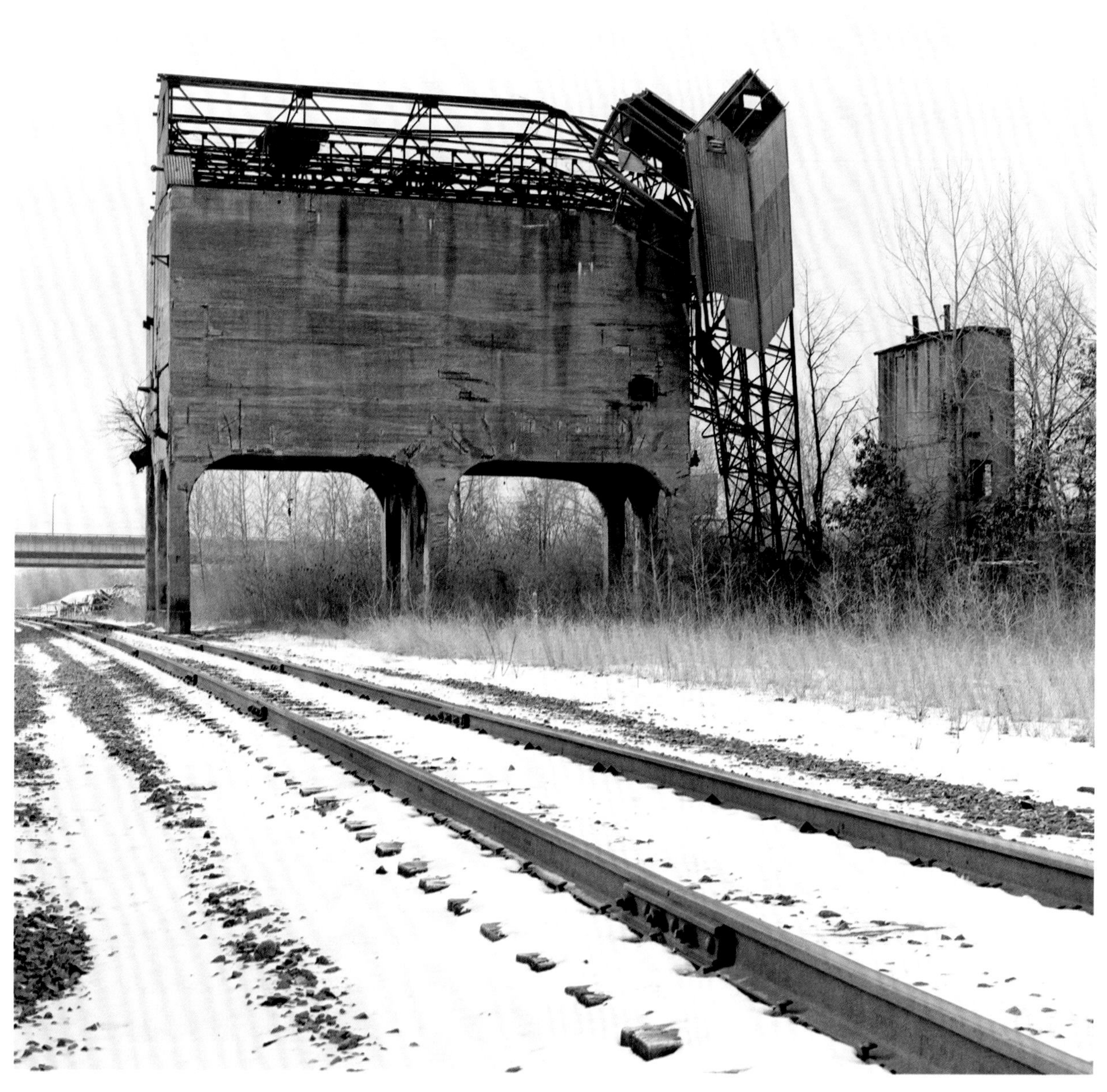

 GIRARD, OHIO Pennsylvania 41°09'01.3"N 80°42'18.2"W

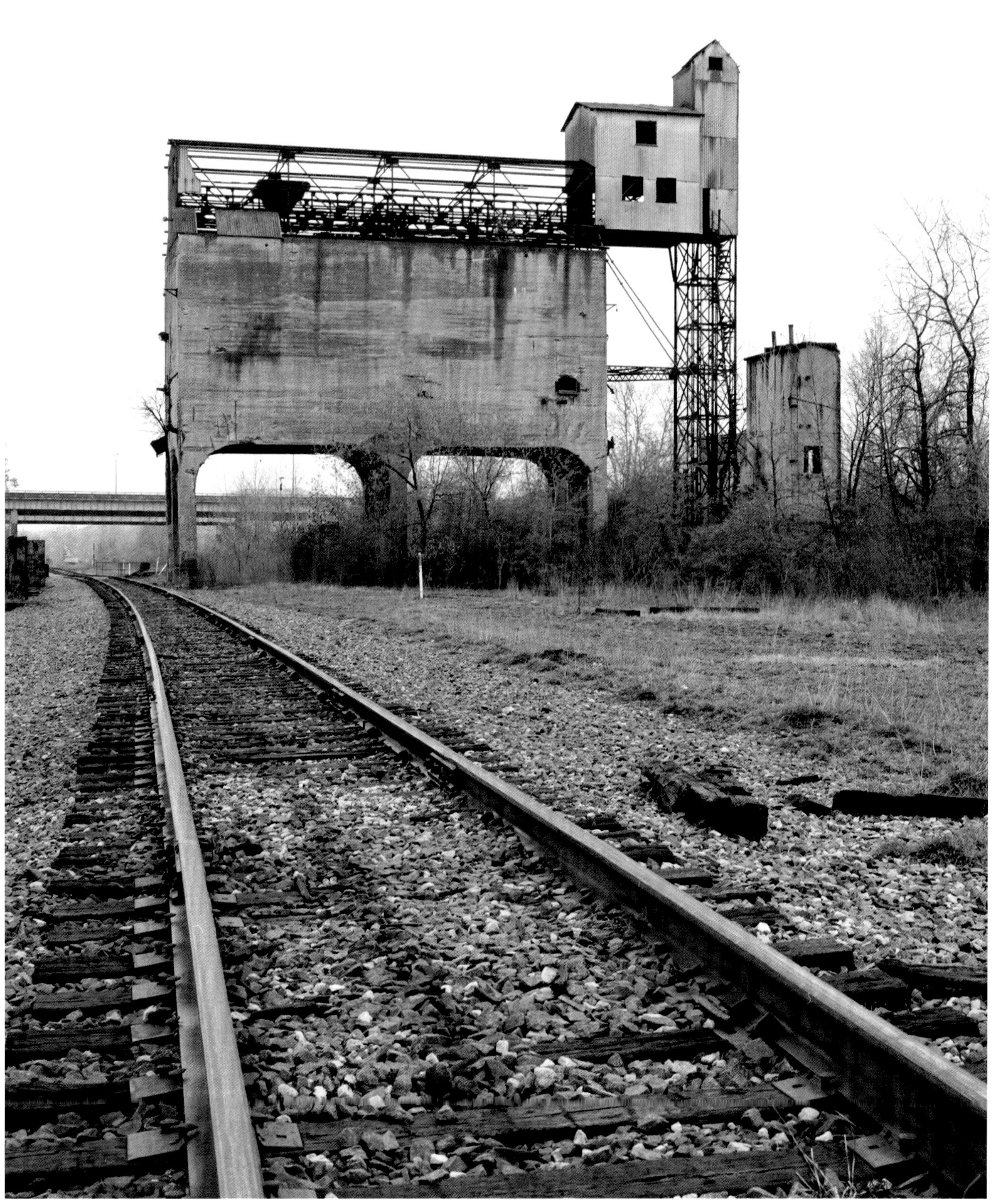

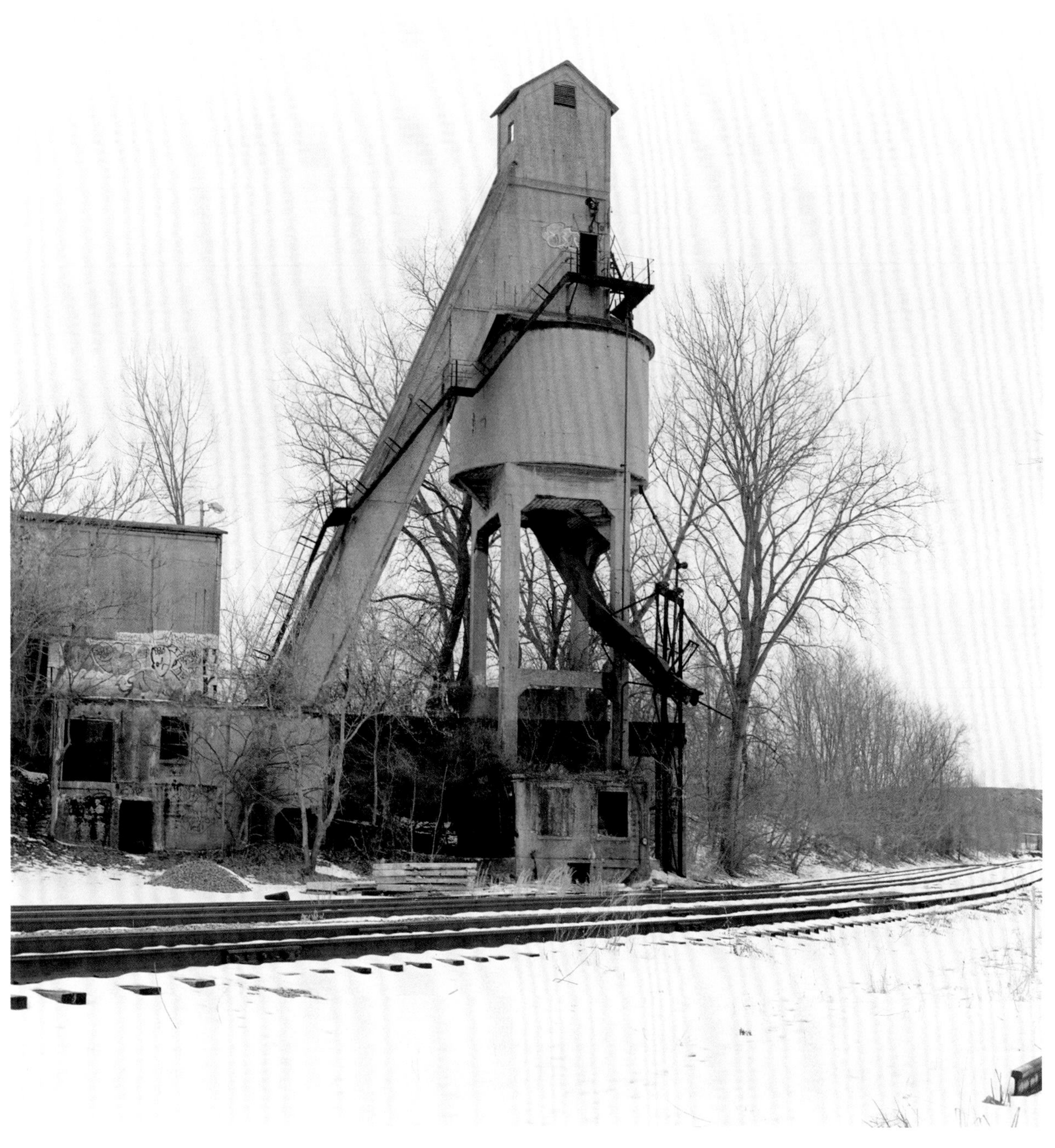

 AKRON JUNCTION, OHIO Baltimore & Ohio 41°05'14.2"N 81°29'14.8"W

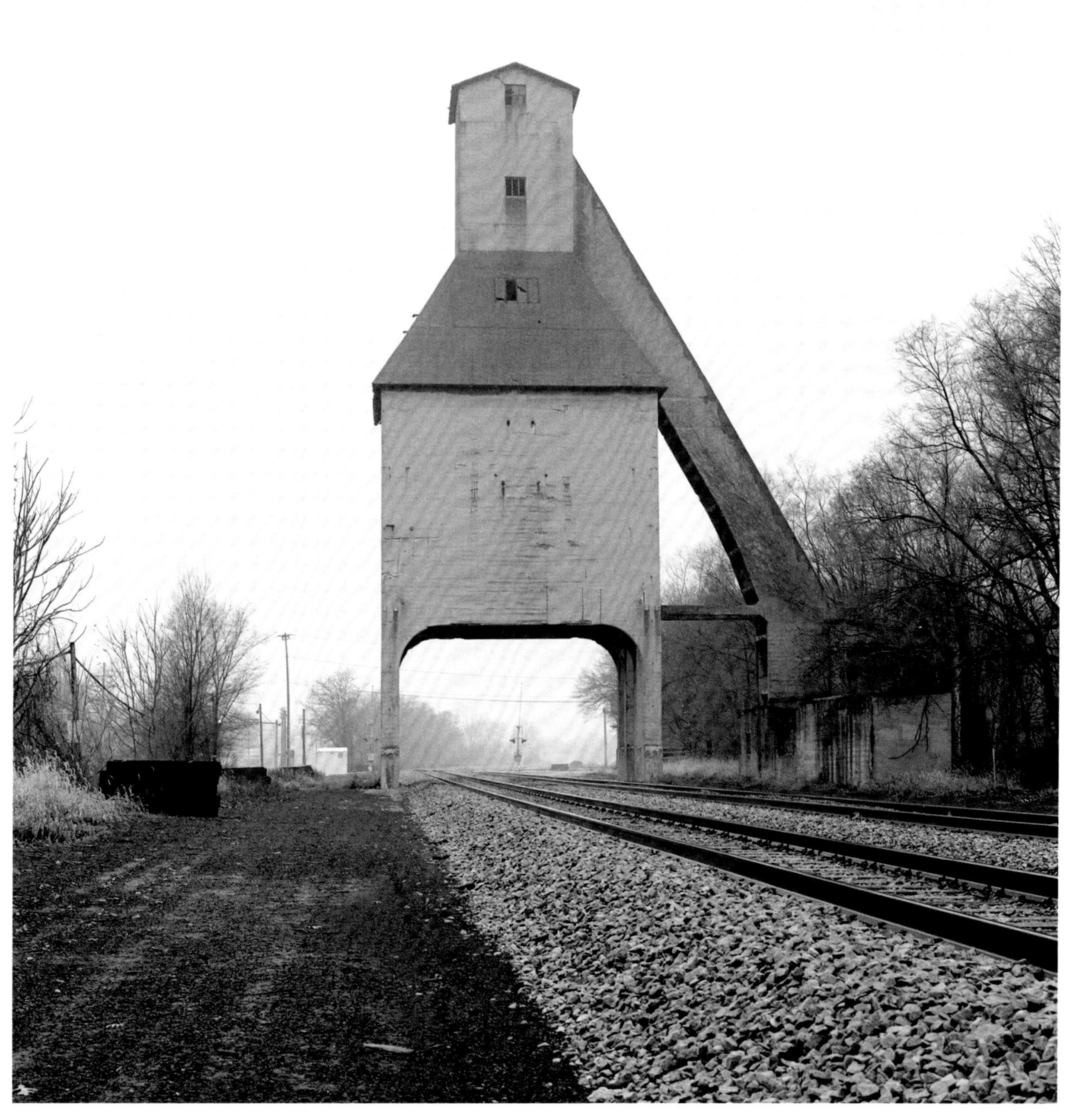

95 **MICHIGAN CITY, INDIANA** Michigan Central 41°43’33.2”N 86°52’31.7”W

COUNCIL BLUFFS, IOWA Illinois Central 41°16’27.5”N 95°51’50.3”W

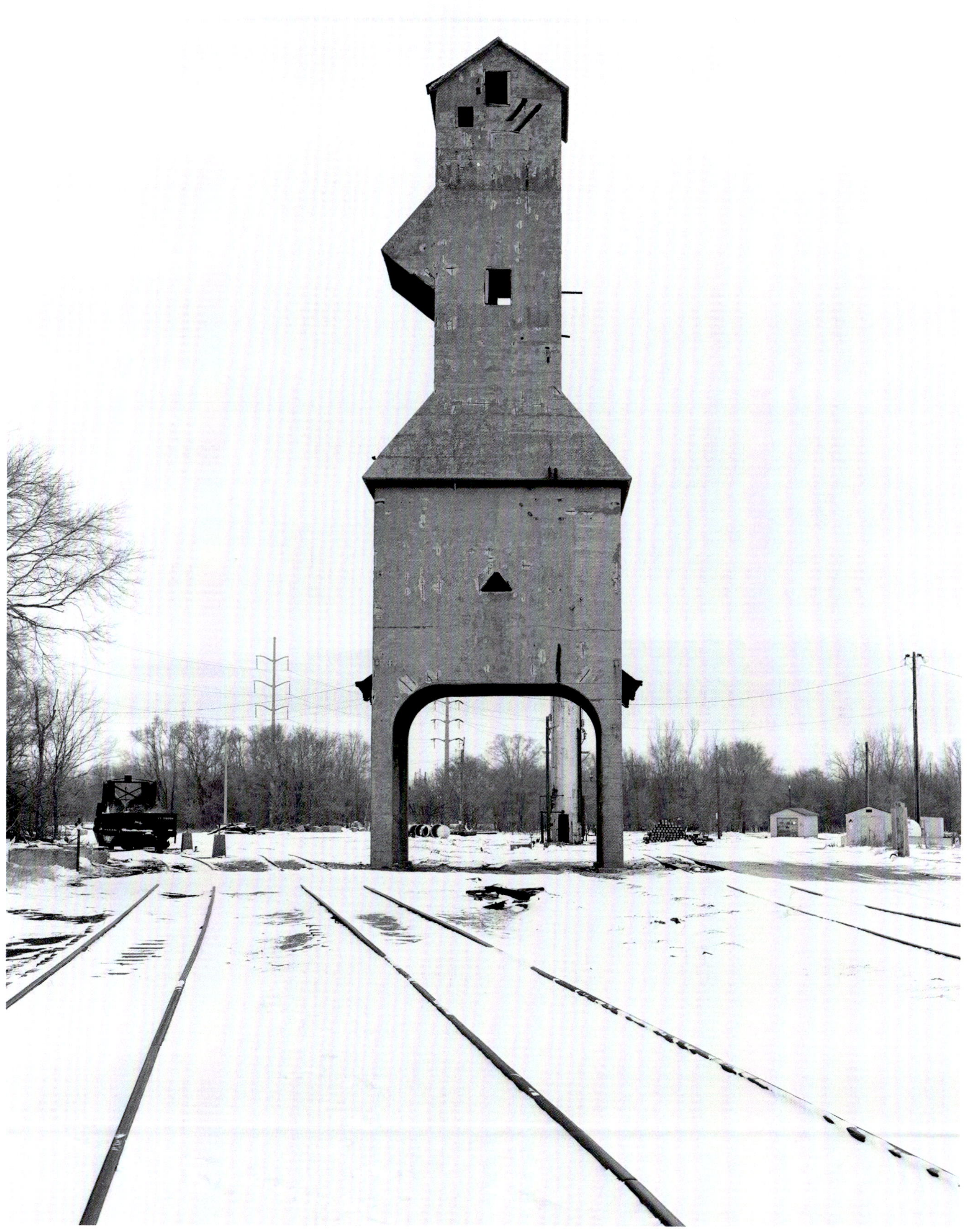

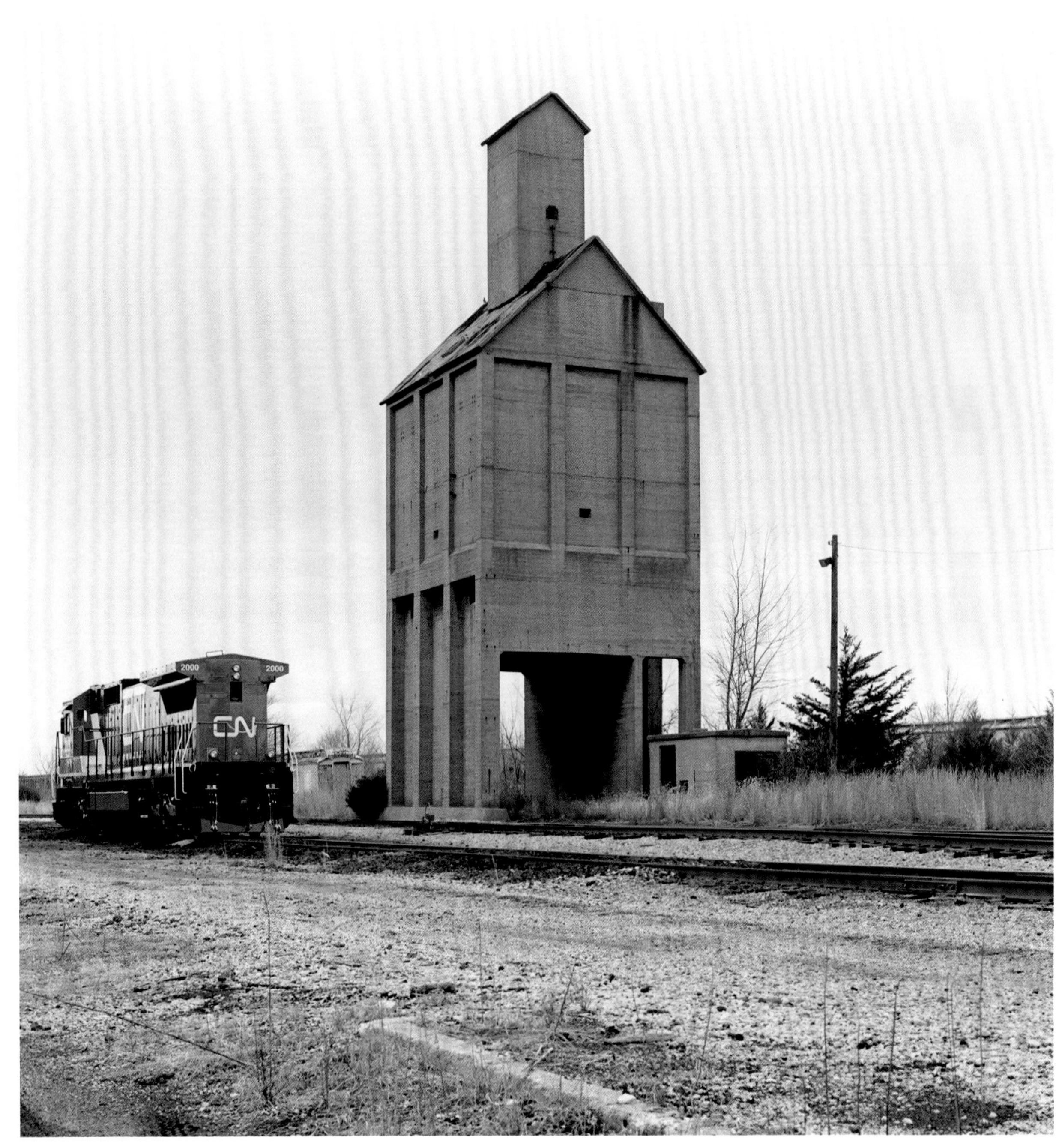

 CENTRALIA, ILLINOIS Illinois Central 38°29’52.4”N 89°08’46.9”W

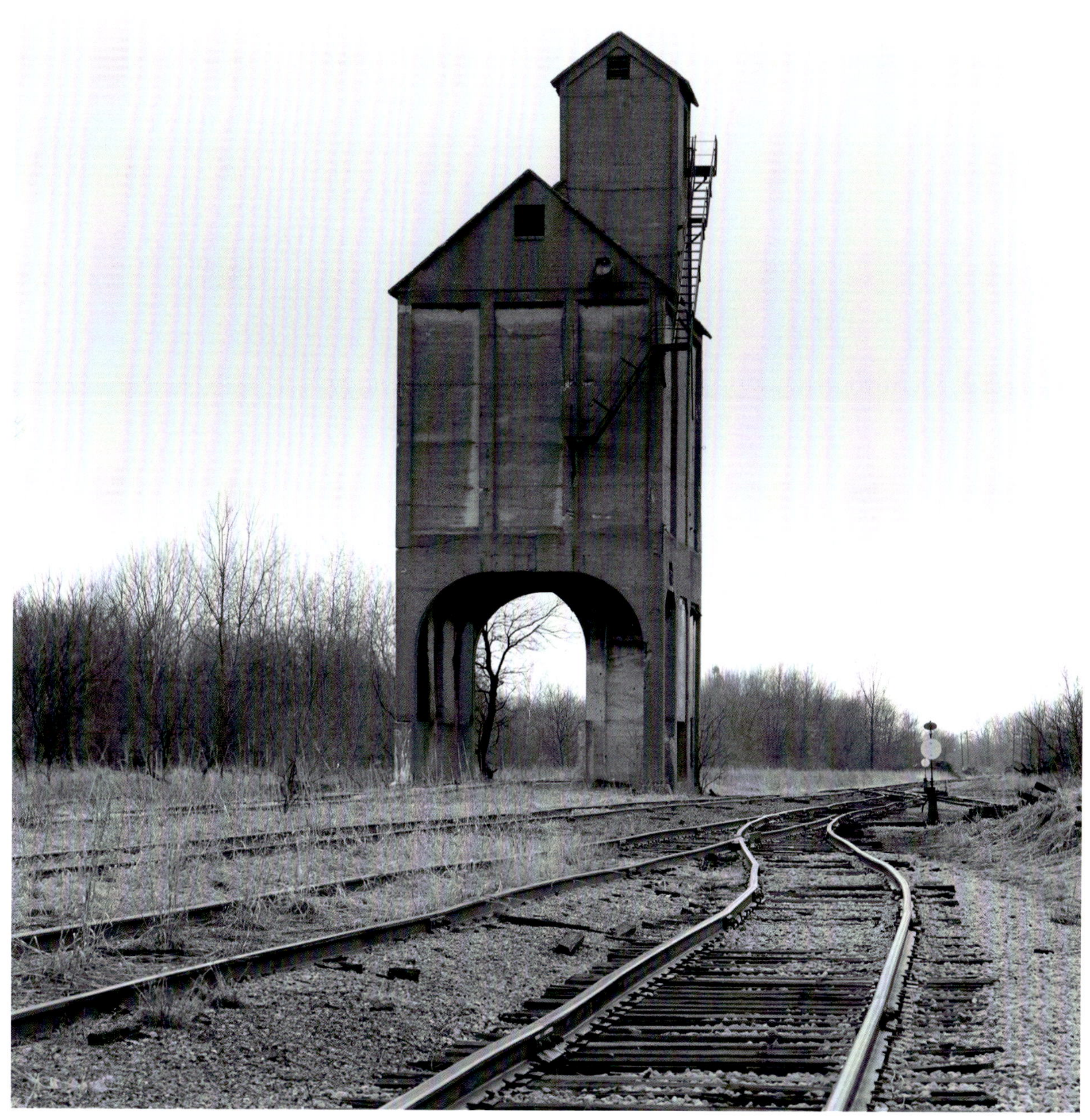

99 **DURAND, MICHIGAN** Grand Trunk Western 42°54’56.5”N 83°59’51.5”W

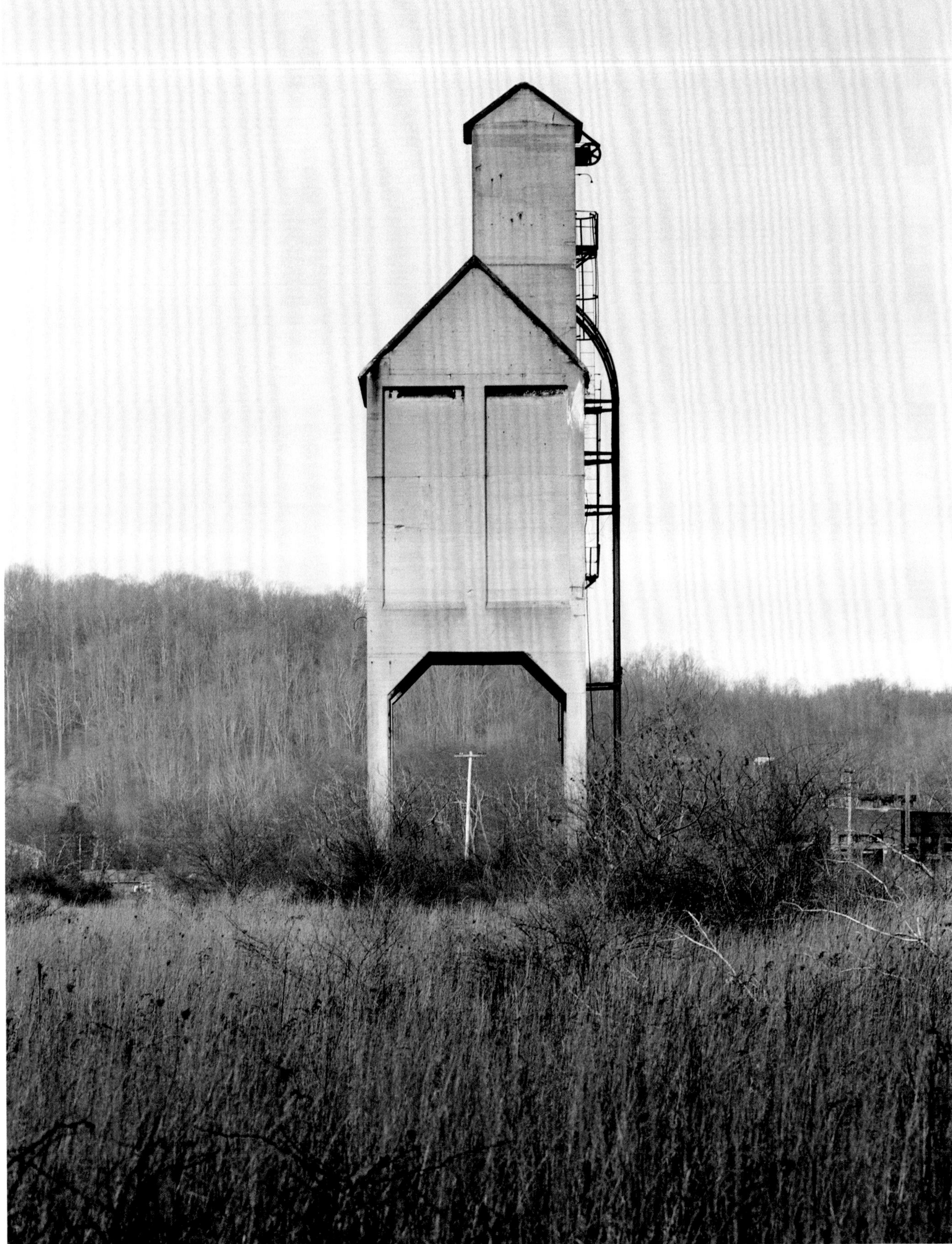

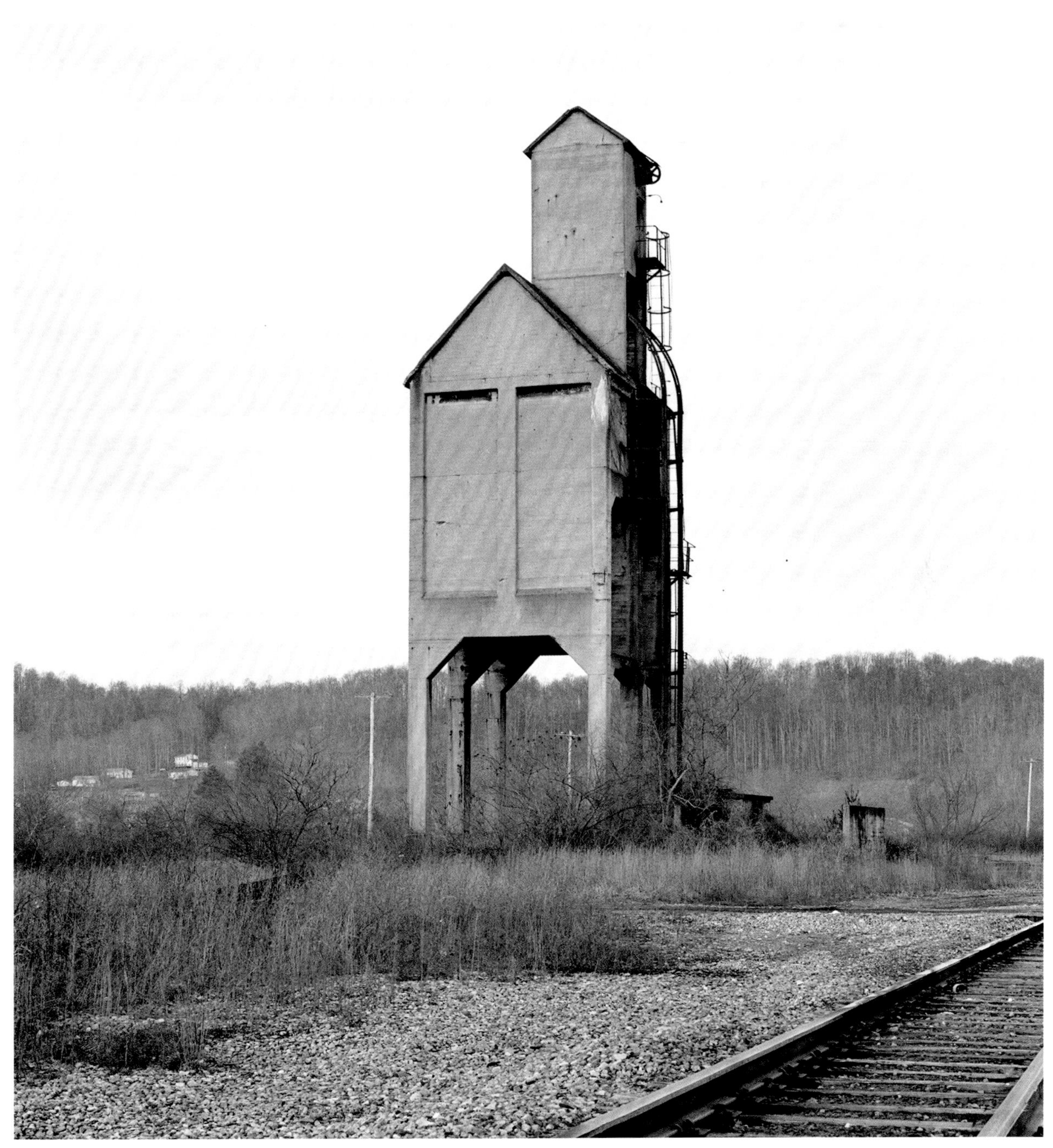

101 **COWEN, WEST VIRGINIA** Baltimore & Ohio 38°25'12.4"N 80°32'55.4"W

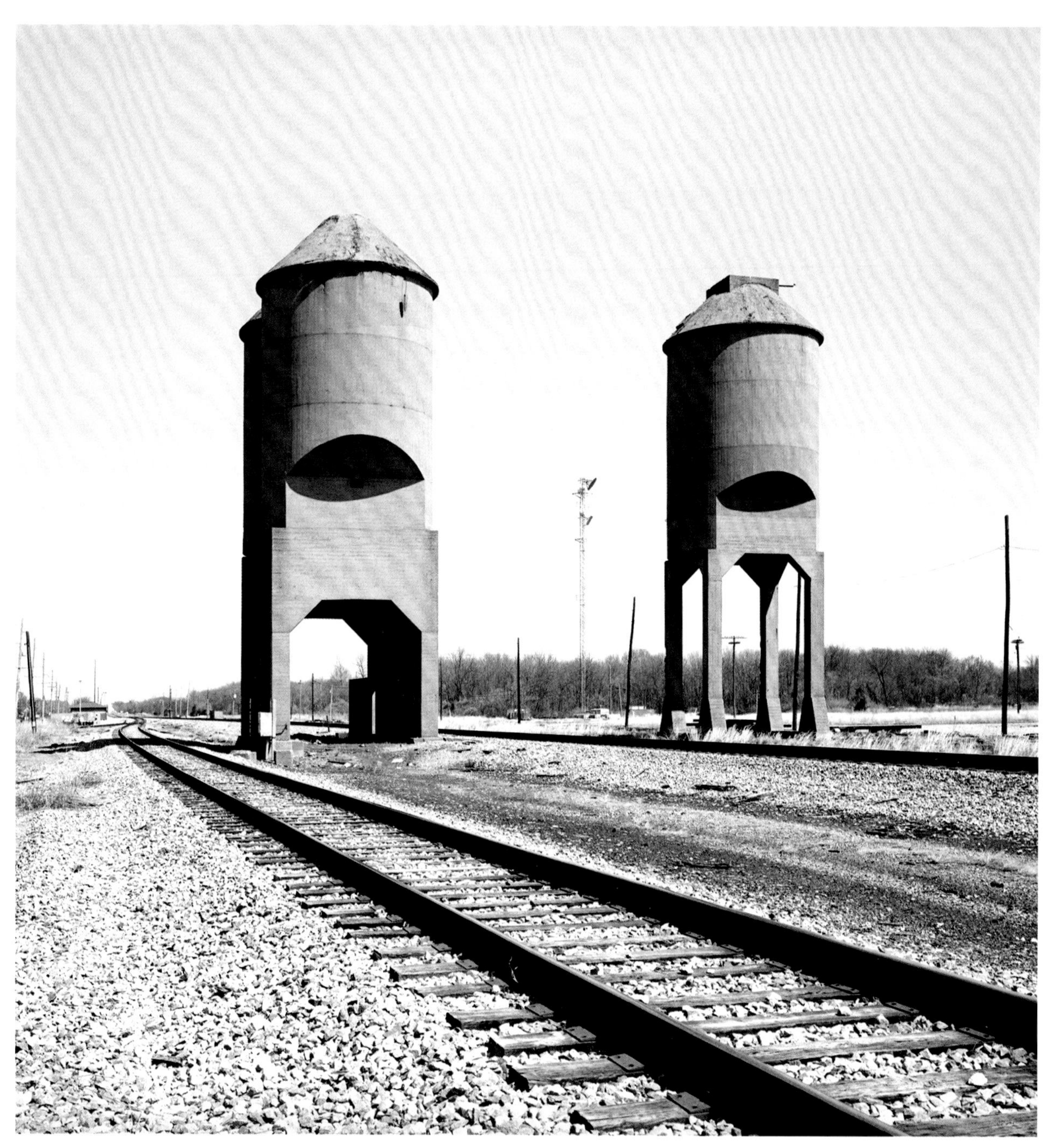

 CARBONDALE, ILLINOIS Illinois Central 37°44'23.5"N 89°13'03.9"W

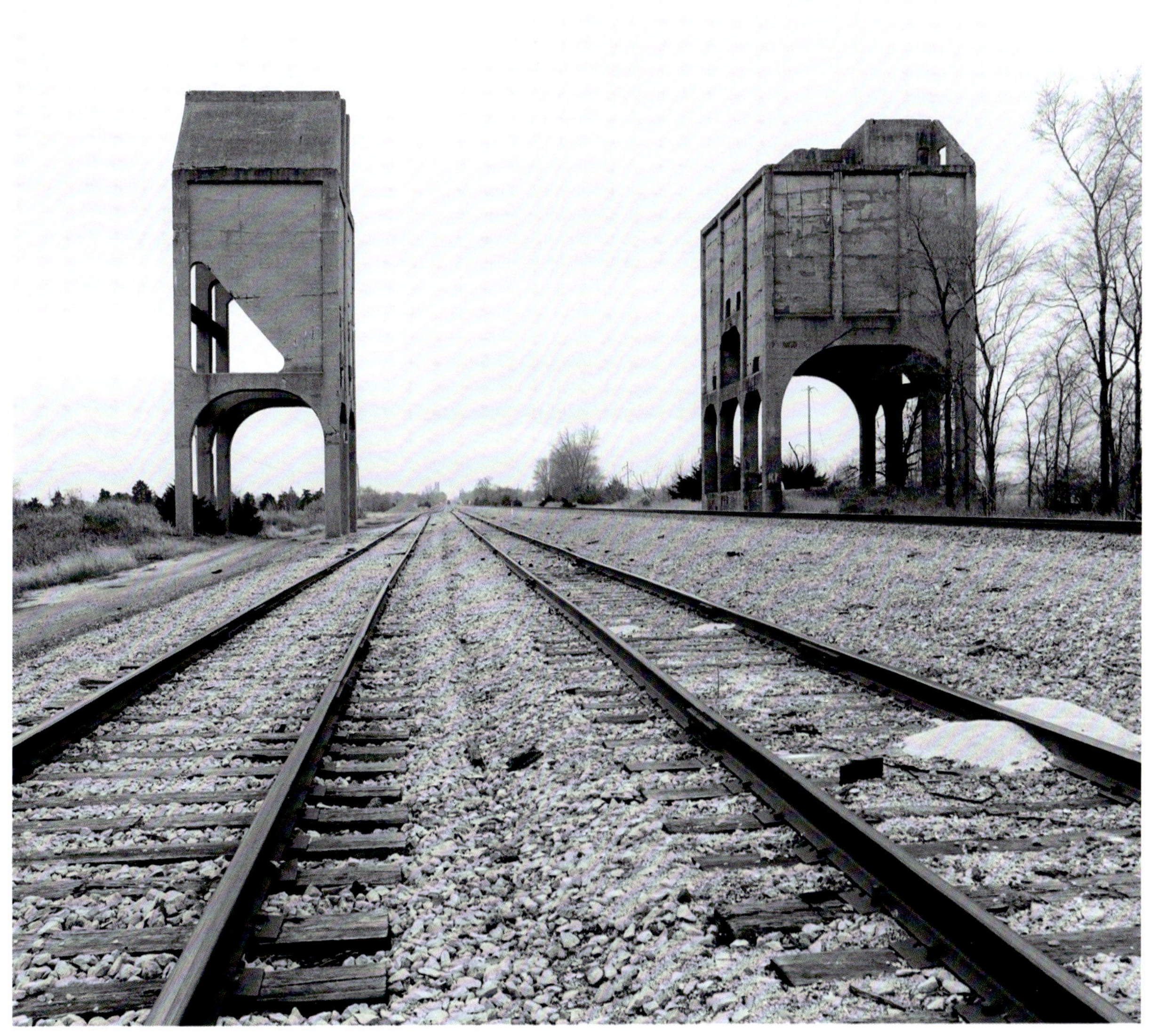

103 **GILMAN, ILLINOIS** Illinois Central 40°47'15.4"N 87°59'22.6"W

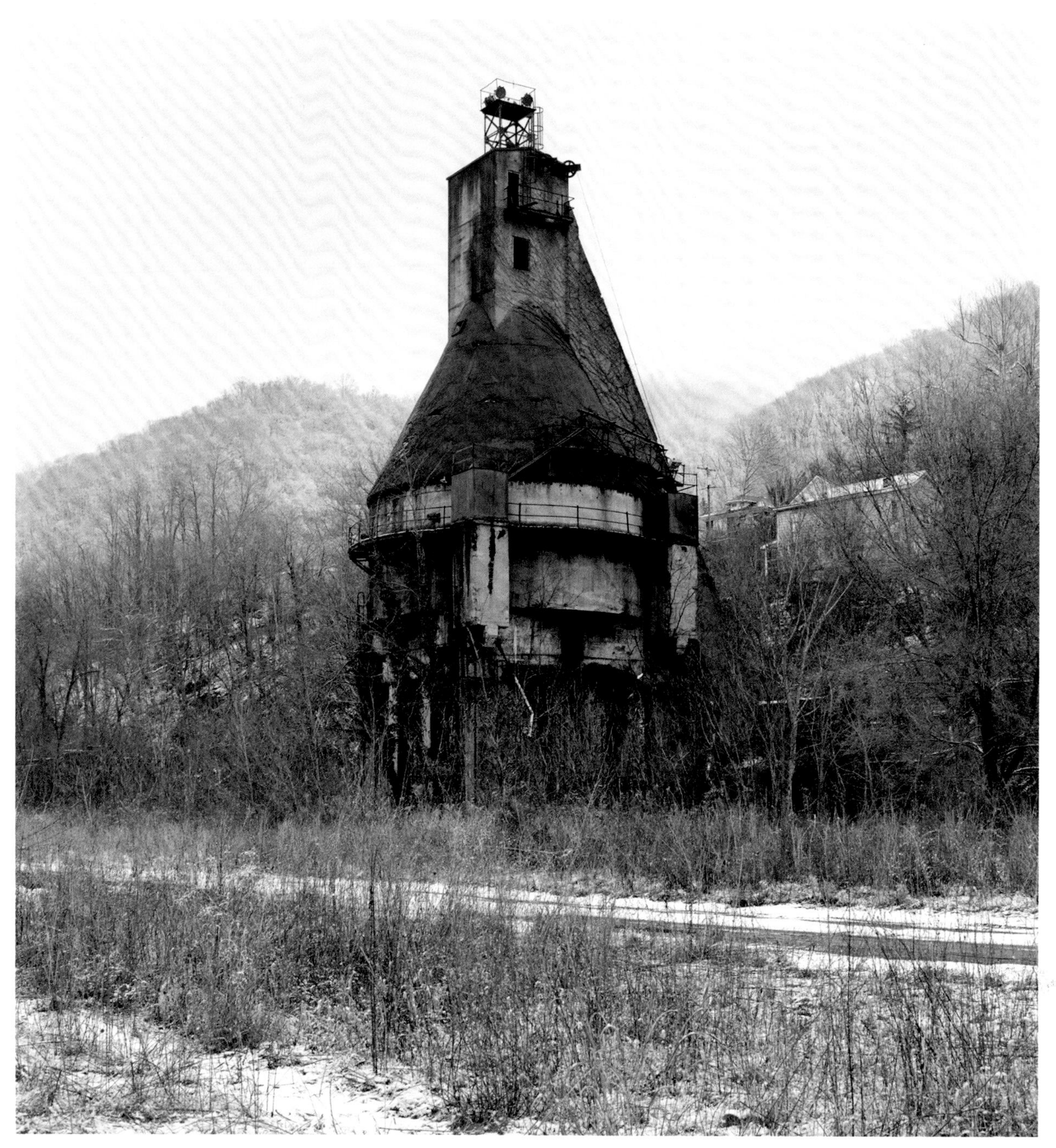

 HINTON, WEST VIRGINIA Chesapeake & Ohio 37°40'41.4"N 80°53'02.1"W

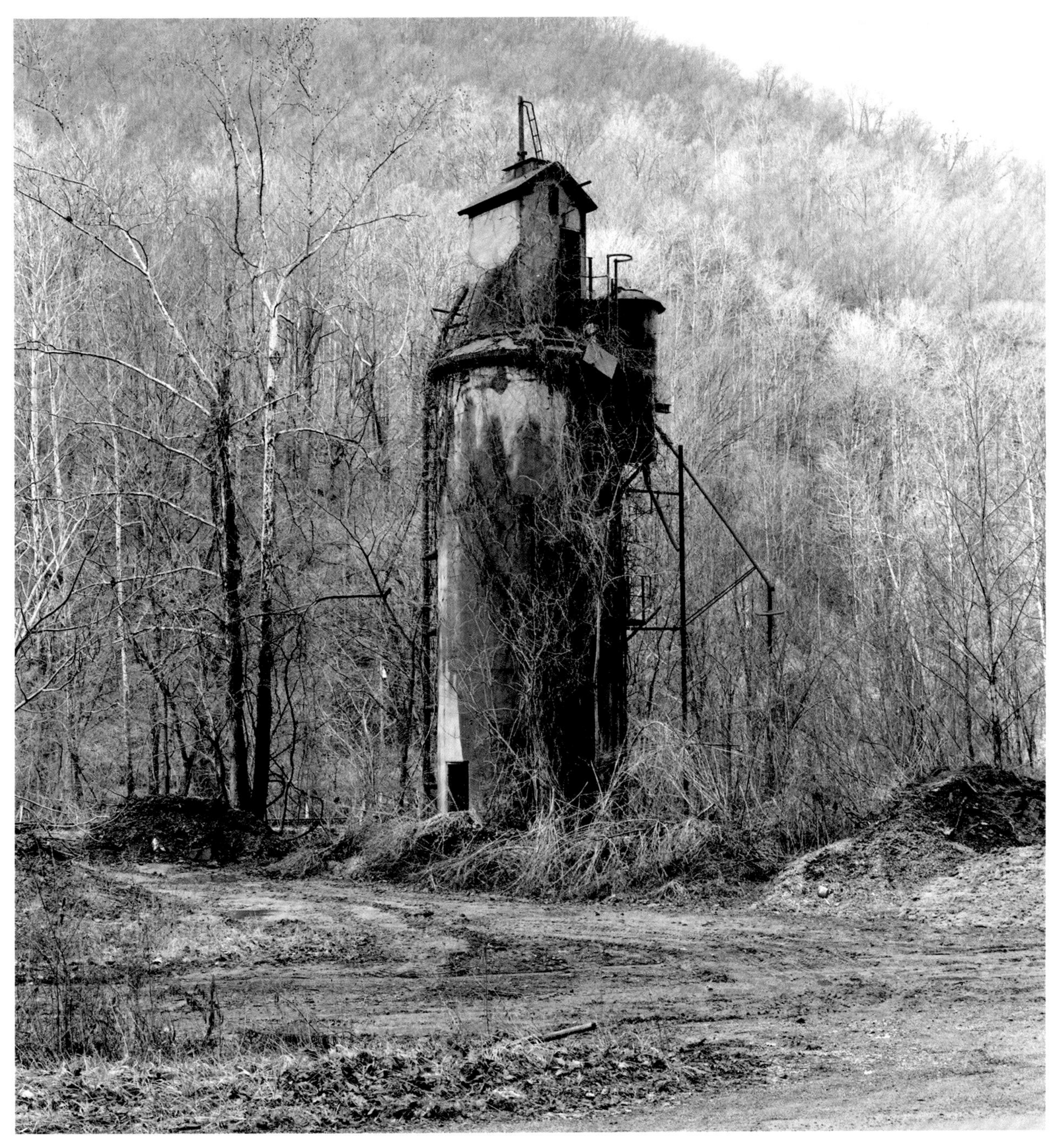

105 **CANE FORK, WEST VIRGINIA** Chesapeake & Ohio 38°05'41.8"N 81°26'29.7"W

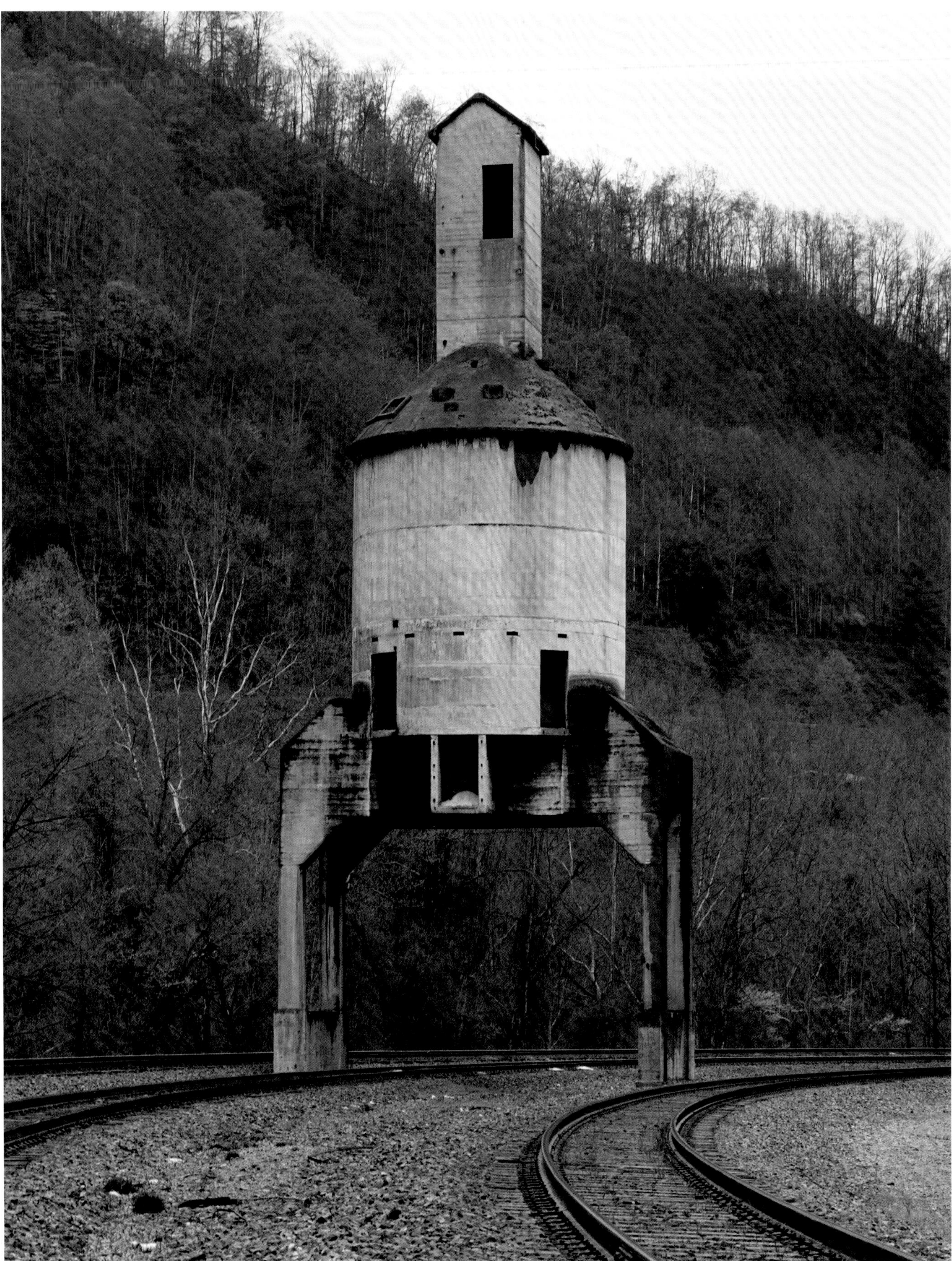

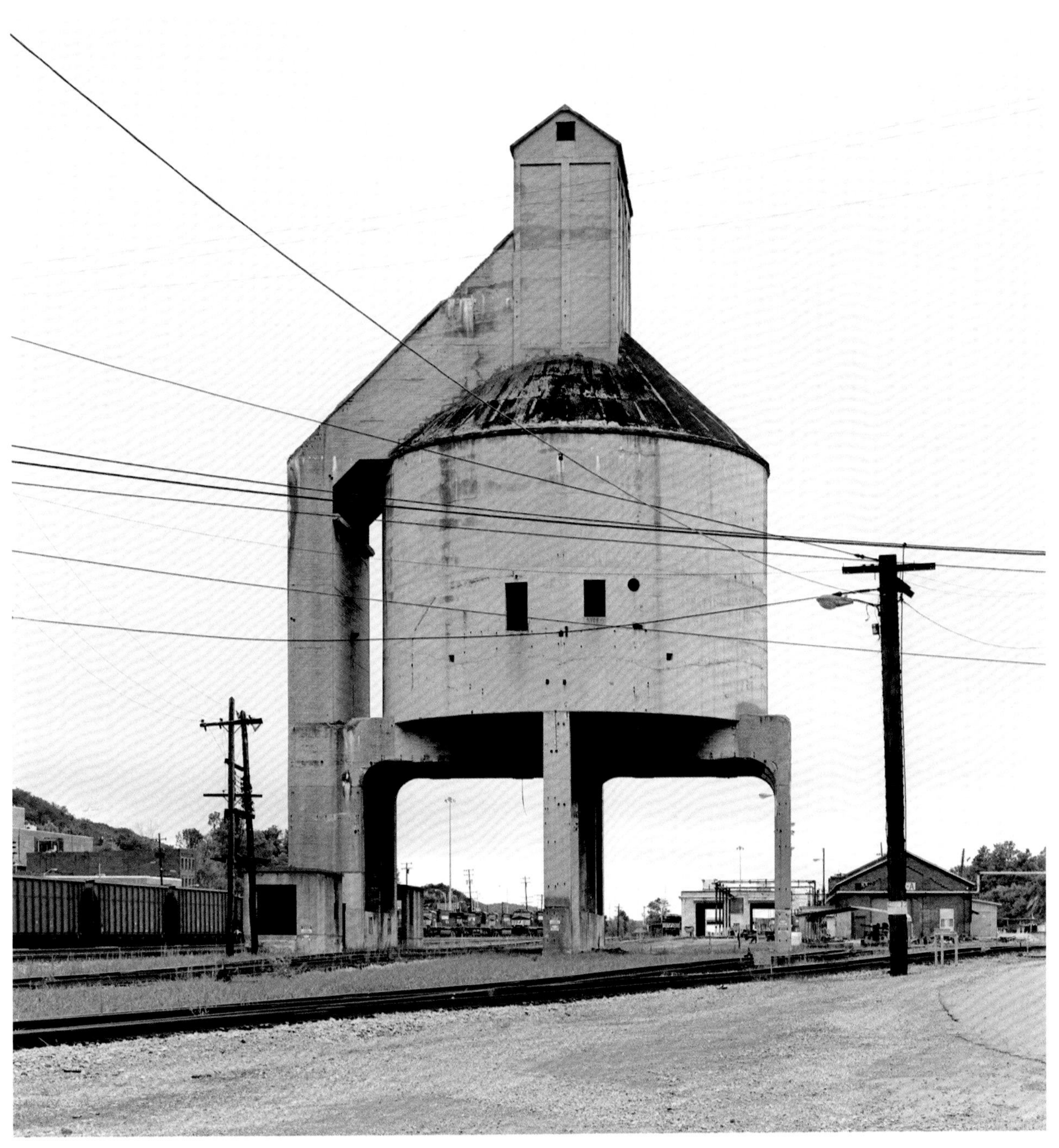

106 **WELCH, WEST VIRGINIA** Norfolk & Western 37°26’56.2”N 81°36’10.8”W (left)

107 **BLUEFIELD, WEST VIRGINIA** Norfolk & Western 37°16’17.5”N 81°13’13.8”W (above)

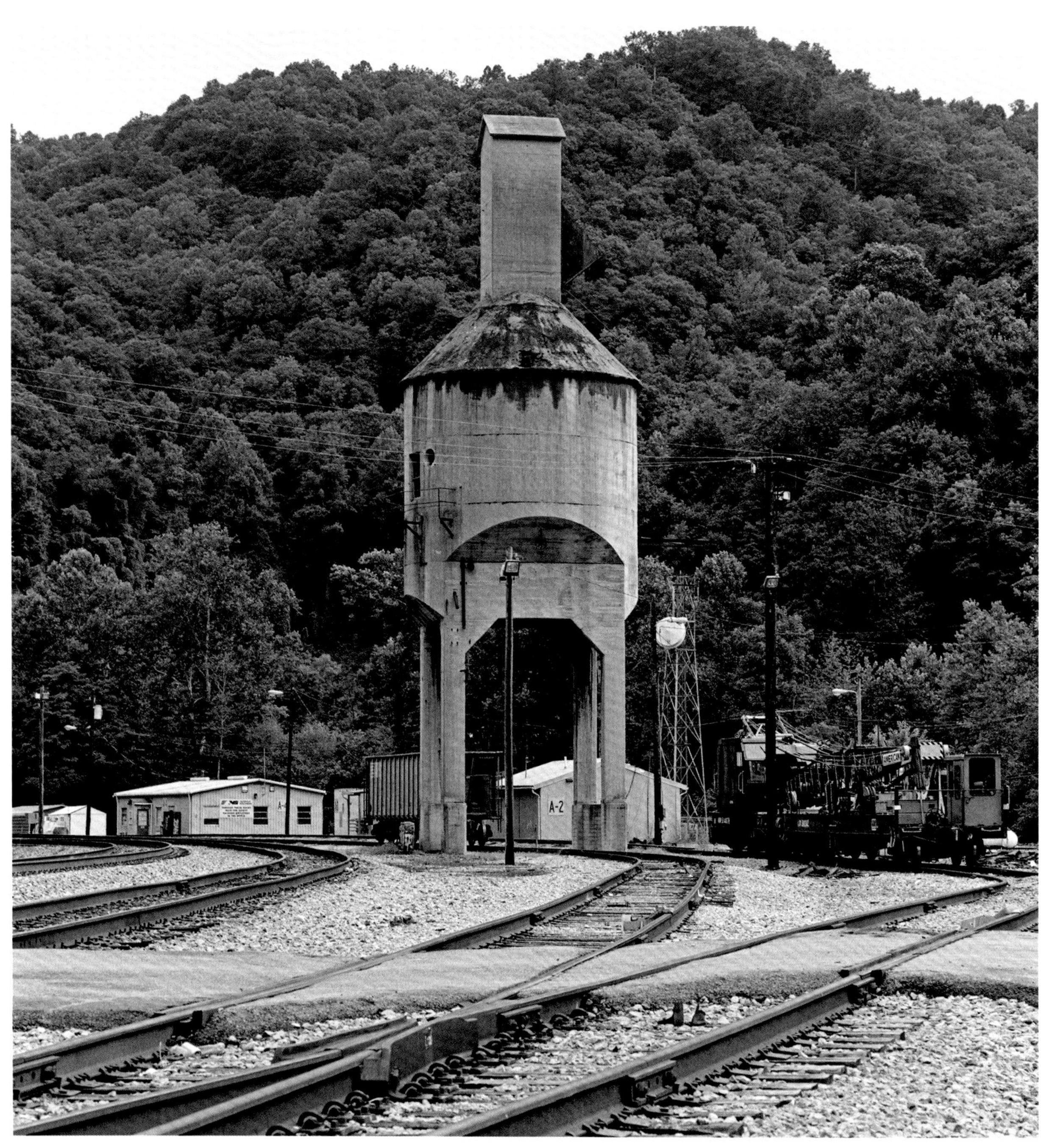

 IAEGER, WEST VIRGINIA Norfolk & Western 37°27’32.8”N 81°49’03.4”W

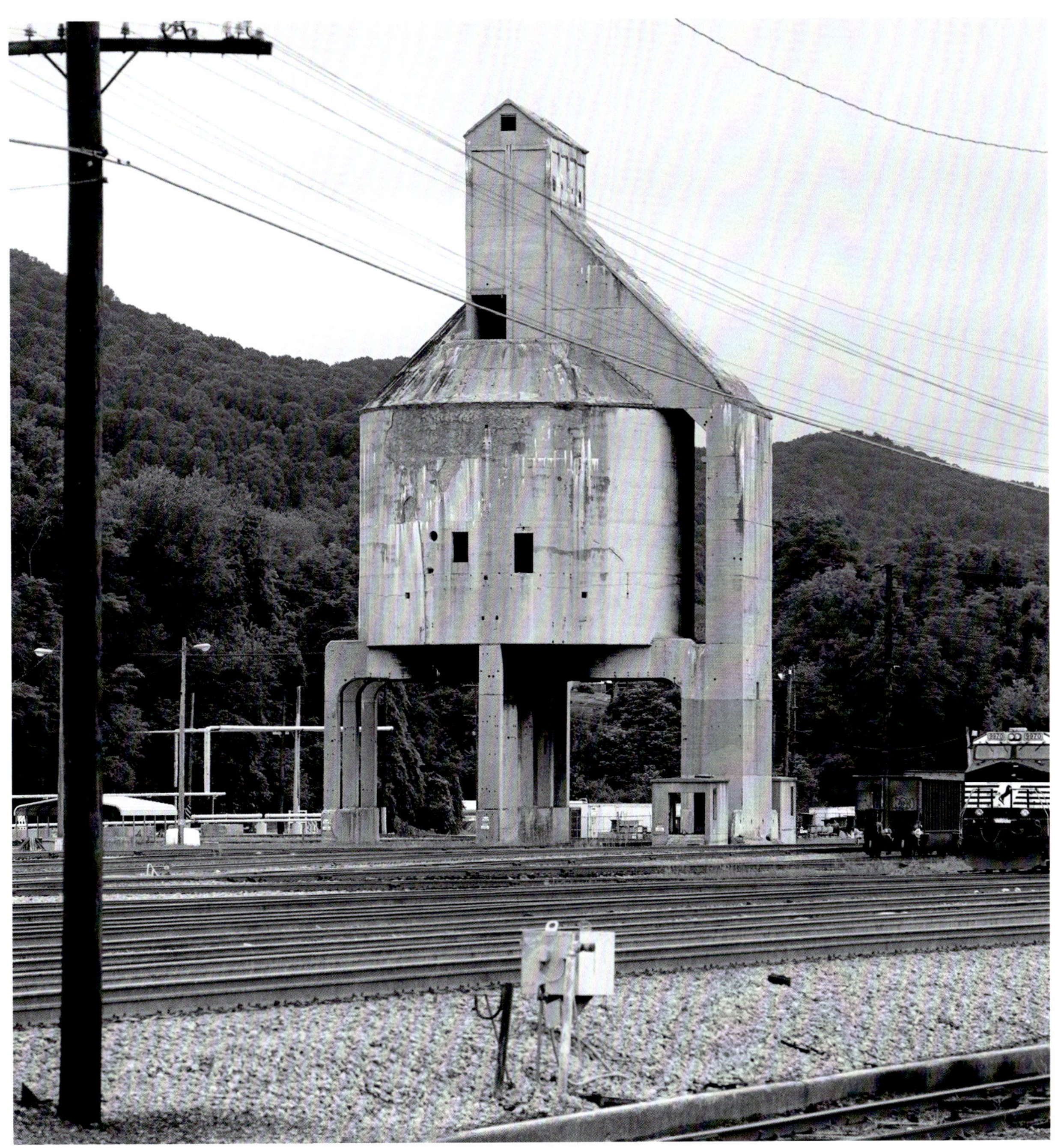

 BLUEFIELD, WEST VIRGINIA Norfolk & Western 37°16’17.5”N 81°13’13.8”W

110 **VICKER, VIRGINIA** Norfolk & Western 37°09'47.1"N 80°29'25.8"W

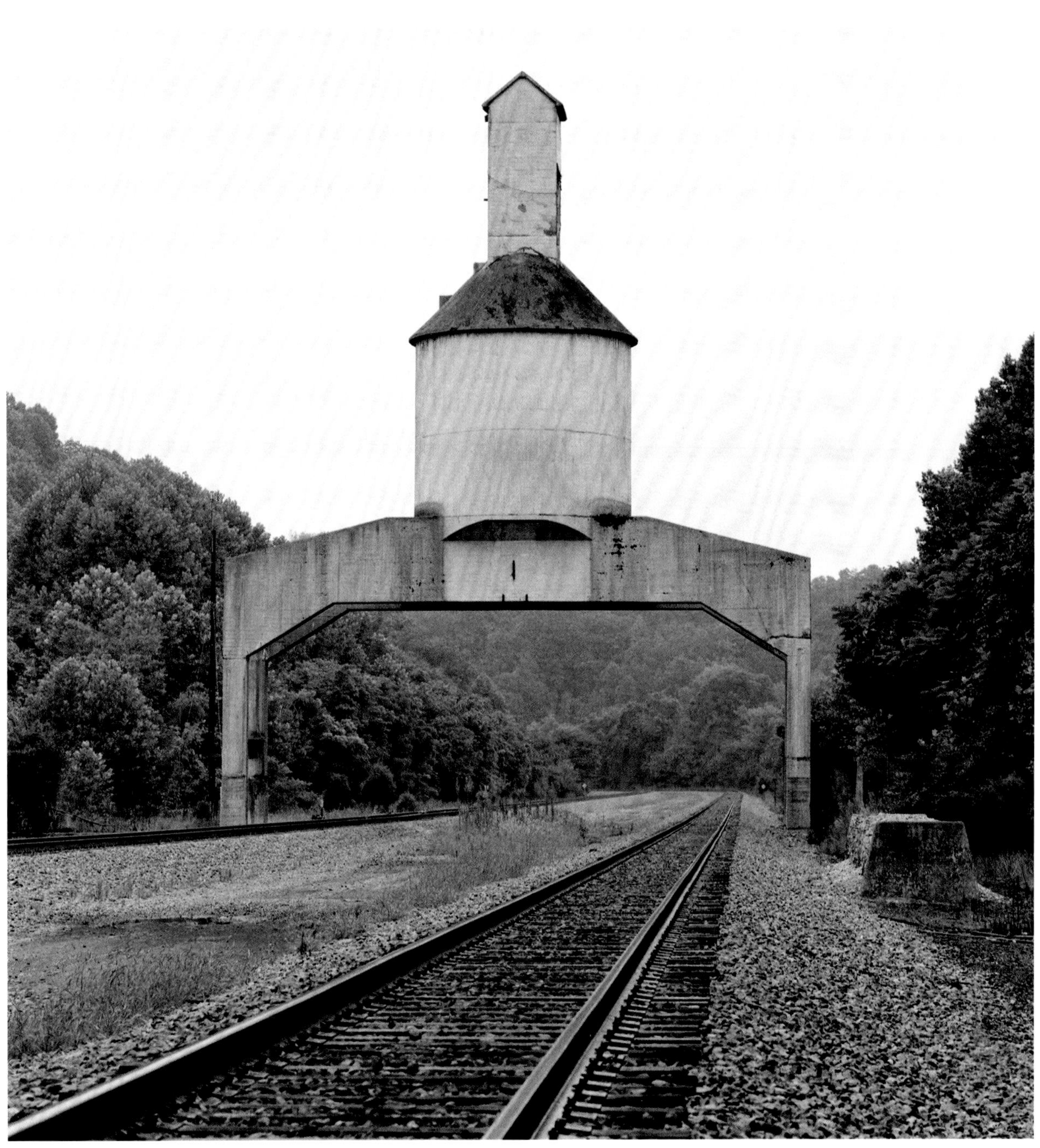

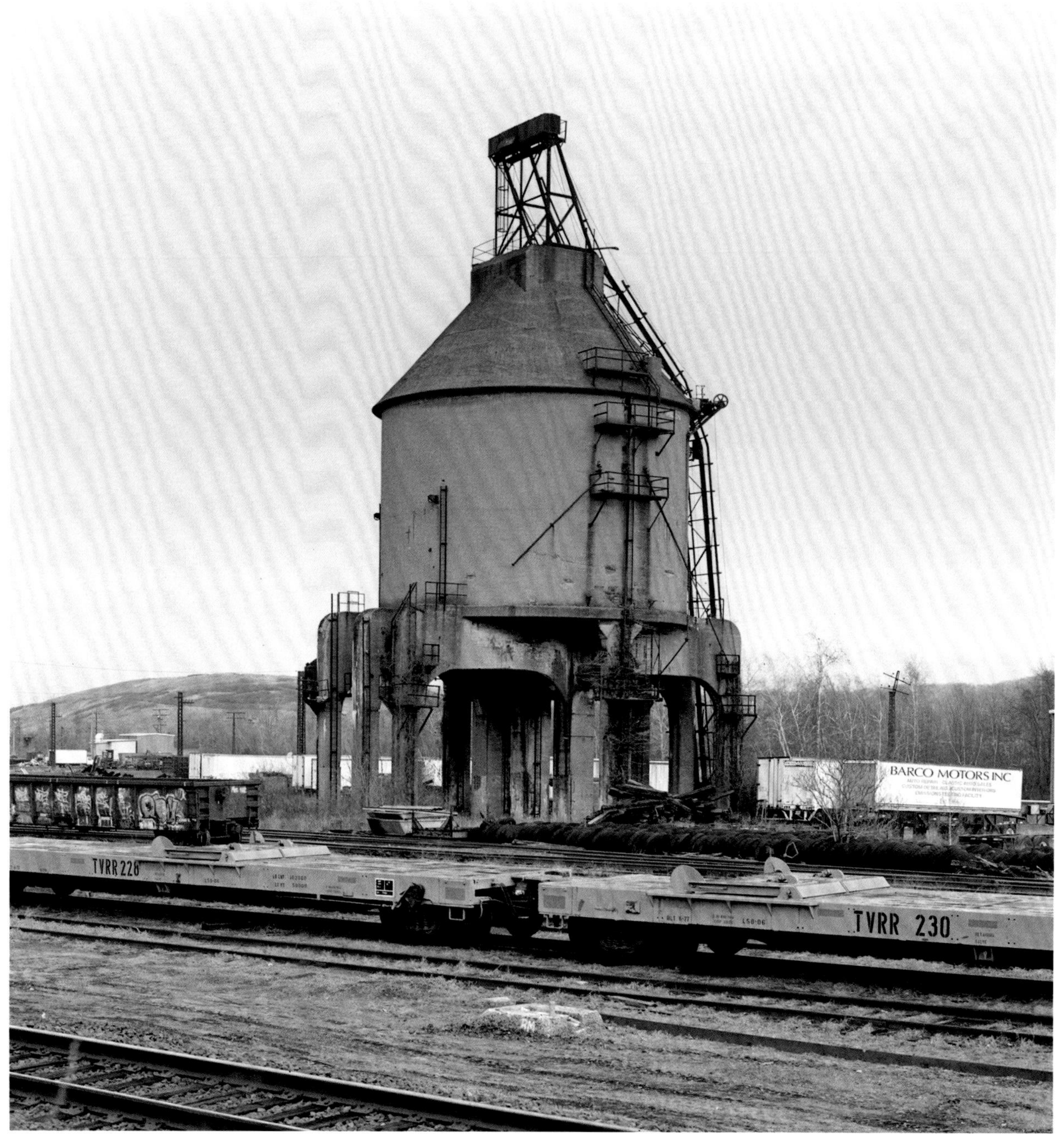

 NEW HAVEN, CONNECTICUT New York, New Haven & Hartford 41°19'25.2"N 72°53'39.5"W

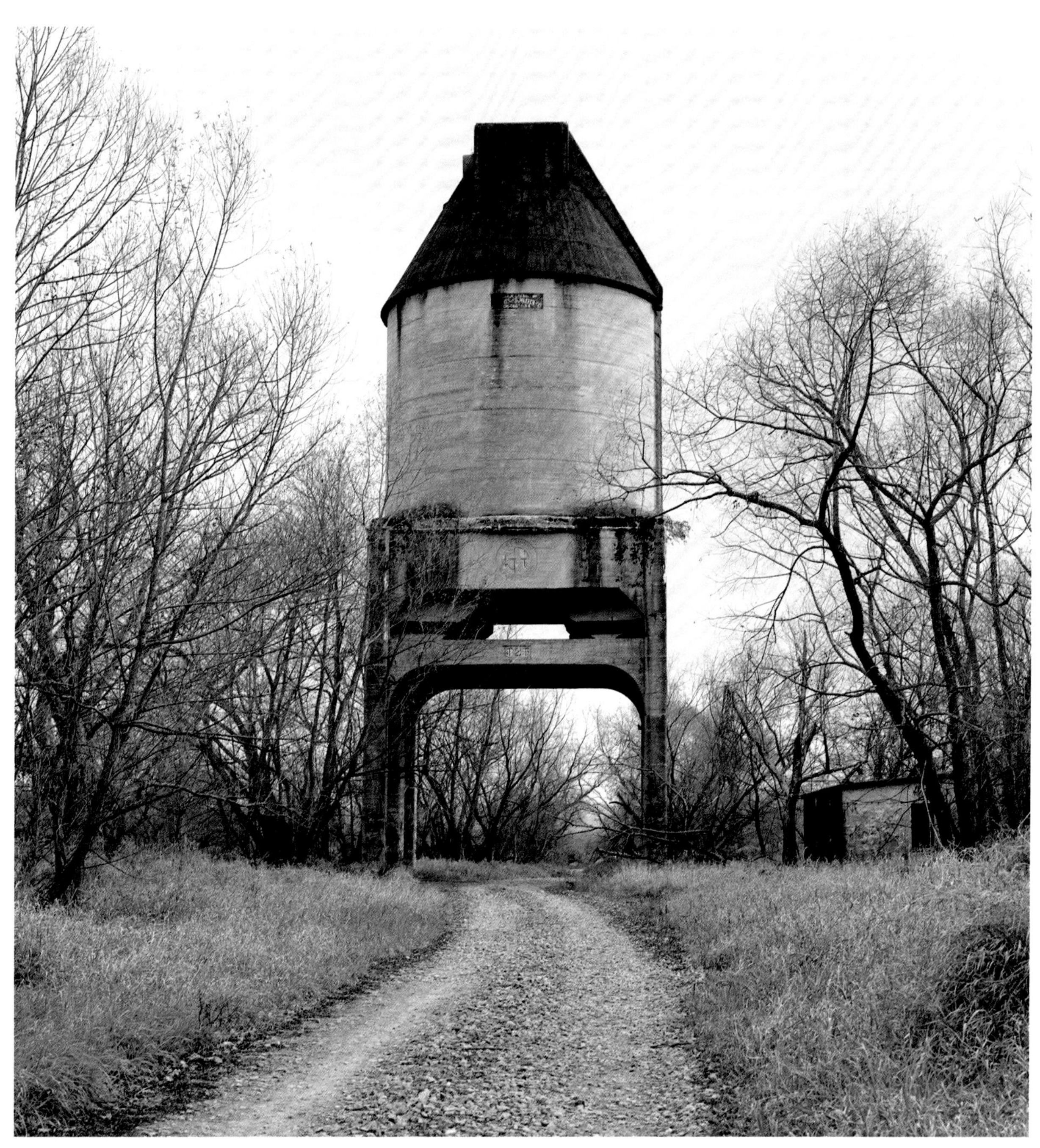

113 **LEADVALE, TENNESSEE** Southern 36°04'44.8"N 83°14'23.4"W

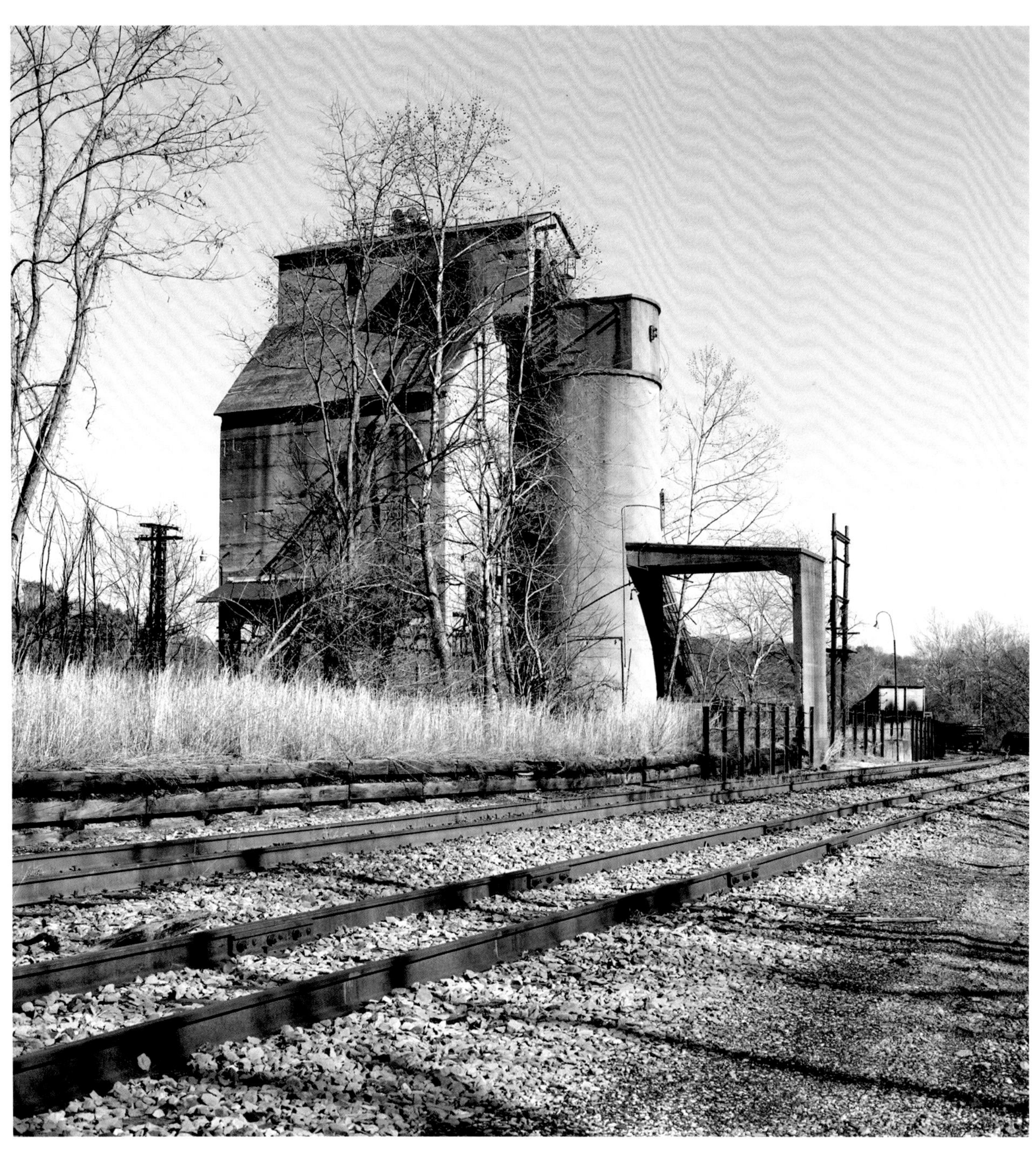

 CLIFTON FORGE, VIRGINIA Chesapeake & Ohio 37°48'39.8"N 79°49'55.7"W

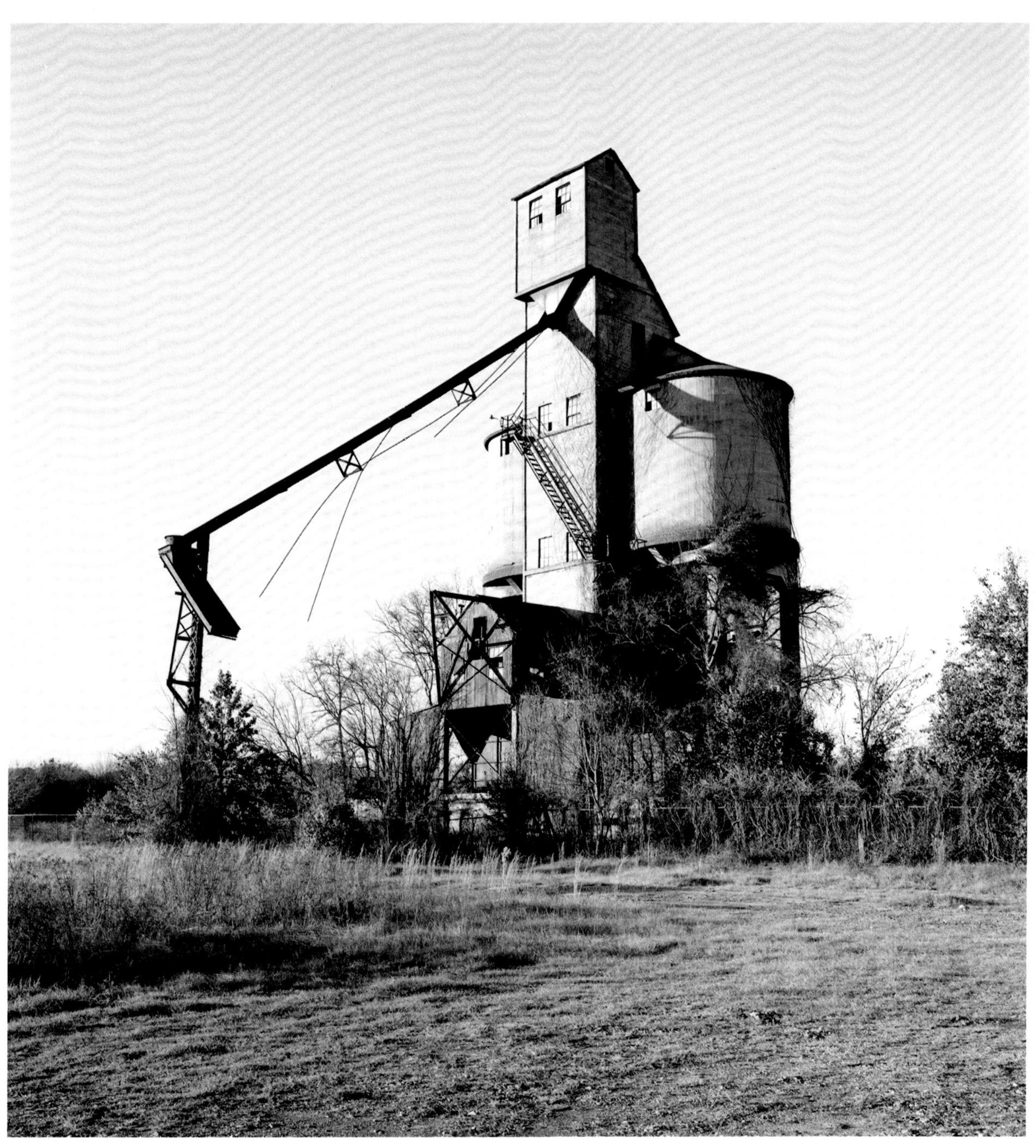

 MACON, GEORGIA Central of Georgia 32°49'31.4"N 83°37'38.3"W

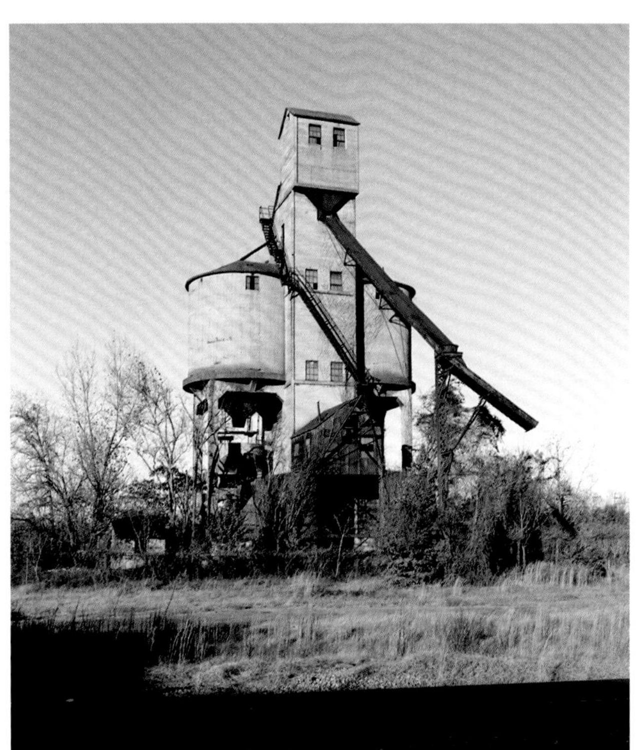

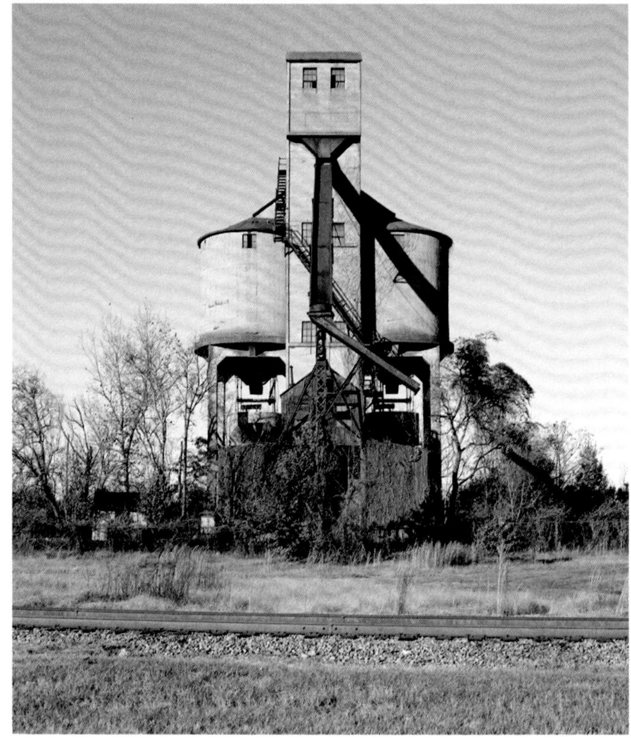

 MACON, GEORGIA Central of Georgia 32°49'31.4"N 83°37'38.3"W

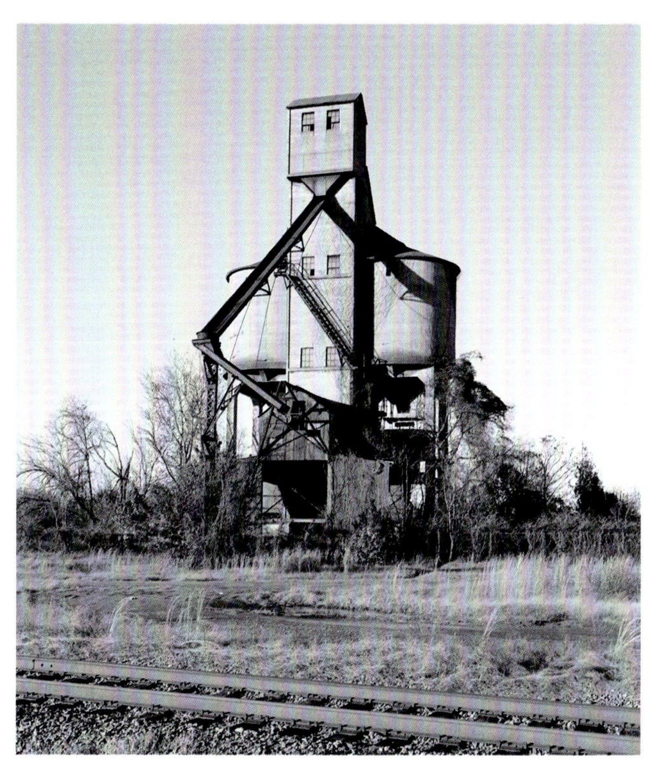

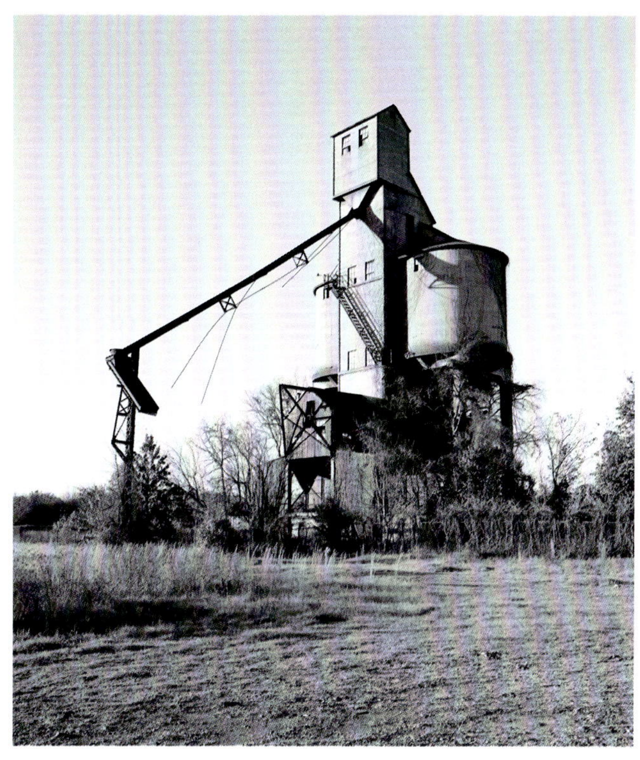

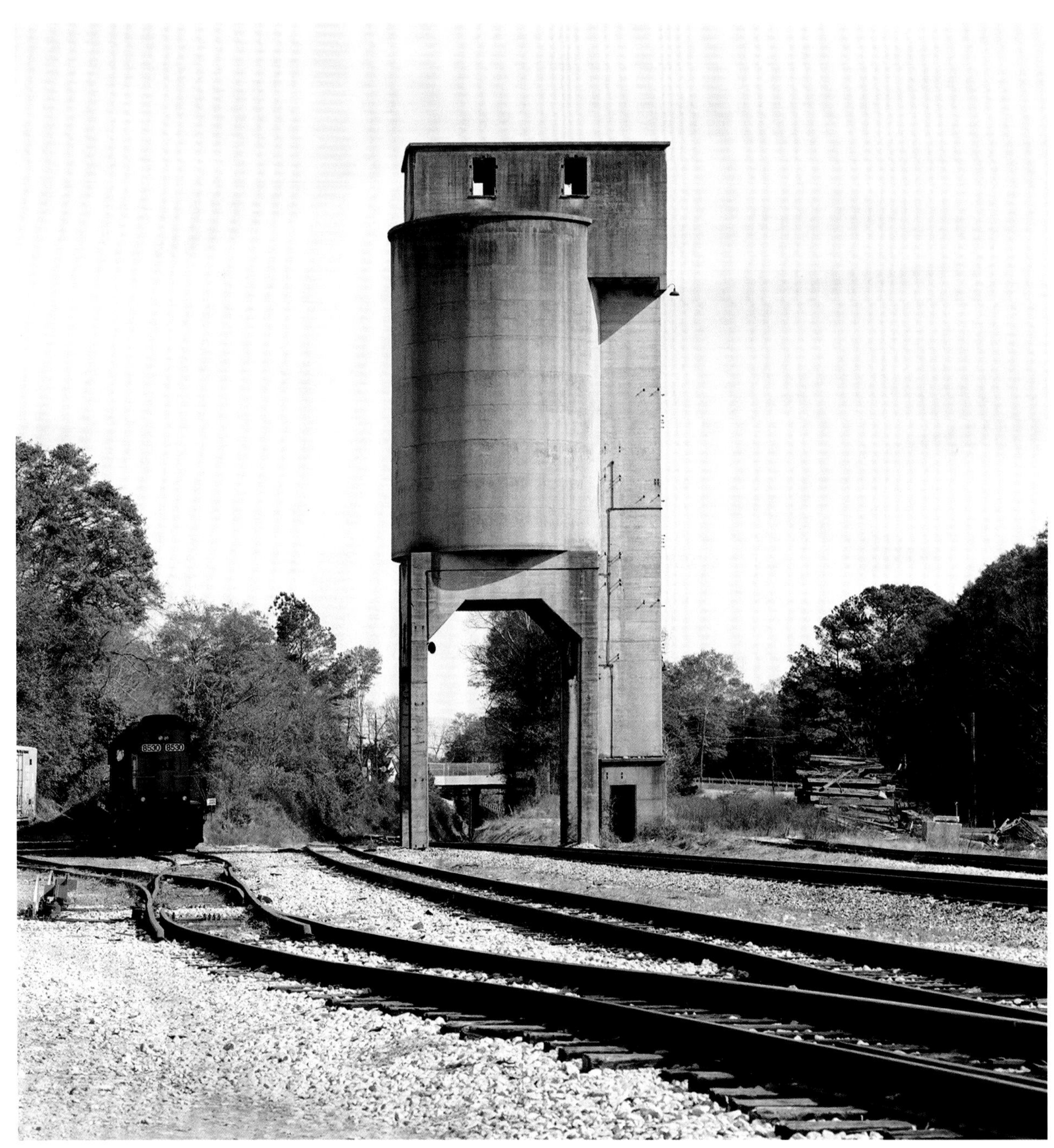

 SOCIAL CIRCLE, GEORGIA (demolished, 2022) Georgia 33°39’13.1”N 83°43’01.5”W

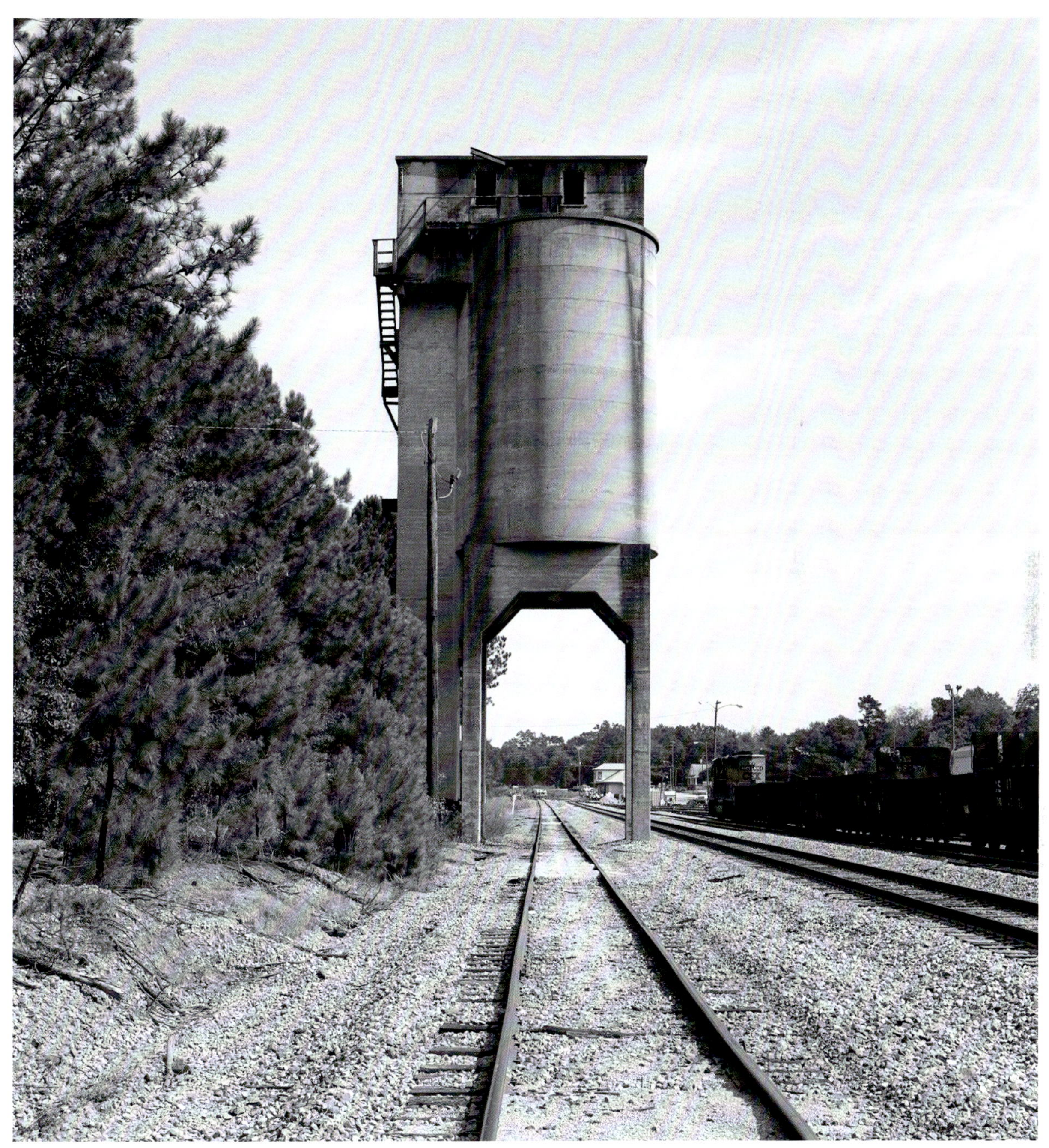

 CAMAK, GEORGIA Georgia 33°27′05.4″N 82°39′01.9″W

CAMAK, GEORGIA Georgia 33°27’05.4”N 82°39’01.9”W

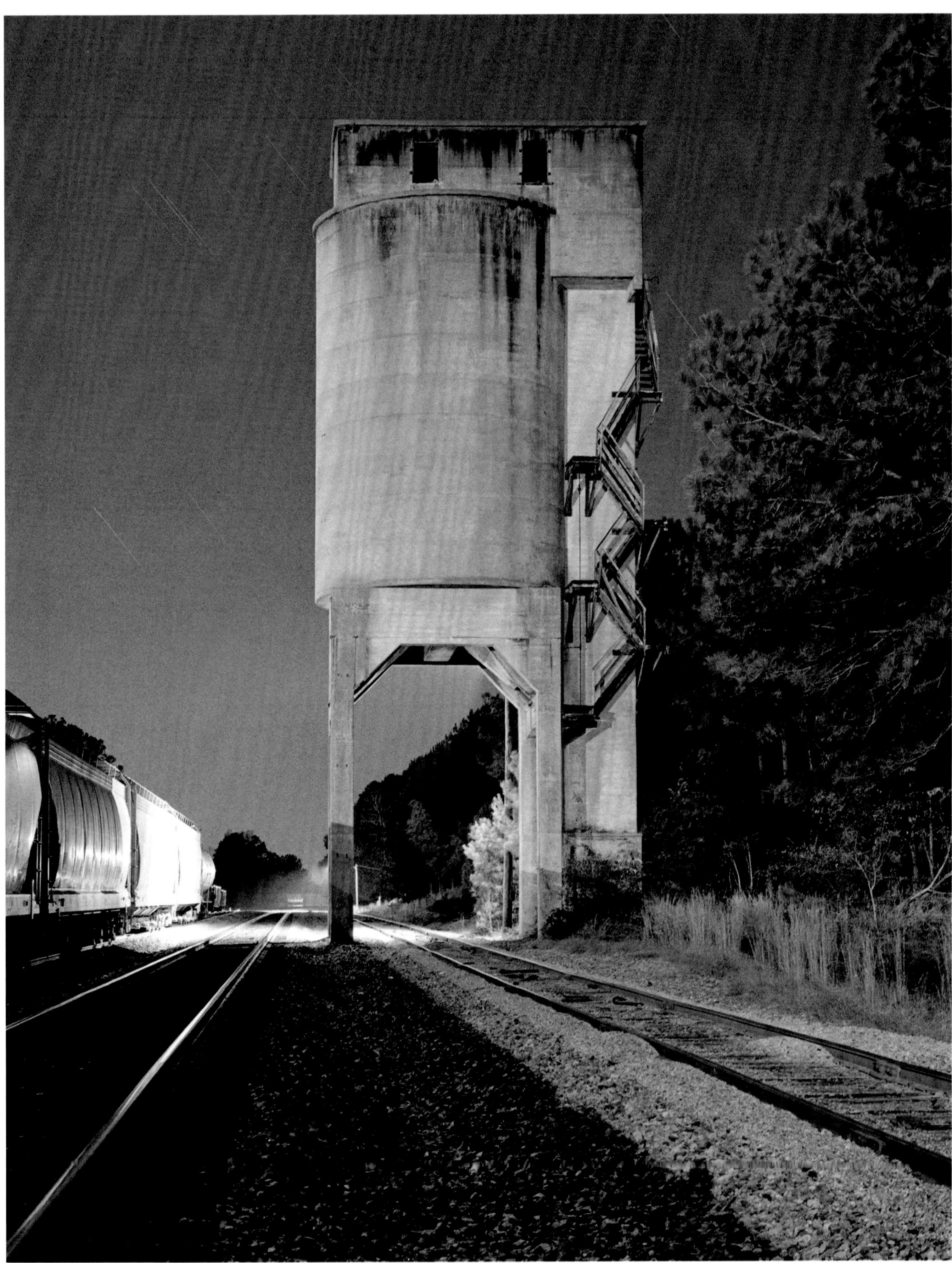

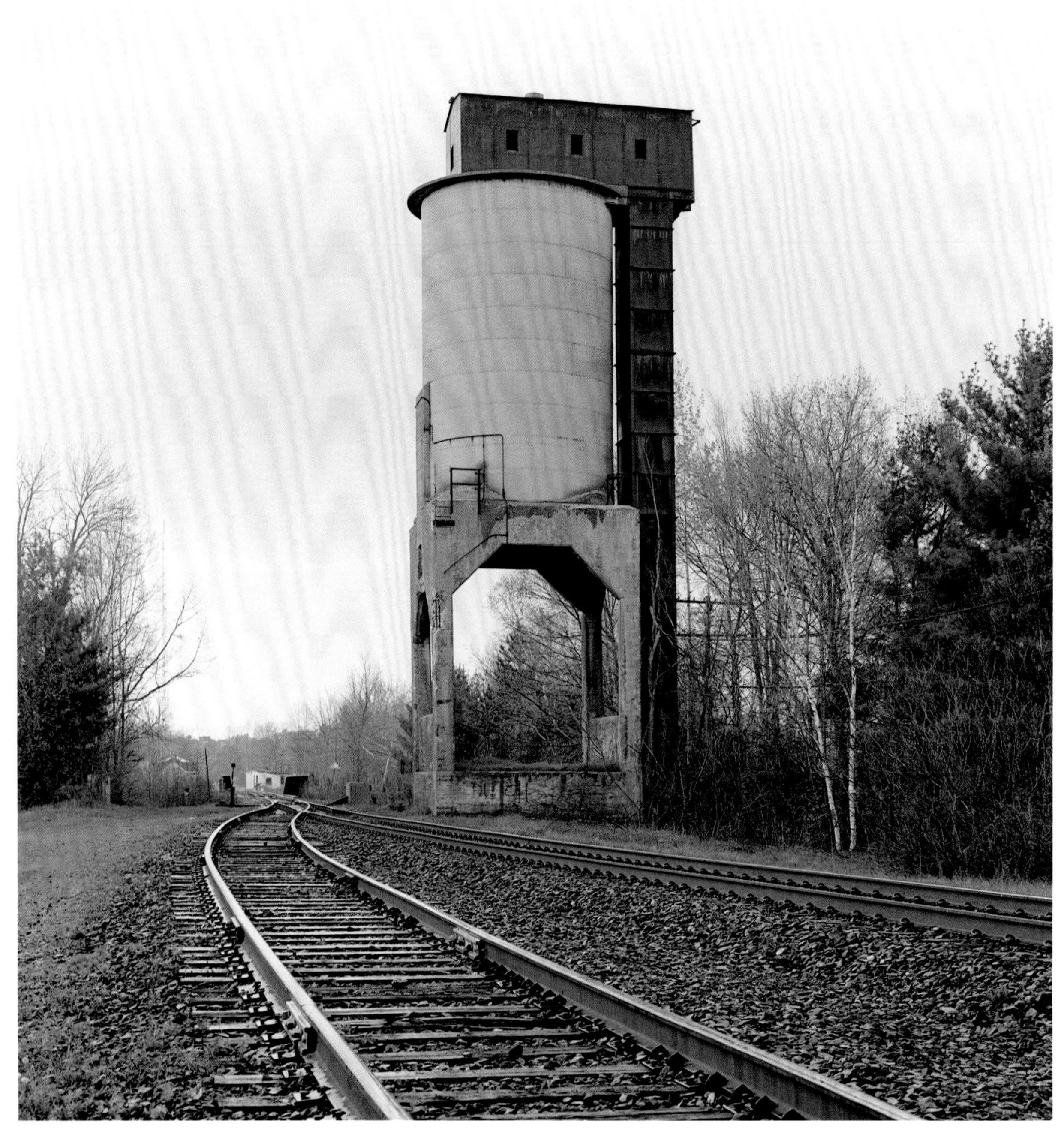

 WASHAGO, ONTARIO Canadian National 44°44'45.7"N 79°20'04.1"W

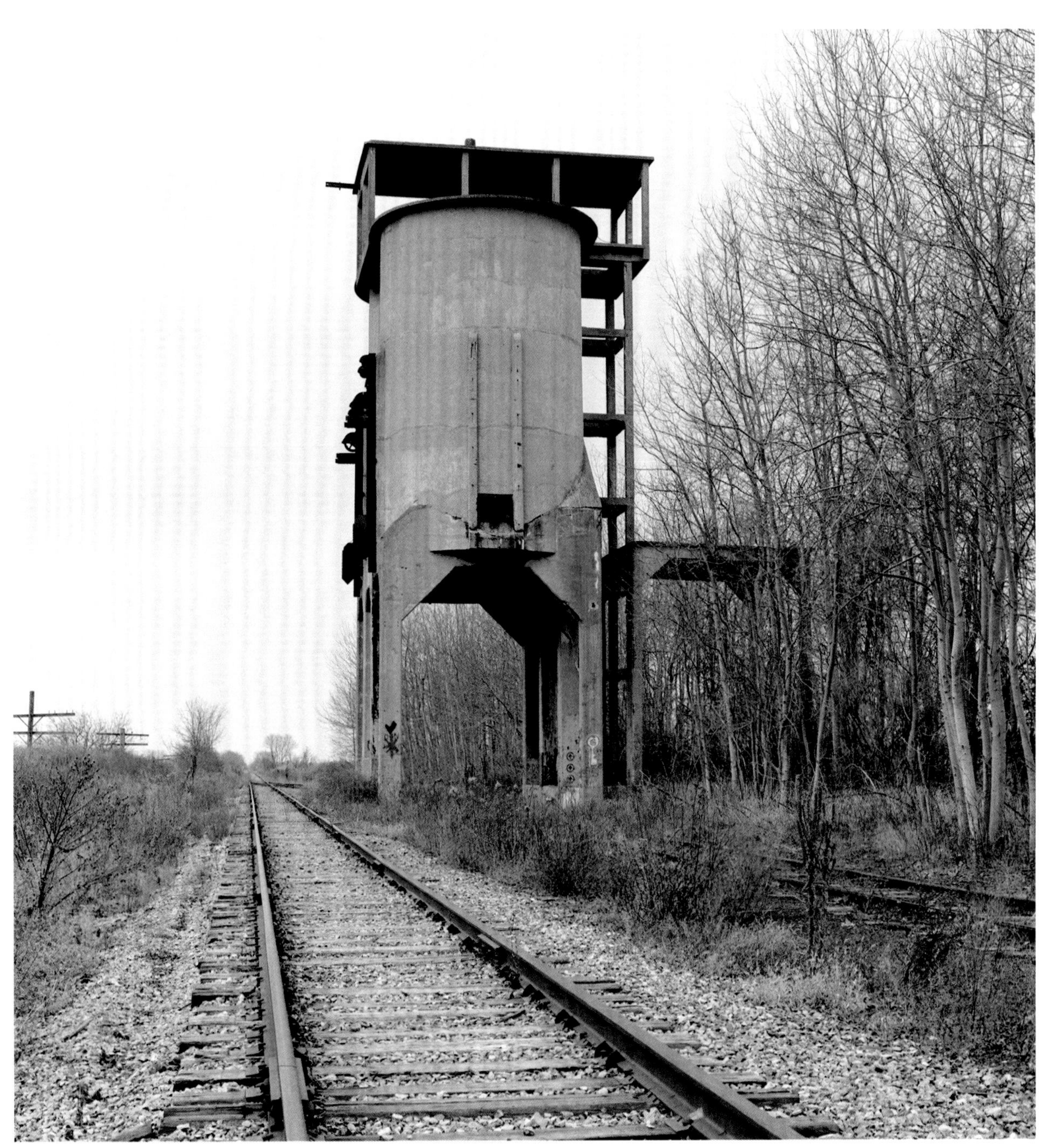

123 **AYLMER, ONTARIO** Canadian National 42°46'49.0"N 80°59'46.4"W

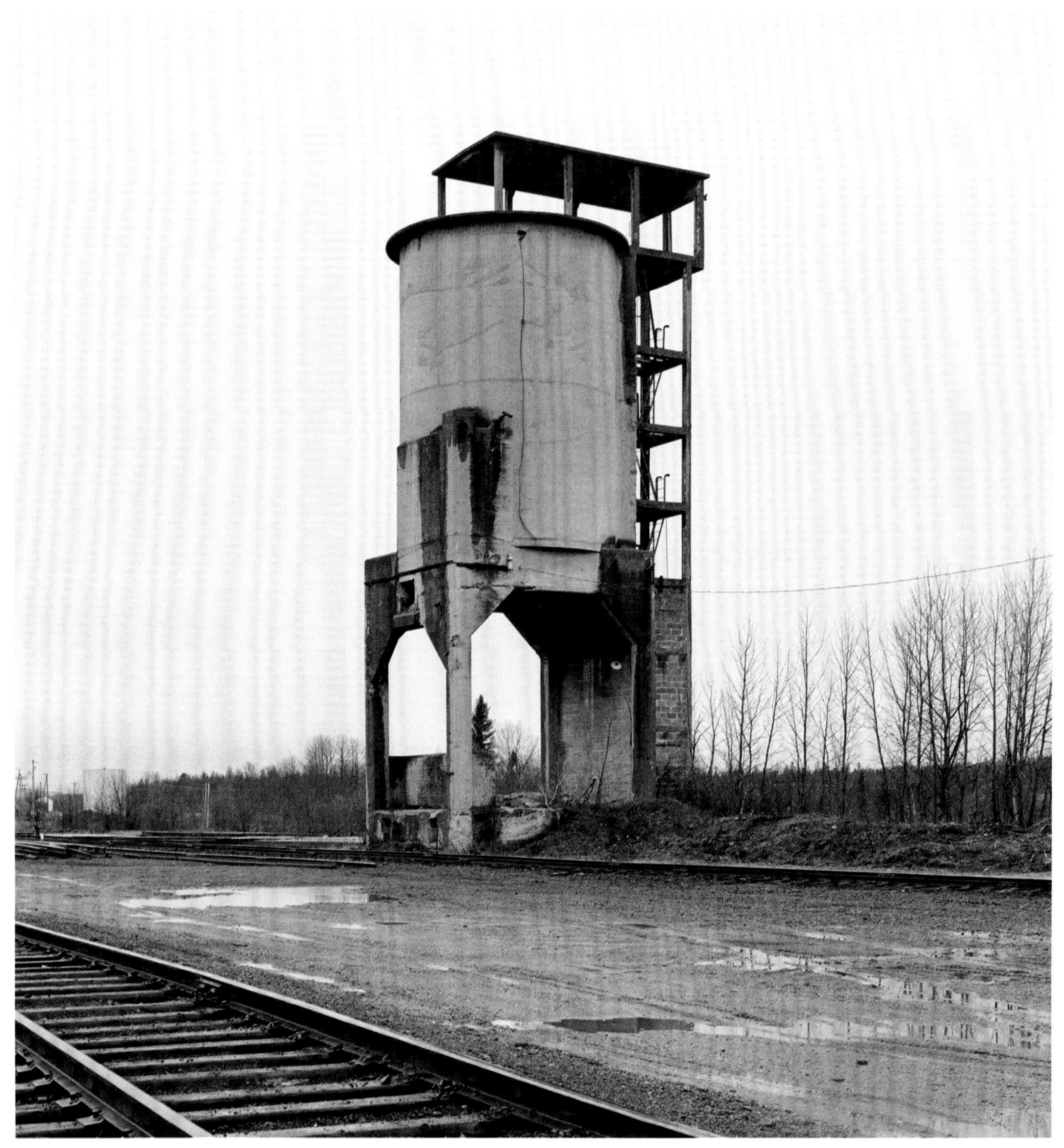

 HORNPAYNE, ONTARIO Canadian National 49°13’14.0”N 84°46’26.0”W

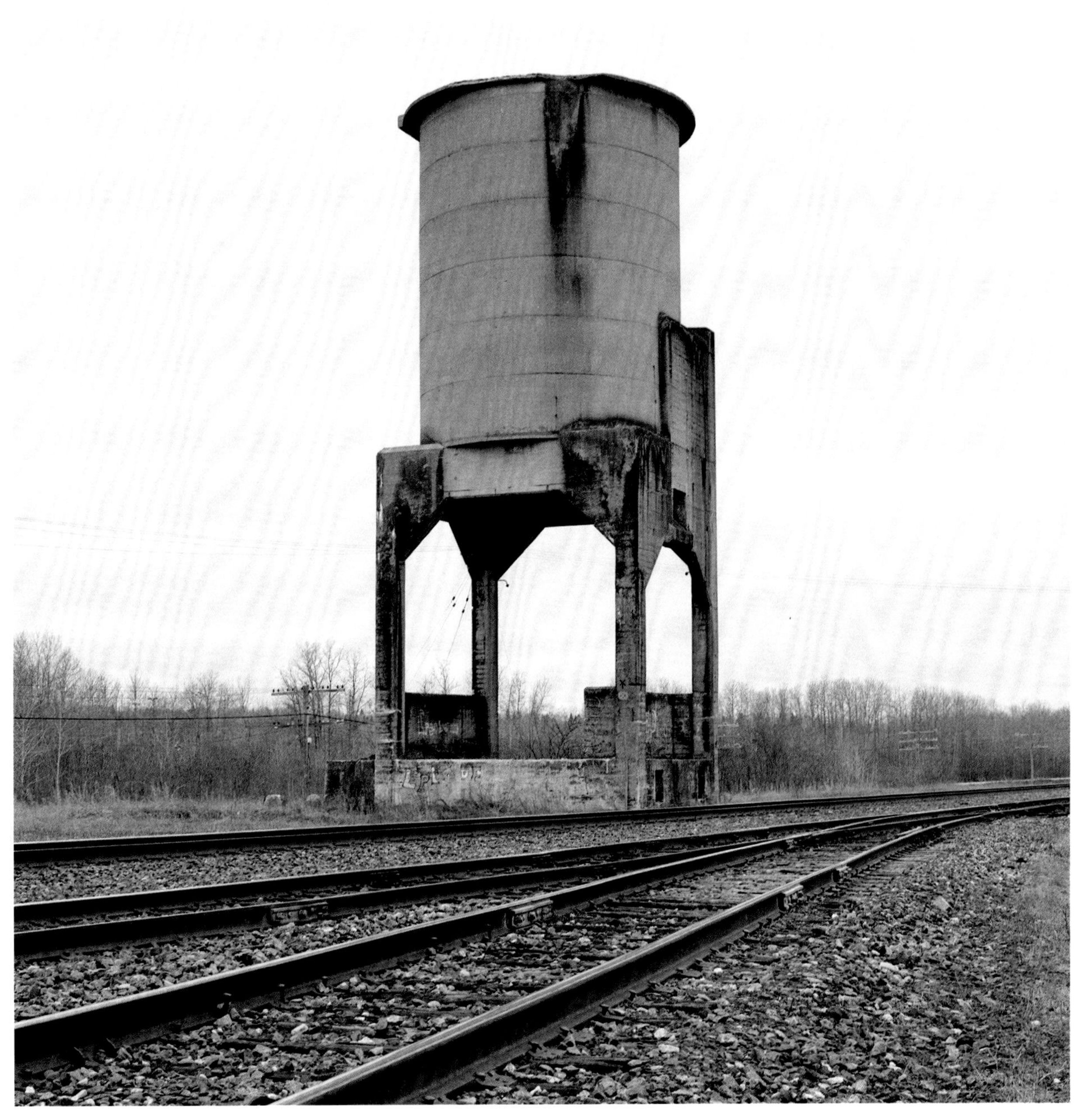

125 **FOLEYET, ONTARIO** Canadian National 48°14'52.3"N 82°26'29.7"W

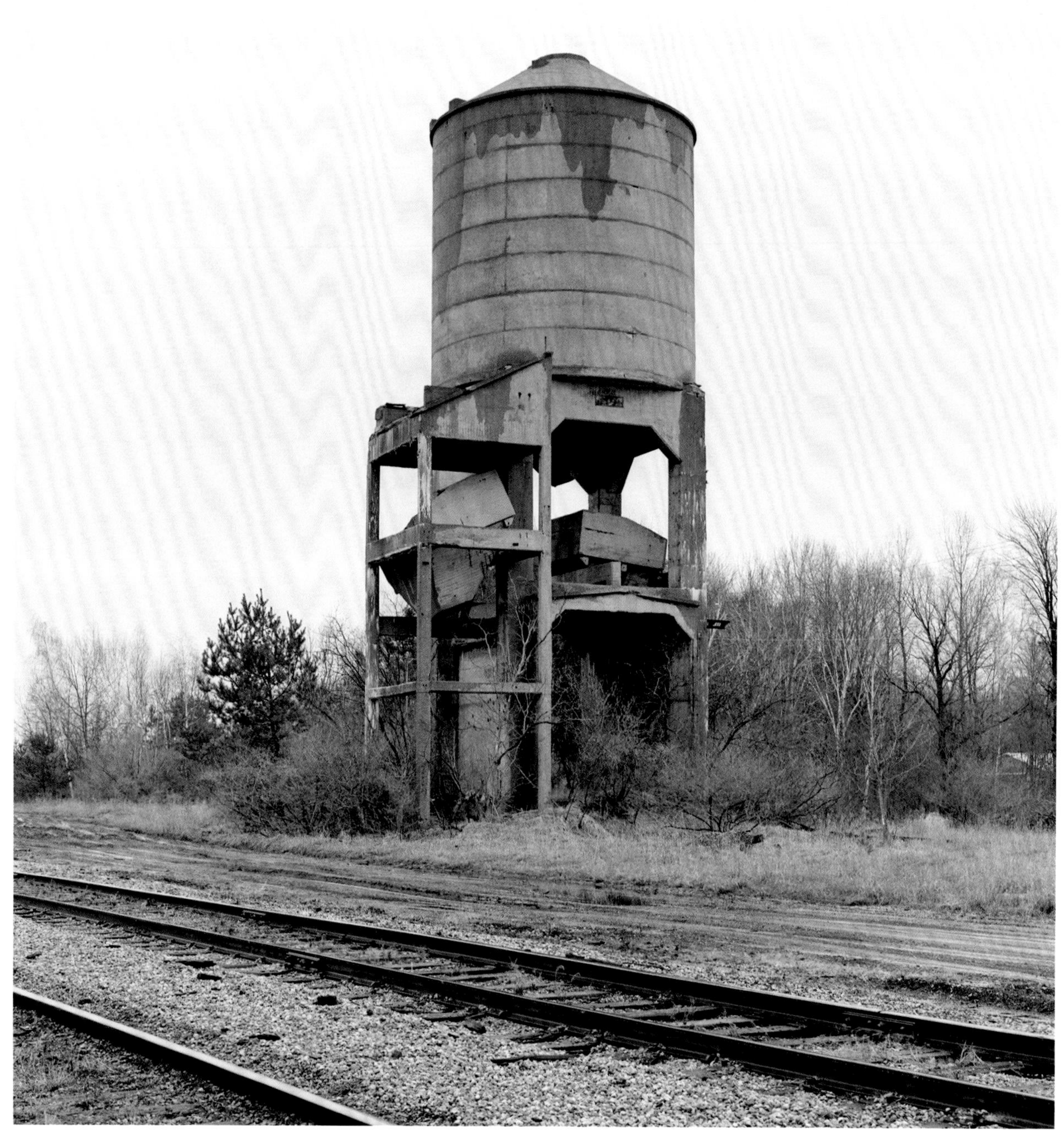

 LUDINGTON, MICHIGAN Pere Marquette 43°56'54.5"N 86°25'53.4"W

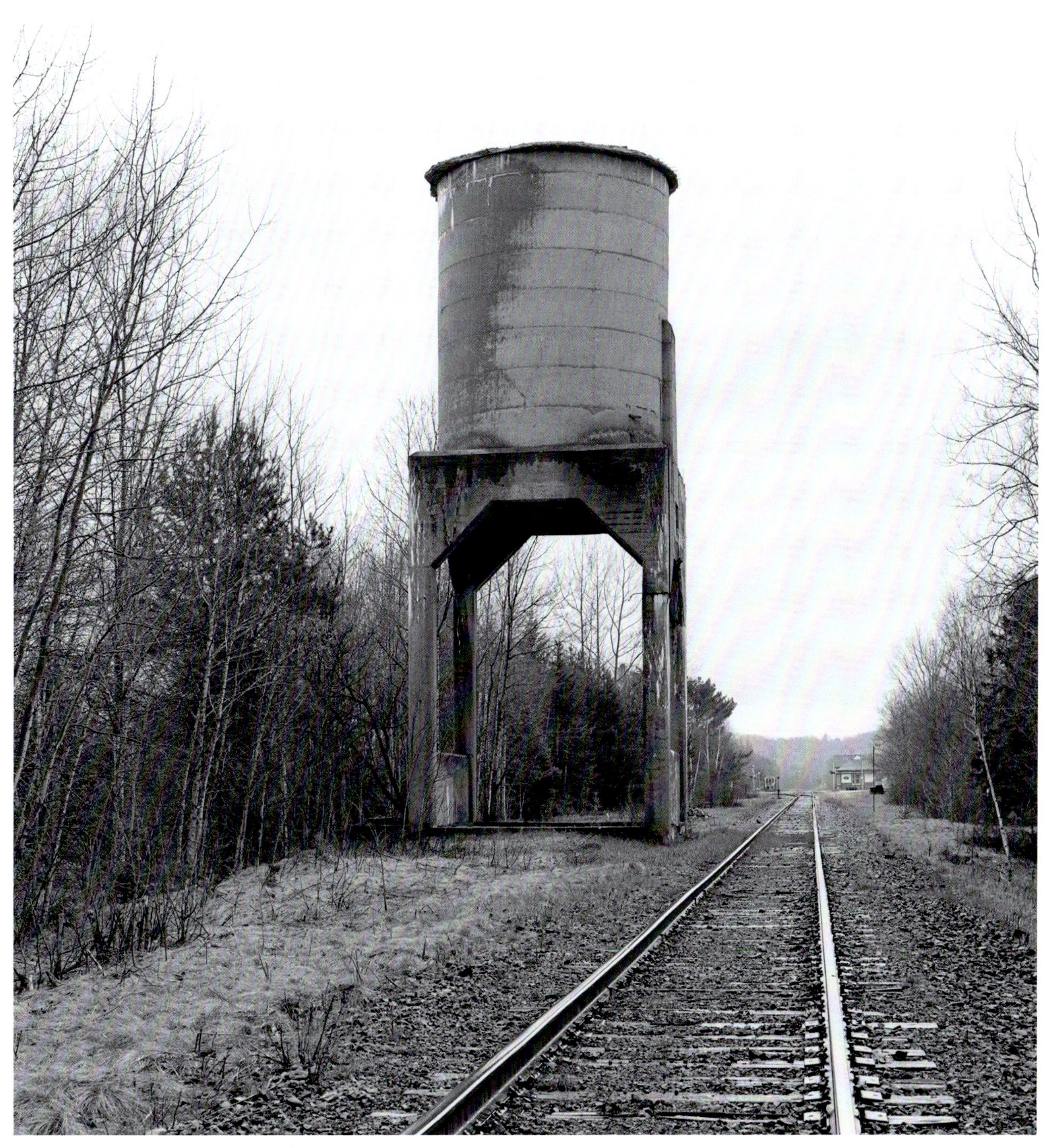

127 **SOUTH RIVER, ONTARIO** Canadian National 45°50’40.4”N 79°22’29.8”W

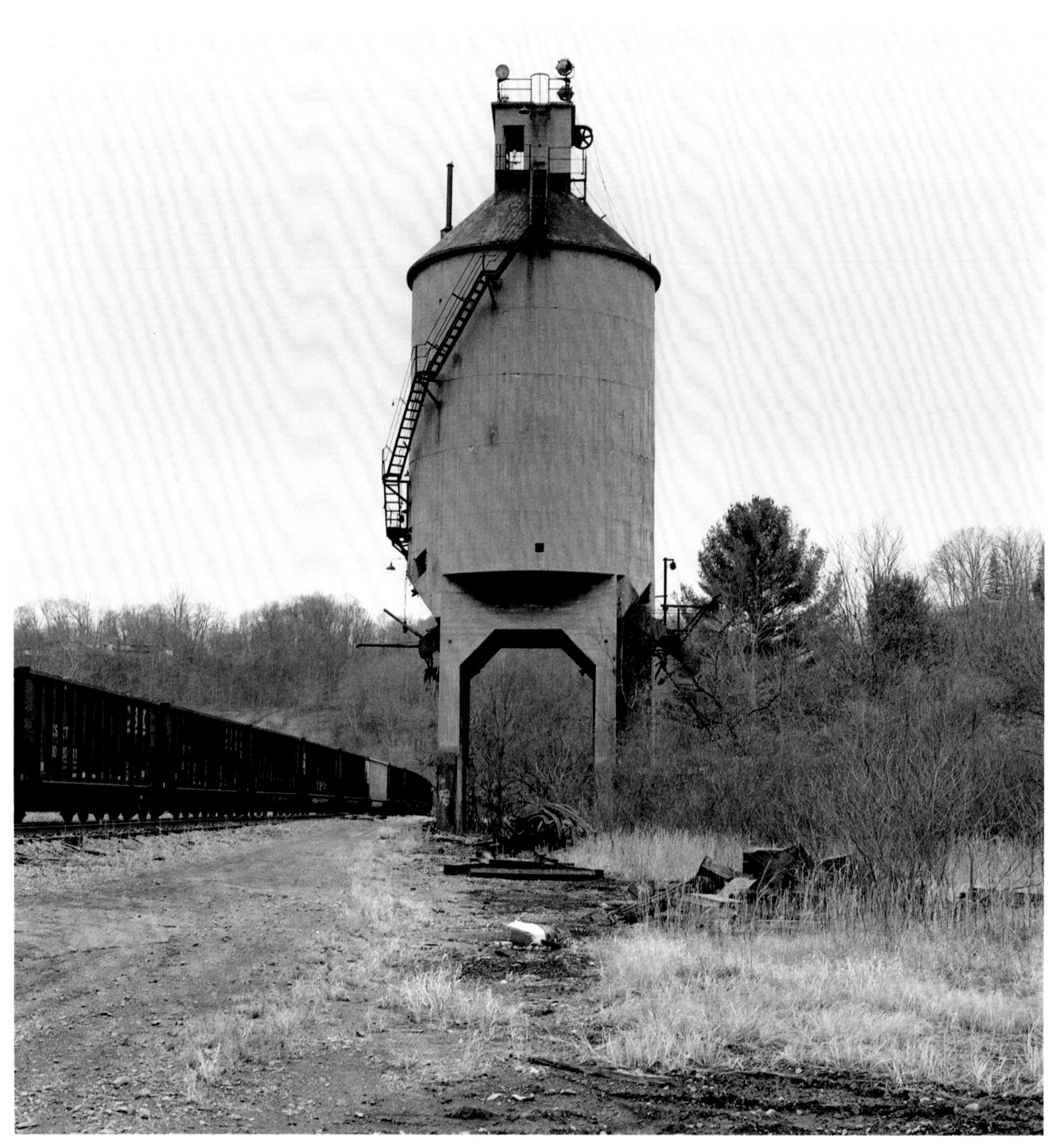

 BECKLEY, WEST VIRGINIA Chesapeake & Ohio 37°45’31.4”N 81°09’40.7”W

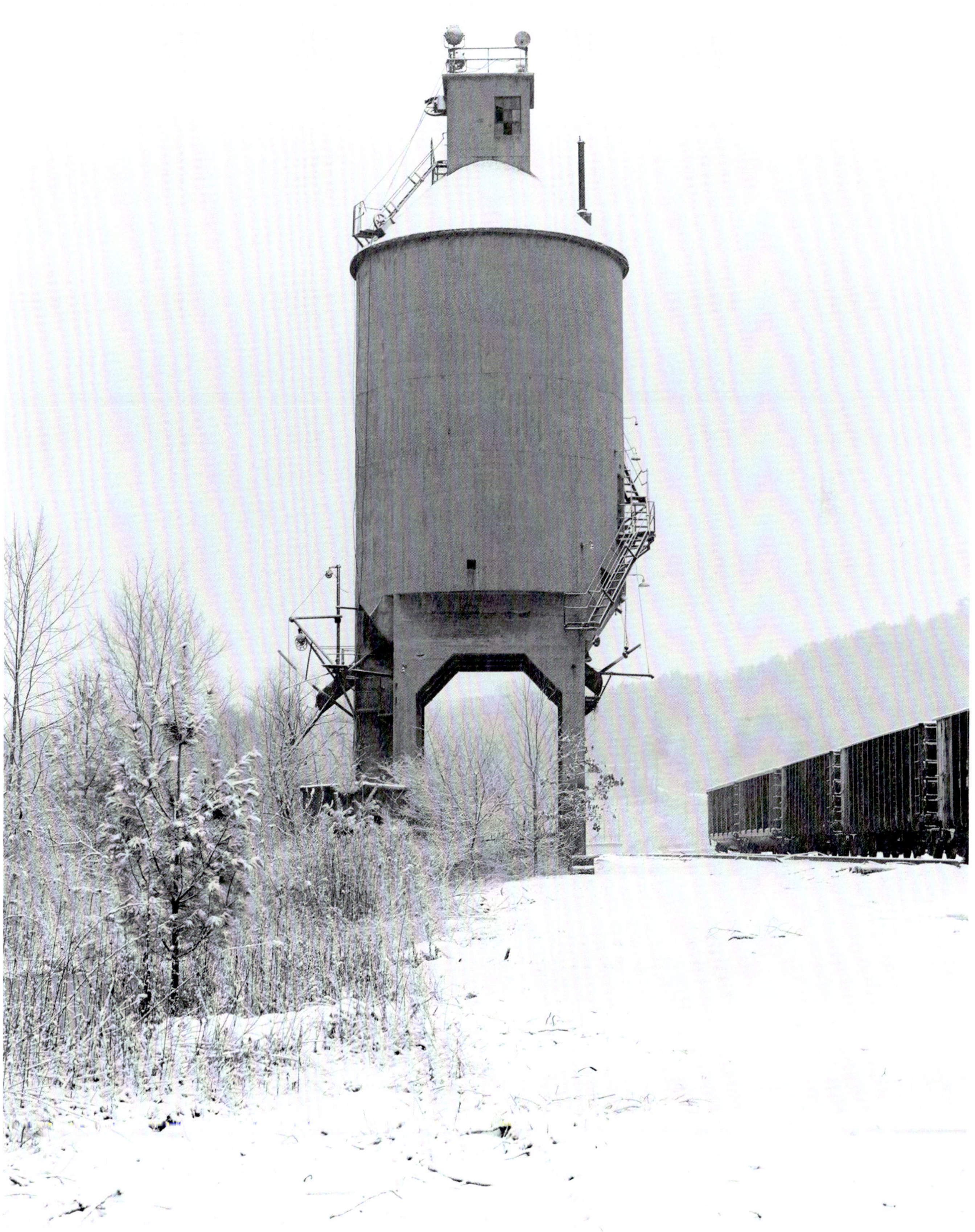

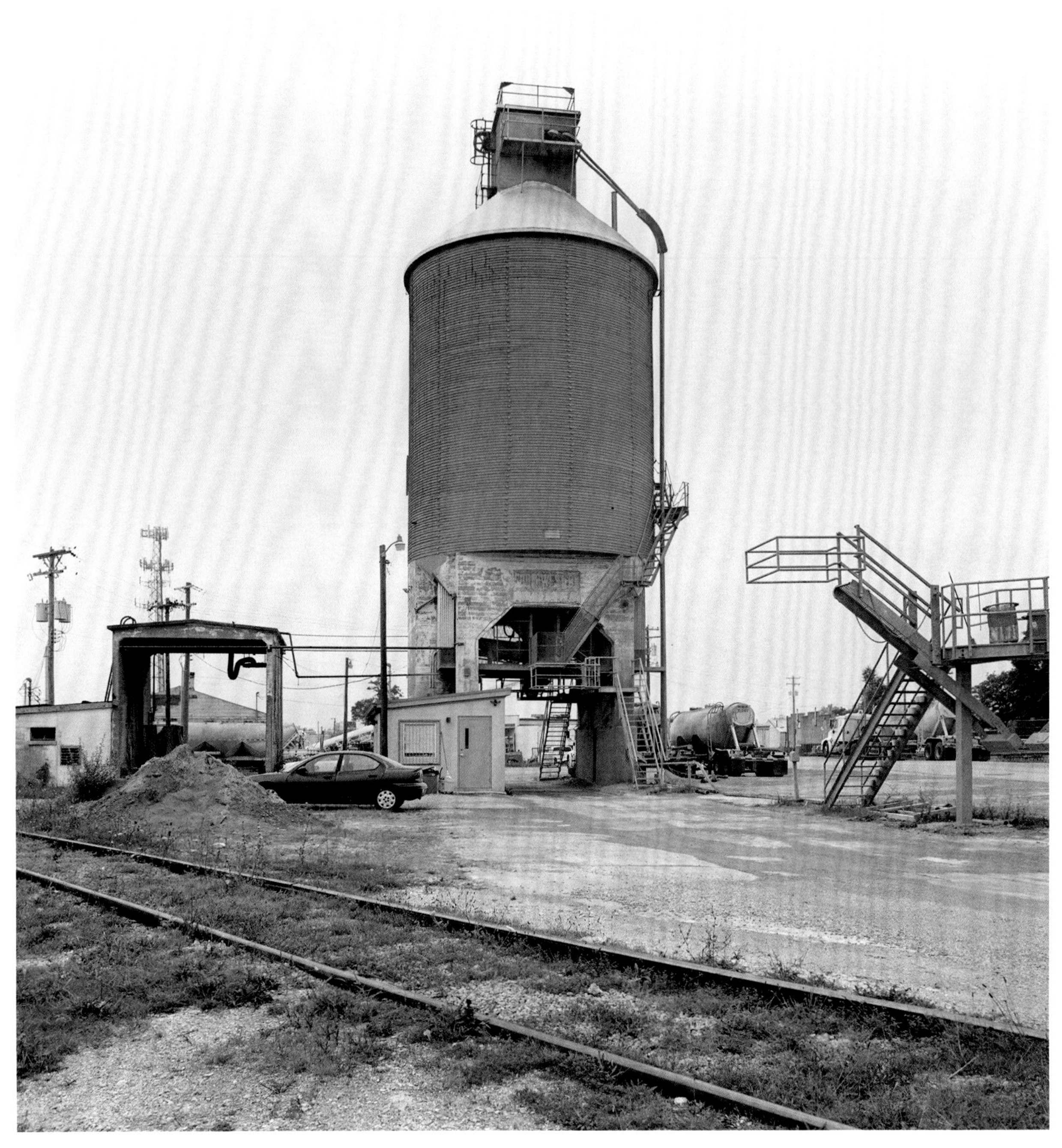

 LEXINGTON, KENTUCKY Chesapeake & Ohio 38°02'21.2"N 84°28'23.5"W

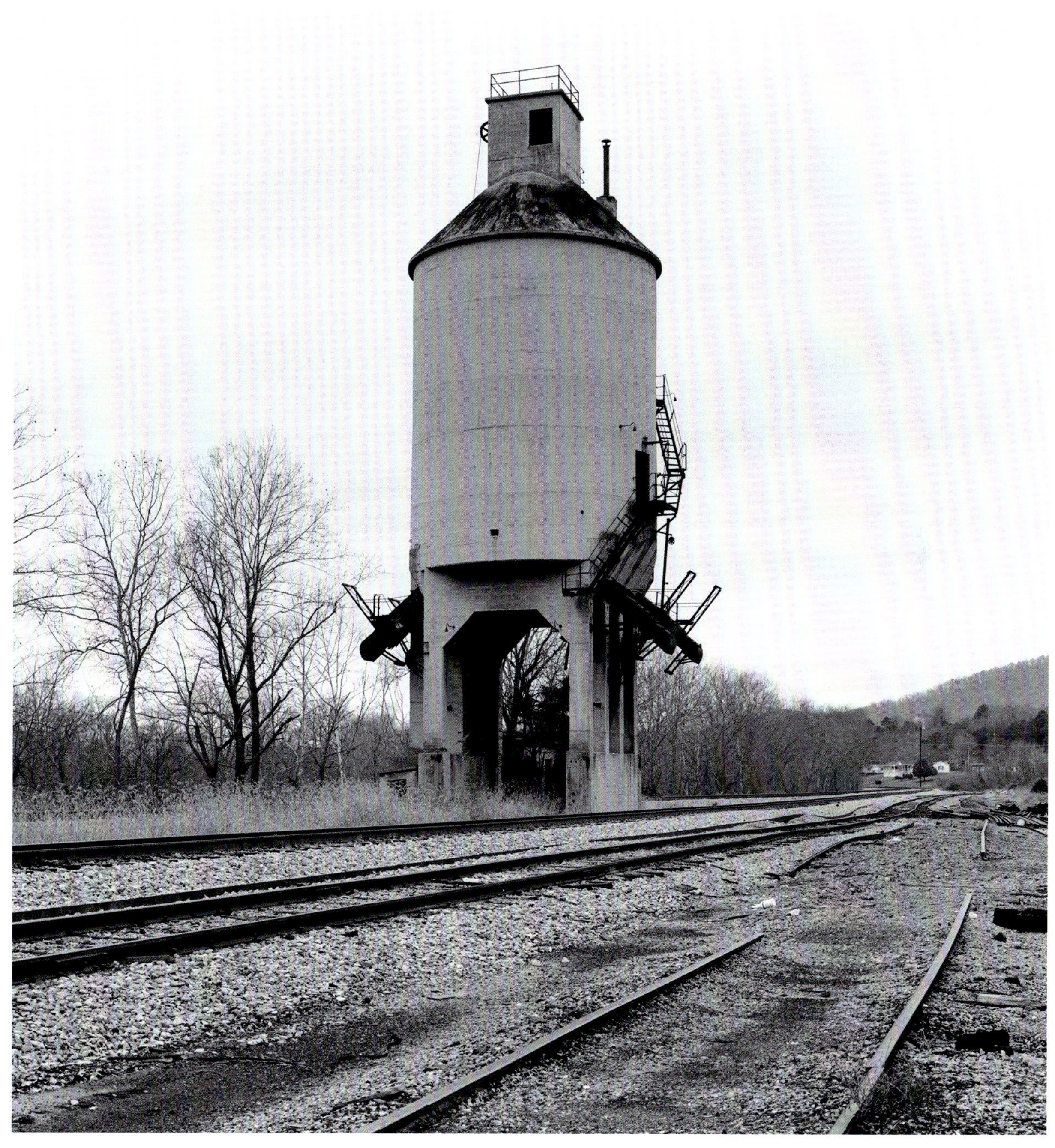

131 **BALCONY FALLS, VIRGINIA** Chesapeake & Ohio 37°37'37.0"N 79°27'27.7"W

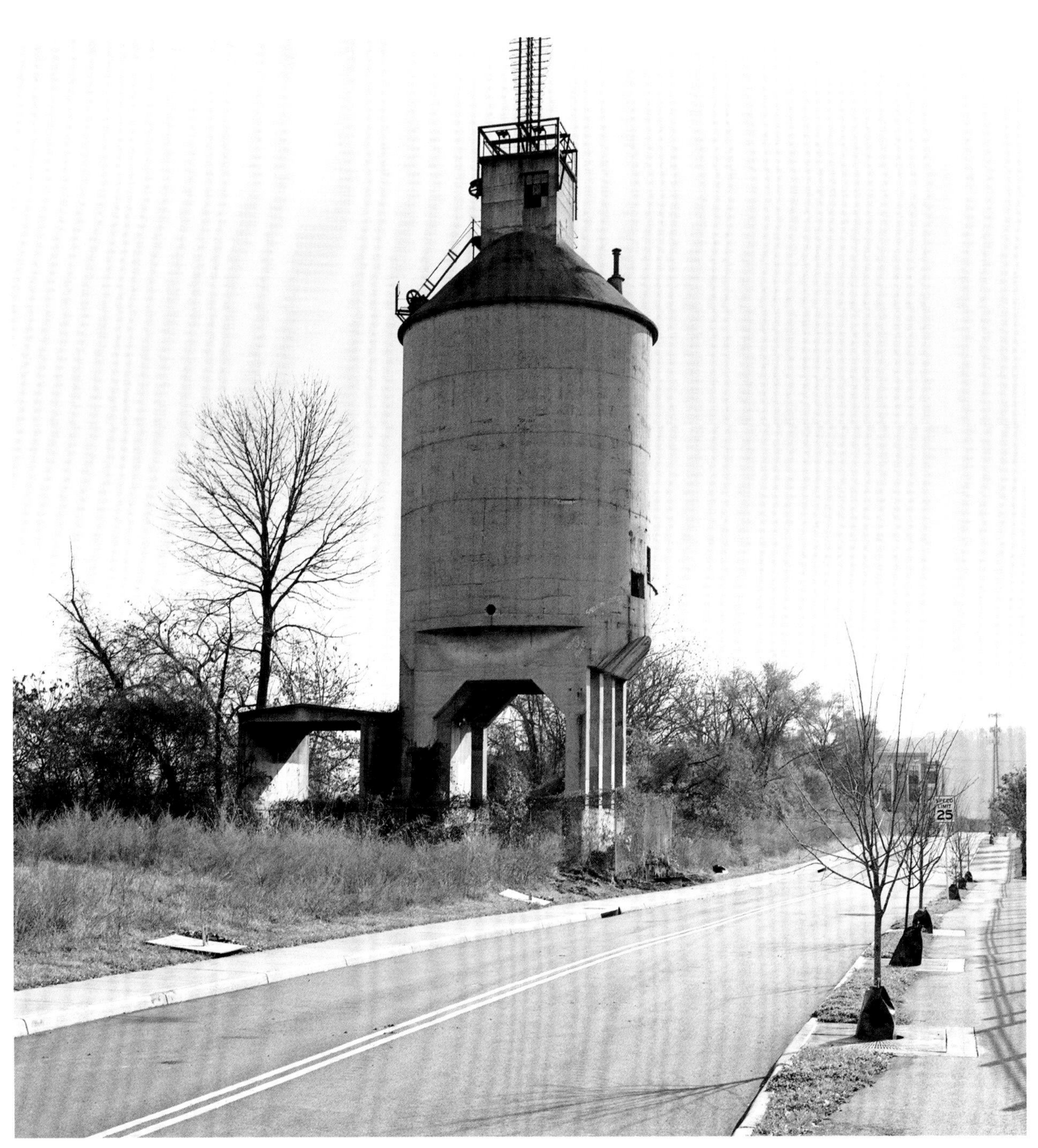

 CHARLOTTESVILLE, VIRGINIA Chesapeake & Ohio 38°01’39.0”N 78°28’20.8”W

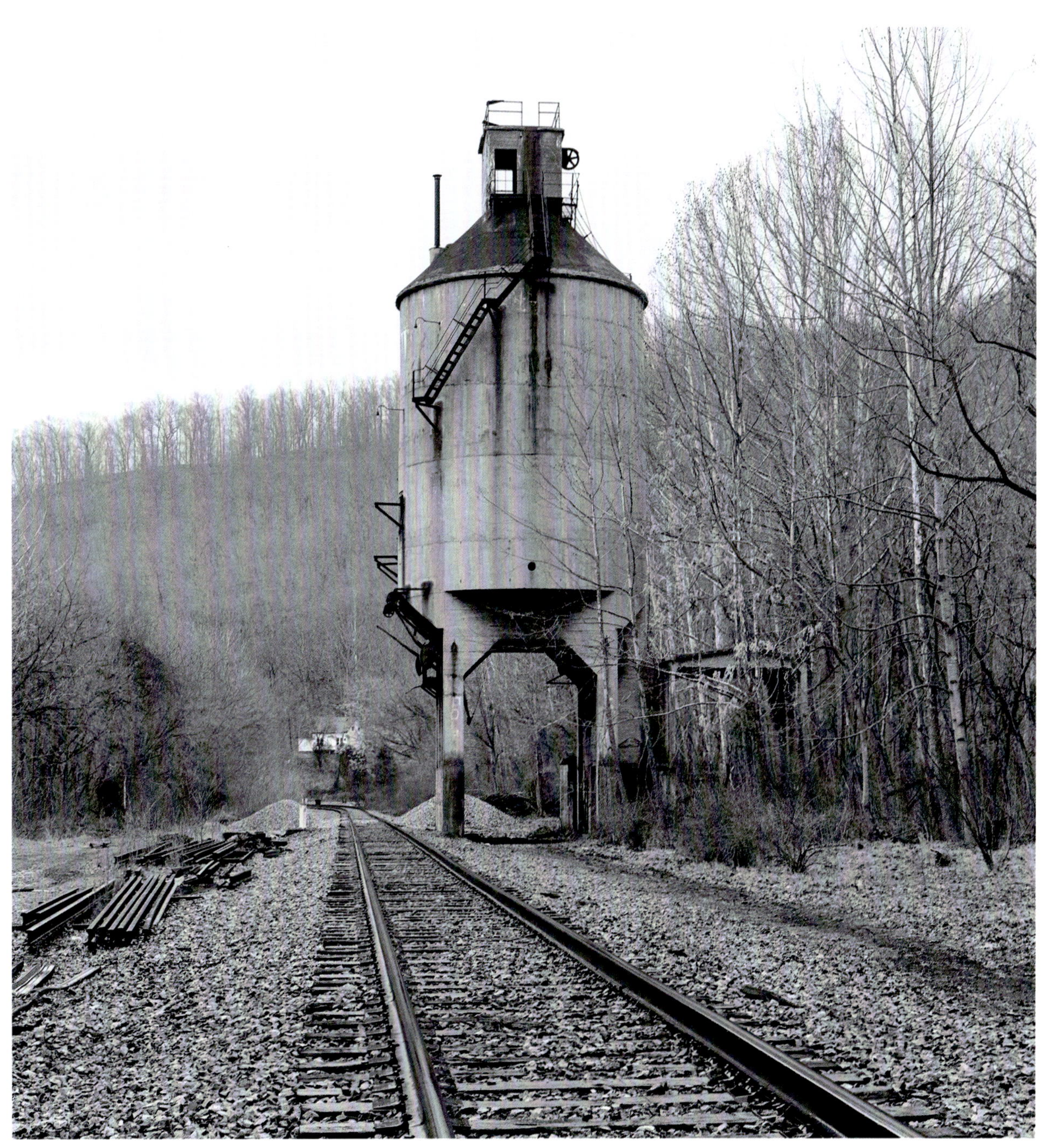

133 **WEST HAMLIN, WEST VIRGINIA** Chesapeake & Ohio 38°17’22.7”N 82°11’35.6”W

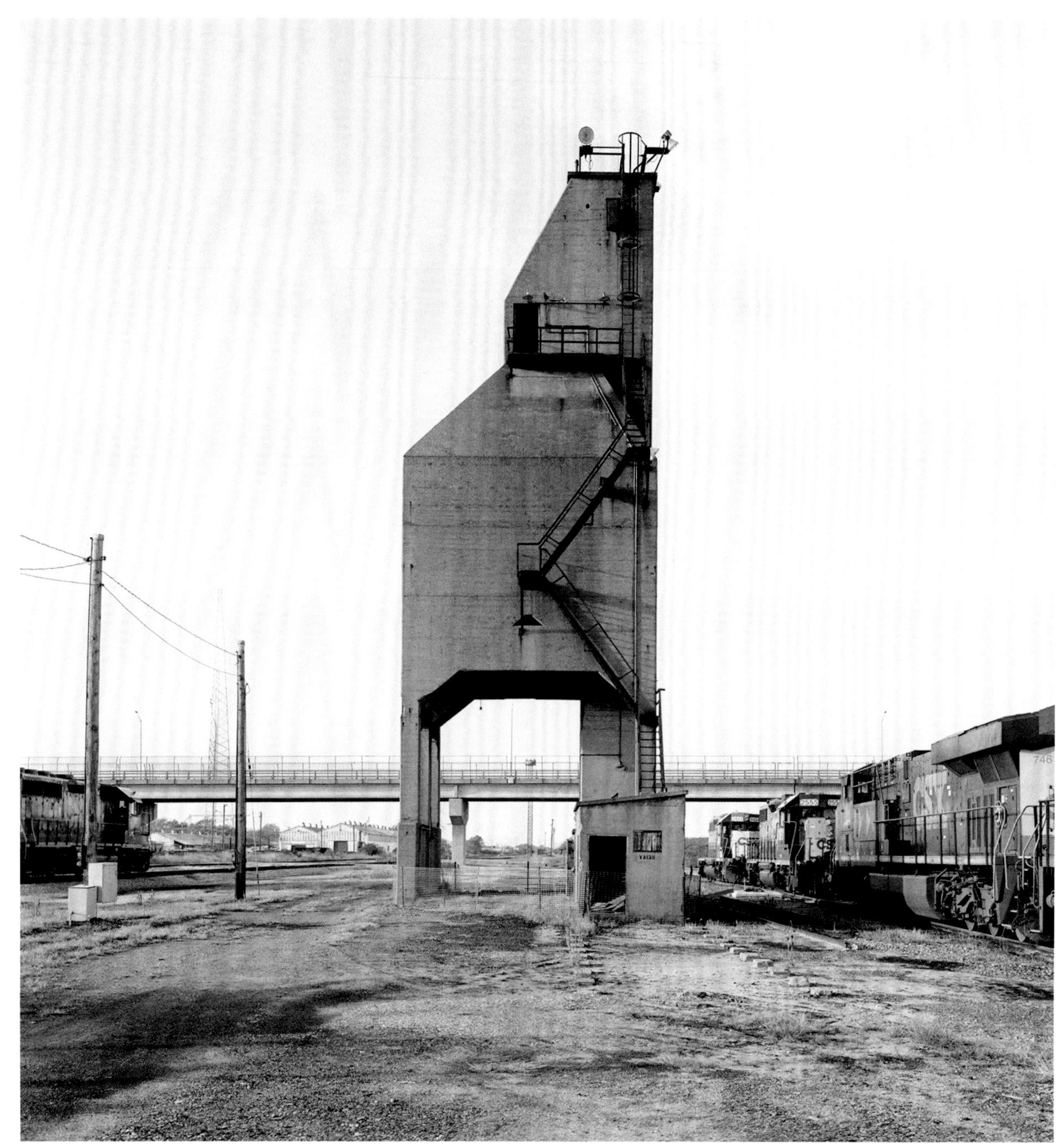

 NEWPORT NEWS, VIRGINIA Chesapeake & Ohio 36°59’16.9”N 76°25’47.2”W

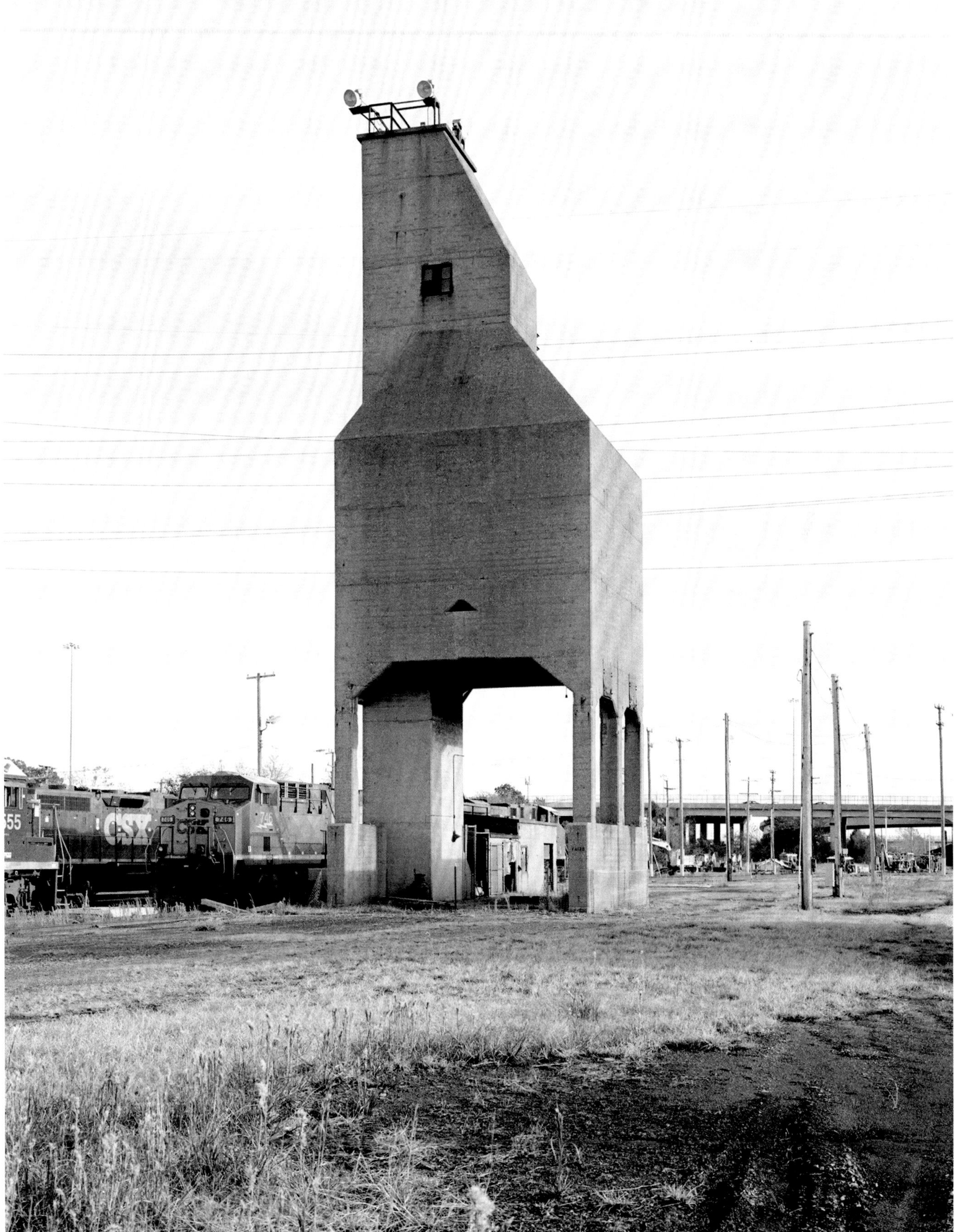
CSX

136 **WILMINGTON, DELAWARE** Pennsylvania 39°44'32.4"N 75°31'29.2"W

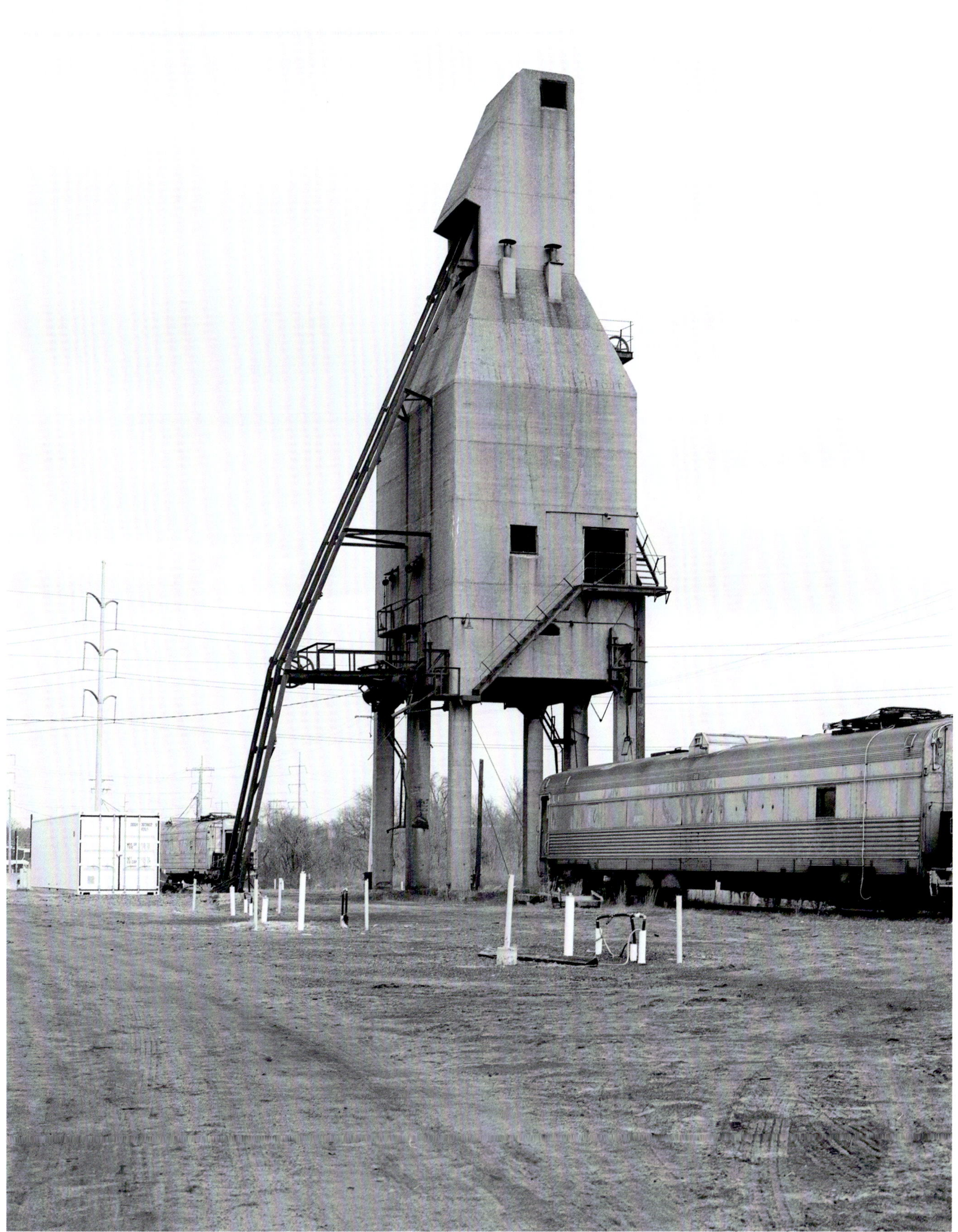

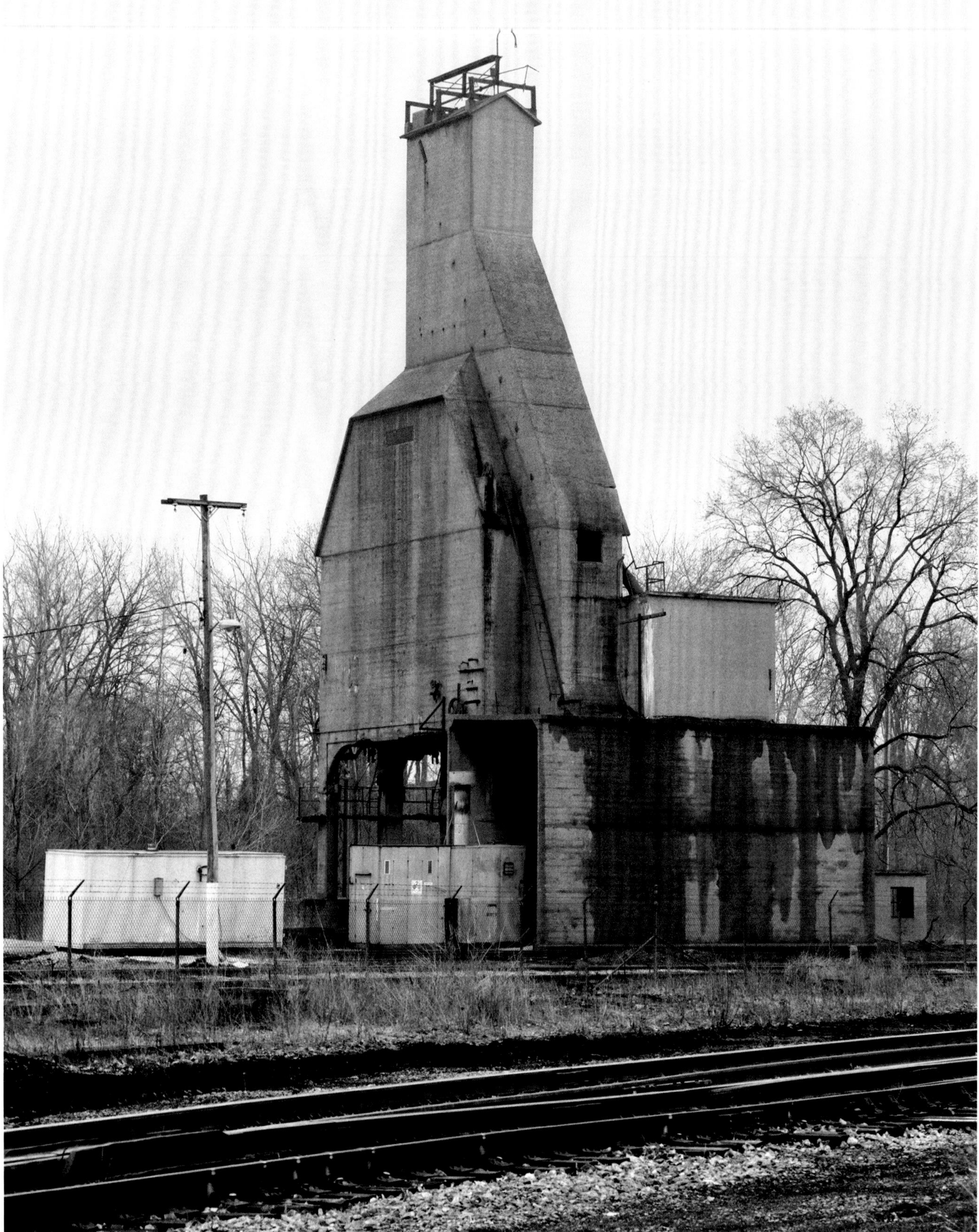

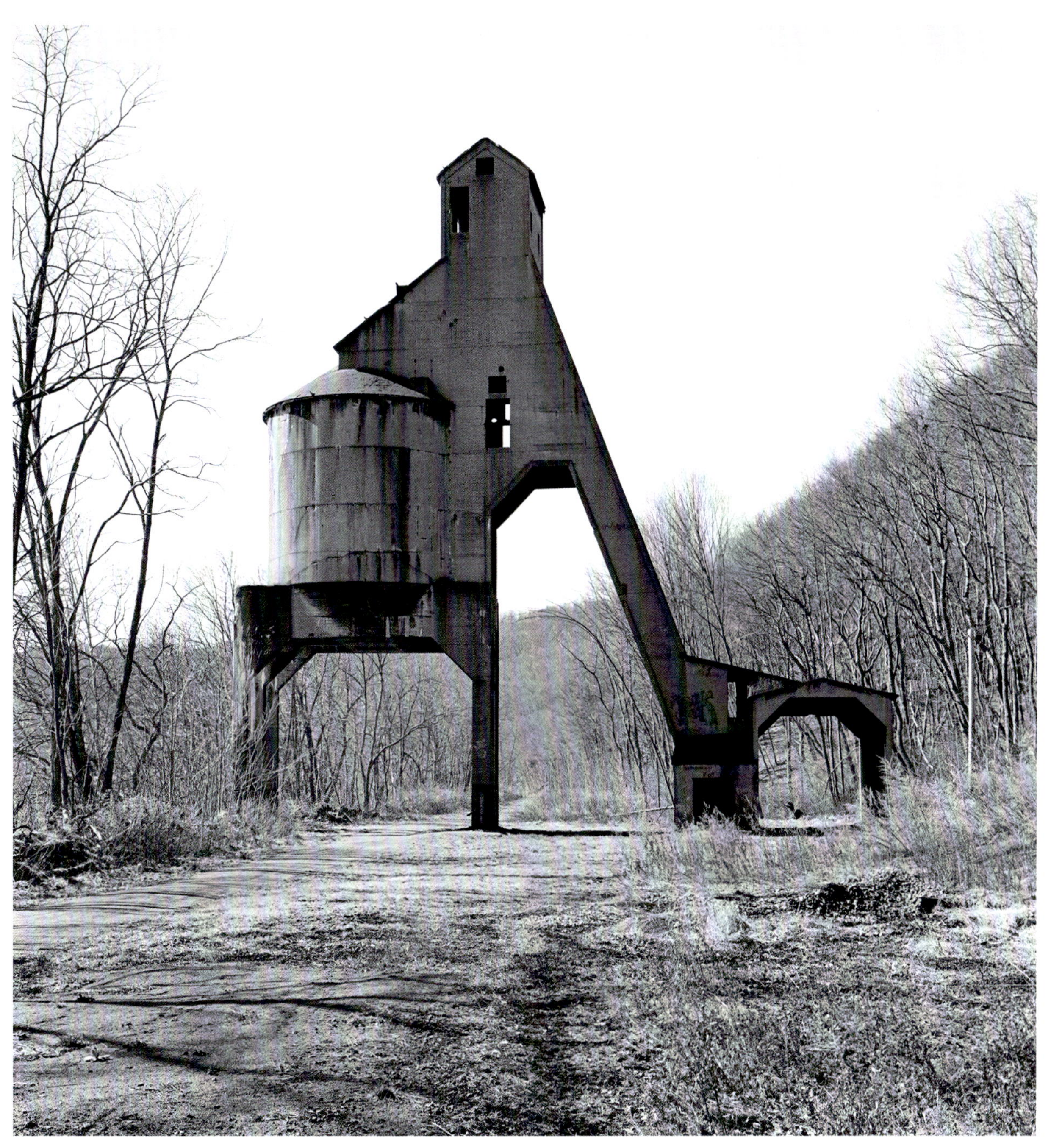

138 **TOLEDO, OHIO (demolished)** Baltimore & Ohio 41°37'15.3"N 83°31'58.9"W (left)

139 **RED BANK, PENNSYLVANIA** Pennsylvania 40°59'07.2"N 79°33'16.5"W (above)

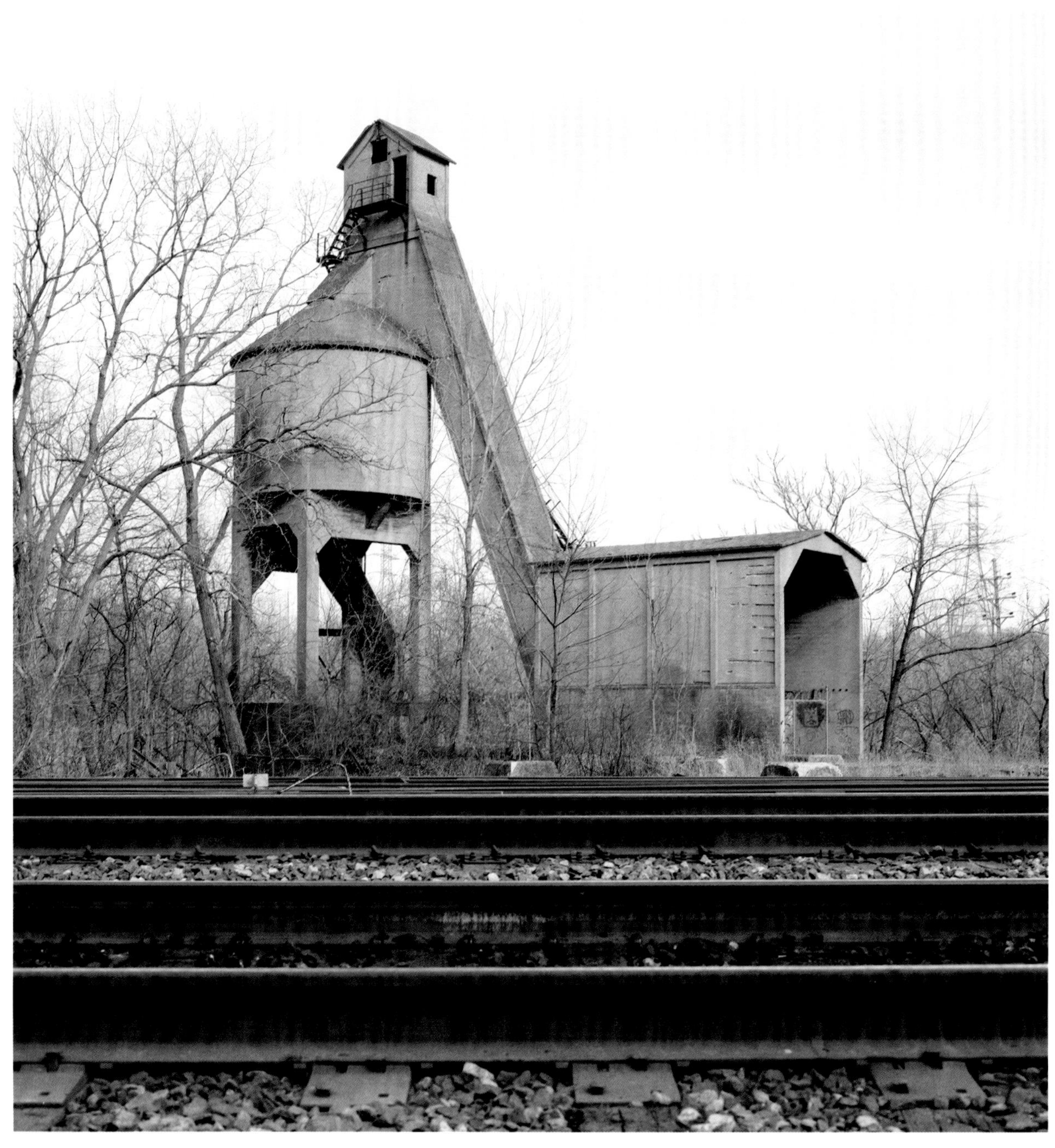

 AKRON JUNCTION, OHIO Baltimore & Ohio 41°05'14.2"N 81°29'14.2"W

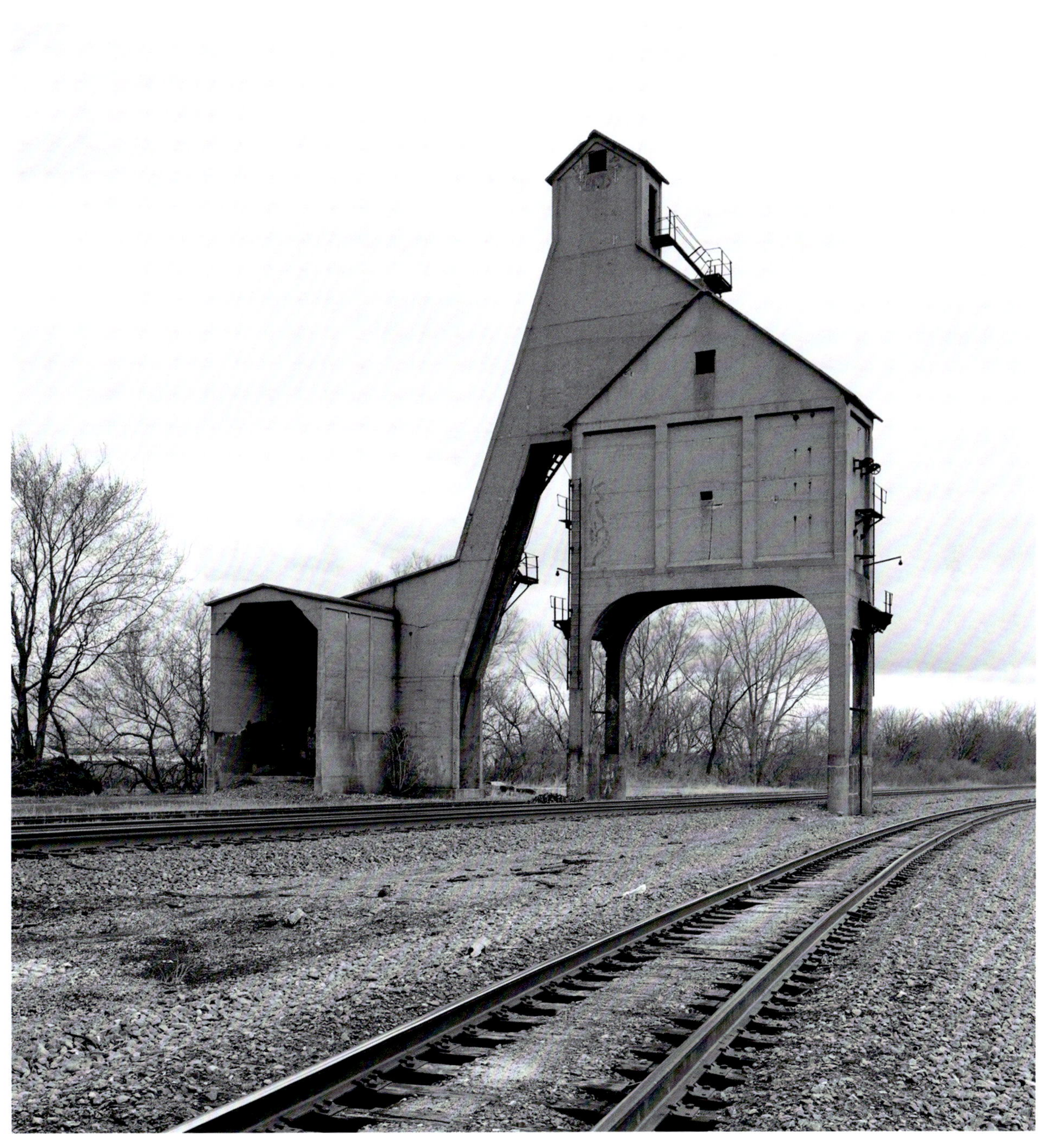

141 **DEKALB, ILLINOIS** Chicago & North Western 41°55'40.1"N 88°44'00.3"W

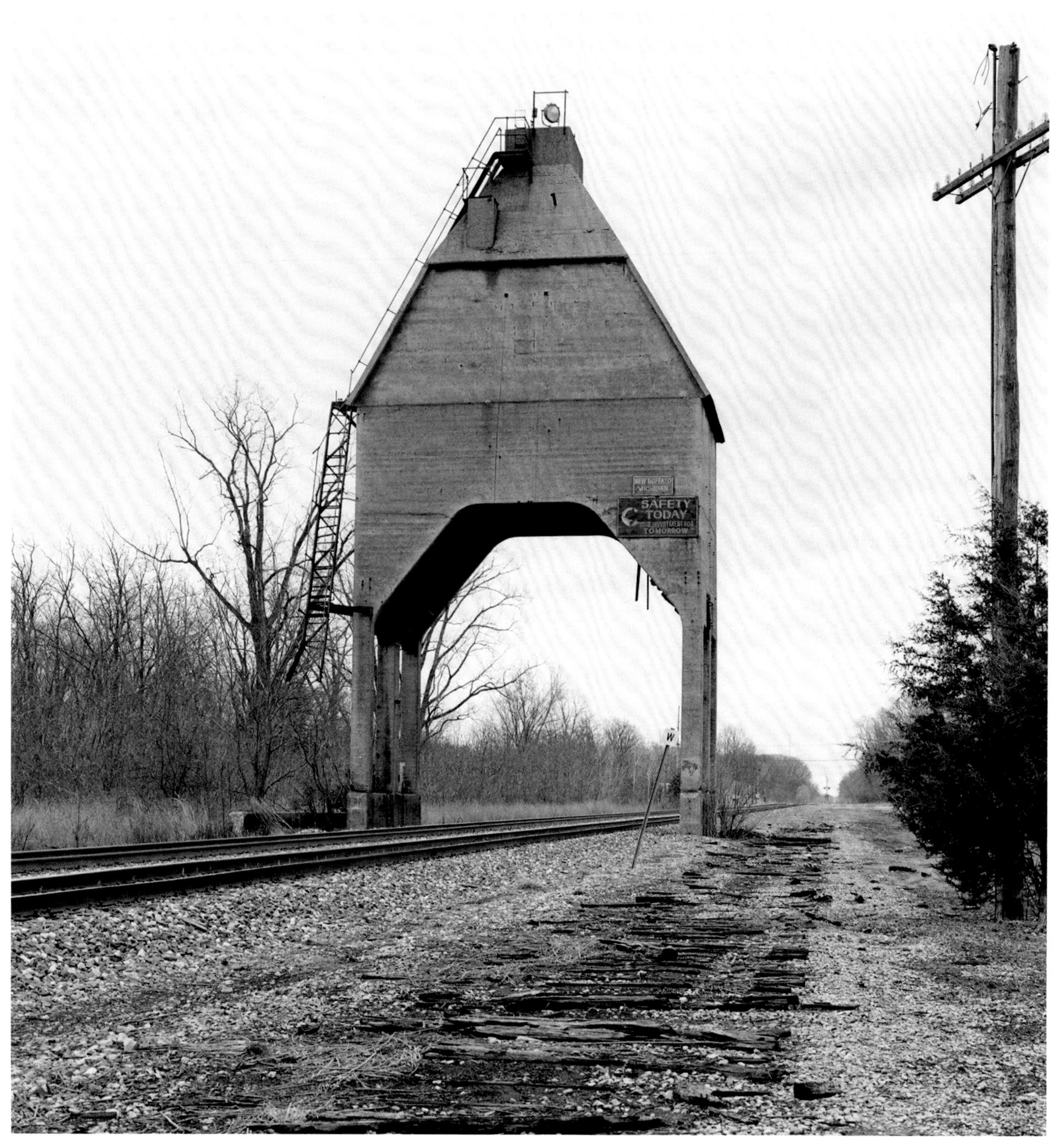

142 **NEW BUFFALO, MICHIGAN** Pere Marquette 41°47′12.4″N 86°44′31.3″W

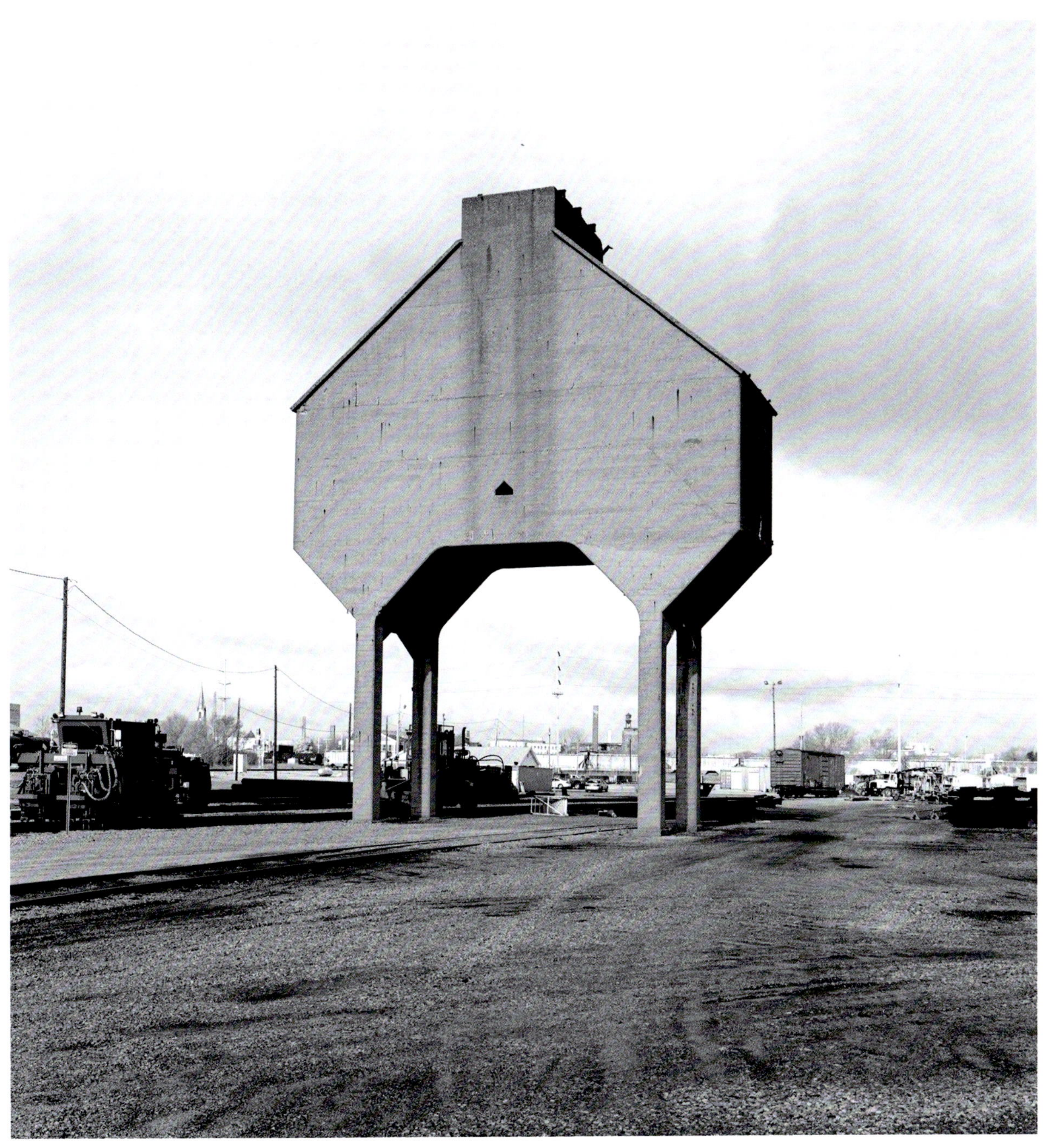

143 **DECATUR, ILLINOIS** Wabash 39°50'53.7"N 88°56'31.0"W

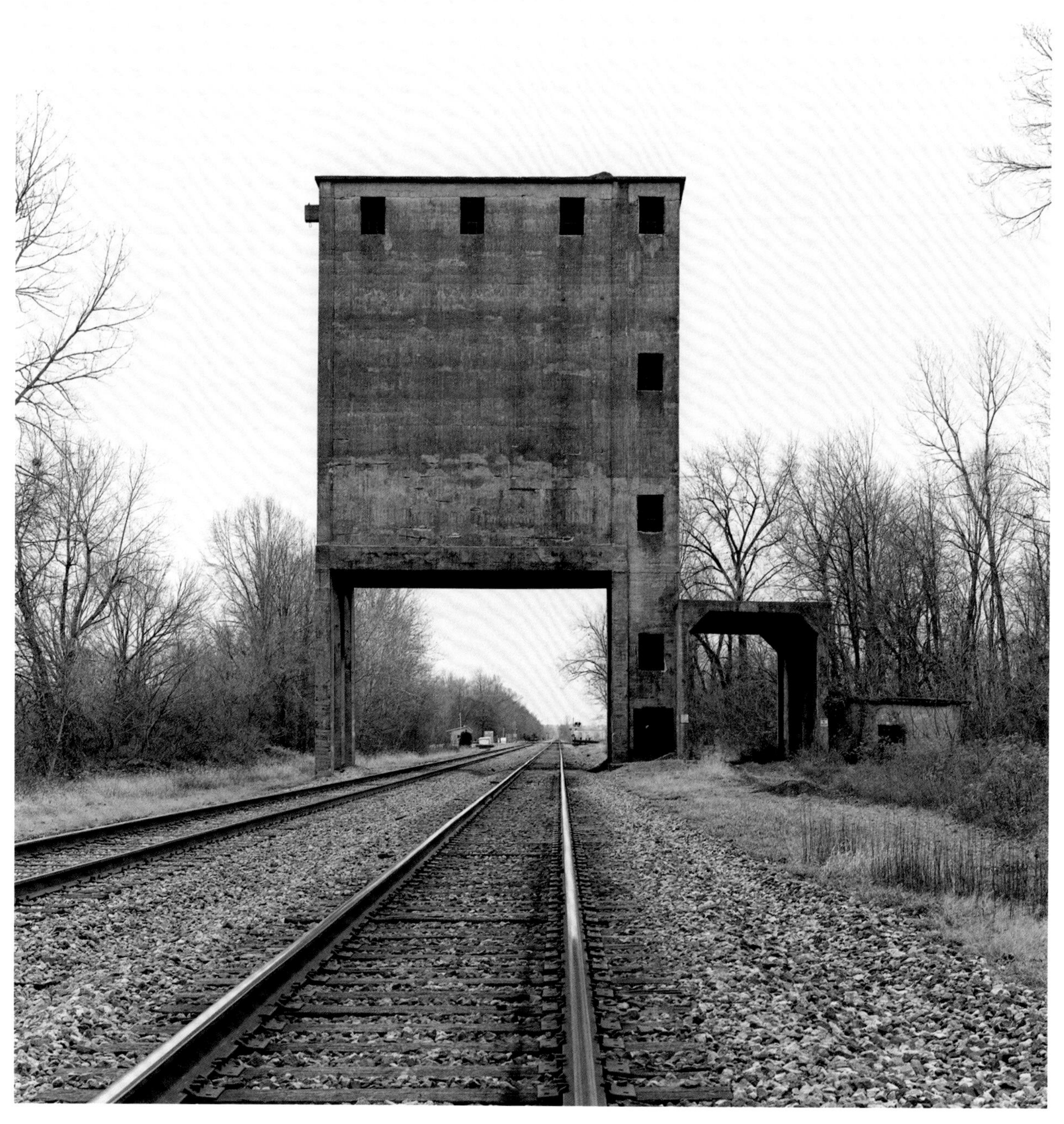

144 **REEVESVILLE, ILLINOIS** Illinois Central 37°20'45.0"N 88°43'04.3"W (above)

145 **BLUFORD, ILLINOIS** Illinois Central 38°18'57.4"N 88°43'43.1"W (right)

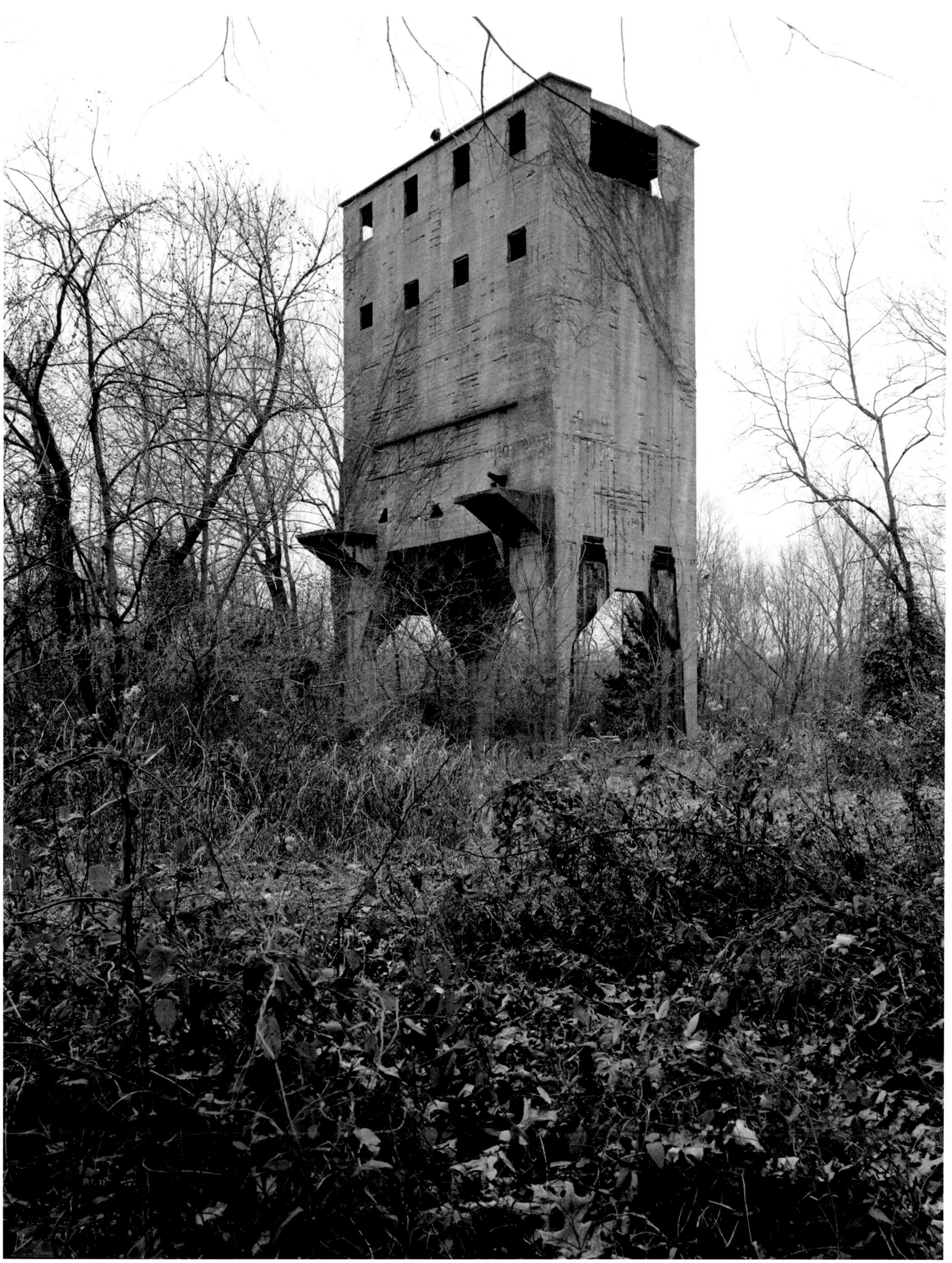

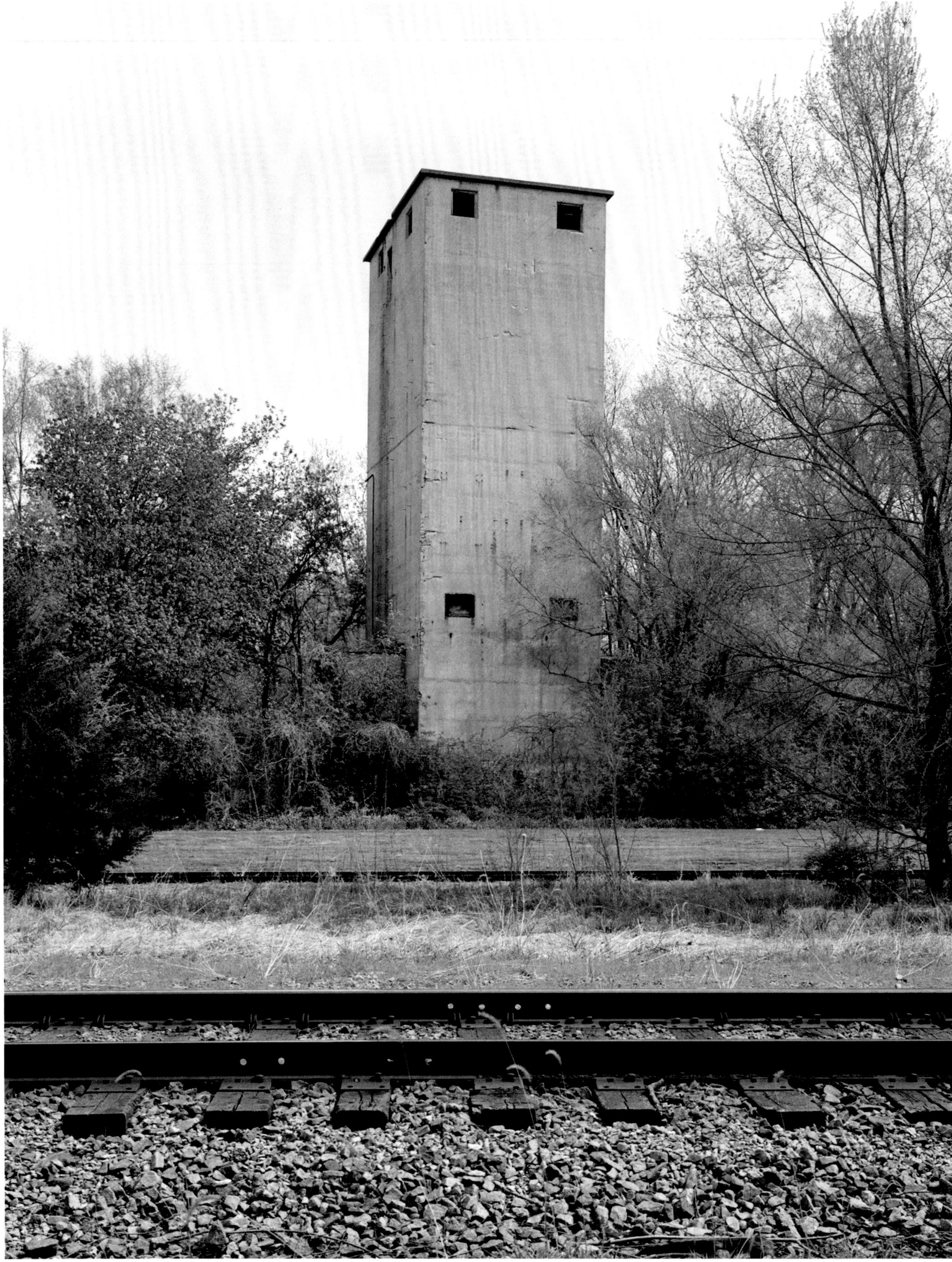

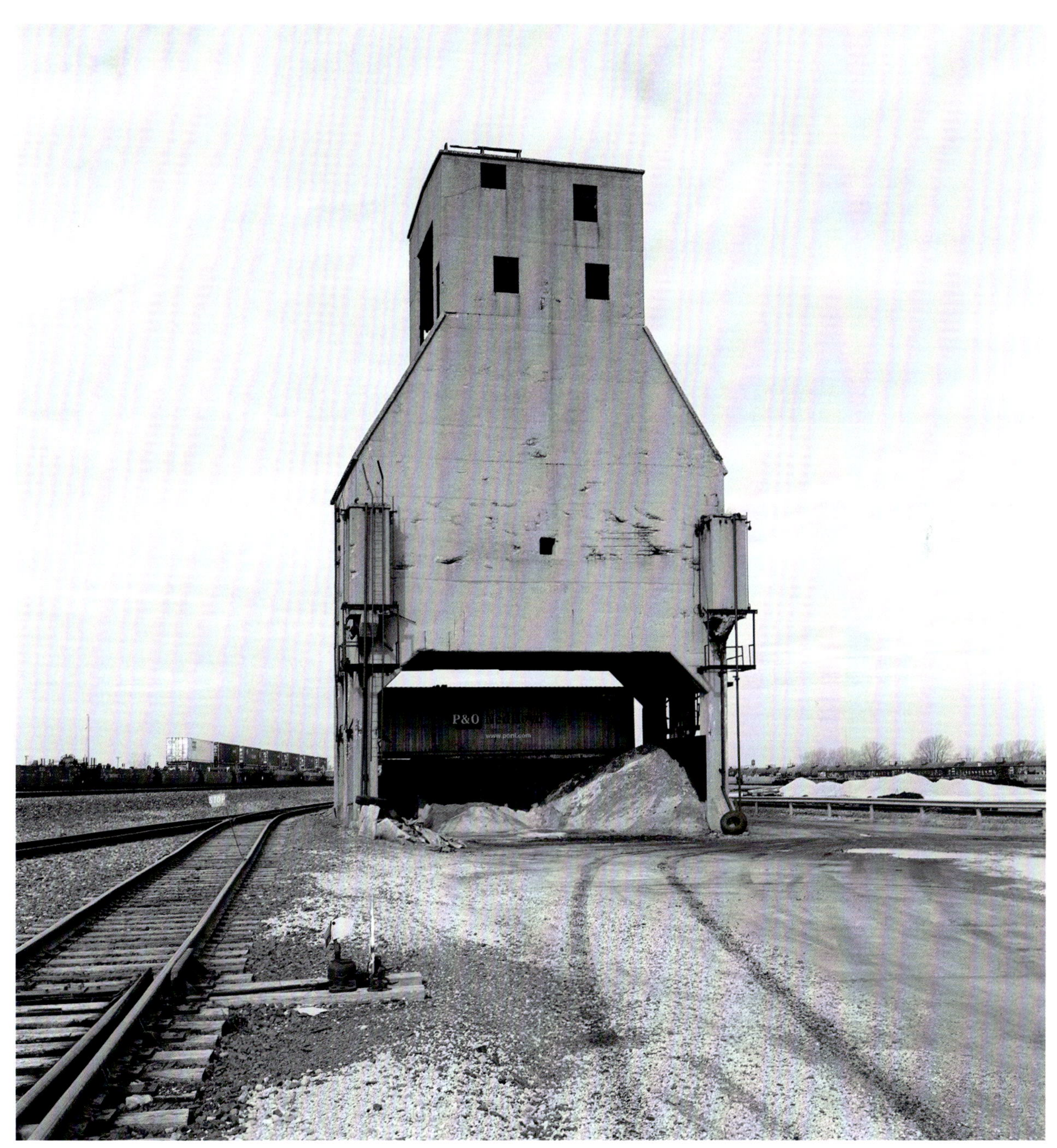

146 **FREEPORT, ILLINOIS** Illinois Central 42°17'48.2"N 89°36'31.4"W (left)

147 **DETROIT, MICHIGAN** New York Central 42°19'16.7"N 83°07'18.9"W (above)

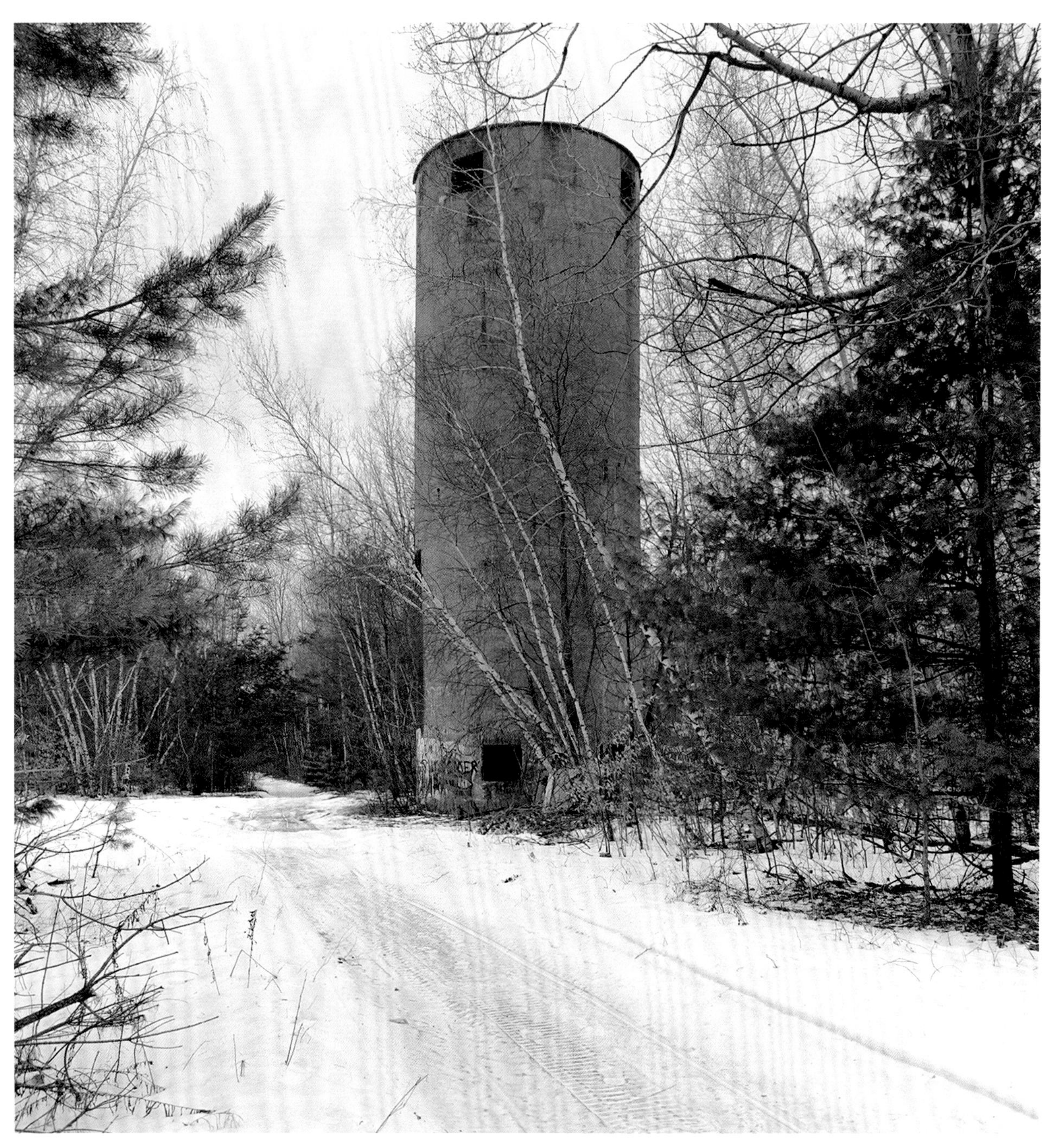

 MALONE, NEW YORK New York Central 44°51’54.2”N 74°16’37.4”W

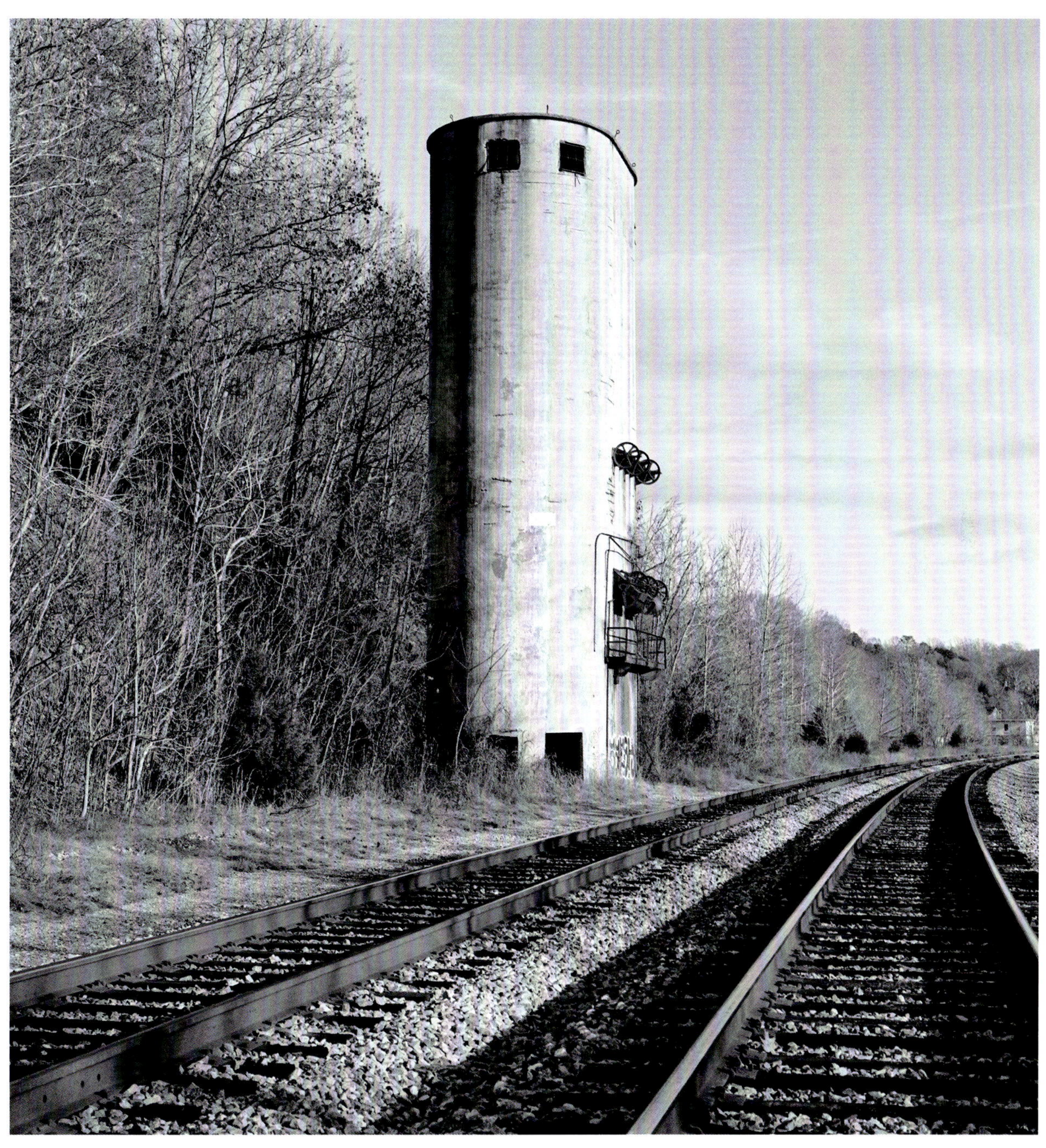

149 **GLADSTONE, VIRGINIA** Chesapeake & Ohio 37°32’52.0”N 78°51’12.4”W

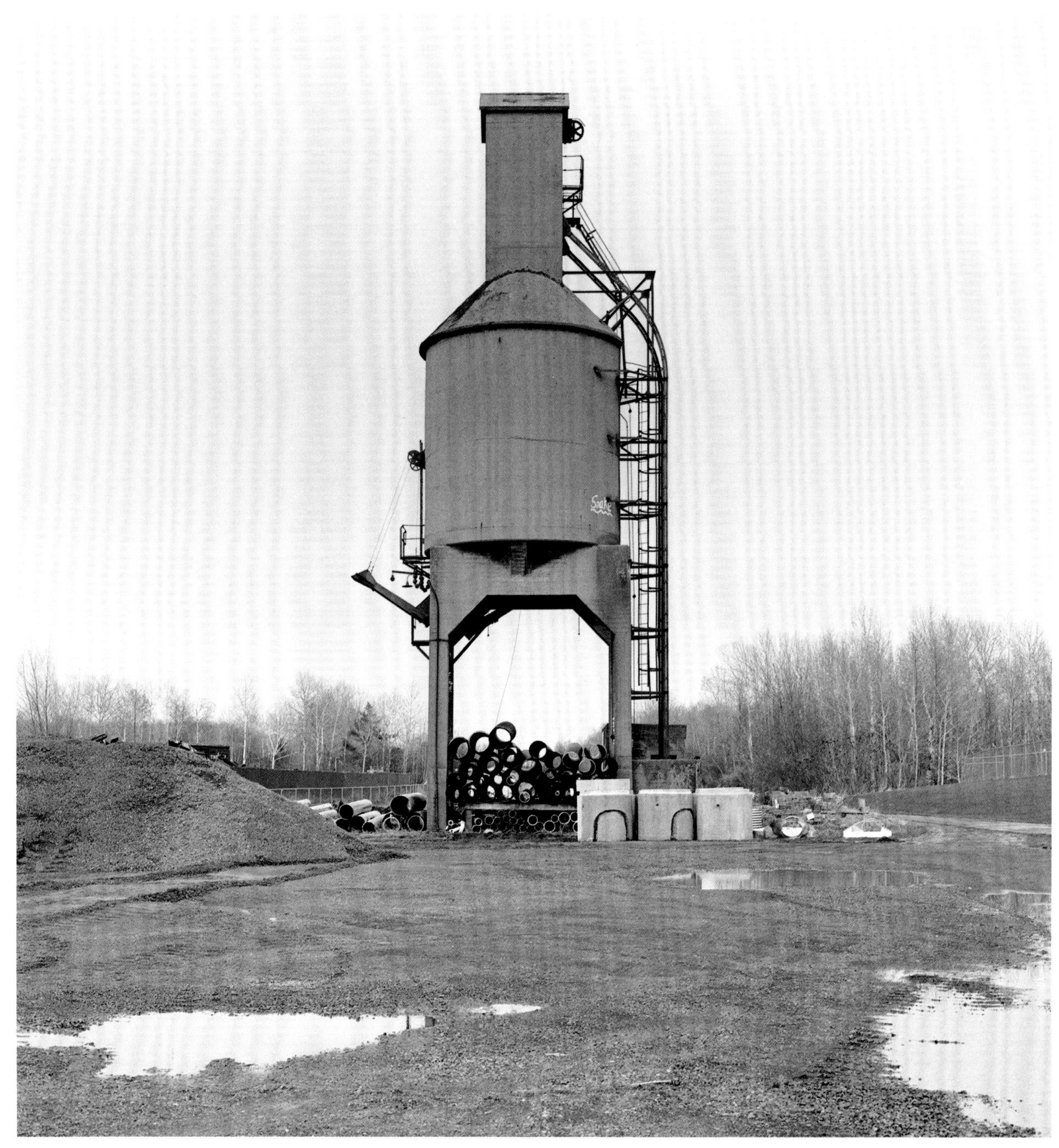

 ASHLAND, WISCONSIN Chicago & North Western 46°35’50.1”N 90°51’09.6”W

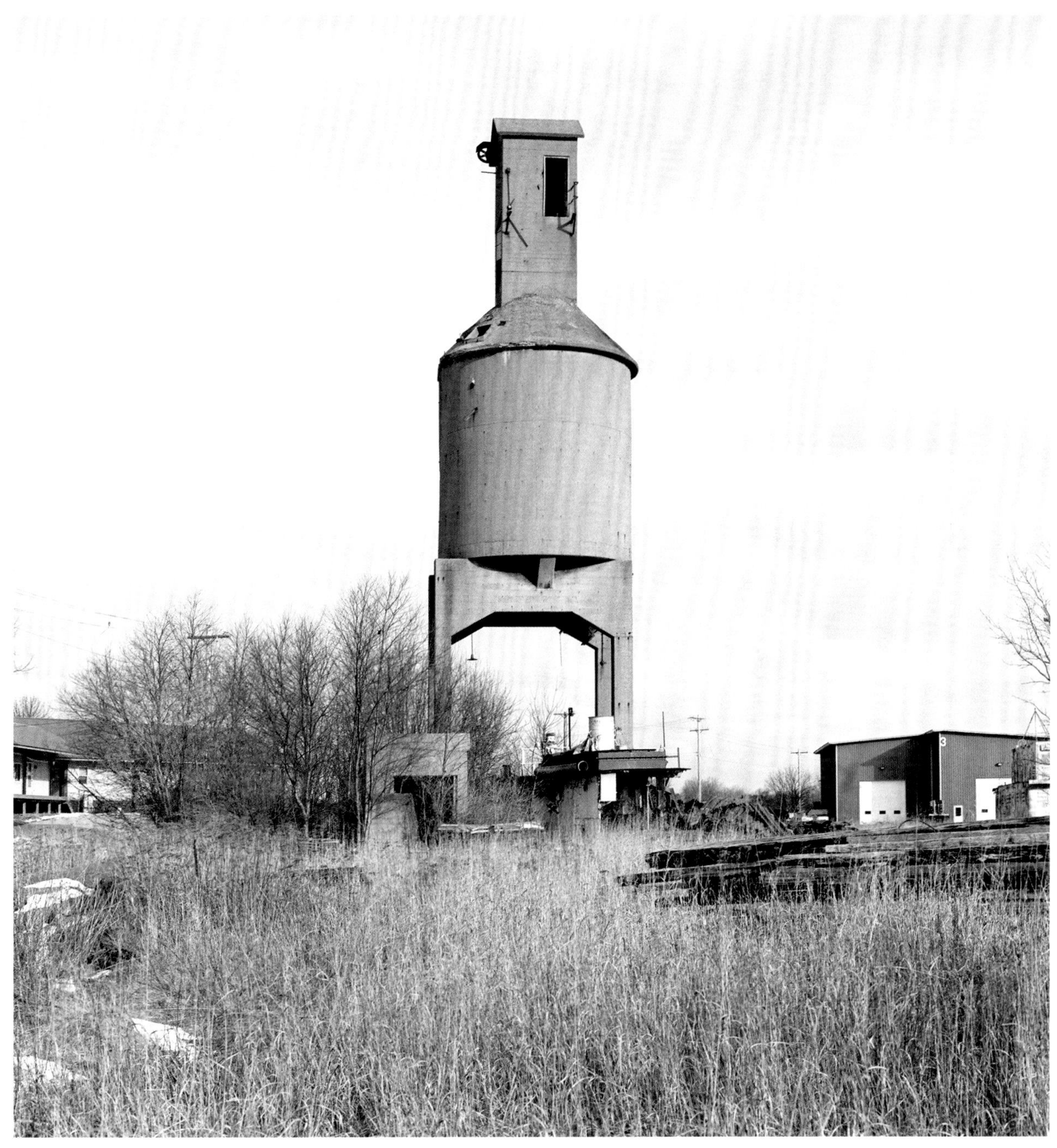

 ESCABANA, MICHIGAN Chicago & North Western 45°44'56.4"N 87°03'35.7"W

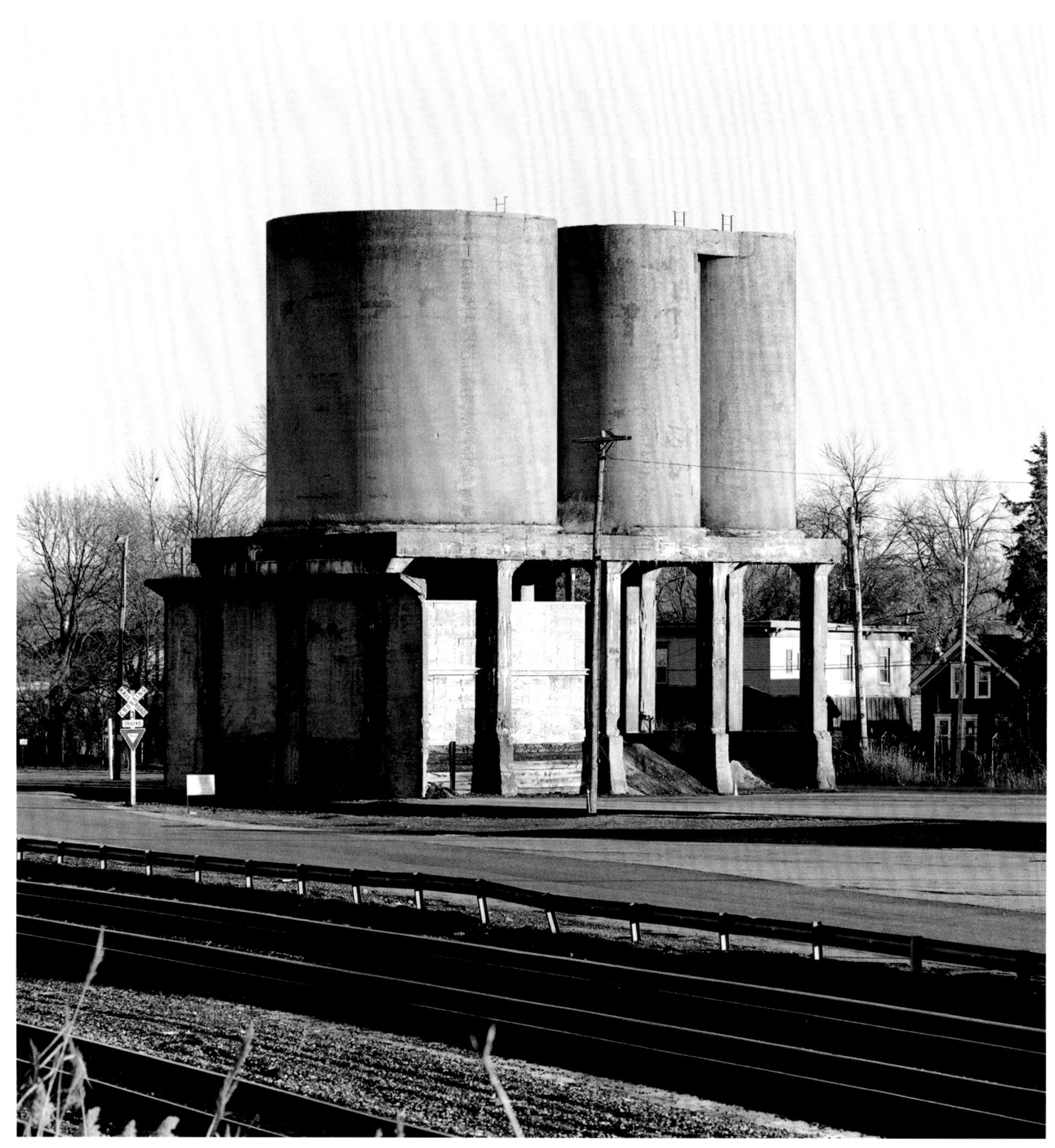

 SOLVAY, NEW YORK New York Central 43°03'45.0"N 76°04'17.6"W

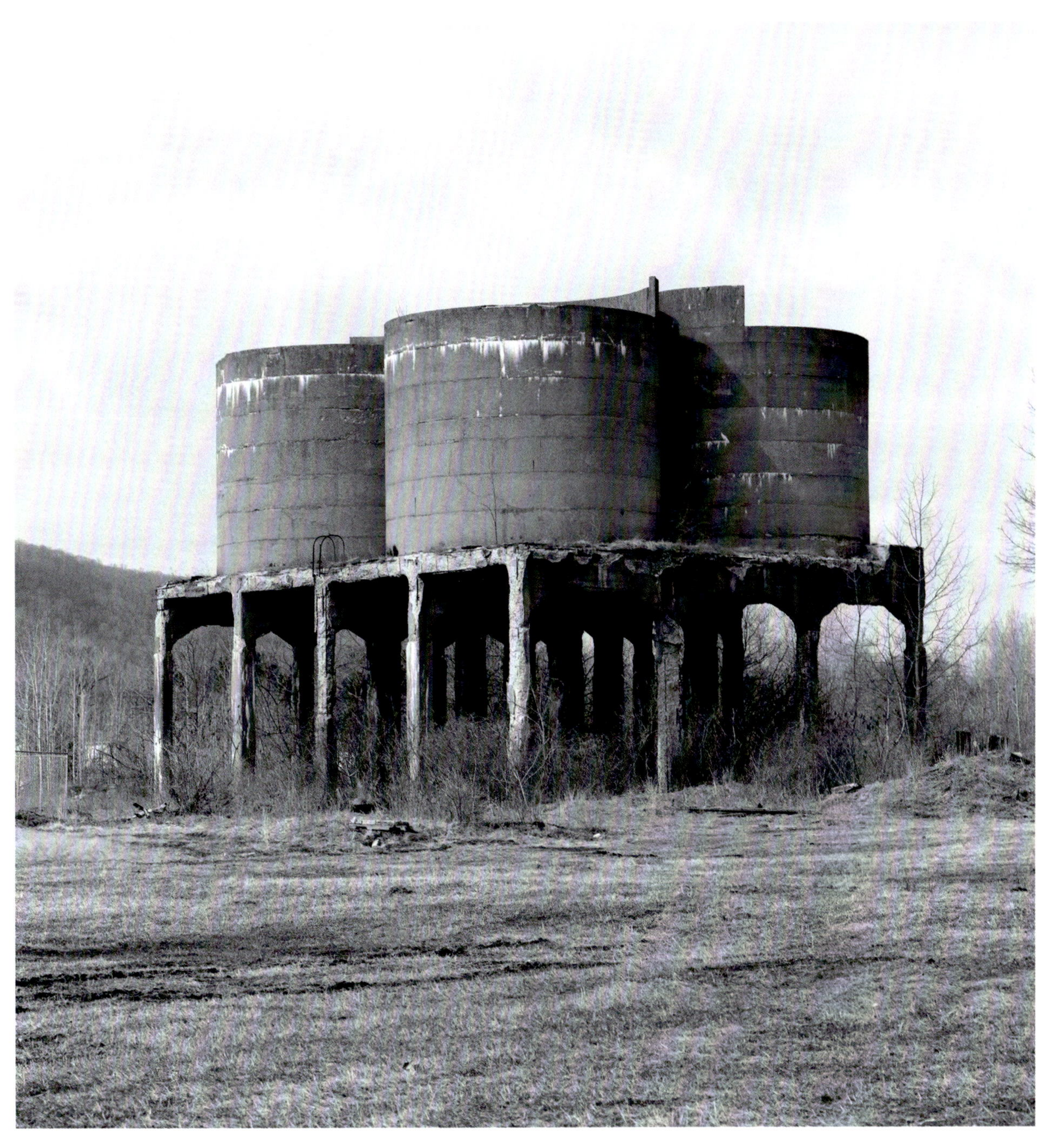

153 **SALAMANCA, NEW YORK** (demolished) Erie 42°09'39.6"N 78°42'55.1"W

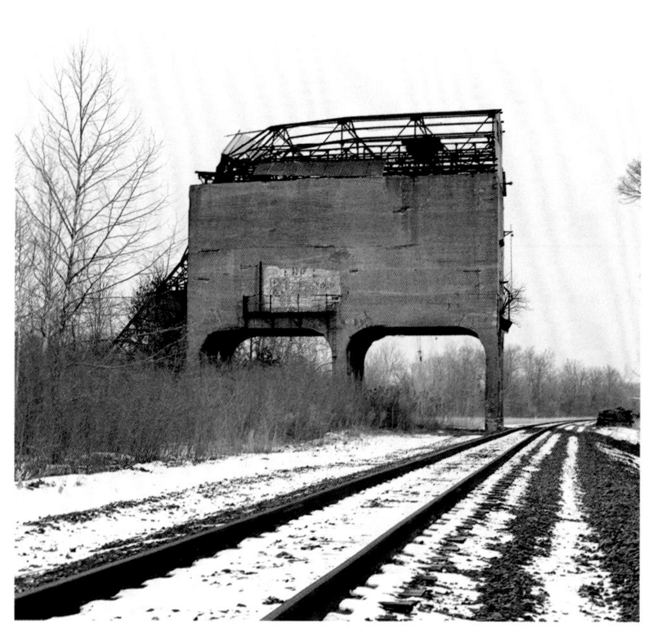

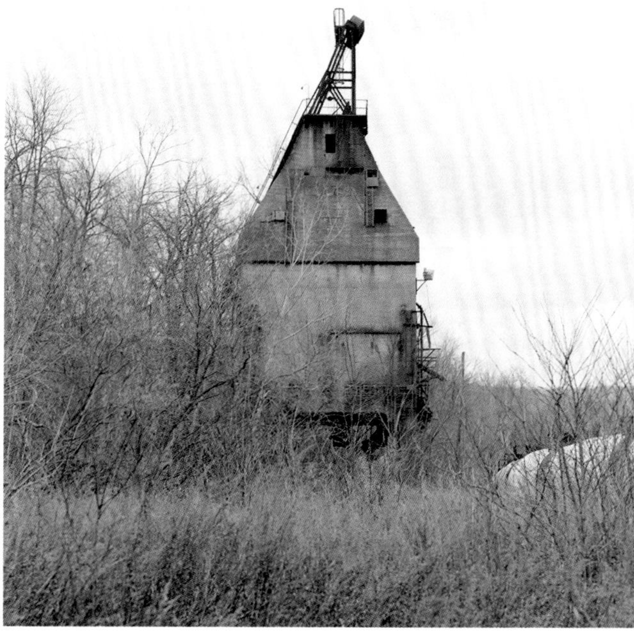

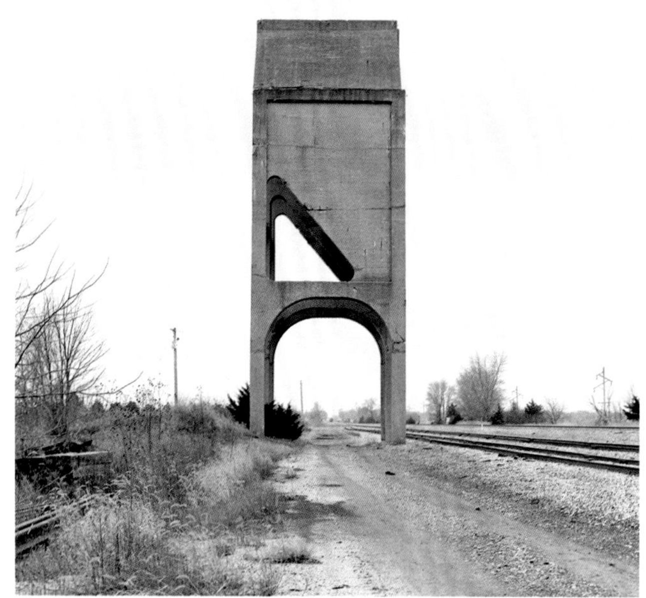

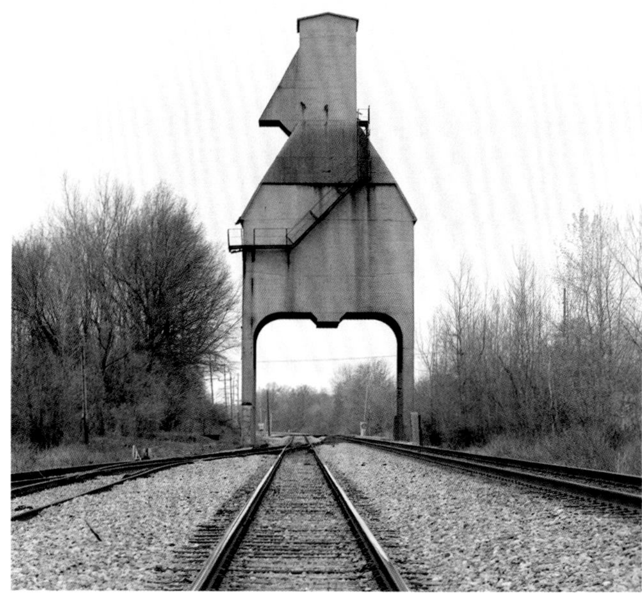

GIRARD, OHIO

COXTON, PENNSYLVANIA

GILMAN, ILLINOIS

SULLIVAN, INDIANA

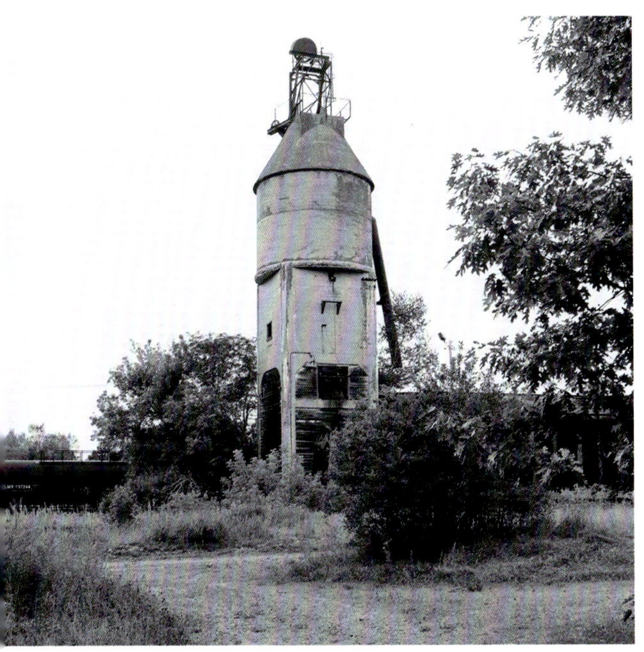

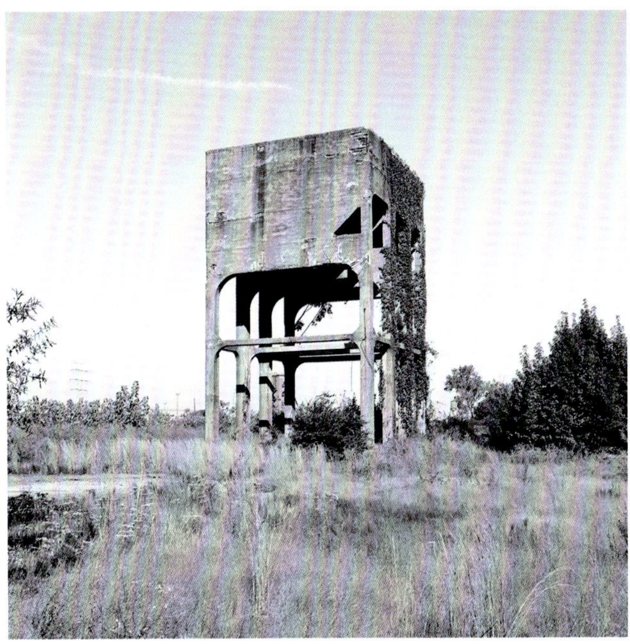

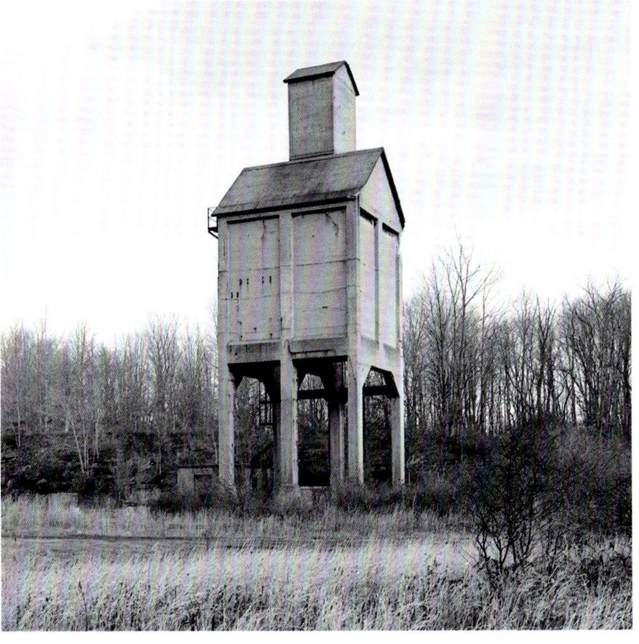

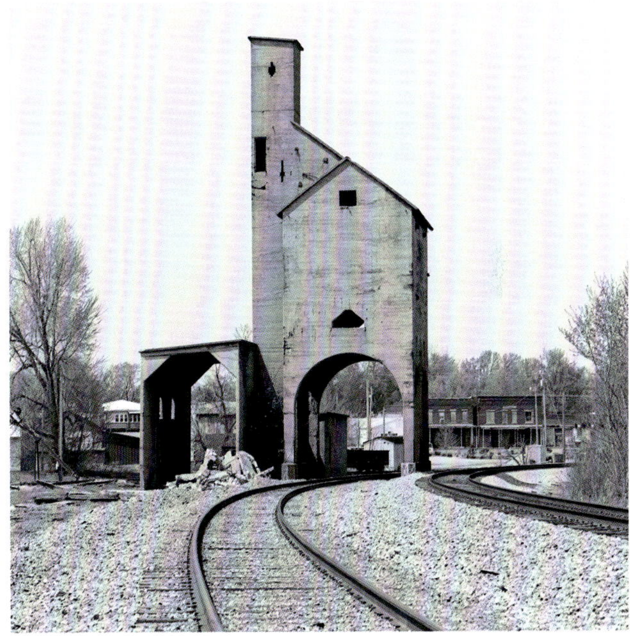

MILLINOCKET, MAINE

COWEN, WEST VIRGINIA

MONTGOMERY, ALABAMA

IRVINGTON, KENTUCKY

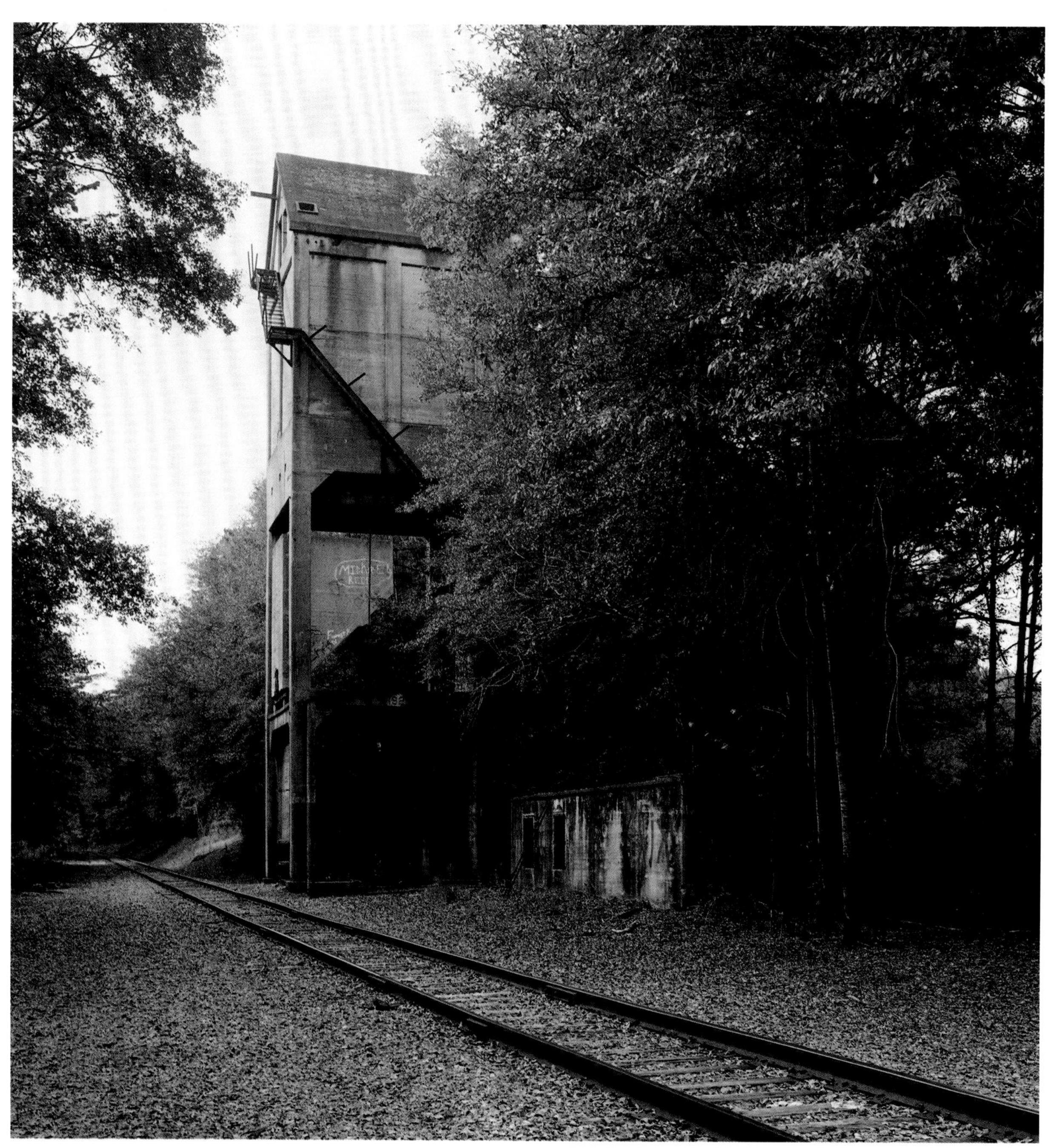

 RAYMOND, GEORGIA Central of Georgia 33°20’24.0”N 84°42’59.3”W

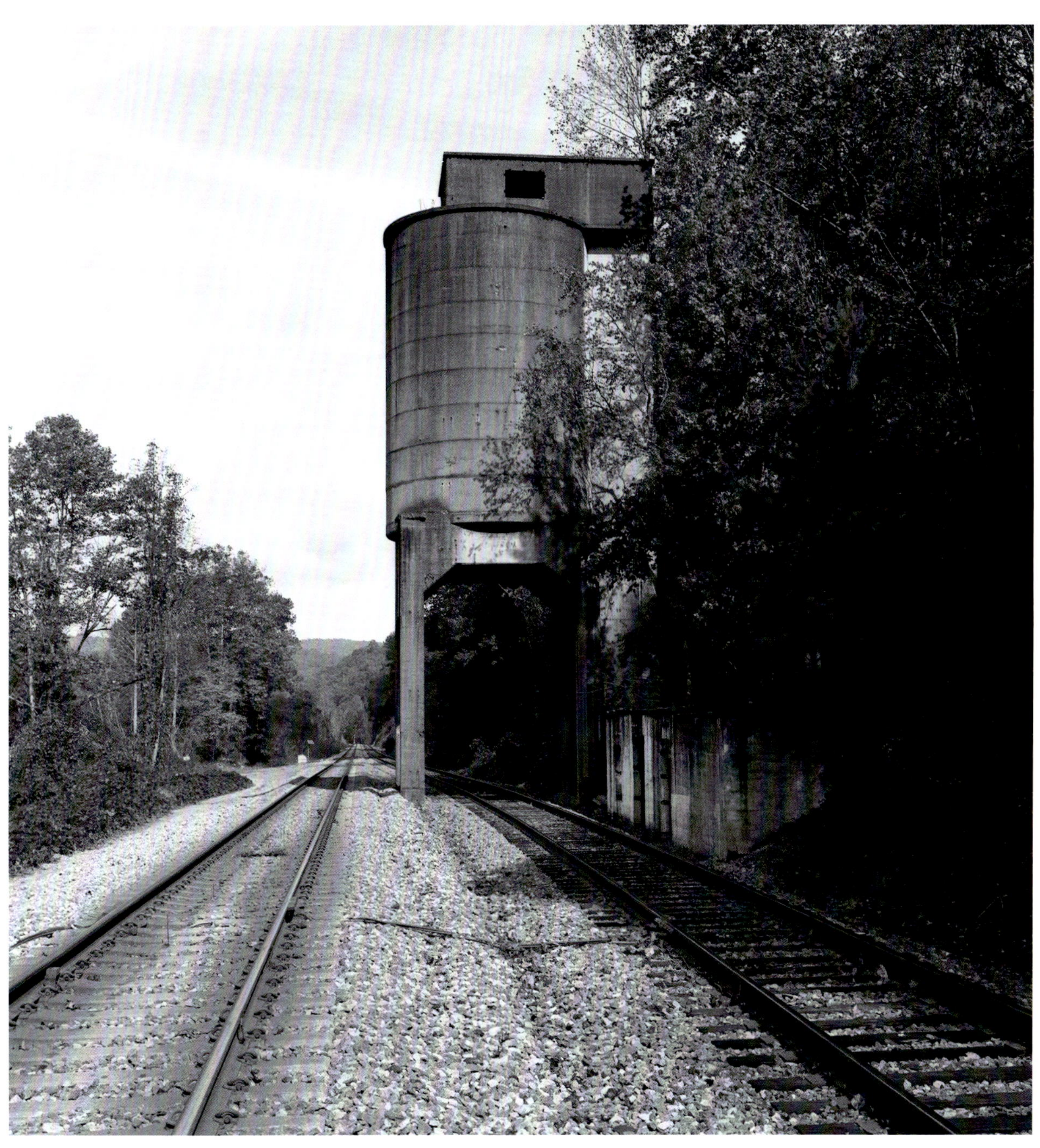

157 **CHASKA, TENNESSEE** Louisvile & Nashville 36°31'42.7"N 84°04'36.1"W

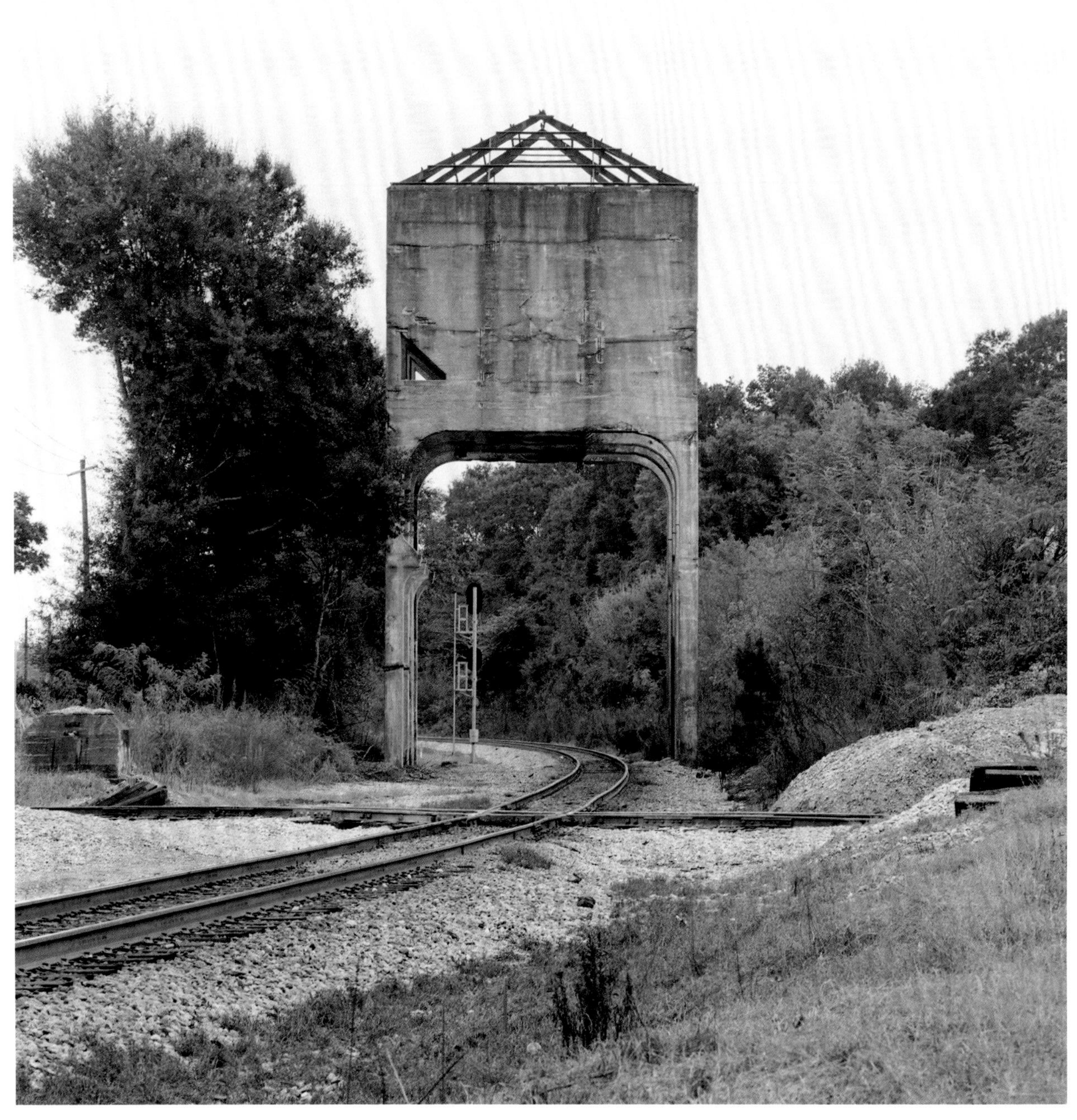

 NEWNAN, GEORGIA Atlanta & West Point 33°22'11.5"N 84°47'48.9"W

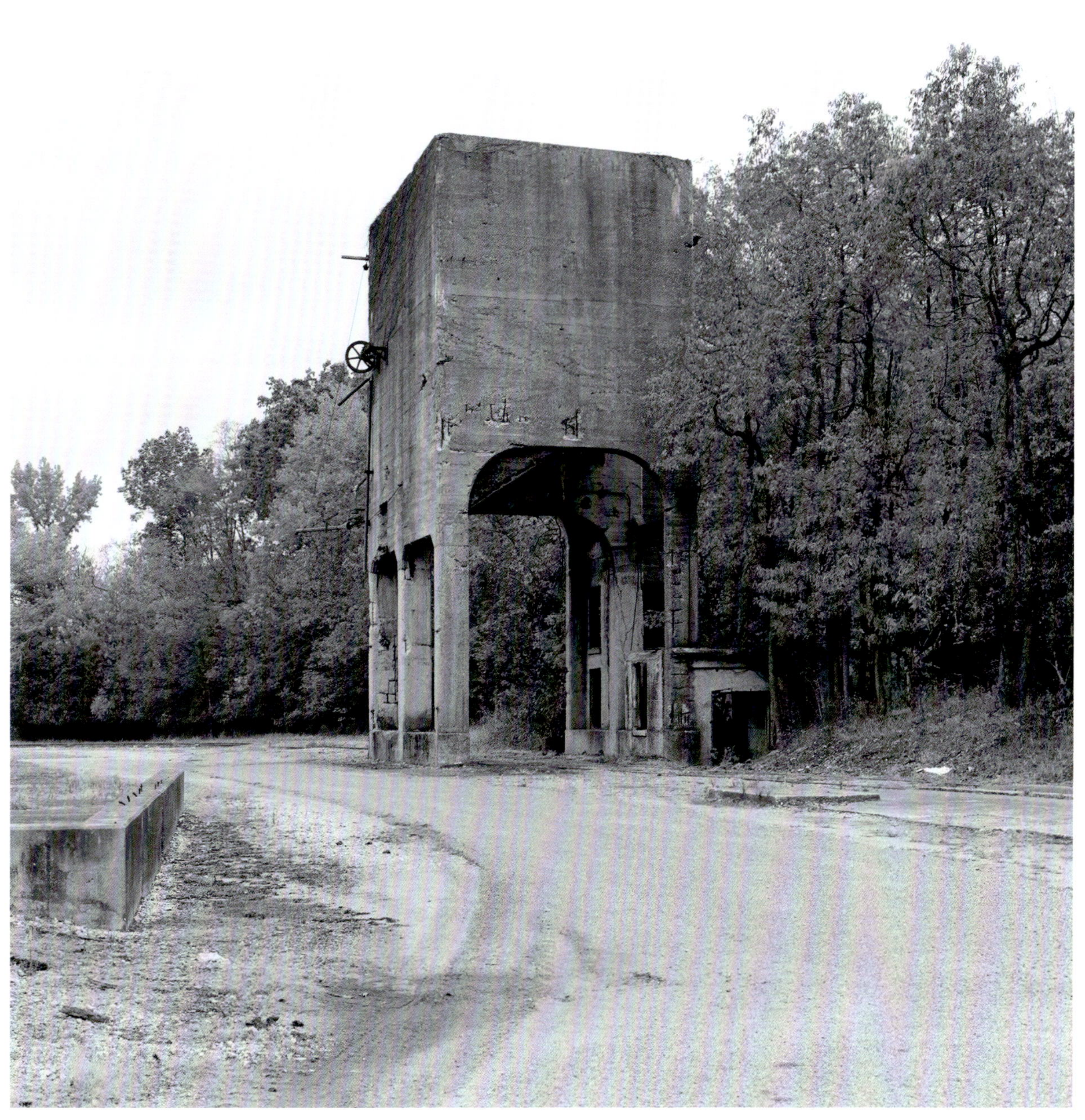

159 **PARIS, TENNESSEE** Louisville & Nashville 36°17’56.8”N 88°20’19.4”W

DAWSON SPRINGS, KENTUCKY Illinois Central 37°09’54.5”N 87°40’41.1”W

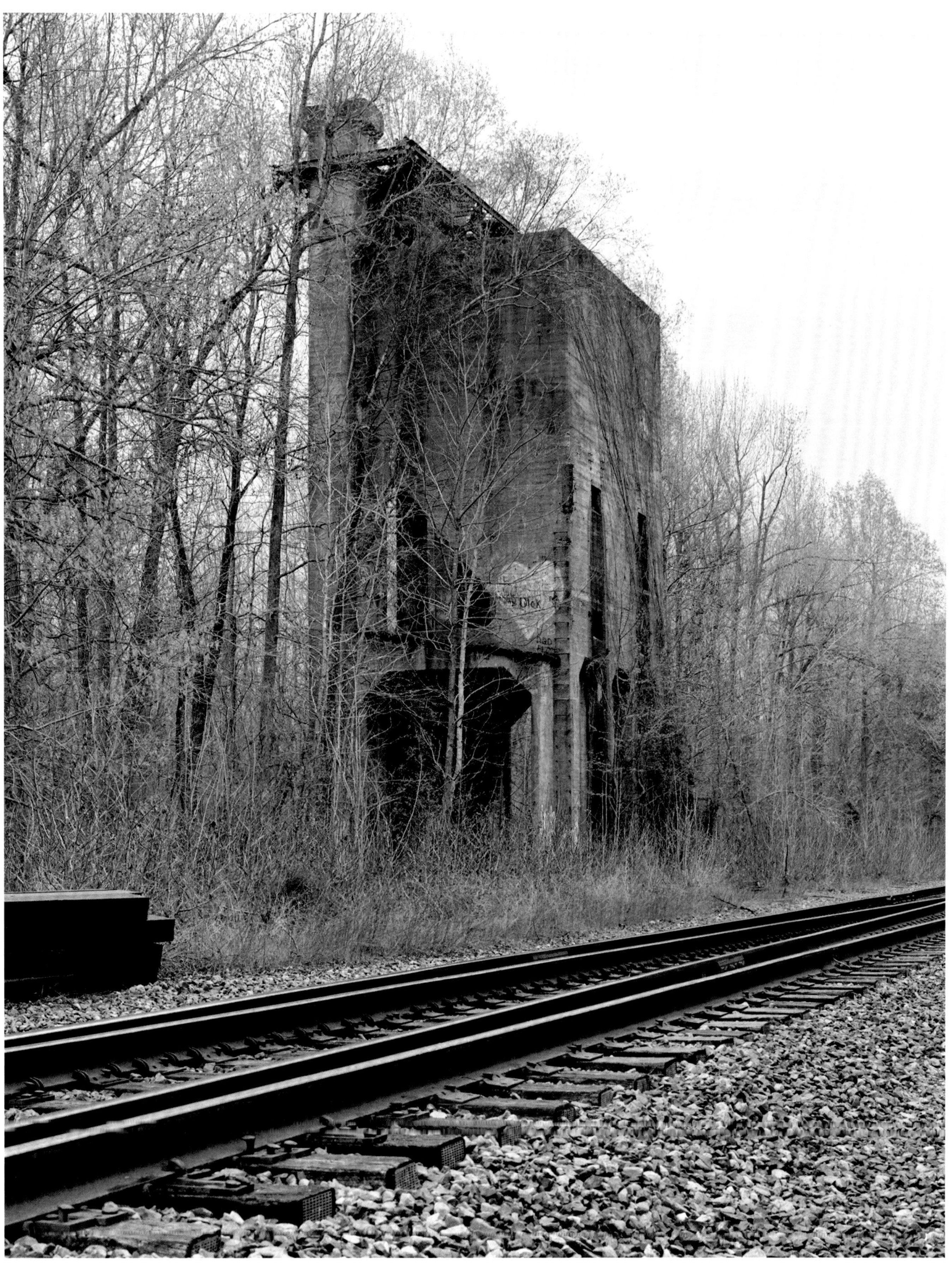

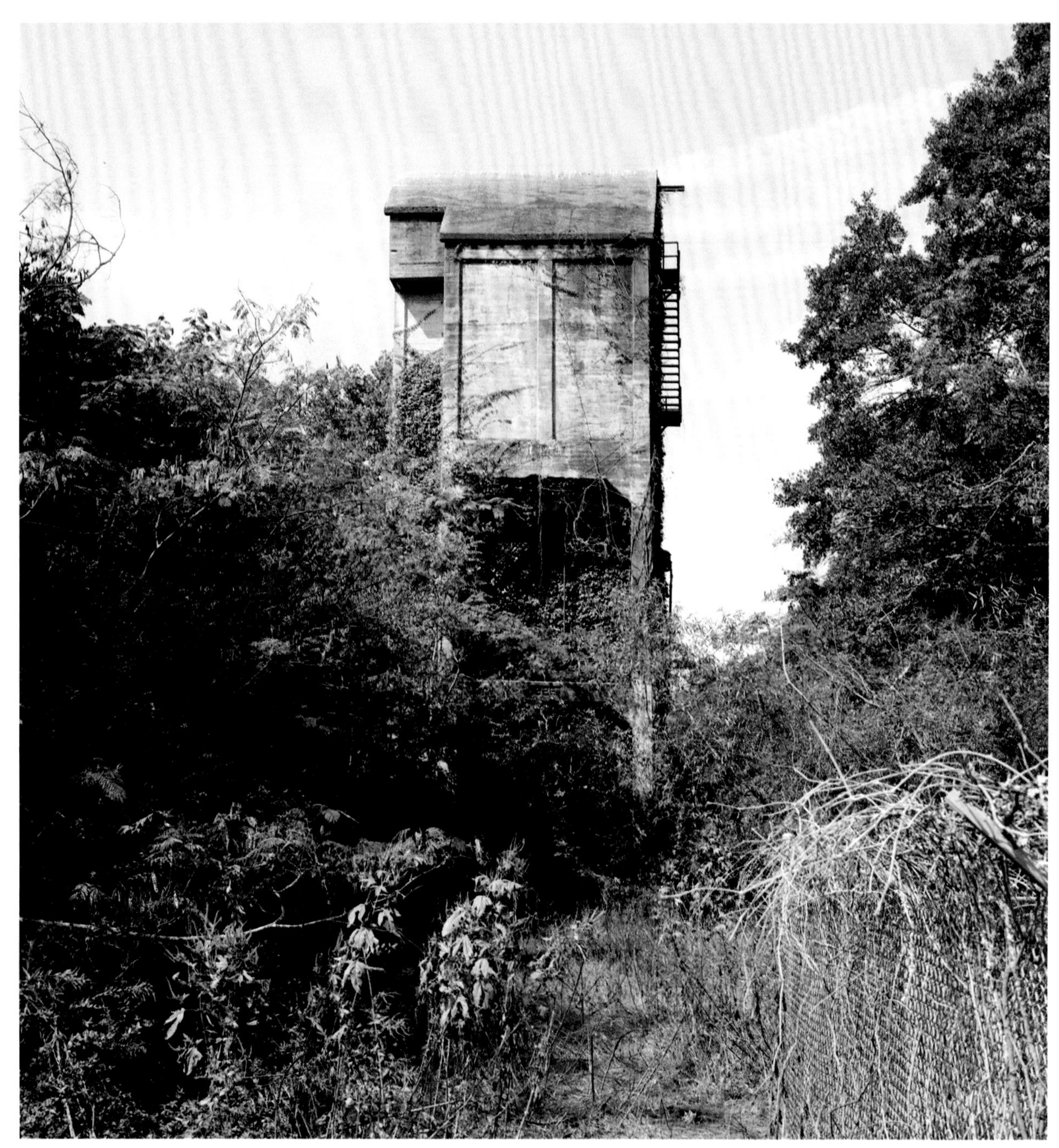

162 **UNION SPRINGS, ALABAMA** Central of Georgia 32°08'22.4"N 85°42'54.8"W (above)

163 **MUSKOGEE, OKLAHOMA** Kansas, Oklahoma & Gulf 35°45'53.8"N 95°22'05.2"W (right)

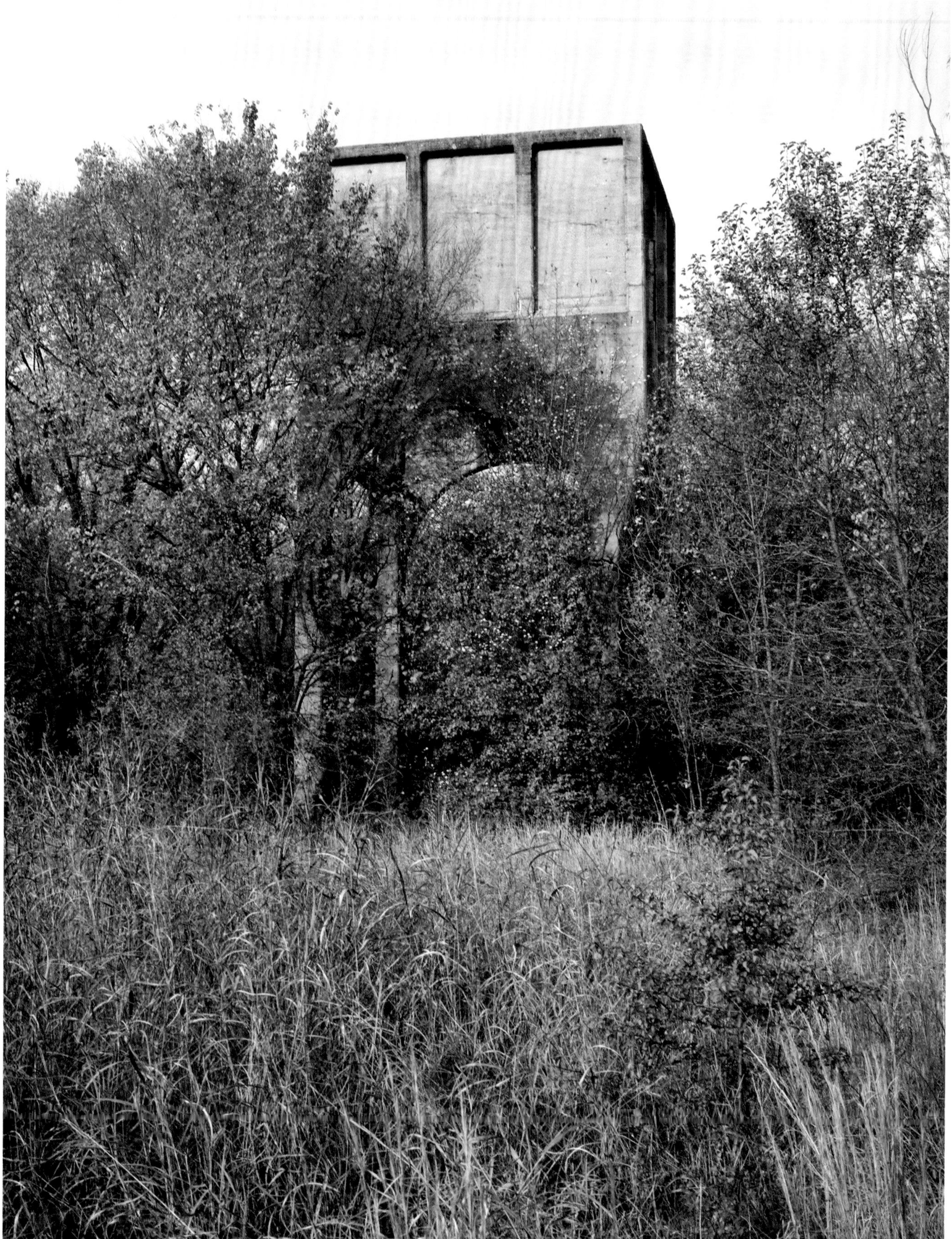

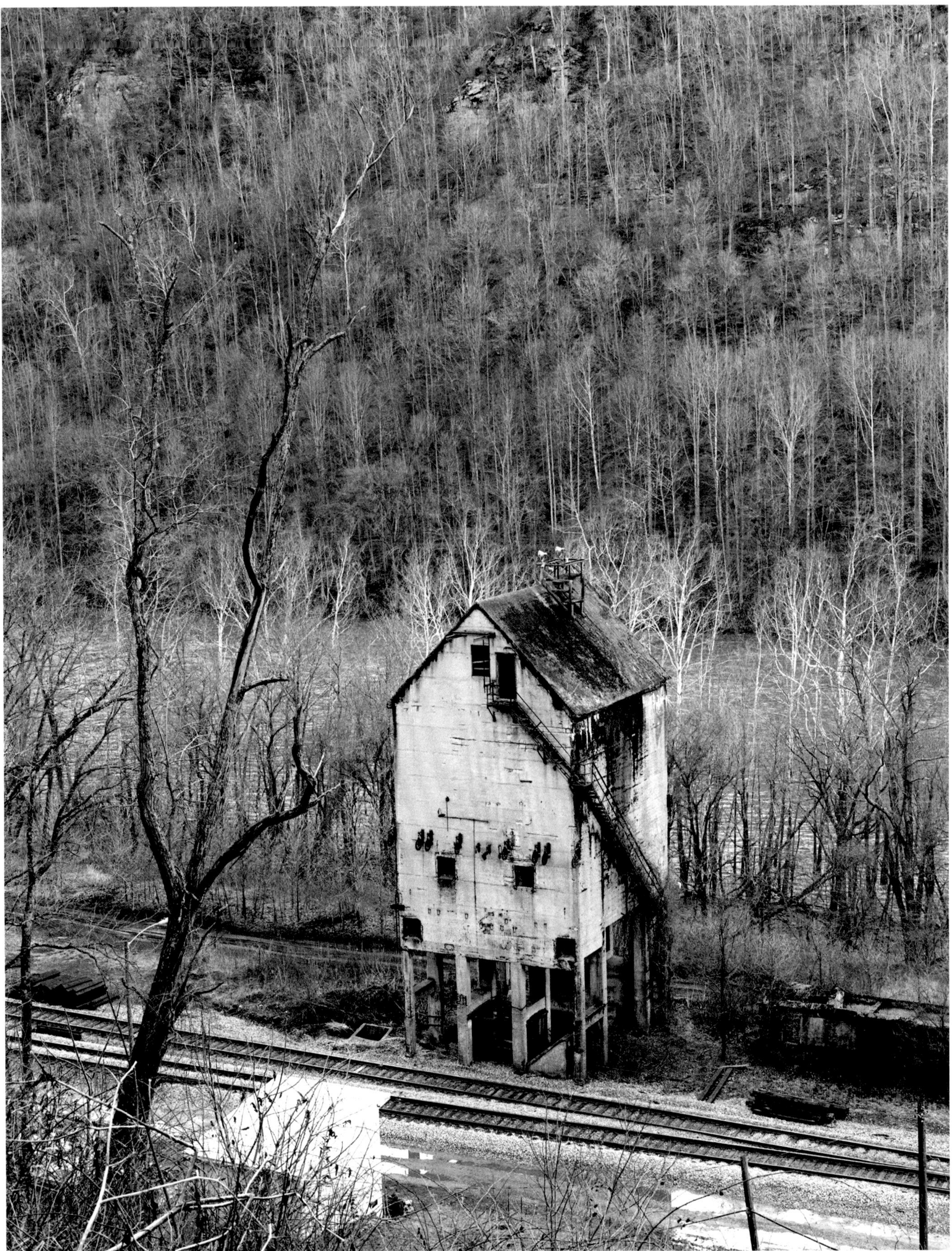

SILENT MONOLITHS
THE COALING TOWER PROJECT

TOPOGRAPHIES

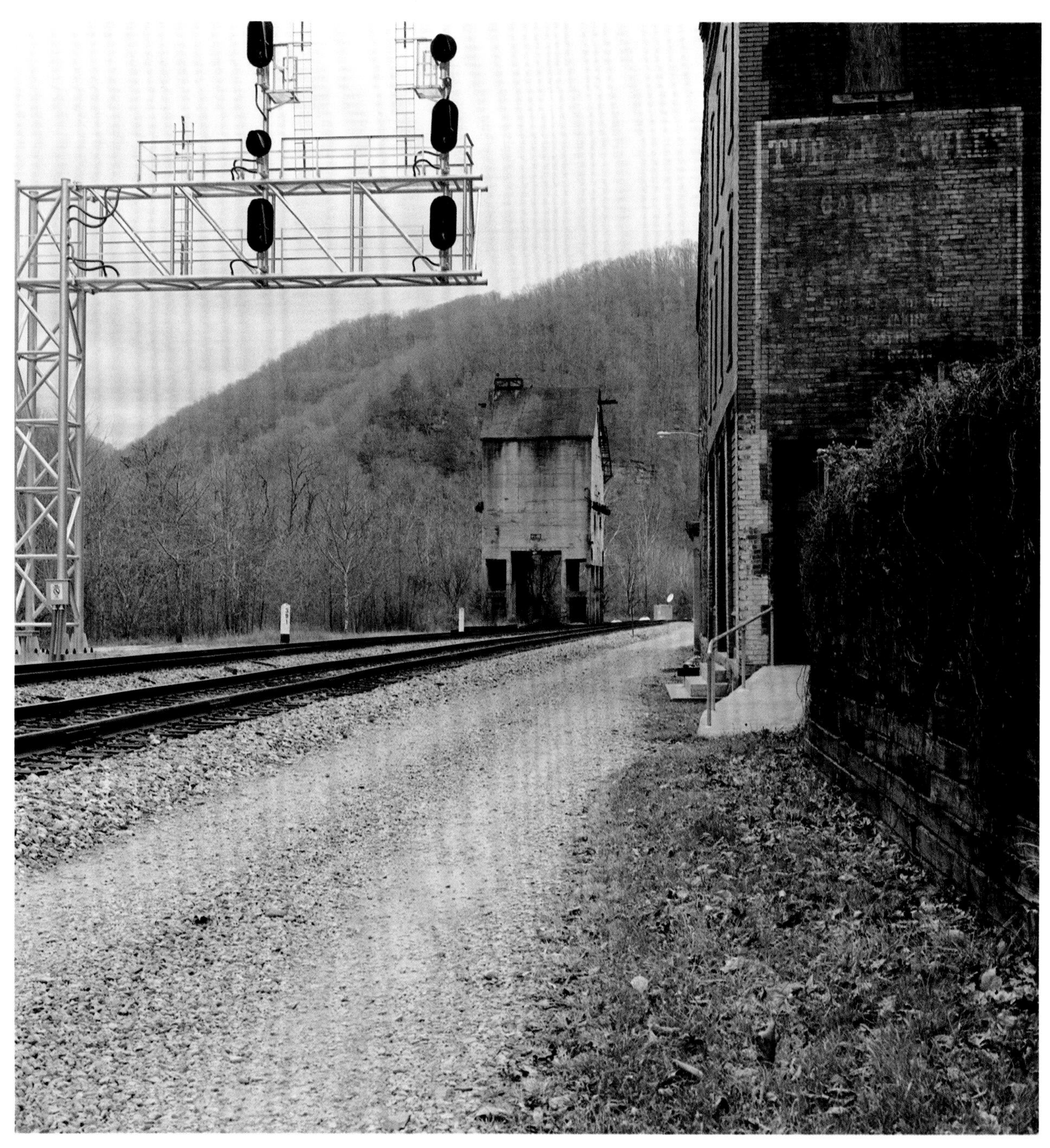

166 **THURMOND, WEST VIRGINIA** Chesapeake & Ohio 37°57'35.6"N 81°04'53.2"W (above and preceding page)

167 **BLUEFIELD, WEST VIRGINIA** Norfolk & Western 37°16'17.5"N 81°13'13.8"W (right)

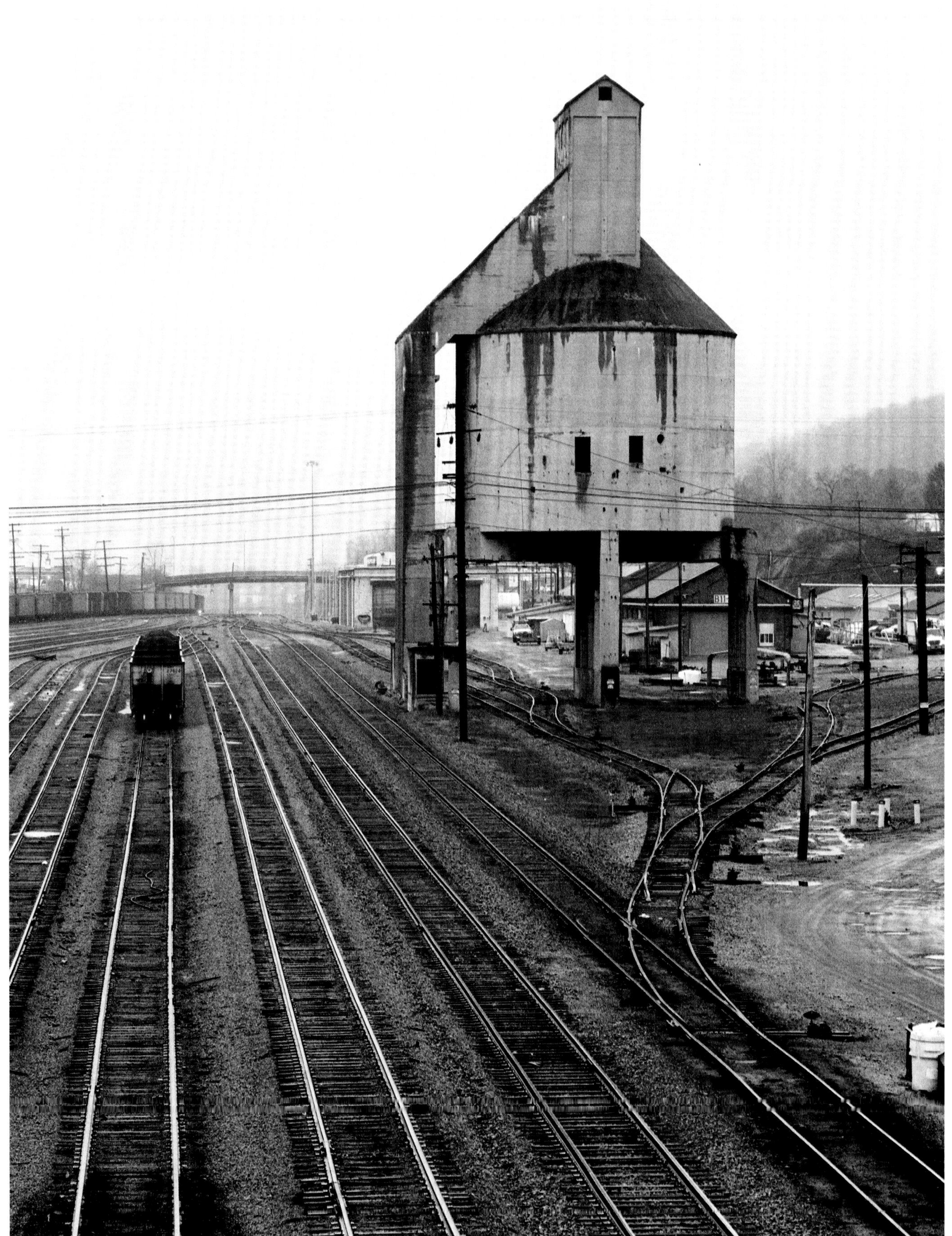

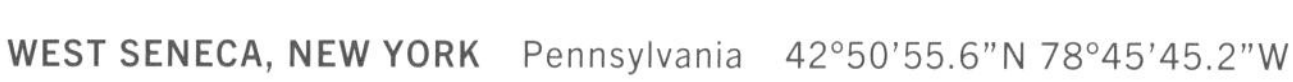

168-169 **WEST SENECA, NEW YORK** Pennsylvania 42°50’55.6”N 78°45’45.2”W

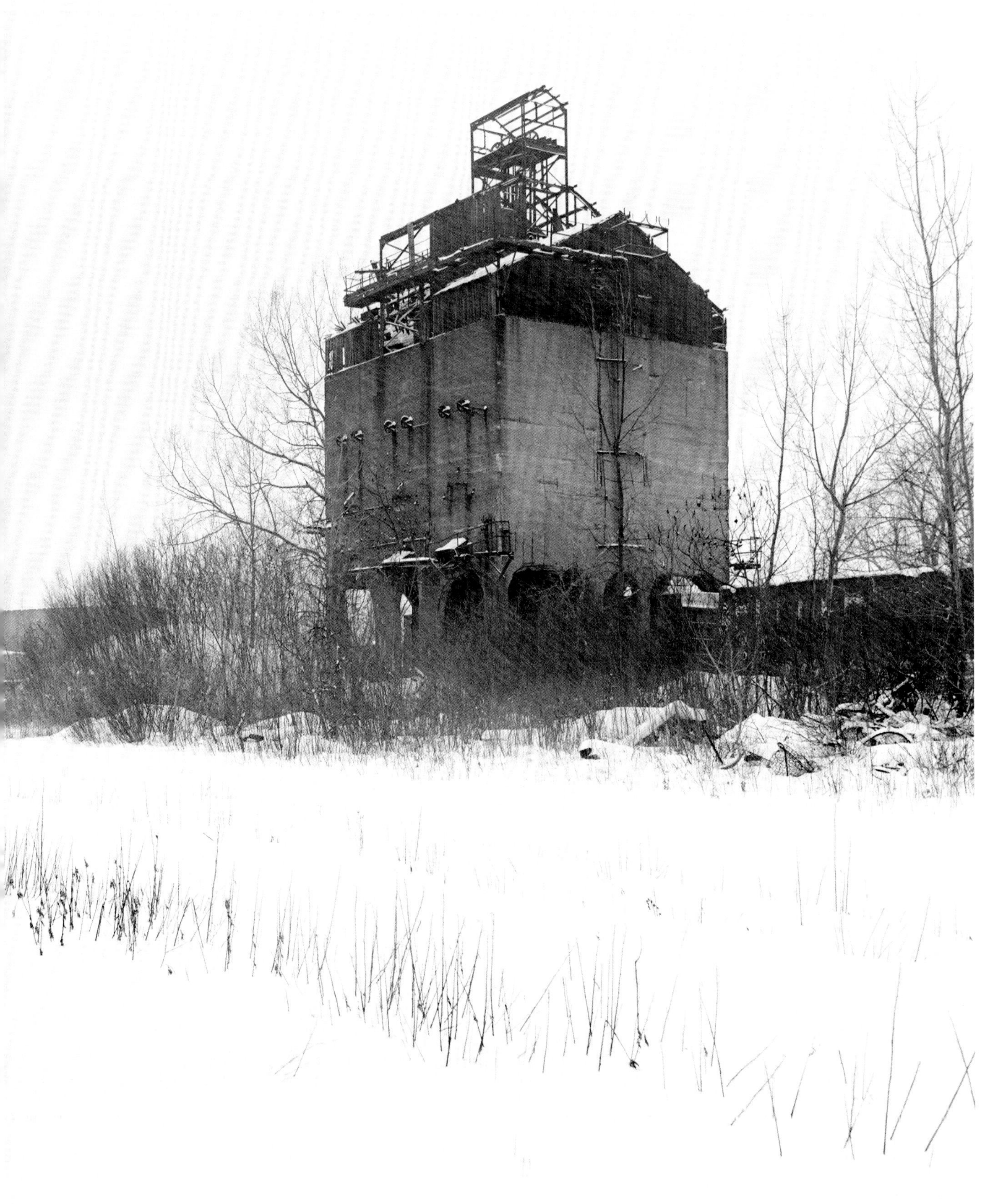

170-171 **GIRARD, OHIO** Pennsylvania 41°09'01.3"N 80°42'18.2"W

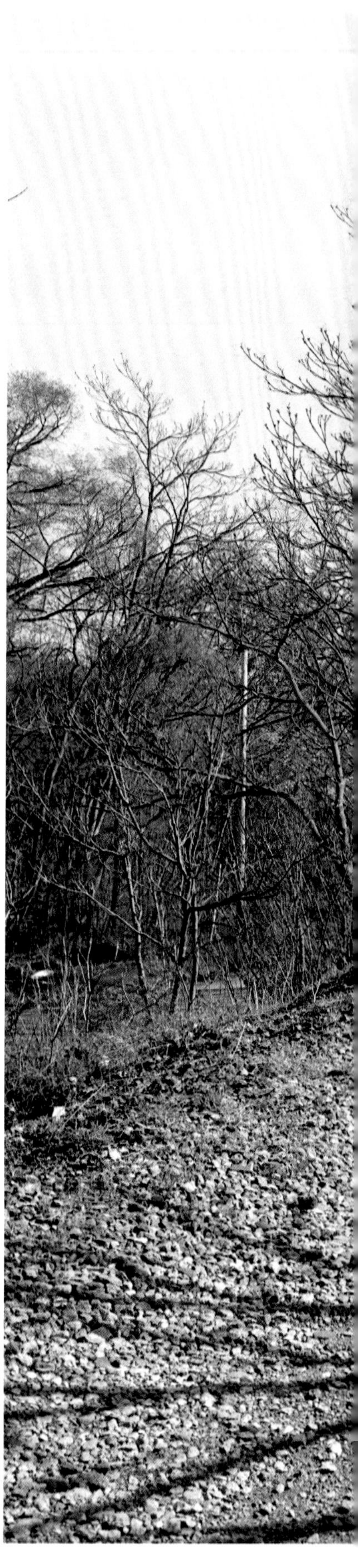

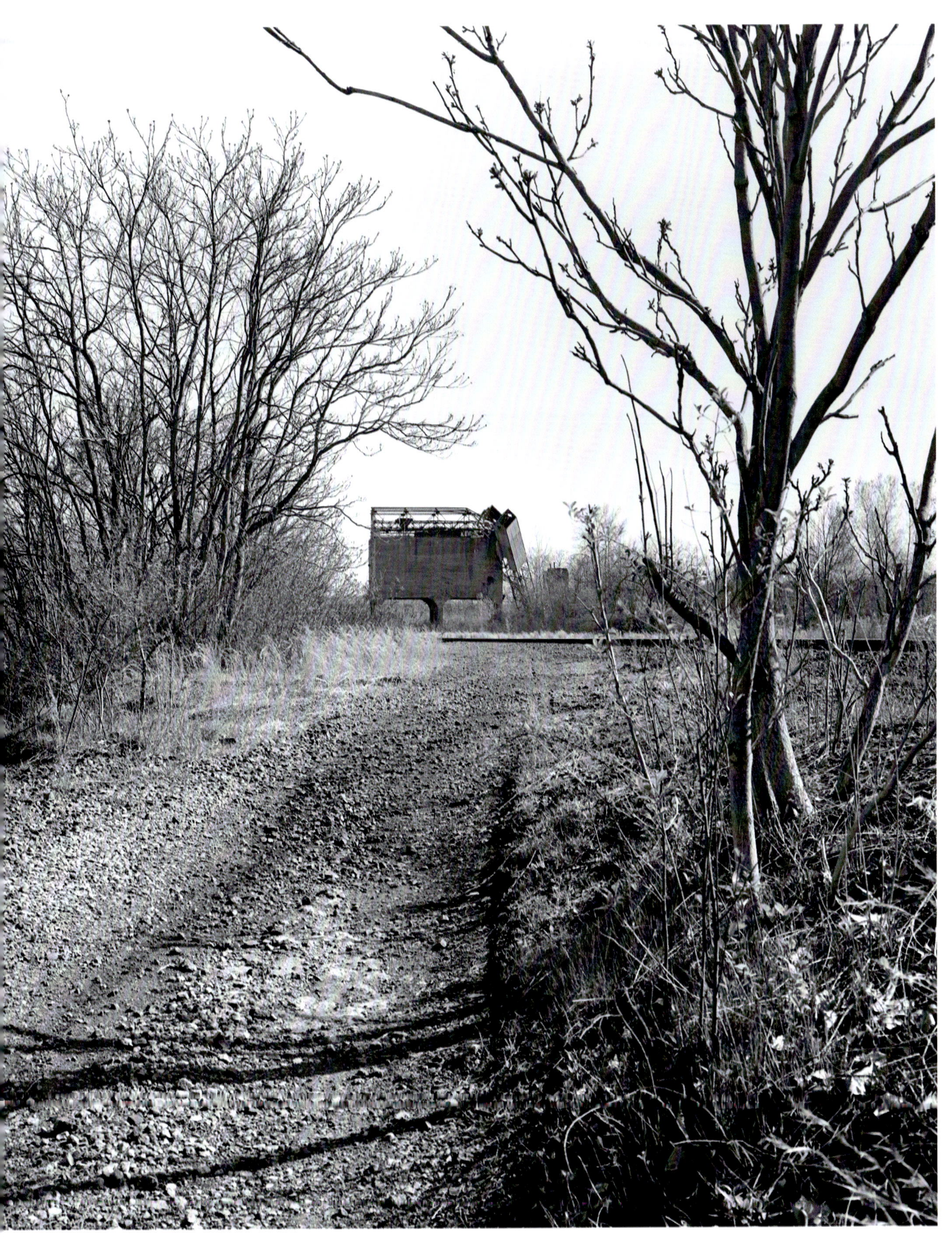

172-173 **CHESTER, MASSACHUSETTS** Boston & Albany 42°17’14.5”N 72°58’56.2”W

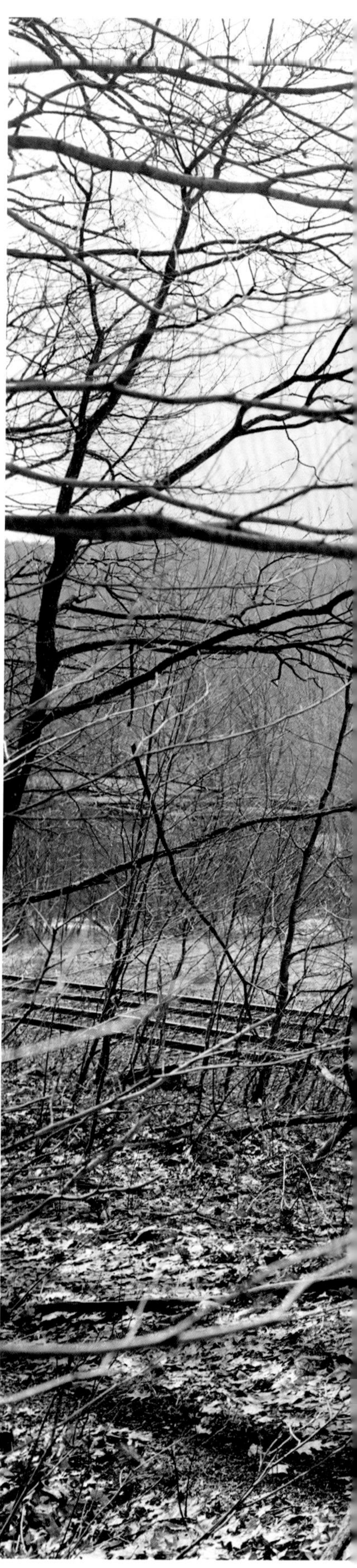

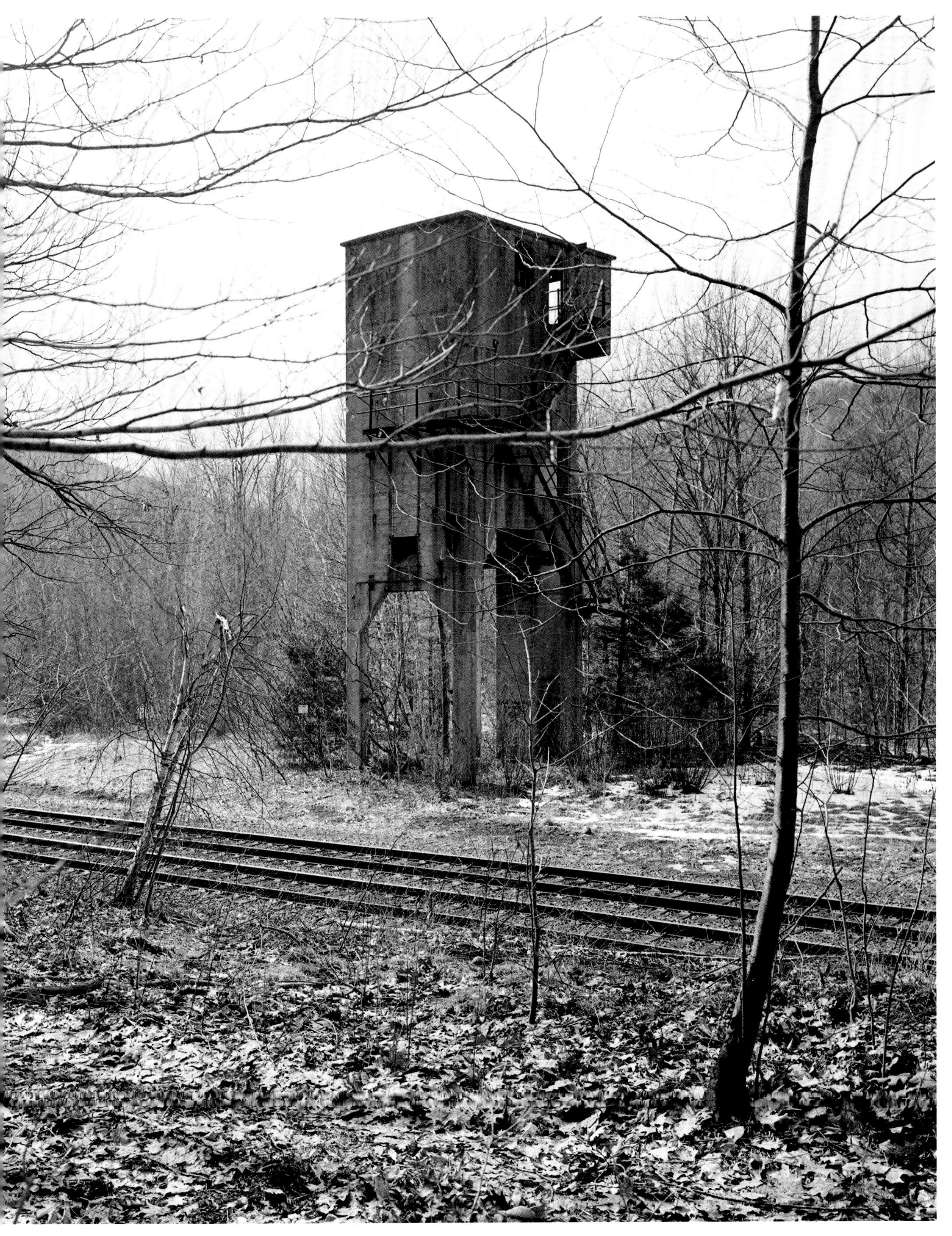

174-175 **MONTFORT, WISCONSIN** Chicago & North Western 42°57'49.6"N 90°24'31.3"W

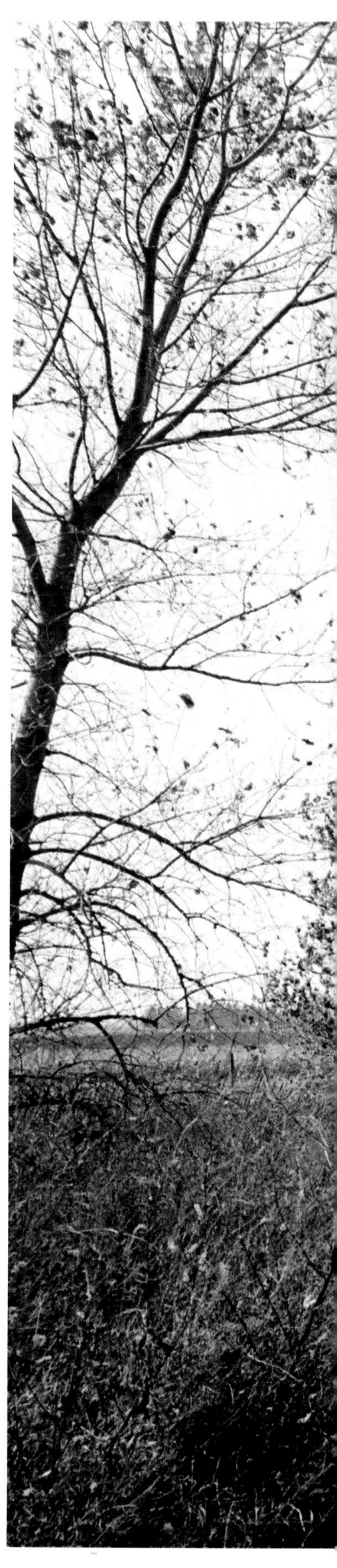

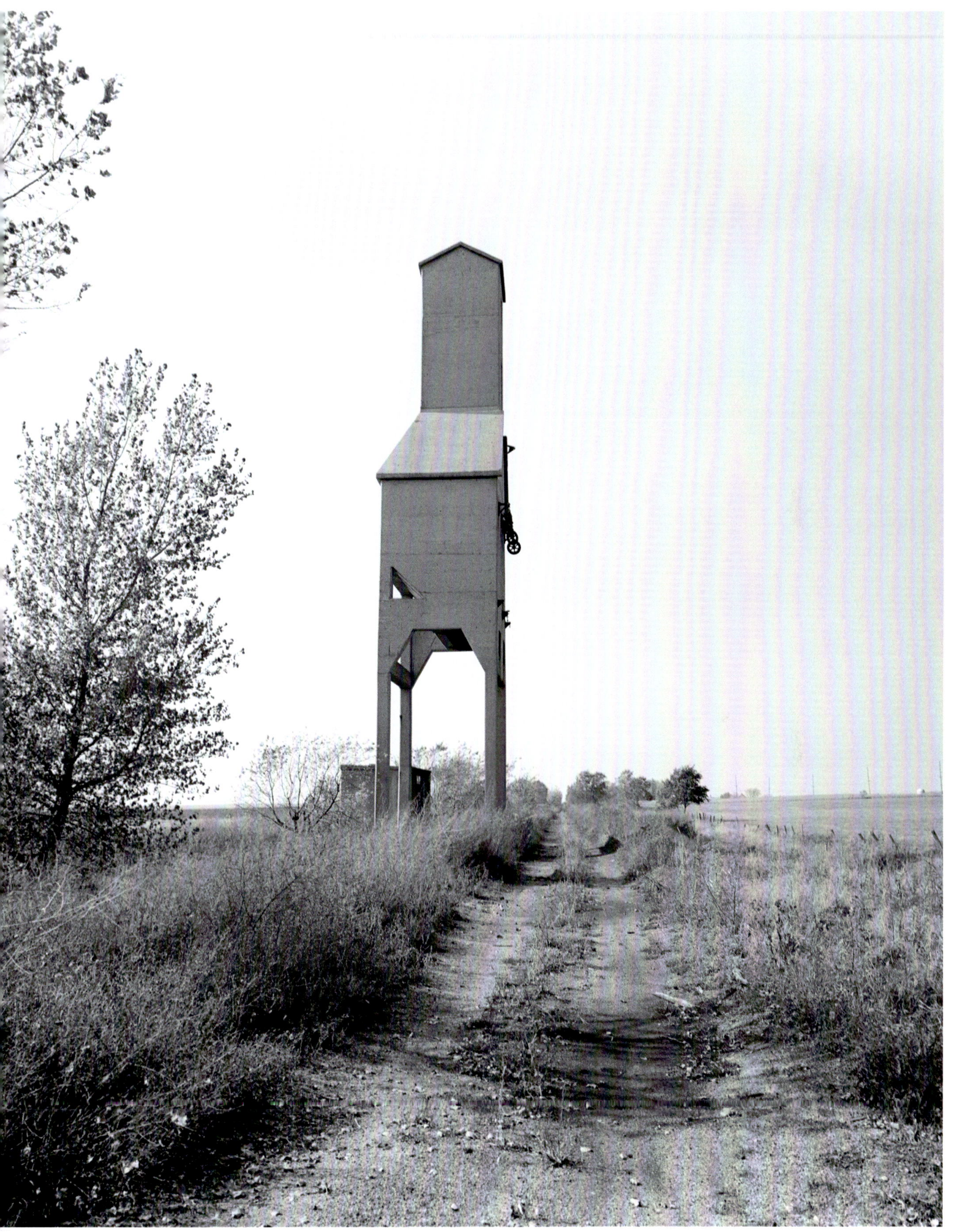

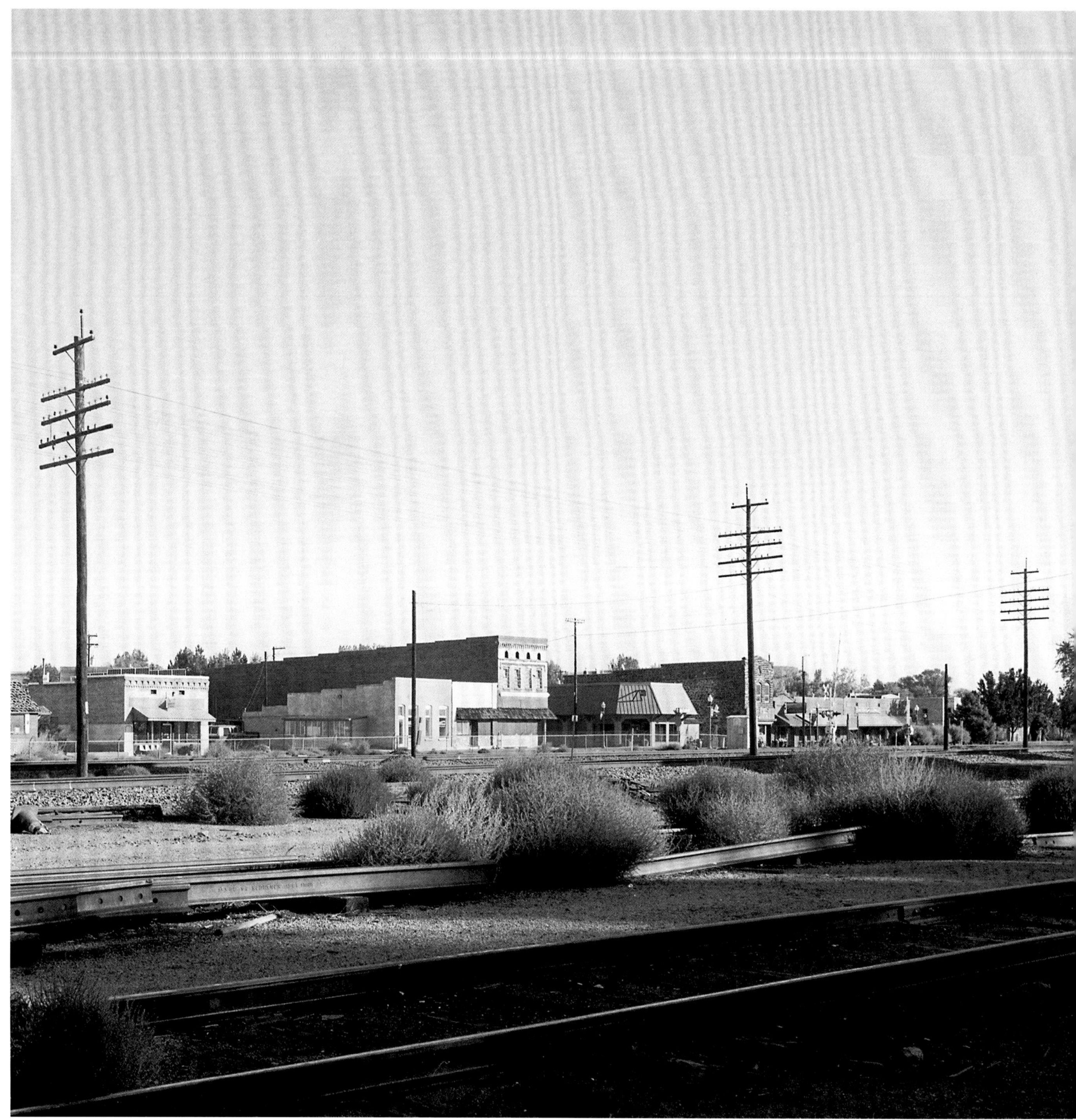

176-177 **GLENNS FERRY, IDAHO** Union Pacfic 42°57'09.8"N 115°18'01.9"W

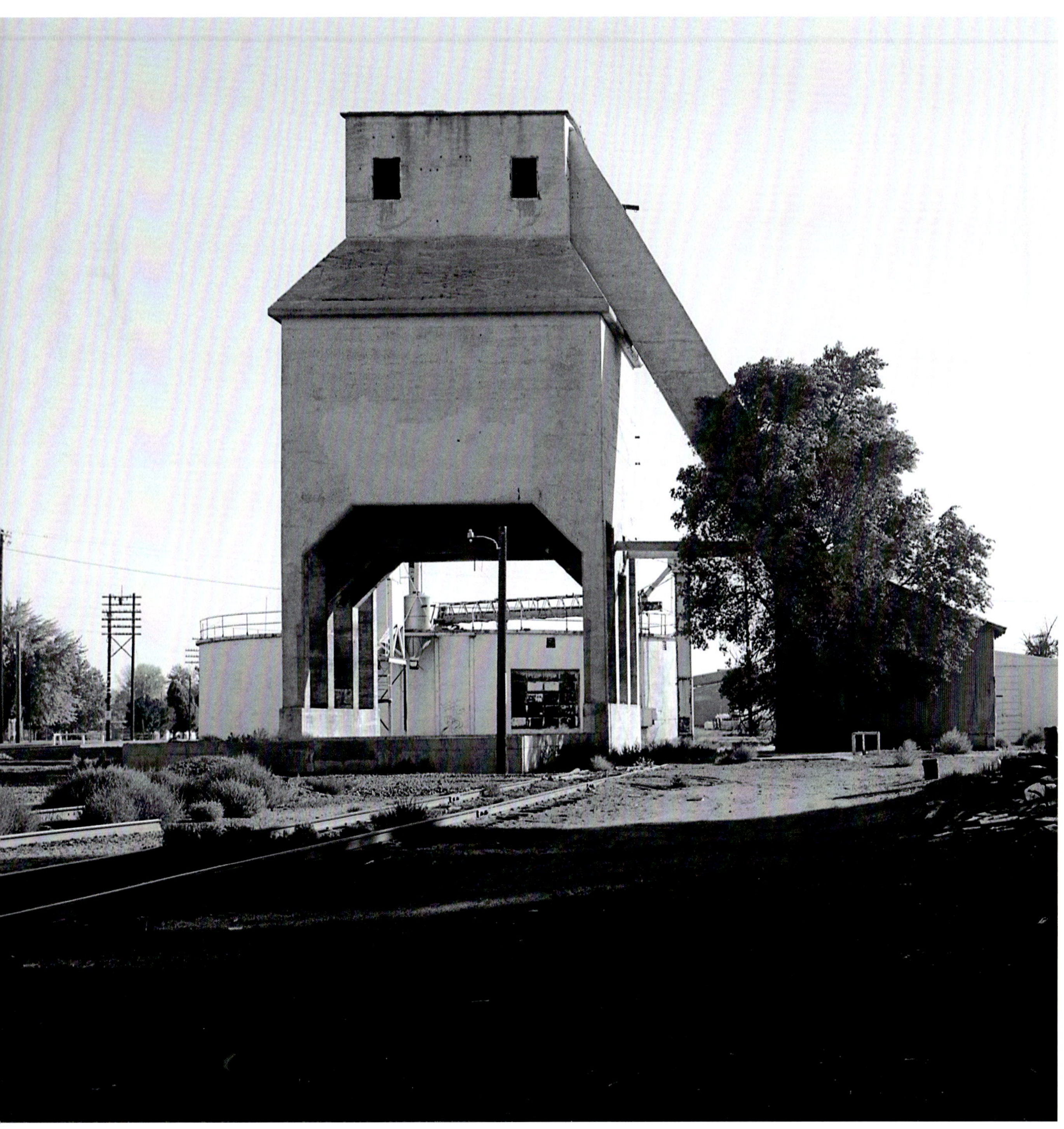

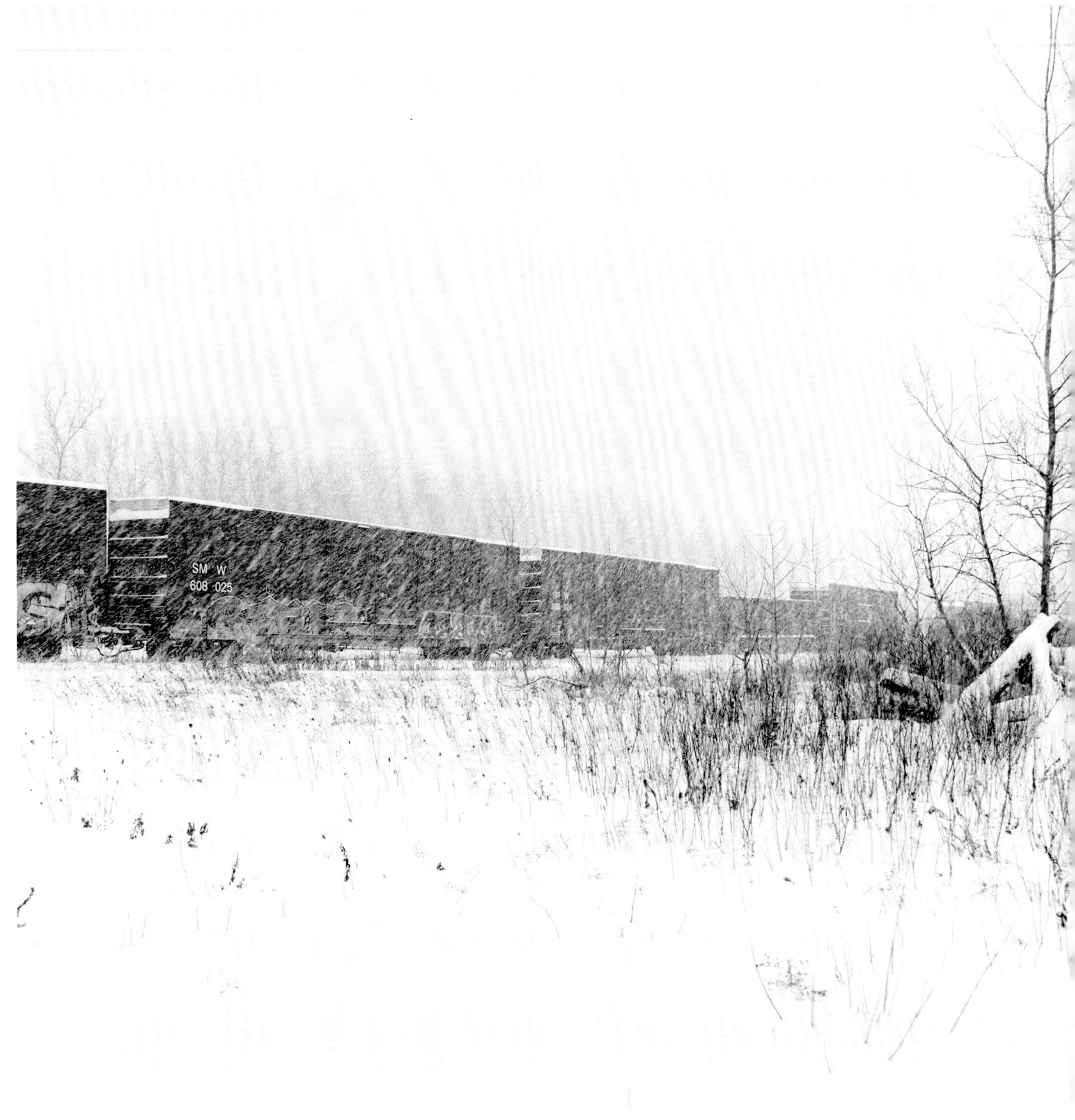

178-179 **WEST SENECA, NEW YORK** Pennsylvania 42°50’55.6”N 78°45’45.2”W

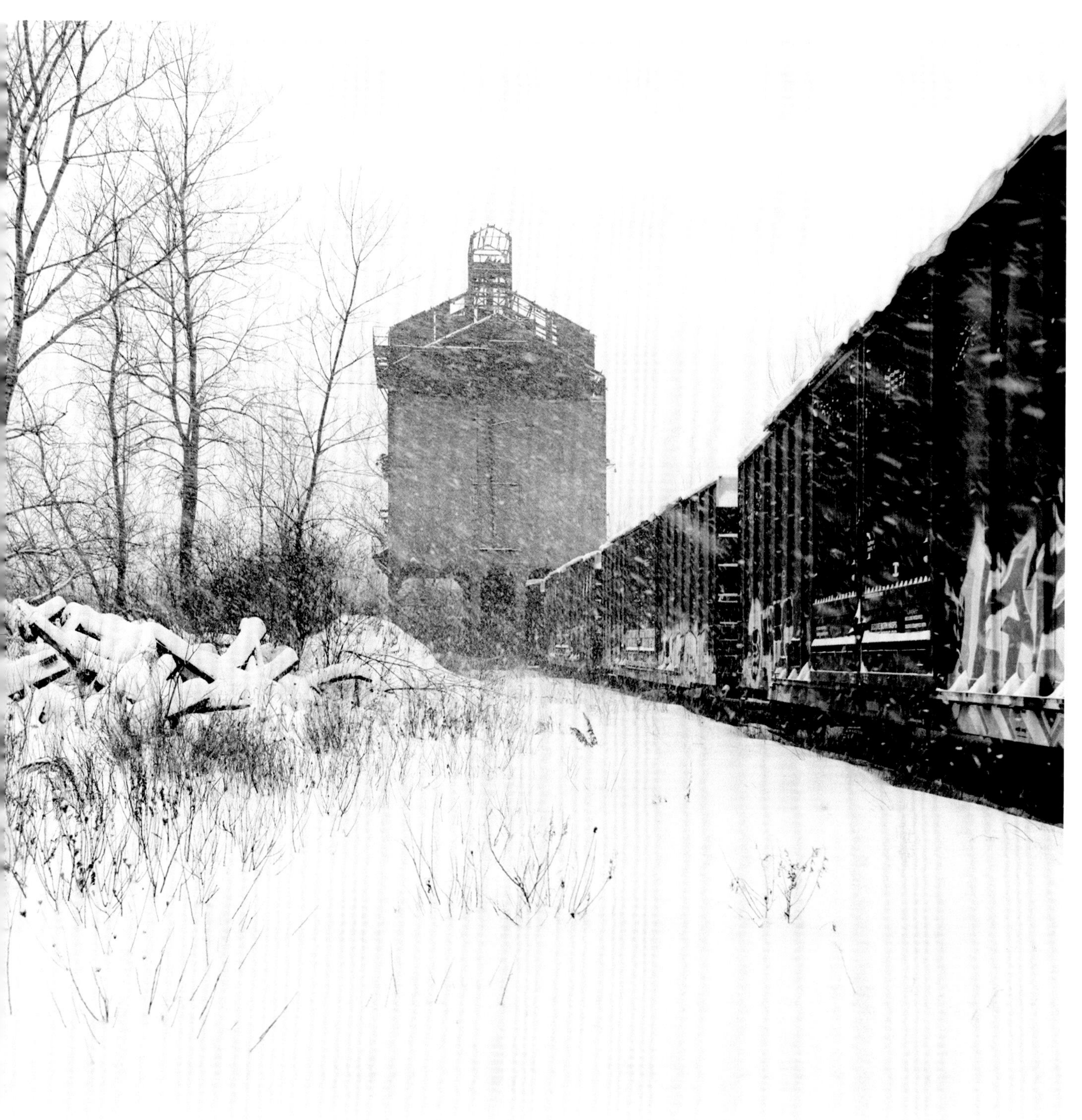

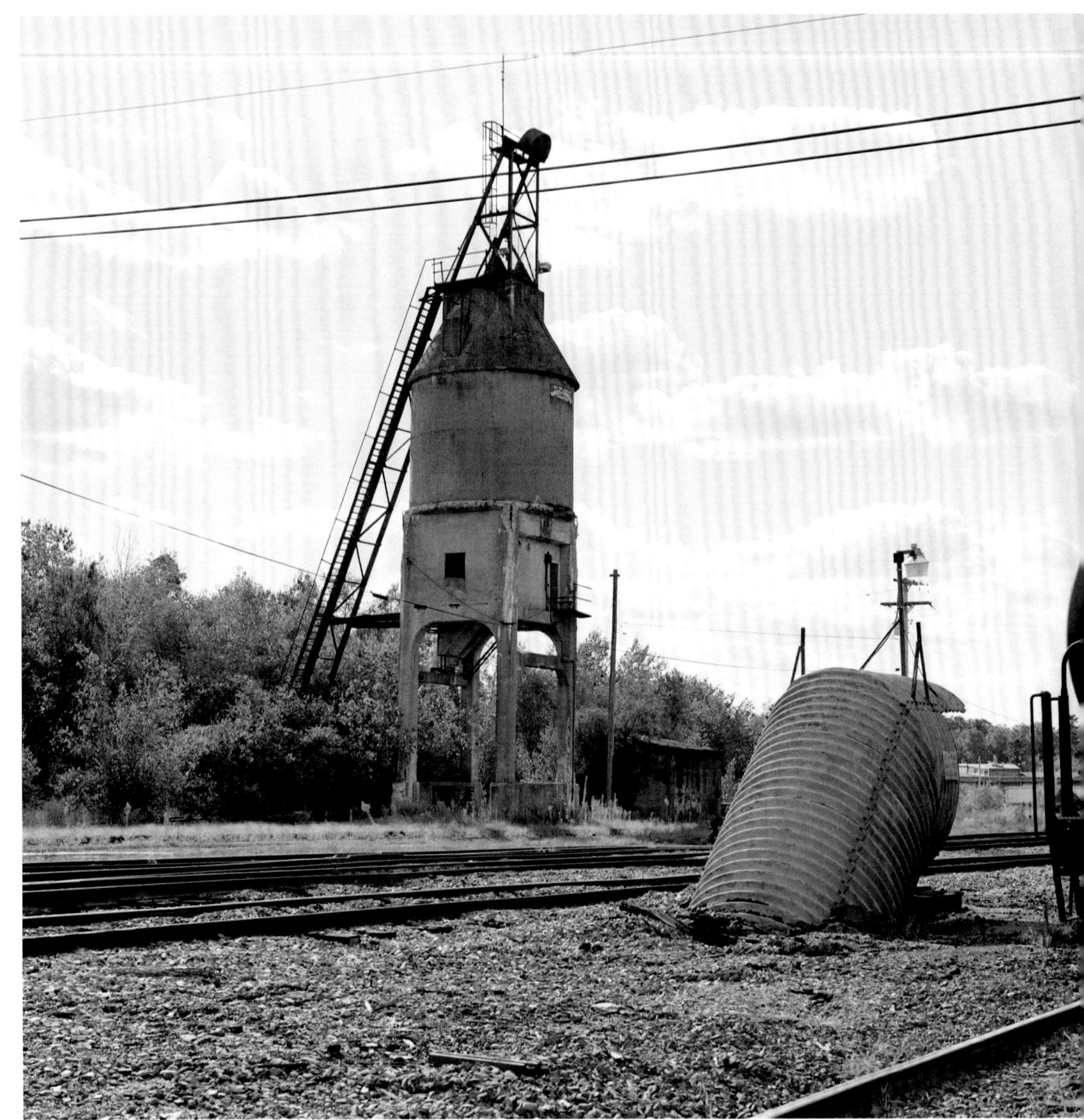

180-181 **NORTHERN MAINE JUNCTION, MAINE** Bangor & Aroostook / Maine Central 44°47'25.2"N 68°51'39.4"W

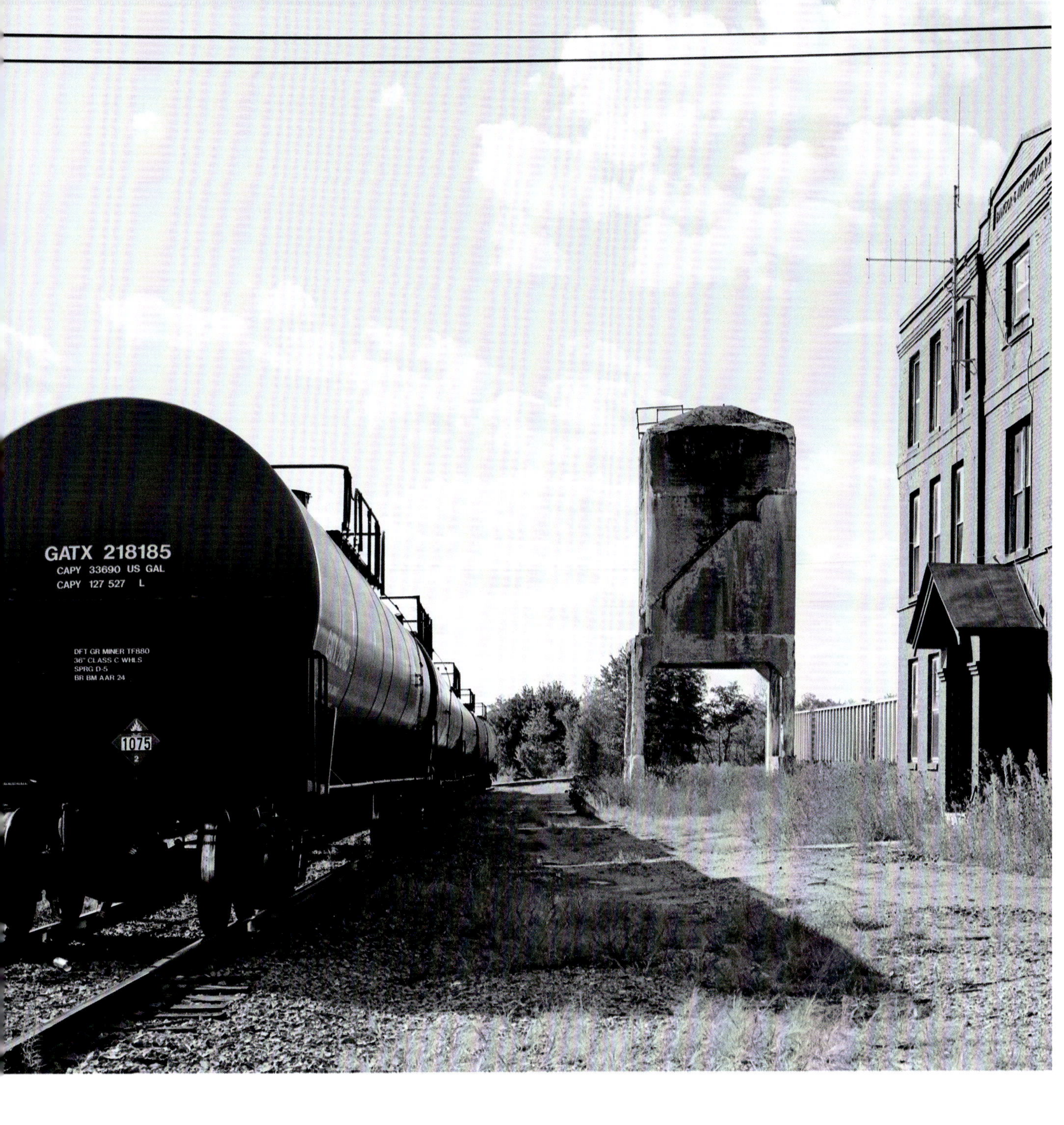
GATX 218185
CAPY 33690 US GAL
CAPY 127 527 L
DFT GR MINER TF880
36" CLASS C WHLS
SPRG D-5
BR BM AAR 24
1075
2

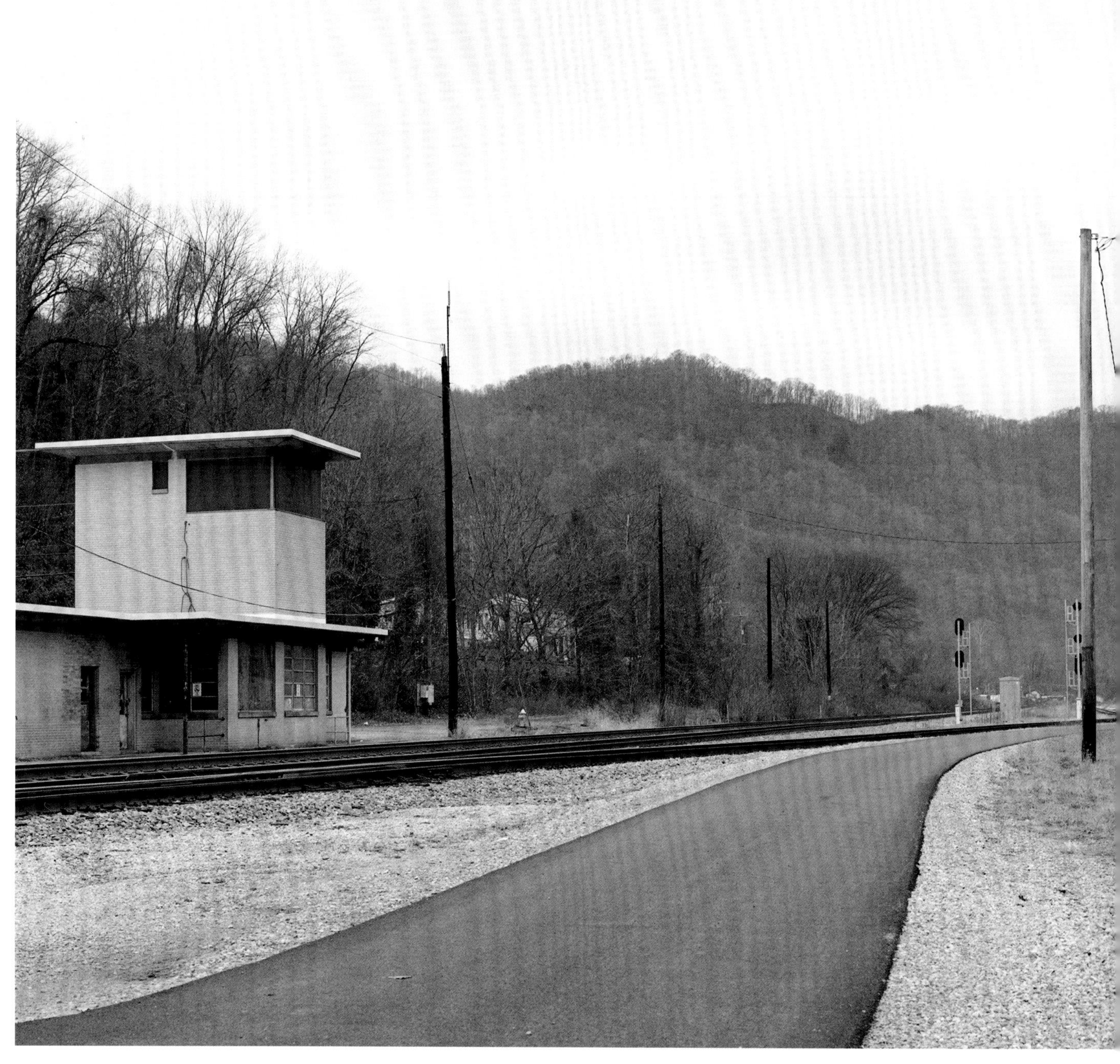

182-183 **HANDLEY, WEST VIRGINIA** Chesapeake & Ohio 38°11'07.4"N 81°21'25.2"W

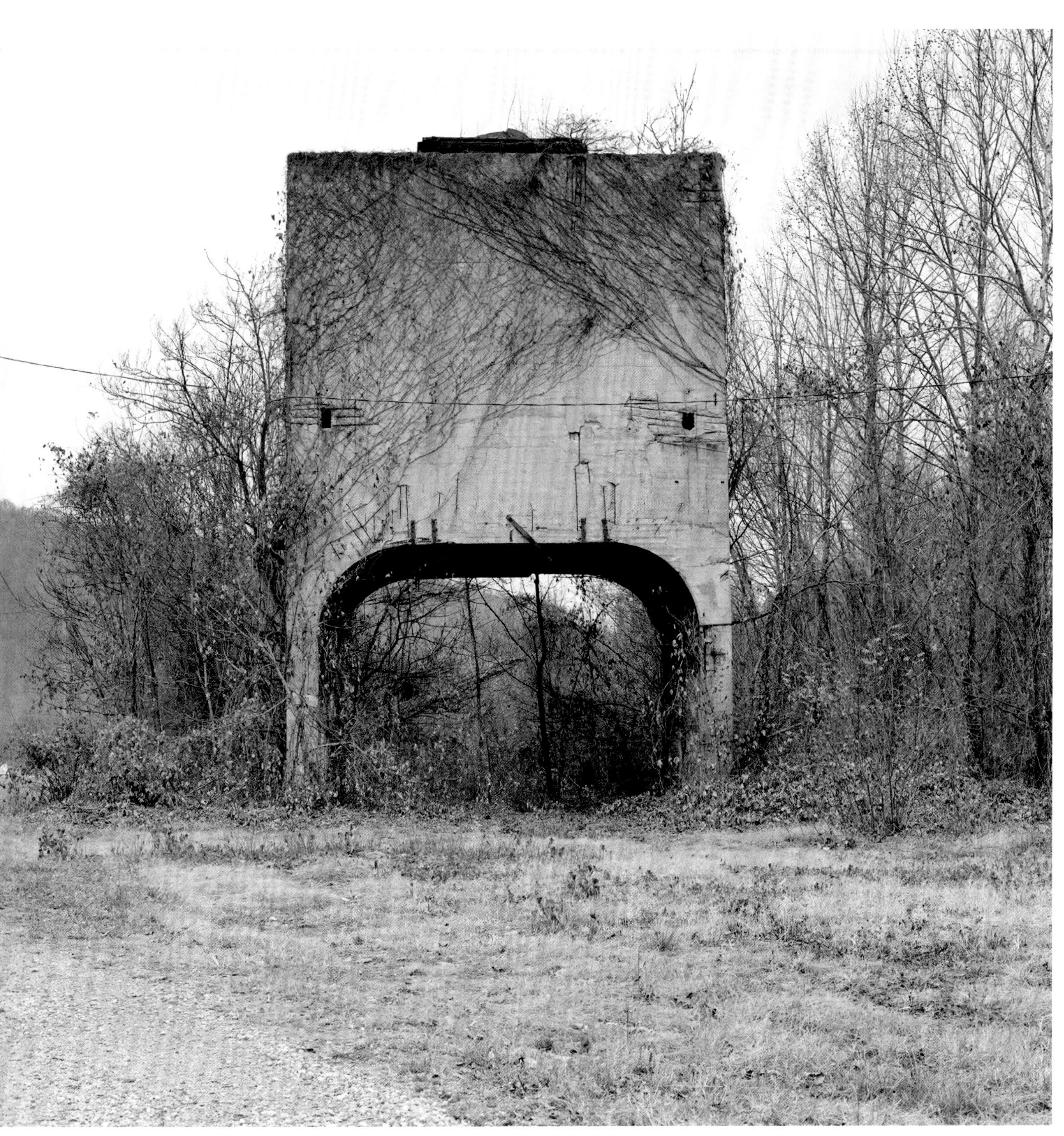

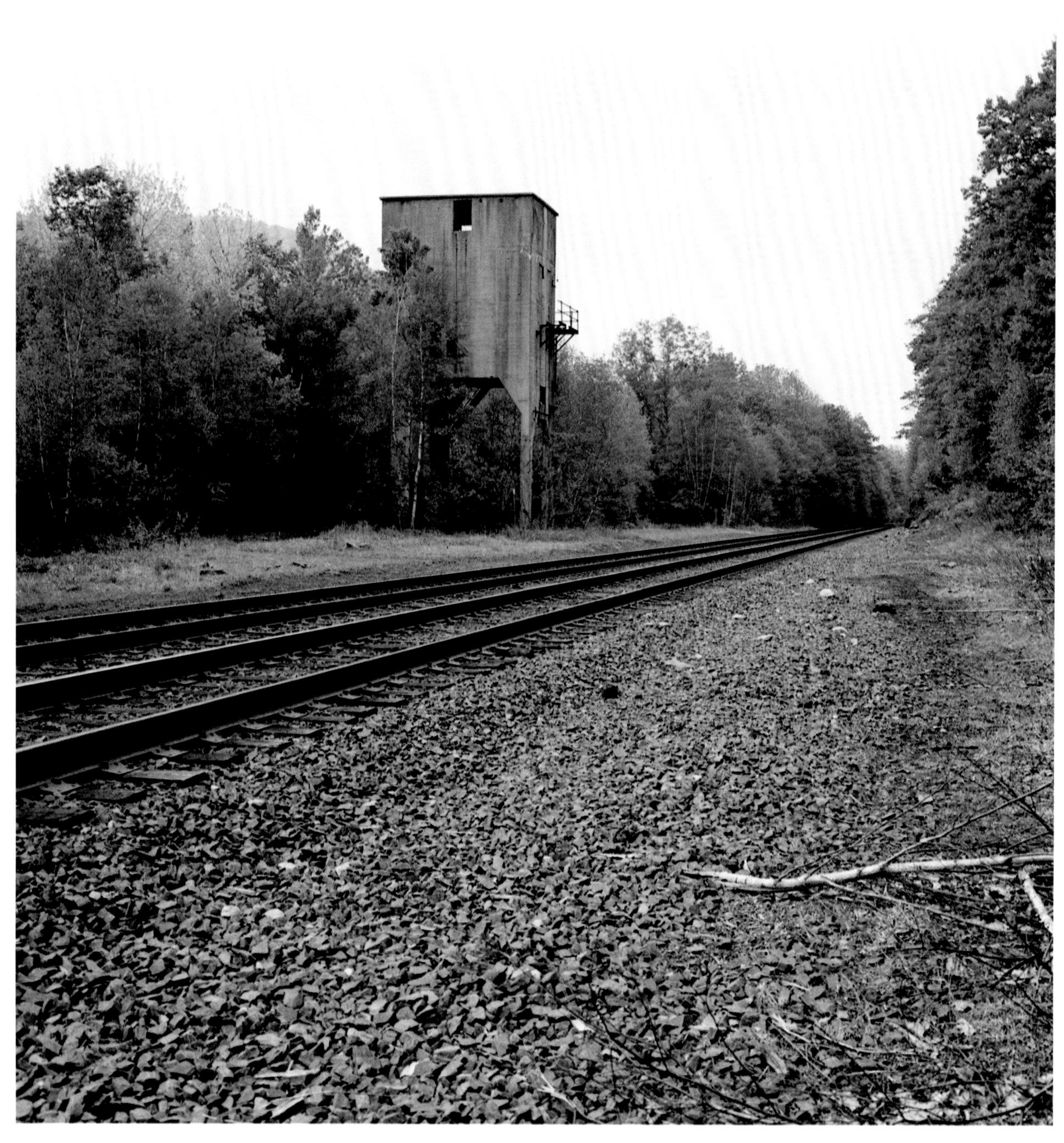

184 **CHESTER, MASSACHUSETTS** Boston & Albany 42°17'14.5"N 72°58'56.2"W (above)

185 **AYLMER, ONTARIO** Canadian National 42°46'49.0"N 80°59'46.4"W (right)

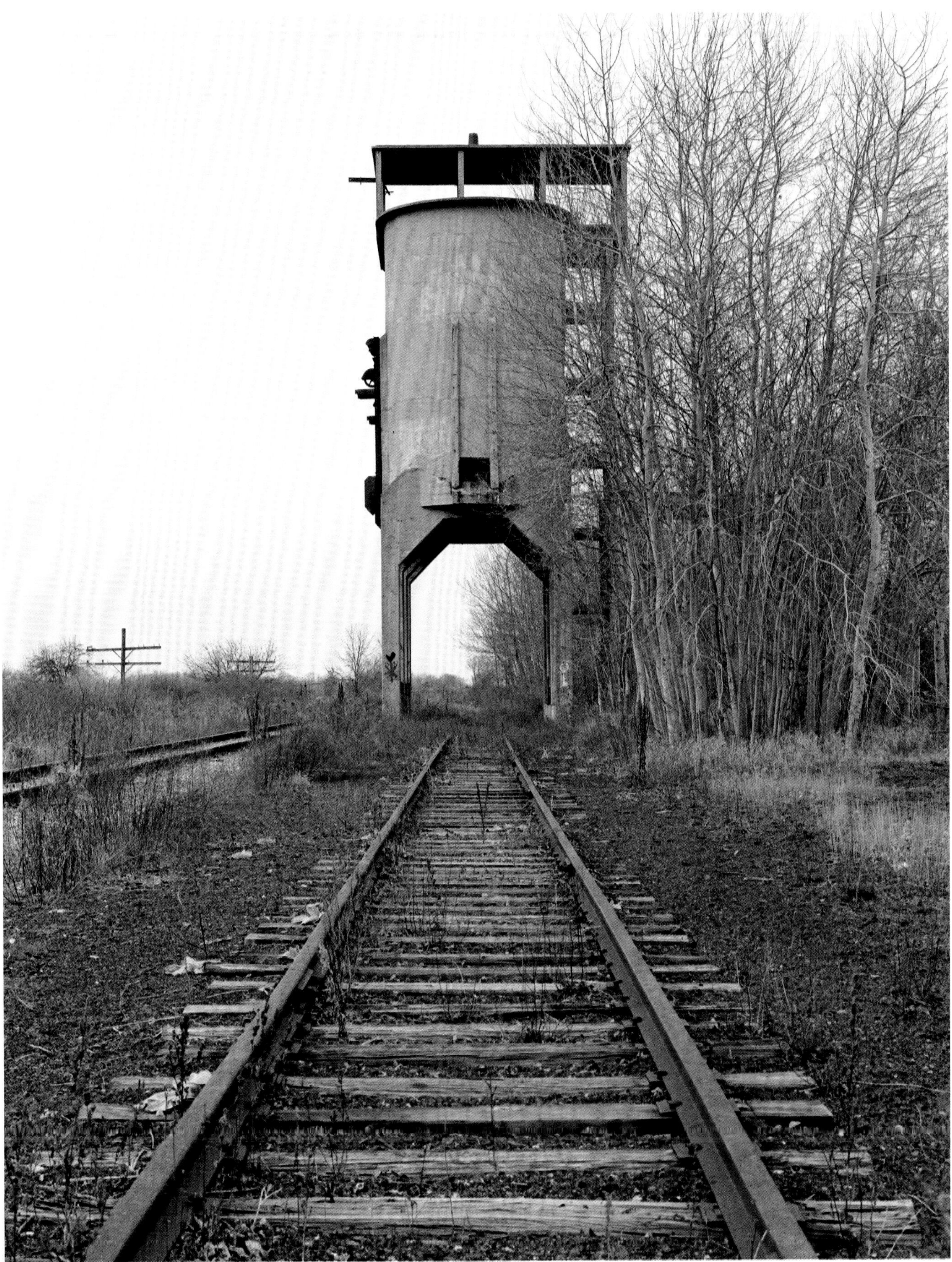

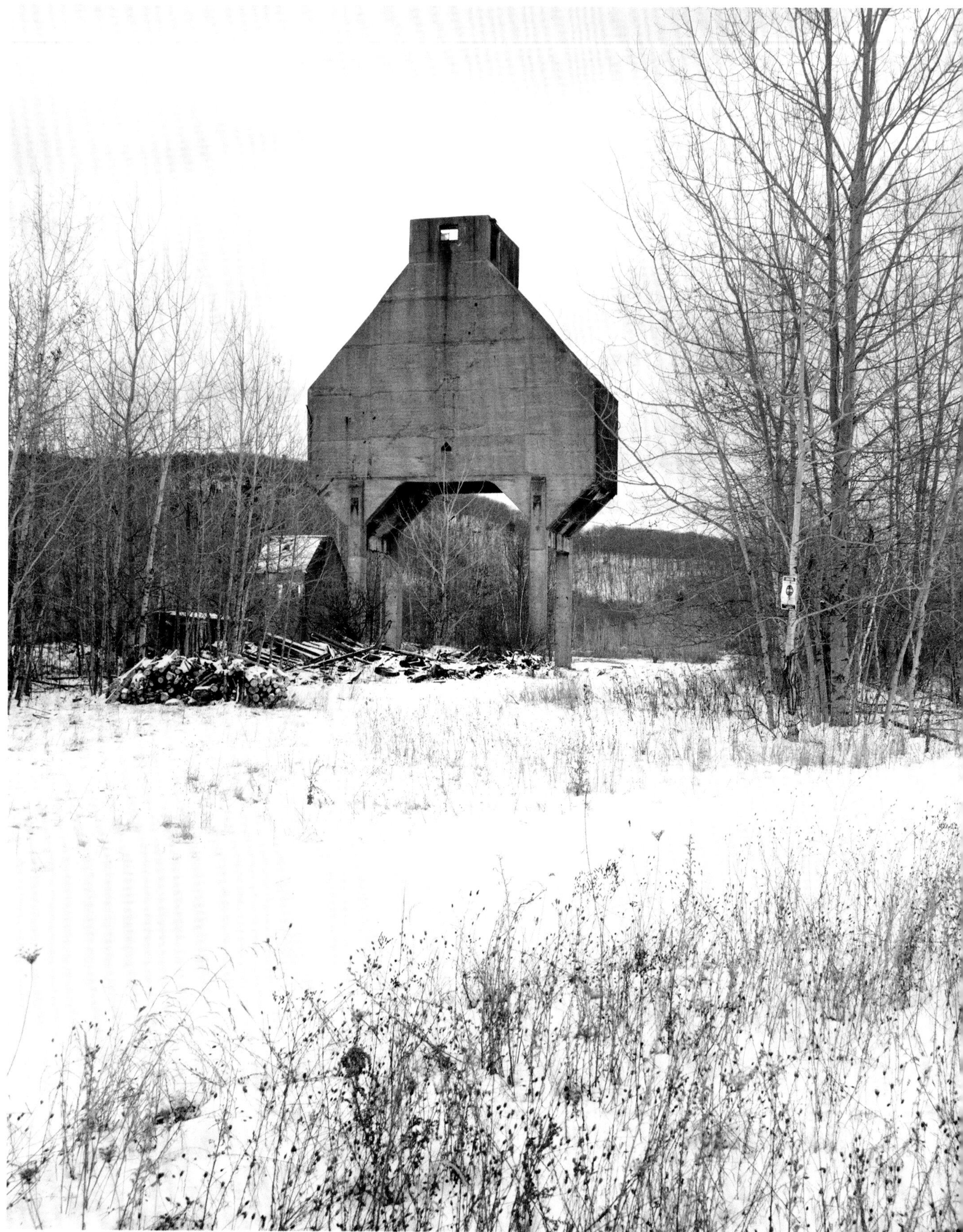

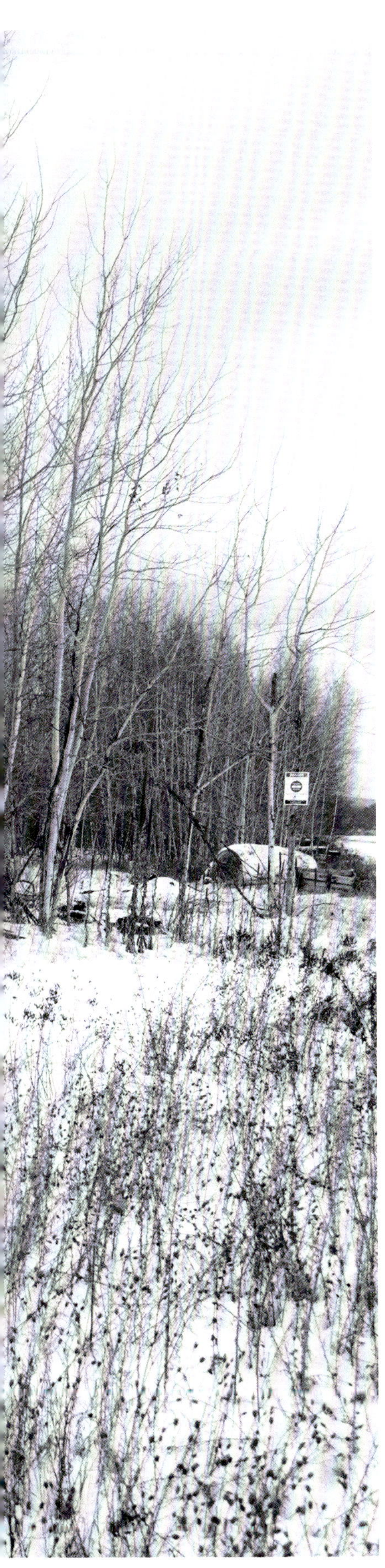

186-187 **ONEONTA, NEW YORK** Delaware & Hudson 42°26’53.2”N 75°05’13.8”W

 BALCONY FALLS, VIRGINIA Chesapeake & Ohio 37°37'37.0"N 79°27'27.7"W

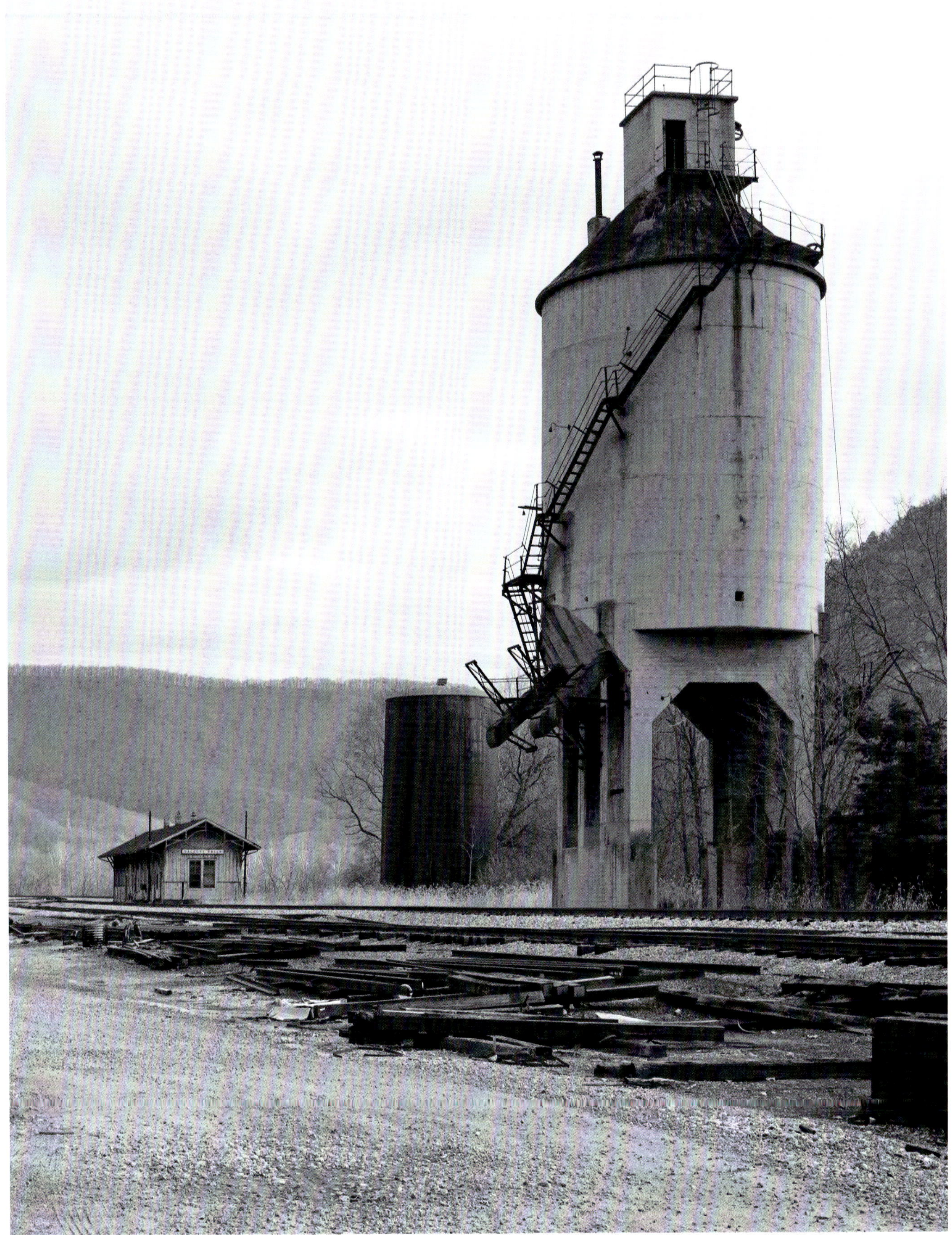

190-191 **AKRON JUNCTION, OHIO** Baltimore & Ohio 41°05'14.2"N 81°29'14.2"W

Following Spread

GILMAN, ILLINOIS Illinois Central 40°47'15.4"N 87°59'22.1"W

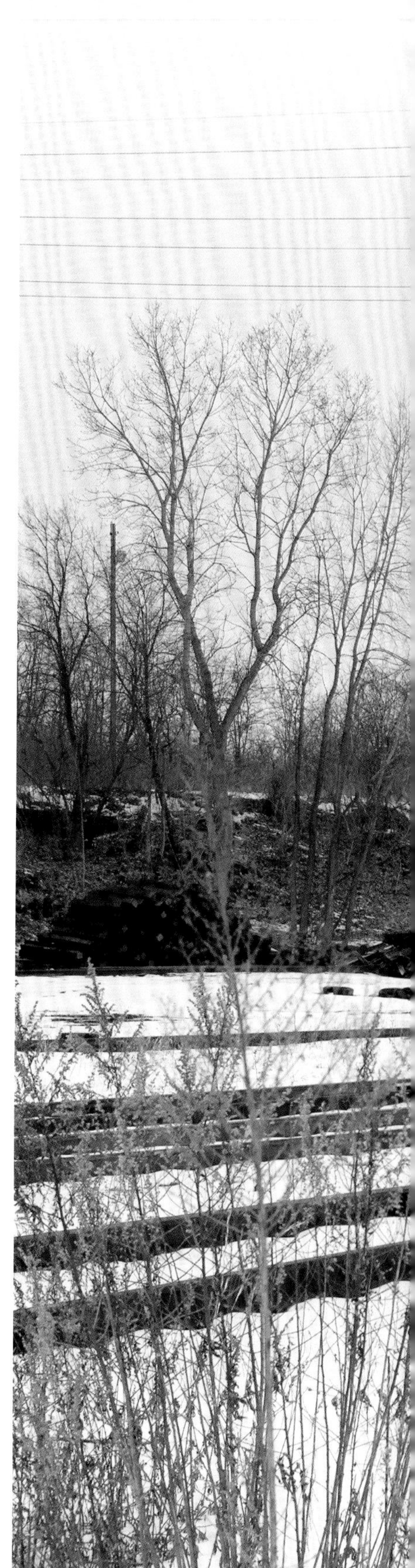

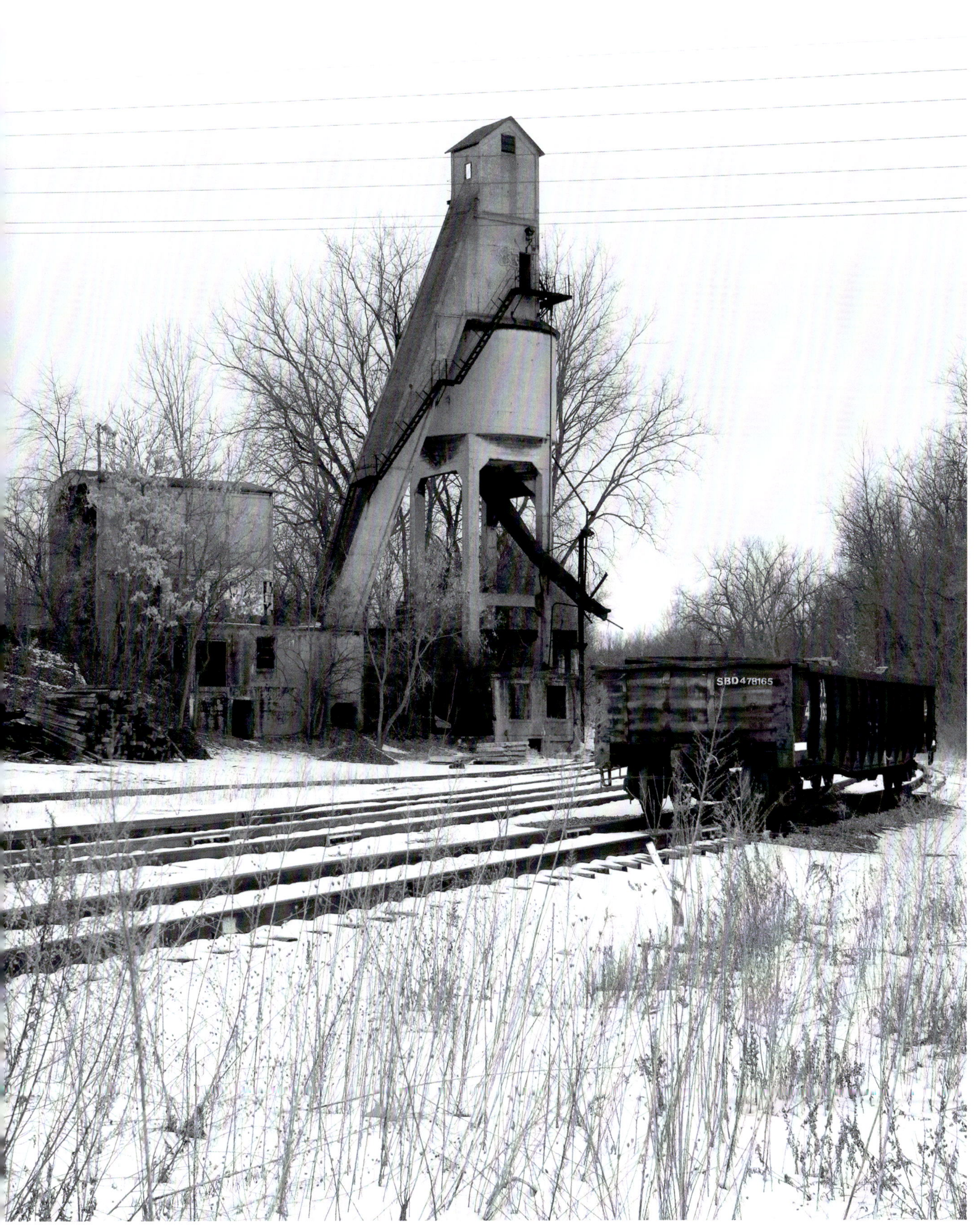
SBD478165

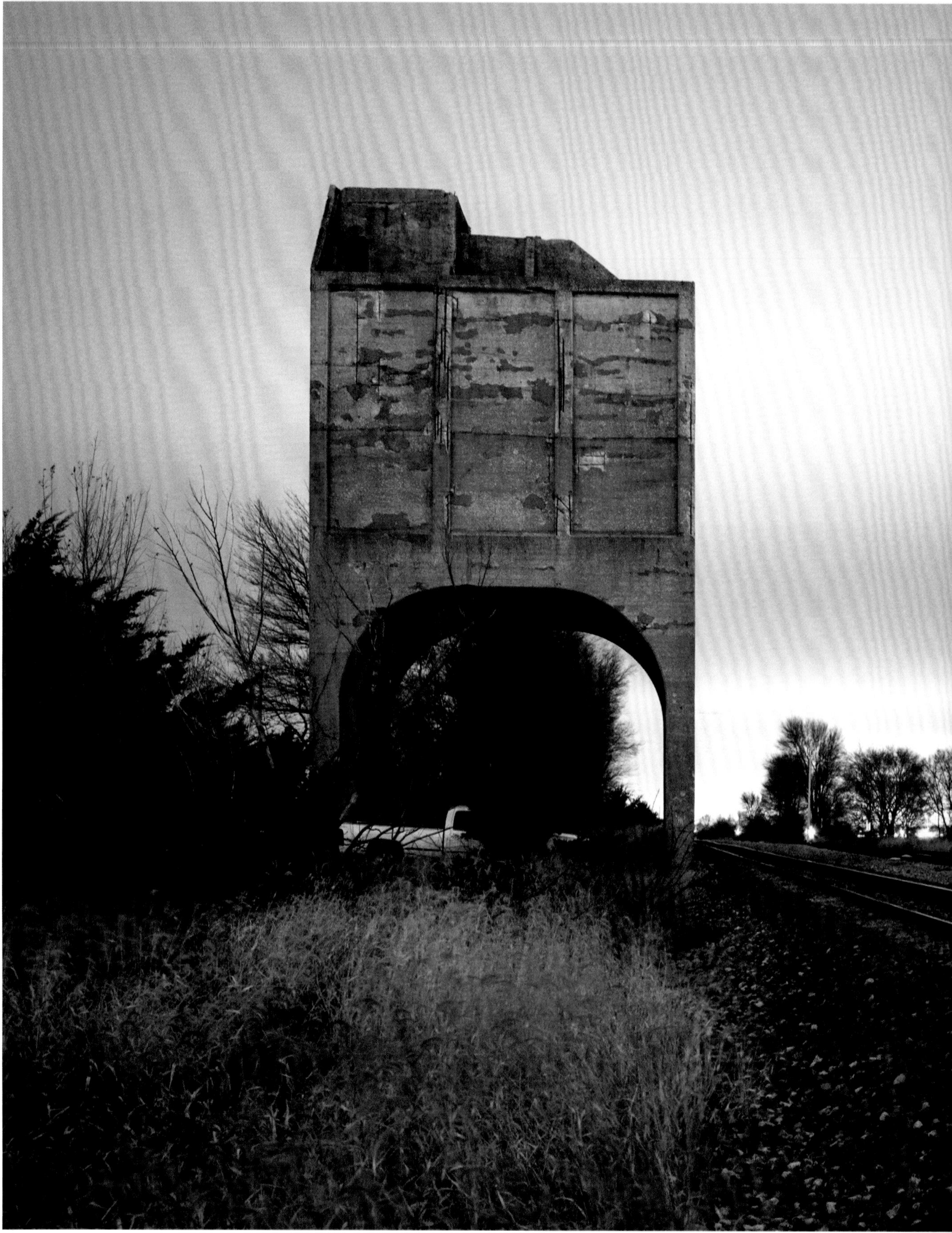

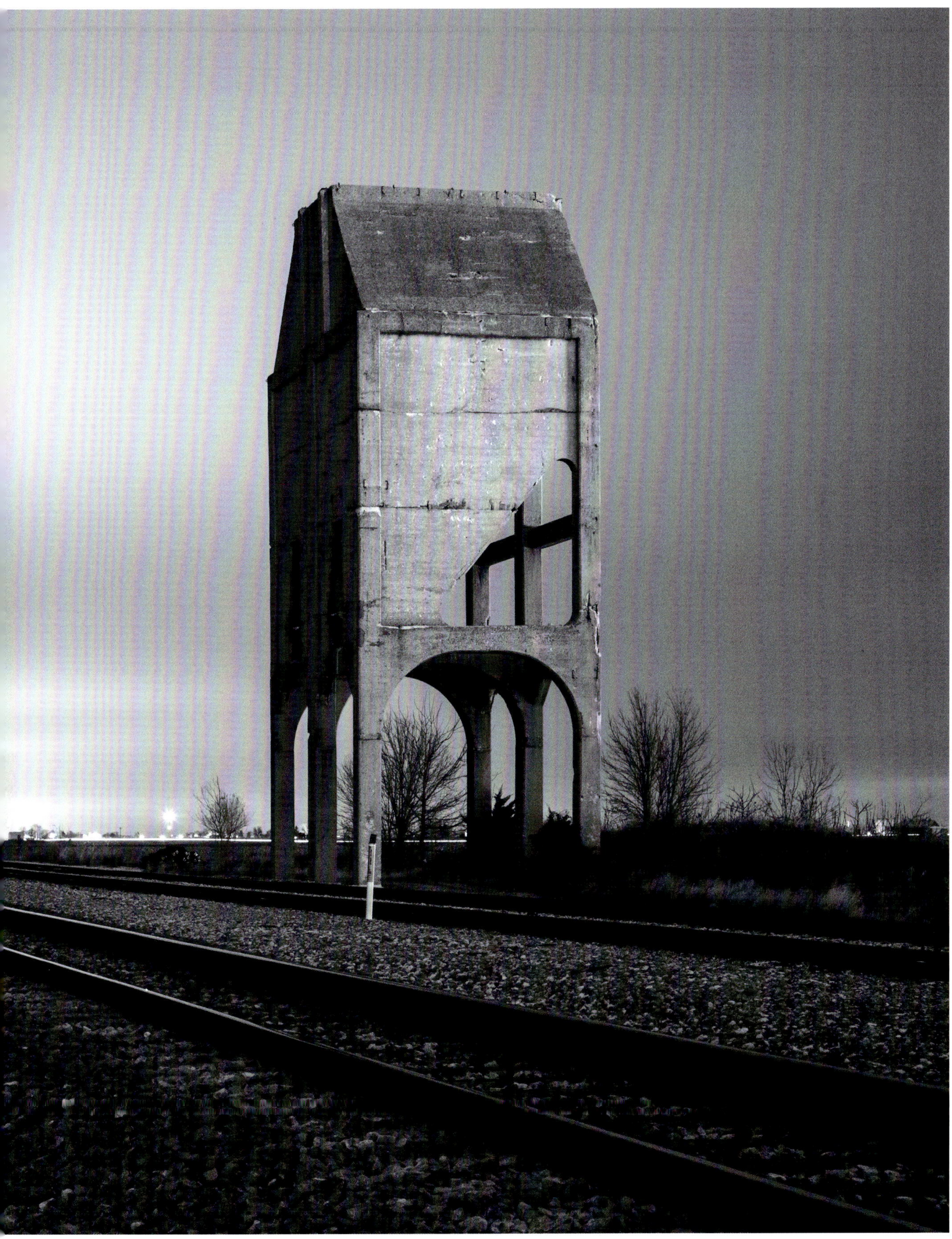

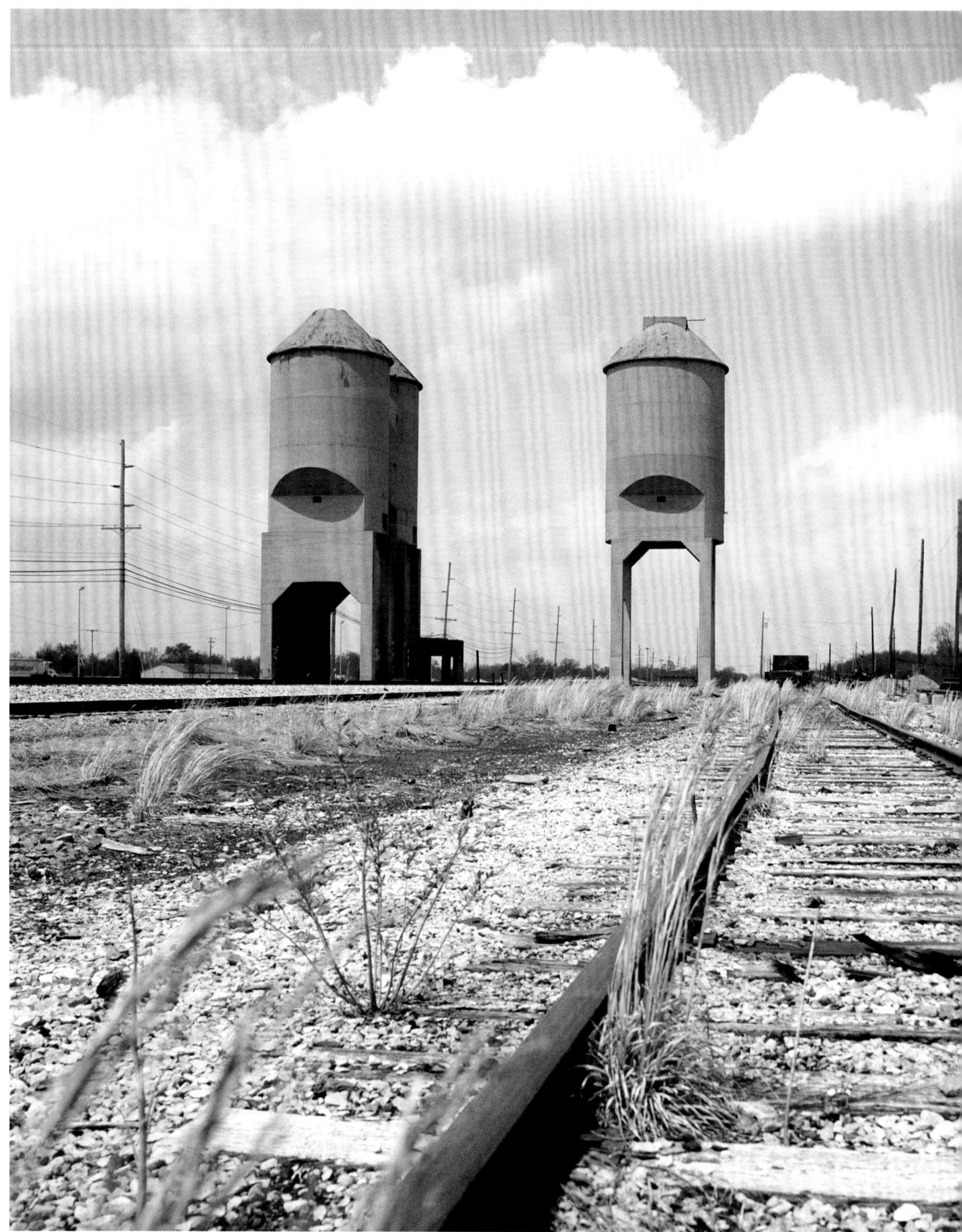

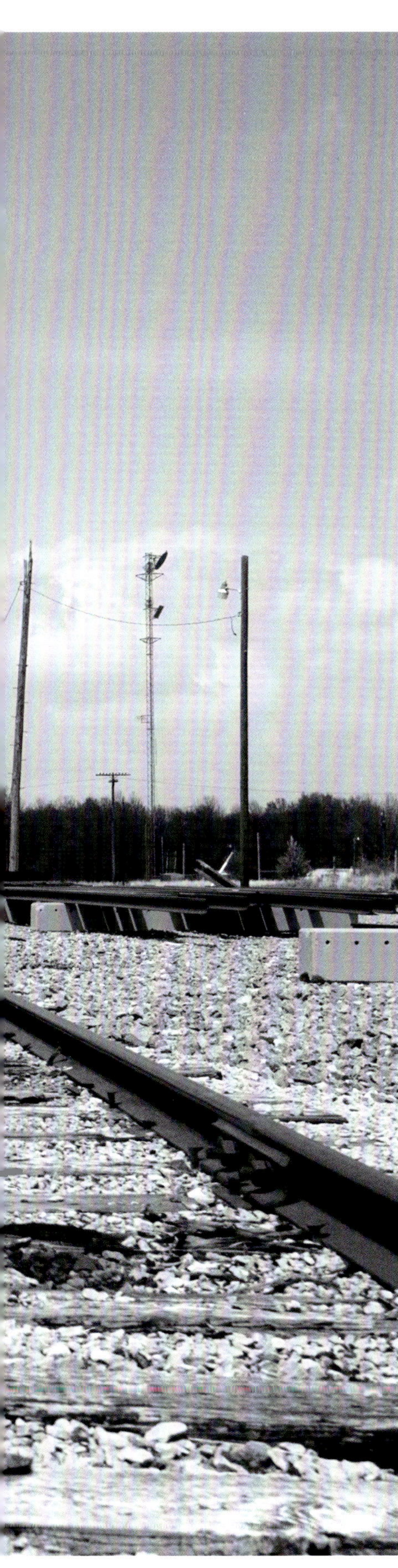

194-195 **CARBONDALE, ILLINOIS** Illinois Central 37°44'23.5"N 89°13'03.9"W

196-197 **LEES, MARYLAND** Baltiimore & Ohio 39°15'13.2"N 76°46'14.6"W

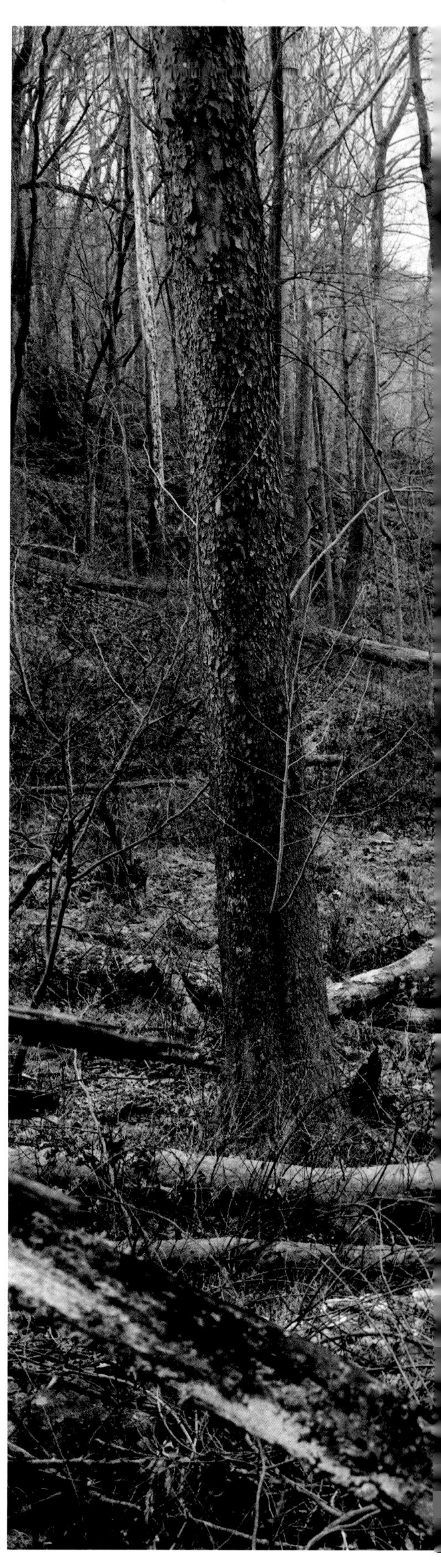

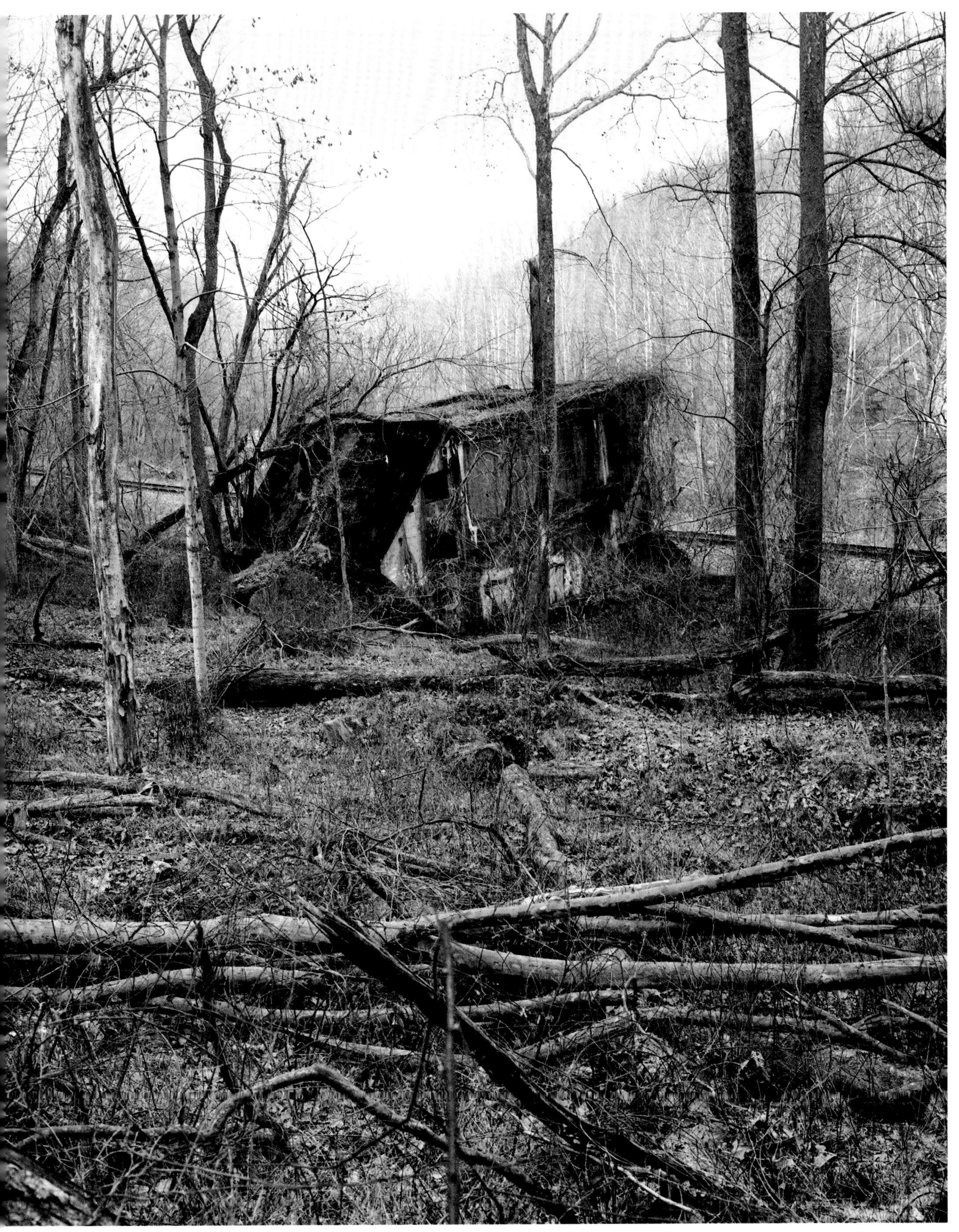

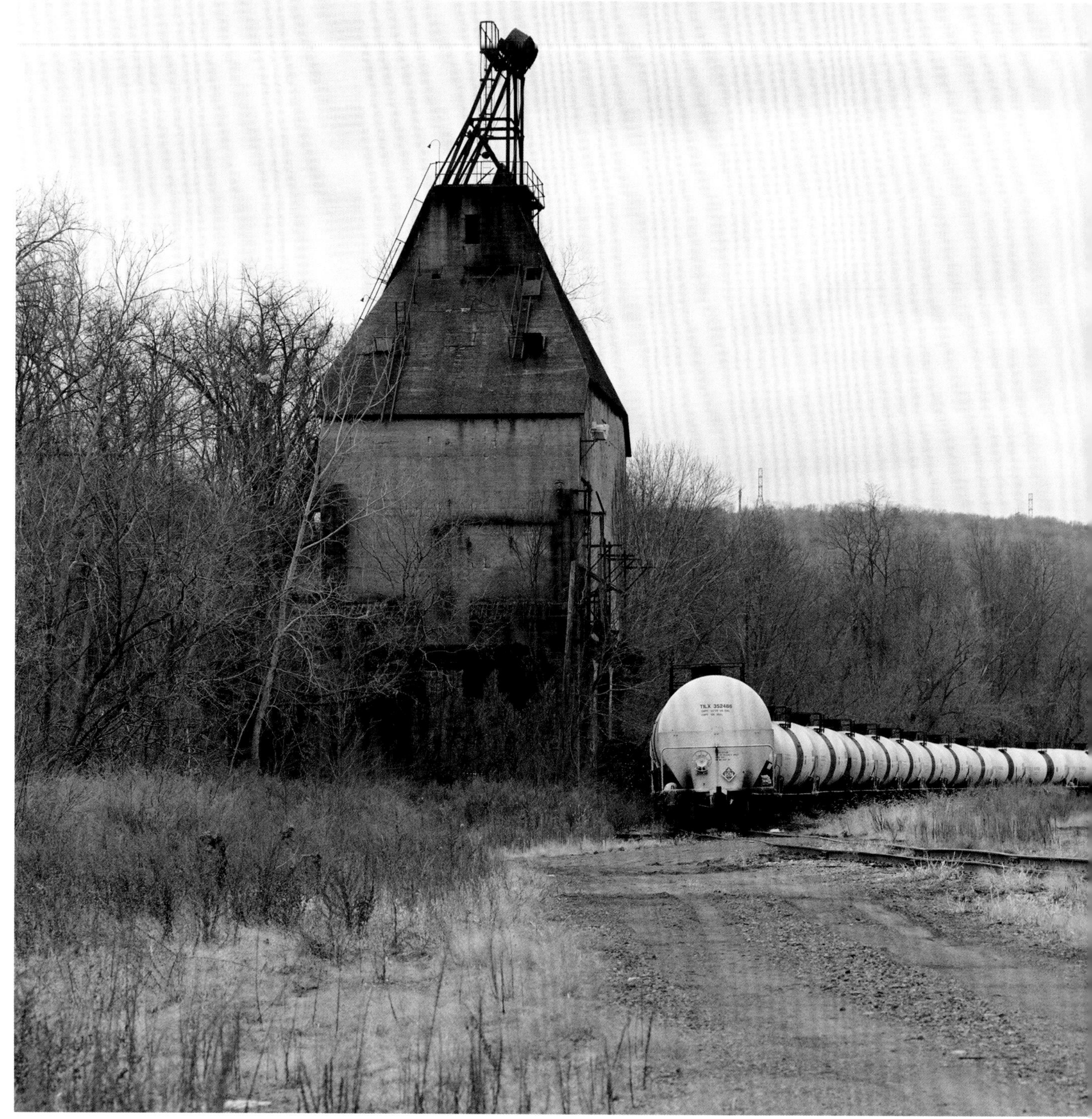

198-199 **COXTON, PENNSYLVANIA** Lehigh Valley 41°21'15.5"N 75°48'08.7"W

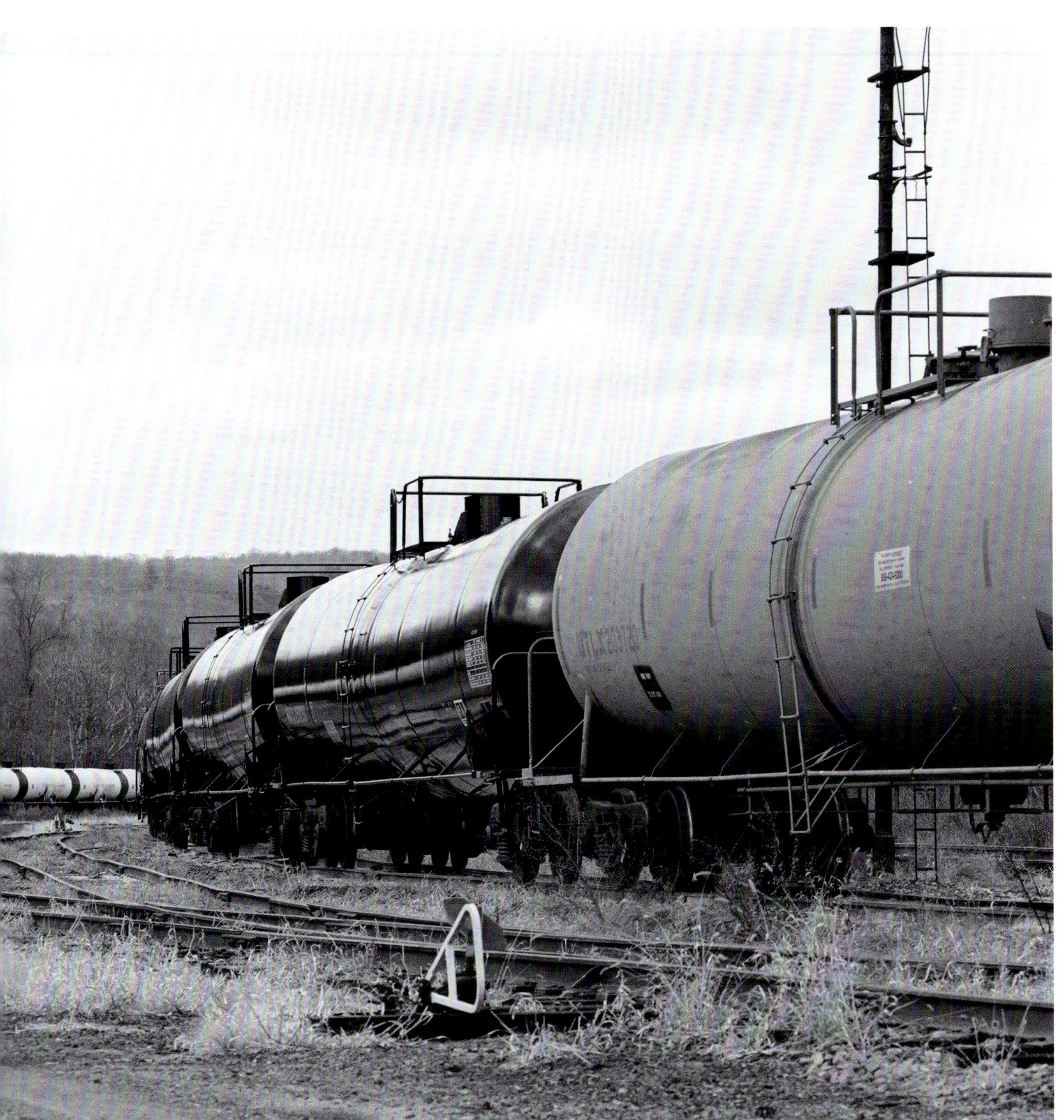

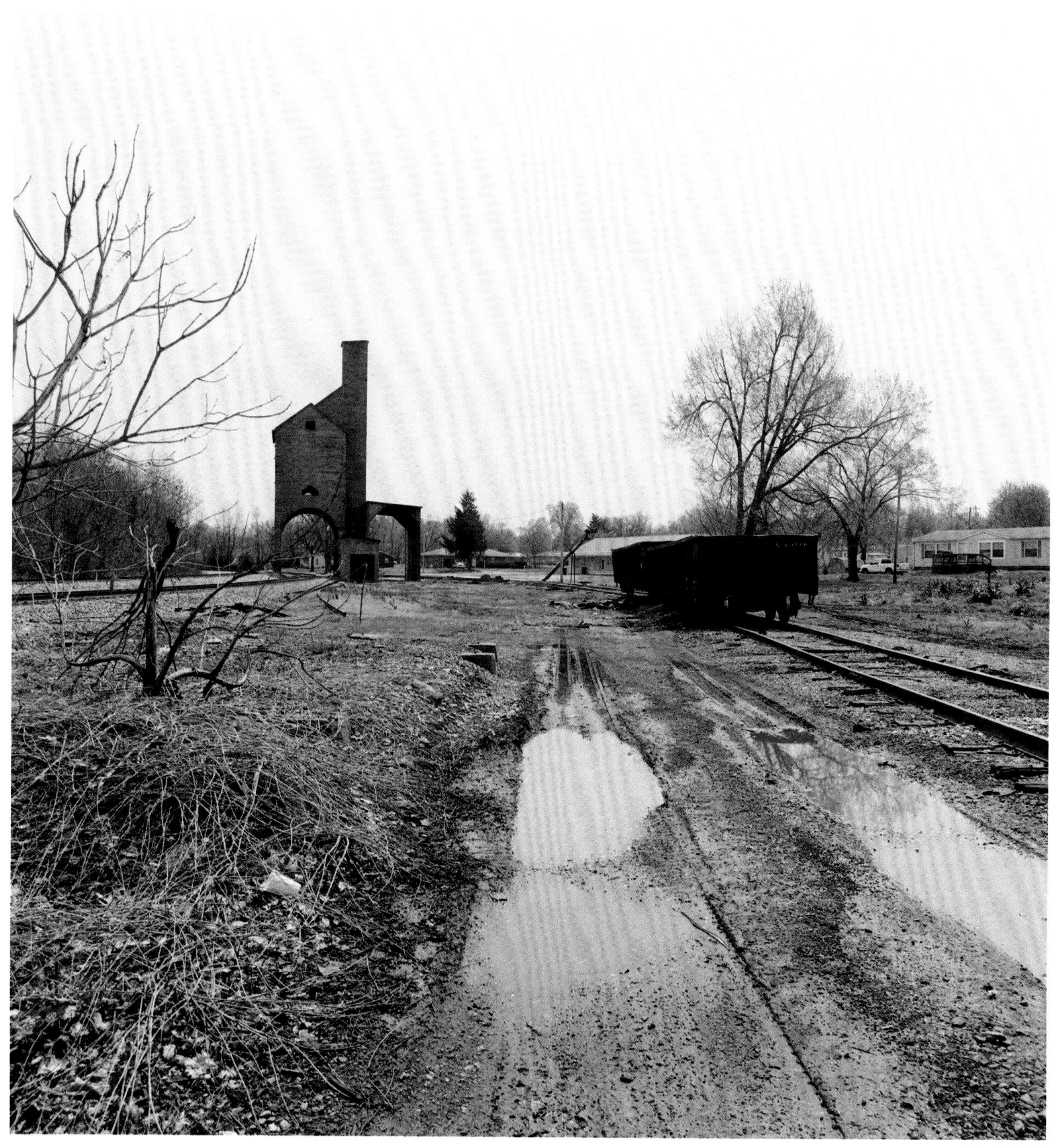

 IRVINGTON, KENTUCKY Louisville & Nashville 37°52’53.9”N 86°16’53.6”W

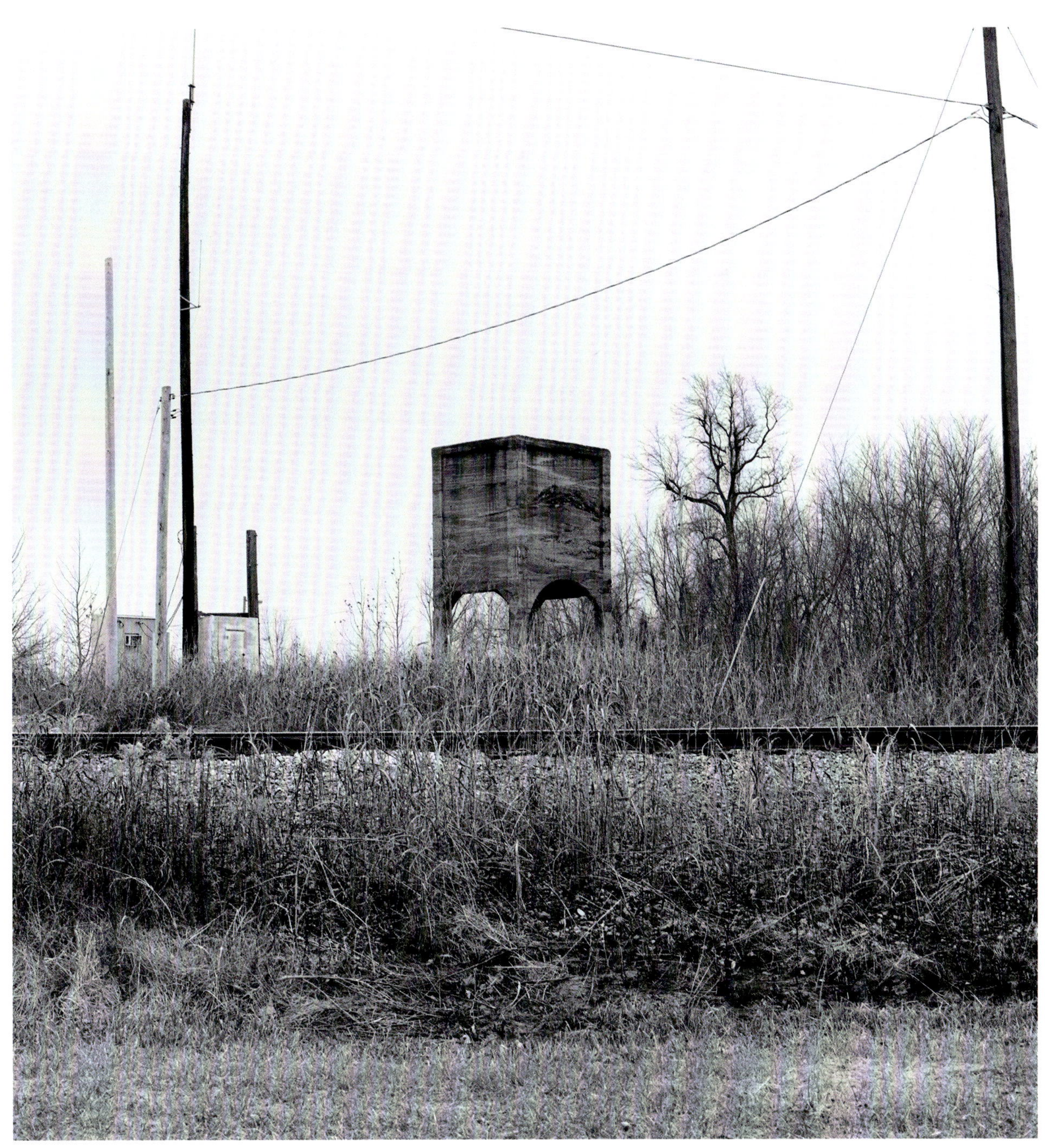

 OWENSBORO, KENTUCKY Illinois Central 37°46'18.0"N 87°05'03.0"W

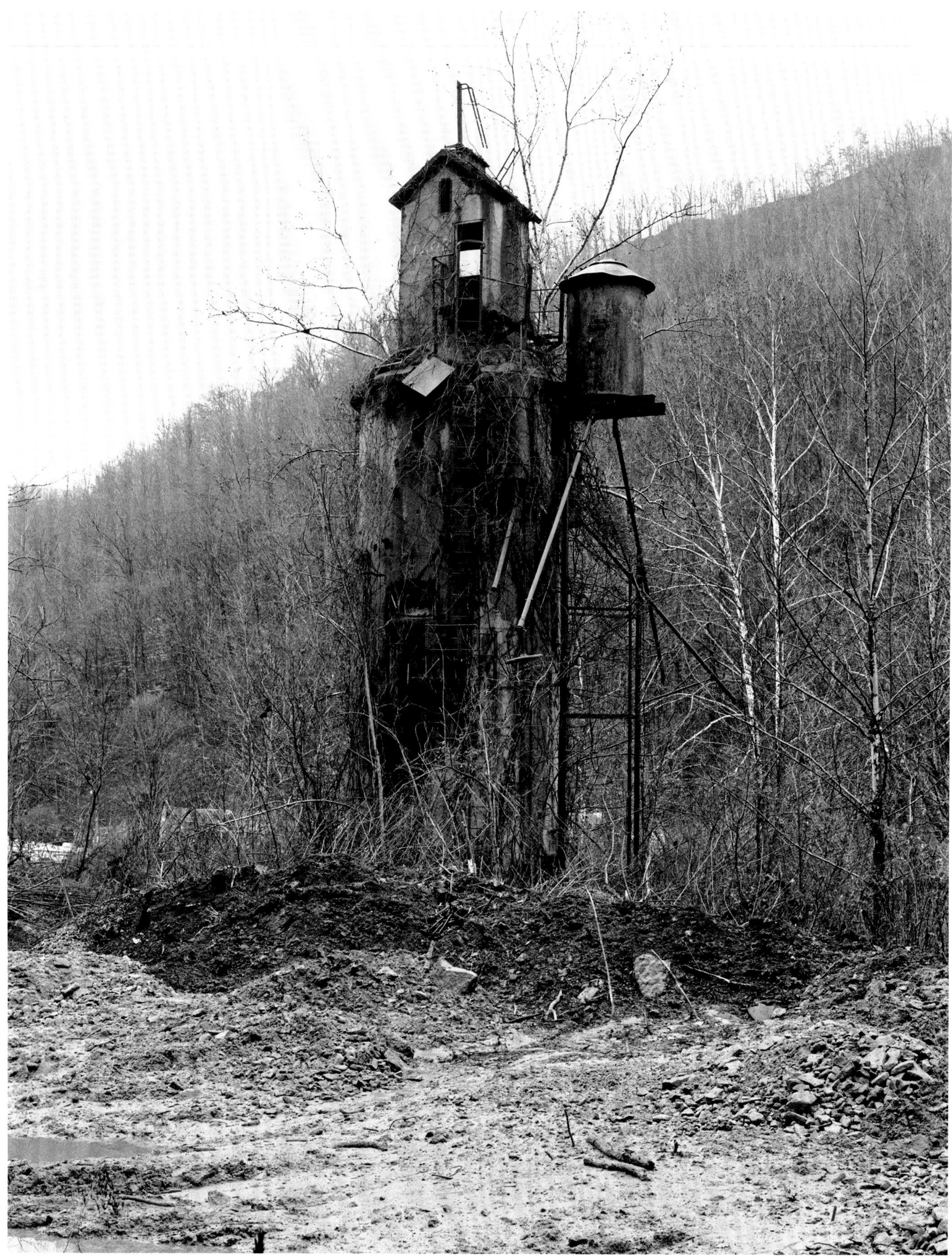

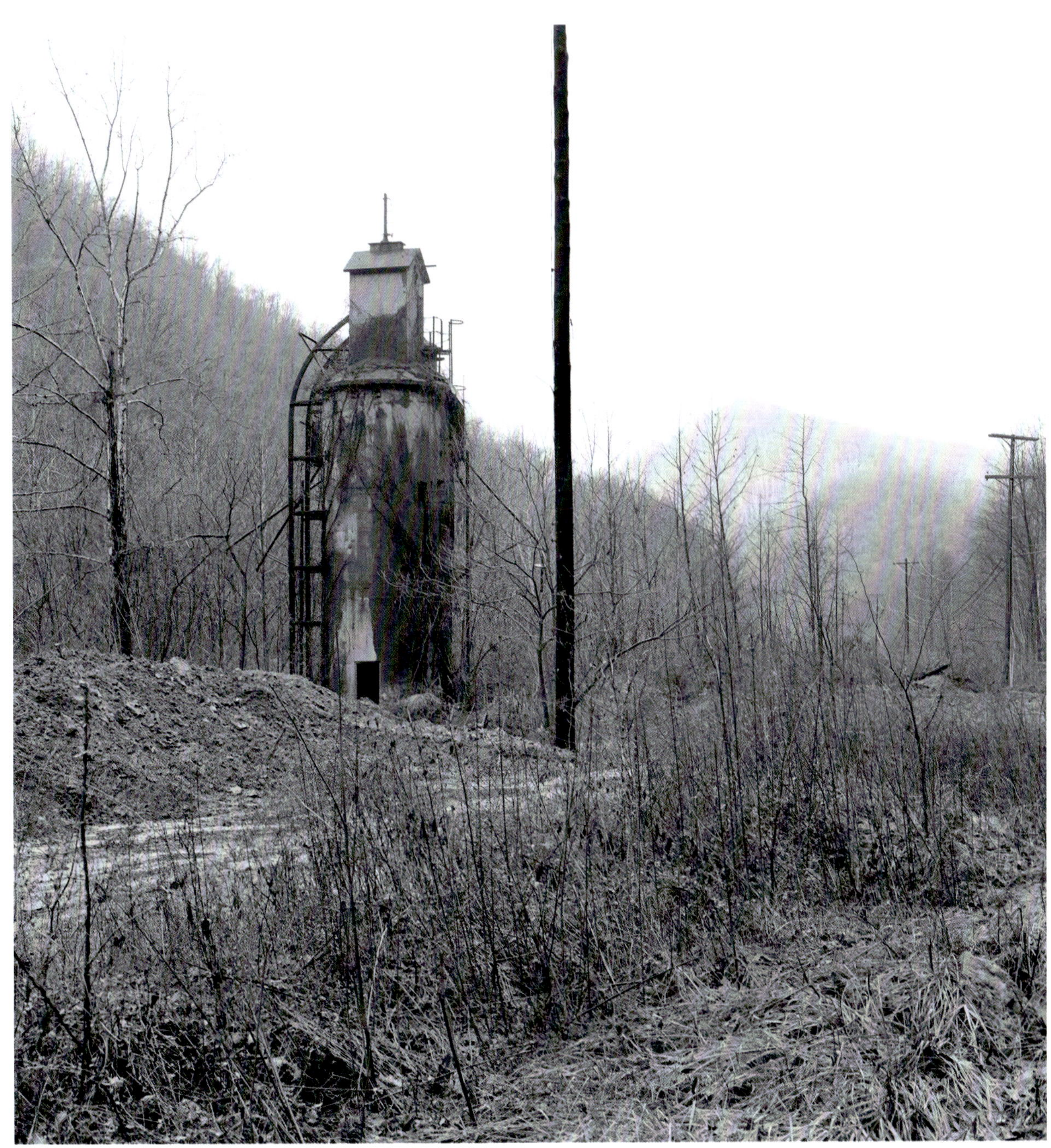

 CANE FORK, WEST VIRGINIA Chesapeake & Ohio 38°05′41.8″N 81°26′29.7″W

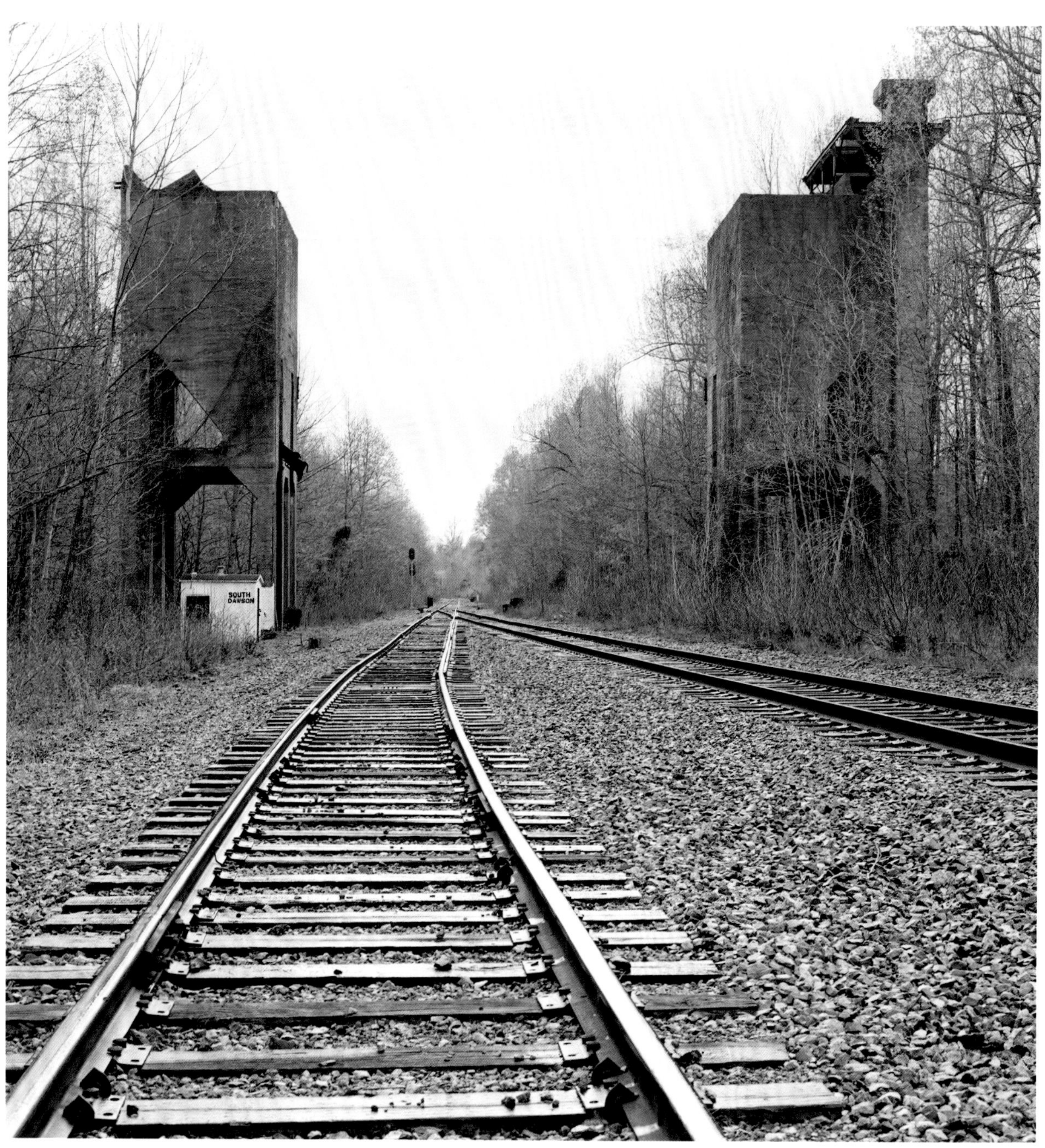

 DAWSON SPRINGS, KENTUCKY Illinois Central 37°09'54.1"N 87°40'41.1"W

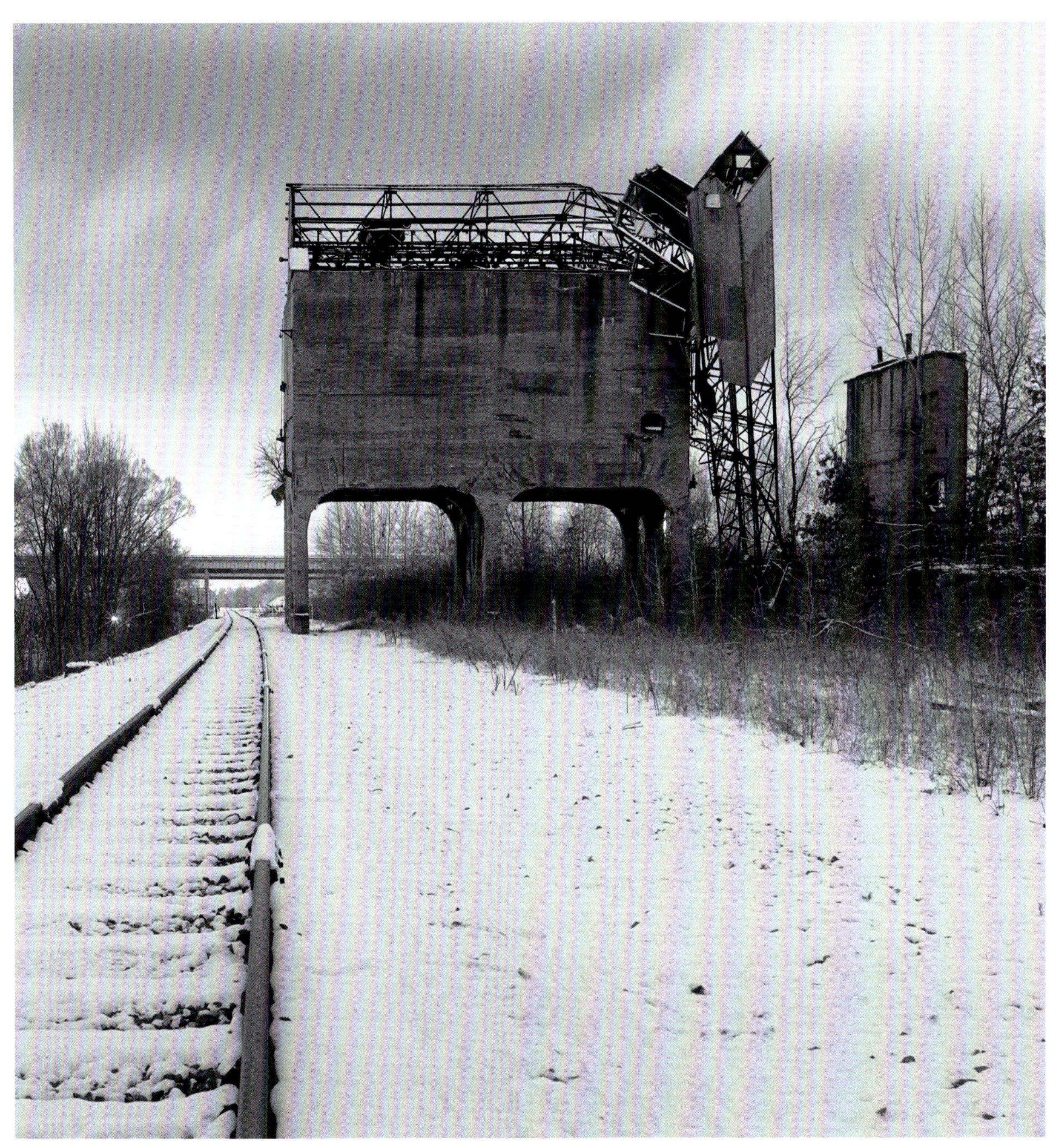

205 **GIRARD, OHIO** Pennsylvania 41°09'01.3"N 80°42'18.2"W

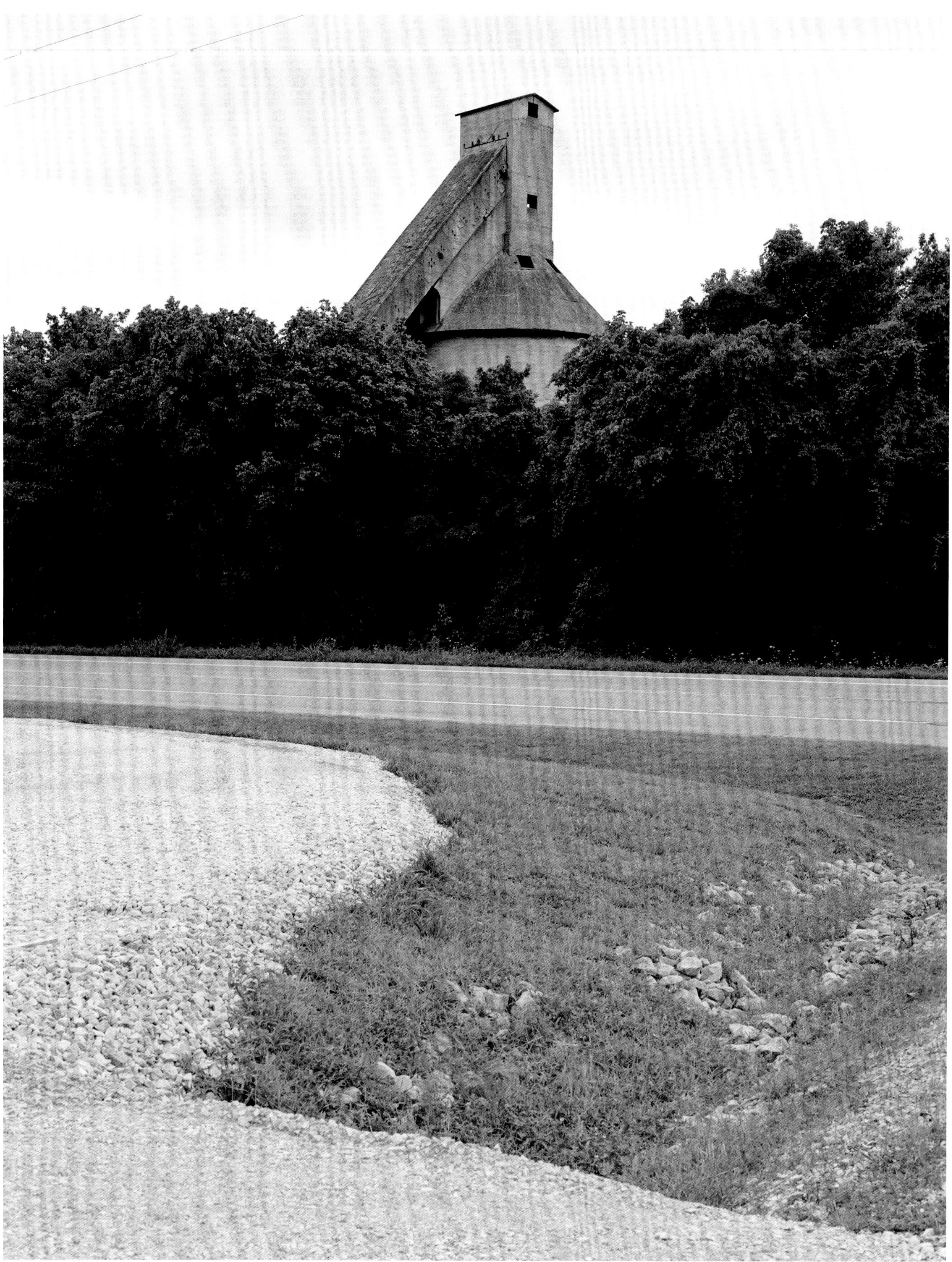

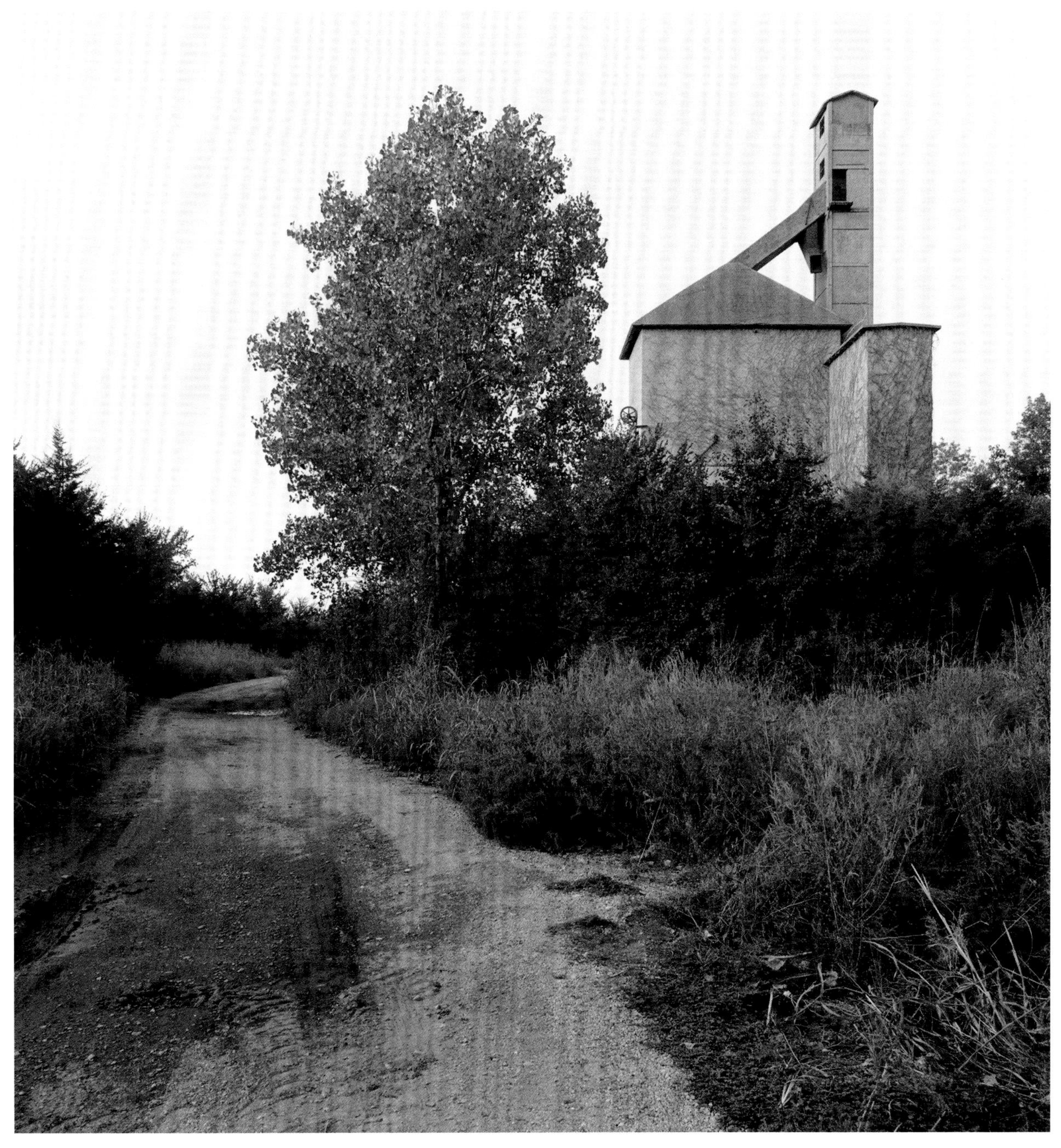

206 **BLUEFIELD, WEST VIRGINIA** Norfolk & Western 37°16'17.5"N 81°13'13.8"W (left)

207 **CUSHING, OKLAHOMA** Atchison, Topeka & Santa Fe 35°58'34.4"N 96°46'29.9"W (above)

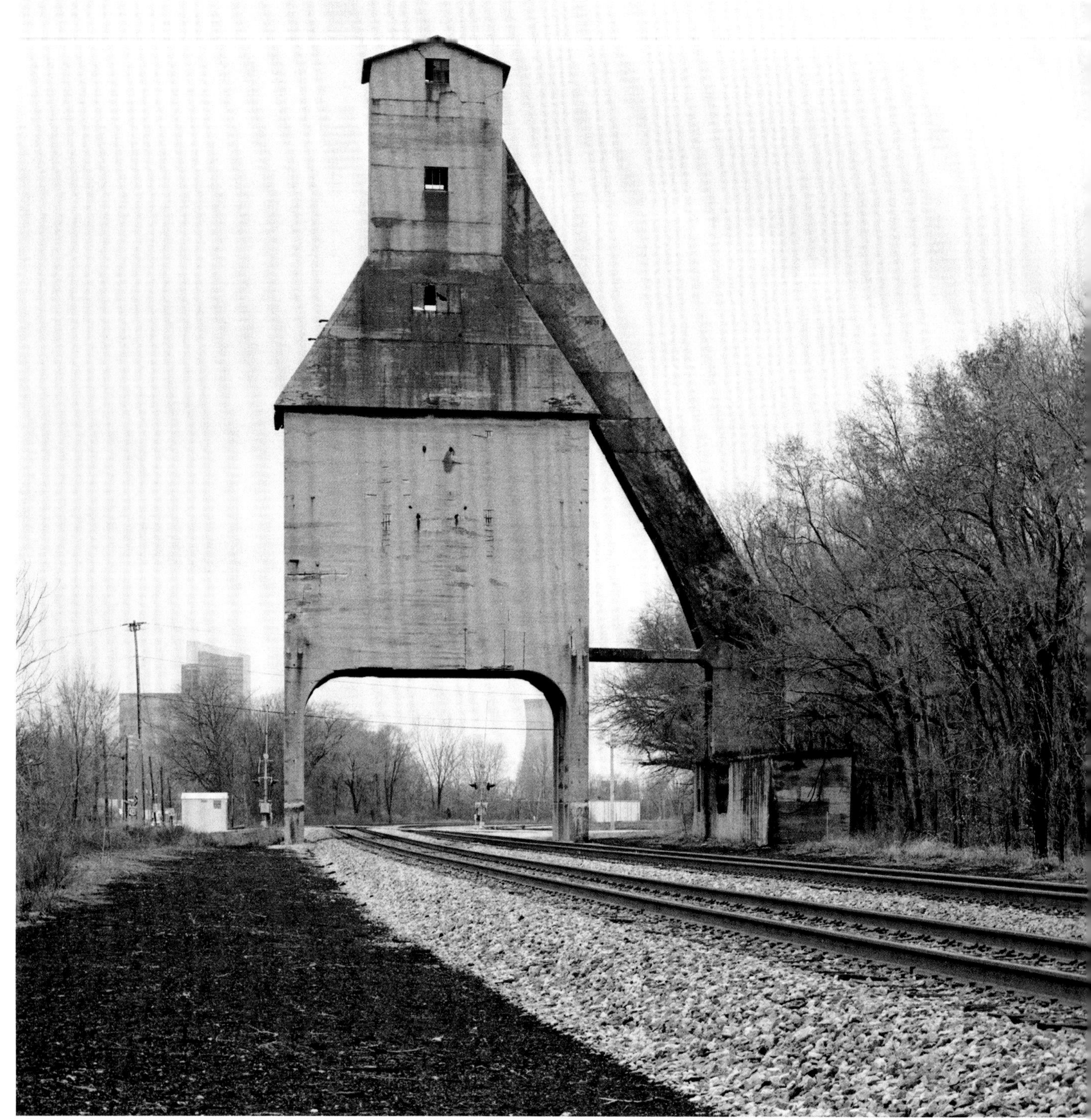

208-209 **MICHIGAN CITY, INDIANA** Michigan Central 41°43'33.2"N 86°52'31.7"W

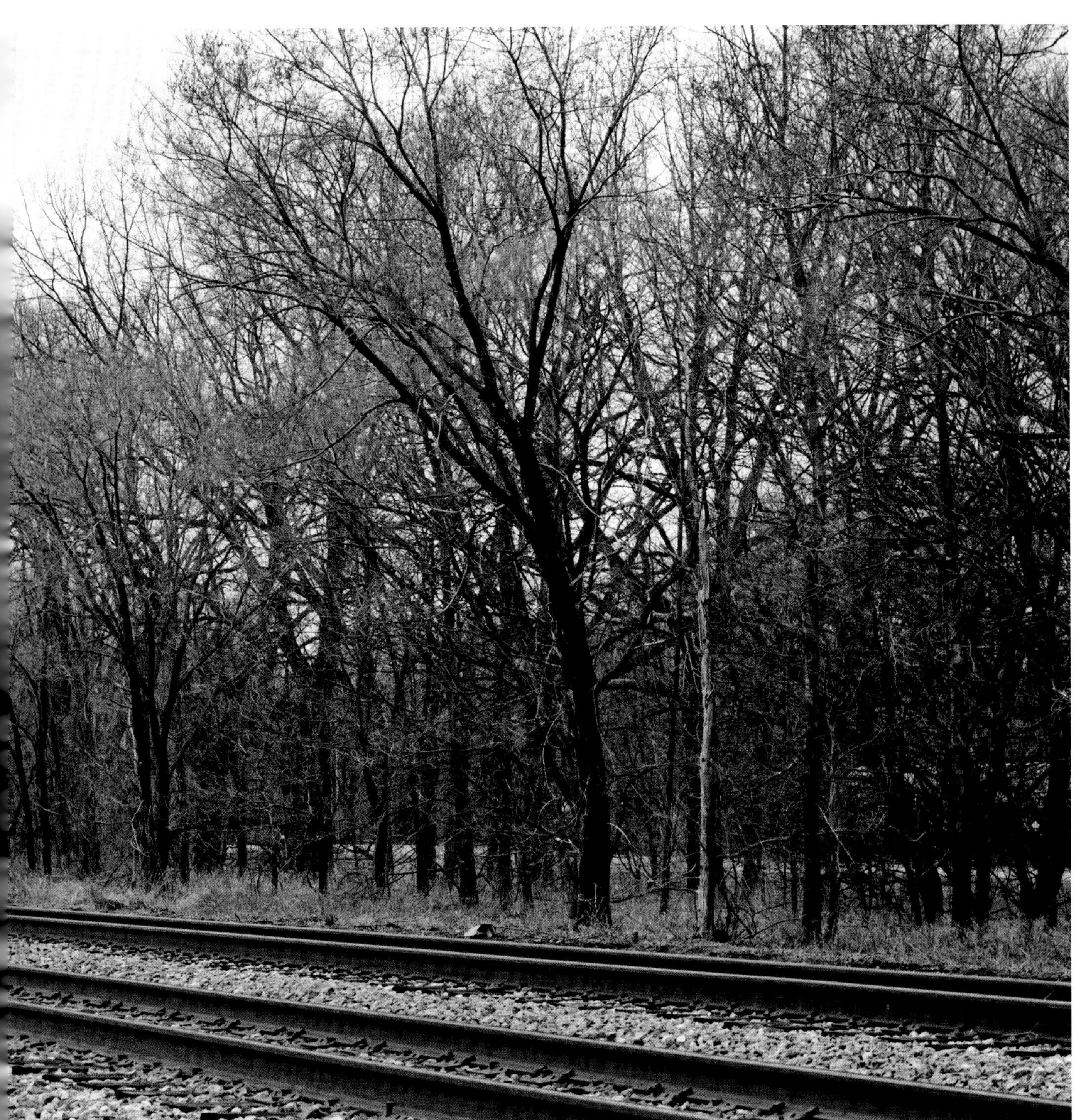

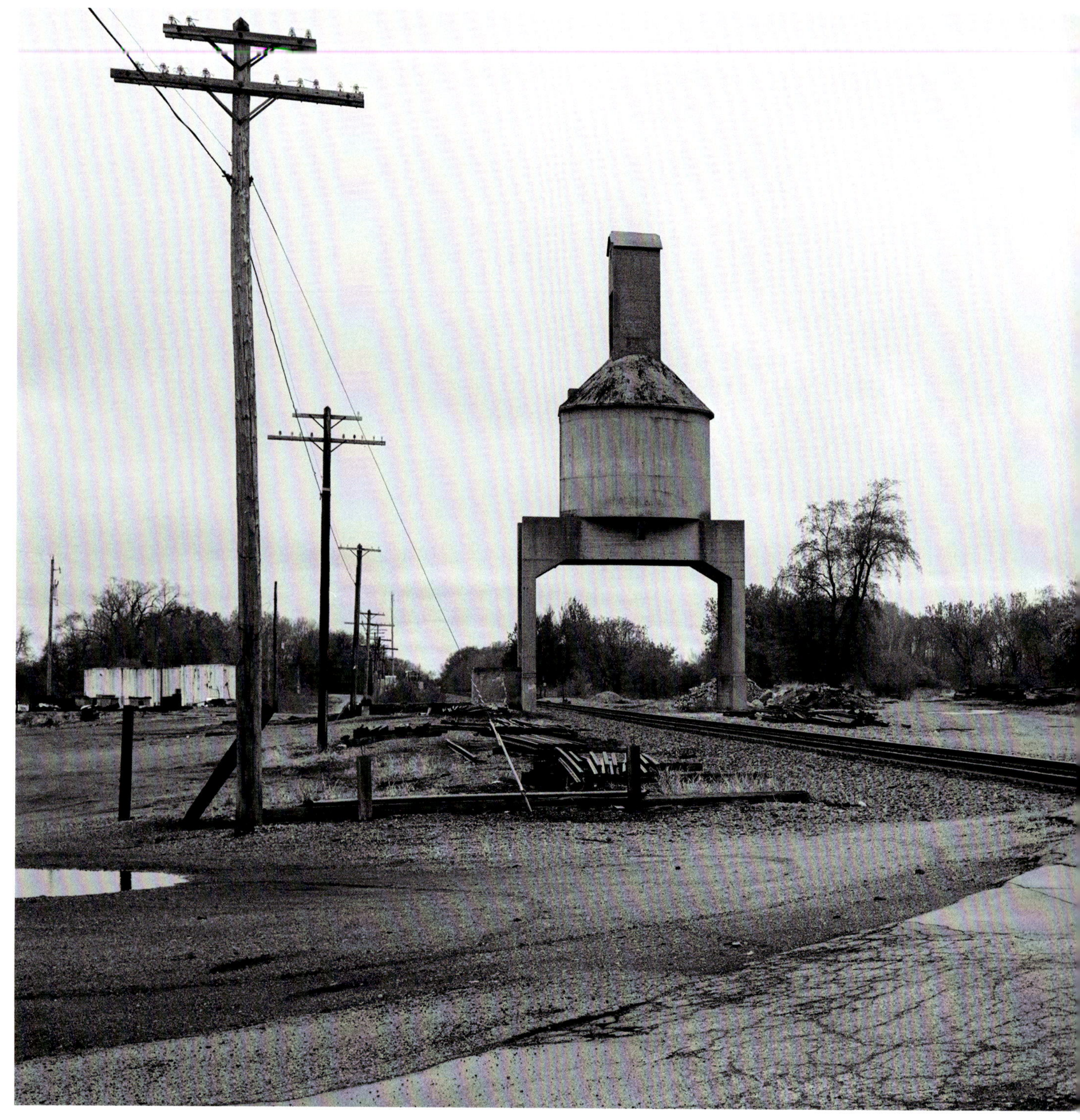

210-211 **CLYMAN JUNCTION, WISCONSIN** Chicago & North Western 43°19′25.0″N 88°42′55.8″W

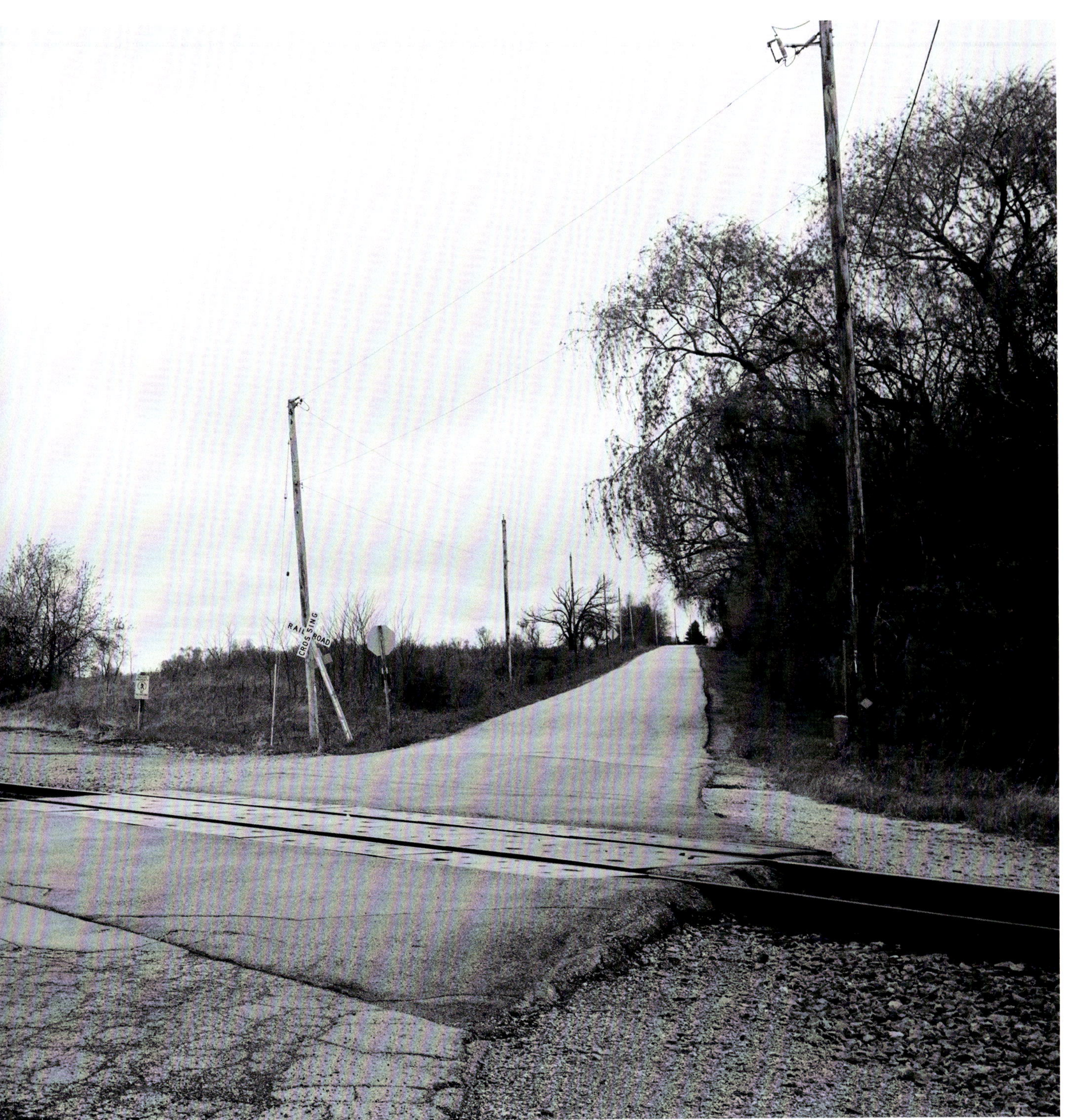
RAILROAD
CROSSING

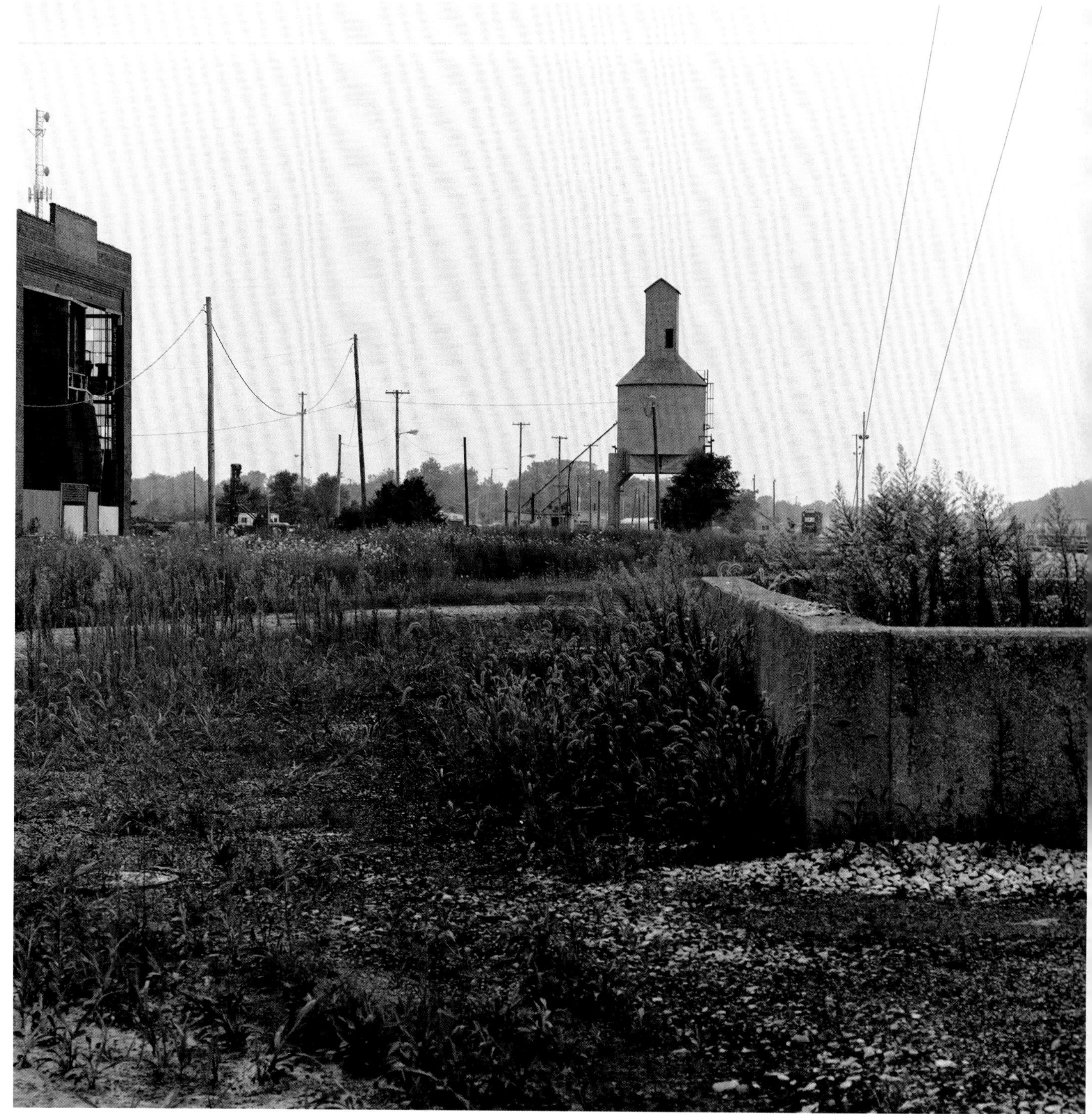

212-213 **FRANKFORT, INDIANA** New York, Chicago & St. Louis 40°16'55.7"N 86°31'30.1"W

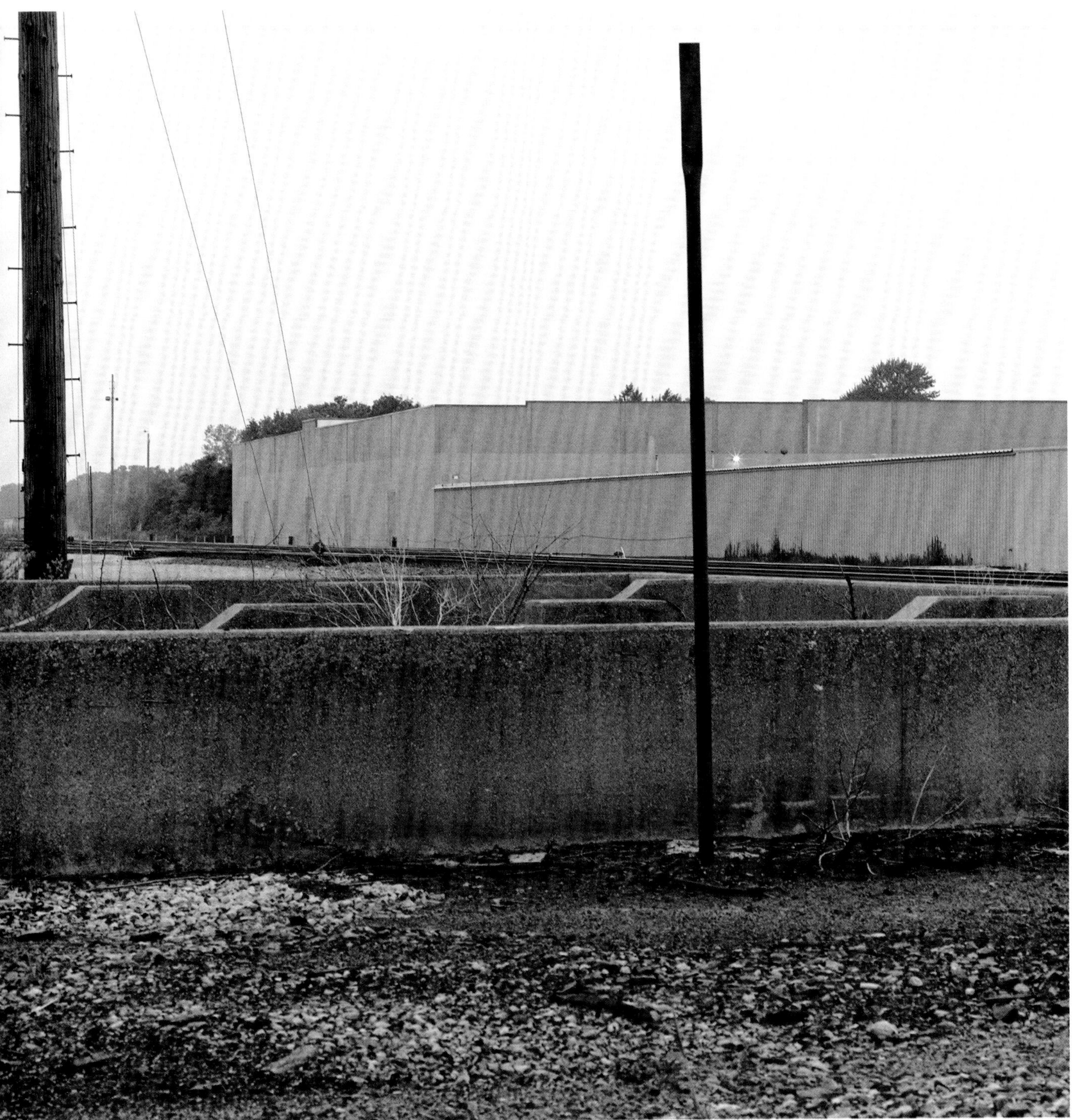

Notes from the Photographer

EVERY PHOTOGRAPHER GARNERS INFORMATION or inspiration from not only their observations of the world but from the images or research done by their predecessors. A friend's photograph of a railroad coaling tower, in a defunct Council Bluffs freight yard, started me thinking about a project documenting these monolithic structures. It was a Sunday afternoon discovery on a Wikipedia entry, listing every coaling tower still upright in North America, that cemented my decision. The list also included place names, coordinates, and satellite views of their locations via Google Earth. These two random, yet synchronistic, occurrences became the genesis for the project, undoubtedly helping chart my path forward.

As a photographer I typically work in a series on specific projects, collecting and compiling a typology of images over many years. The information gleaned from that internet search also revealed, amazingly enough, that 105 coaling towers still stood, scattered far-and-wide across the continent. It became clear early on, with so many coaling towers to potentally photograph, that a long-term project requiring much time and travel would be necessary. In fact, it took five years and 20,000 miles to complete.

Photographing the coaling towers, and the land they sat upon, represented a return to my roots. While in my mid-twenties I shot my first de-industrialized landscape—Southern Pacific's Bayshore Yard near San Francisco—documenting its transformation for over a decade. Once a vital rail hub, its closure was hastened by consolidation and contraction within the railroad industry. Inevitably, it became a site of slow decay and decline, then finally lapsed into total abandonment. So the contemporary scenes and situations I witnessed on my coaling tower tour—like those seen at Frankfort, Indiana, or Girard, Ohio, plus a host of others—were not unfamiliar territories to me. Like Bayshore Yard, these places and in-between spaces were ripe for investigation.

THE FIRST TOWER I VISITED was in Susquehanna, Pennsylvania, arching high over a former Erie mainline. Its massive size—easily one of the largest towers I encountered—inspired awe. Its scale and monumentality made one feel rather small and insignificant in its presence. Representitive of one of the last standing examples of steam-era infrastructure, its stature remained undiminished despite the fact that it, along with many of its brethren, had been out of service and retired-in-place (RIP) sixty to eighty years ago. Over the course of the project, as I shot each one of these architectural remnants from railroading's past, revisiting several of them numerous times, I admired their longevity. Who could have imagined that these now anomalous behemoths of America's heavy industrial era, many erected in the first three decades of the twentieth century, would still be standing in the third decade of the twenty-first century? Their out-sized physicality is in stark contrast to our present day world,

At our best and most fortunate we make pictures because of what stands in front of the camera, to honor what is greater and more interesting than we are.

—Robert Adams
Why People Photograph

which is increasingly based on digitization and miniaturization. But just like microchips, silicon wafers, robotics, and AI—signifiers of today's major technological advances—in their day the coaling towers were thought of similarly and helped transform an industry in transition.

I BEGAN THE PROJECT KNOWING I would utilize two approaches to the work—the first being an evidentiary / typological mode of picture-making. This methodology was inspired by Hilla and Bernd Becher, the German husband-and-wife team, who worked for fifty years assembling photographic inventories of industrial structures throughout Europe and the United States. Employing a deadpan style, they photographed in flat light, exclusively in black and white, with the intention of rendering an accurate, unadorned record of what was in front of them. While my approach aligned with their documentary and aesthetic objectives, it also differed slightly. I was farther away from my subject, included more of the surrounding area, occasionally photographed in soft or bright sunlight, and made several images at night. Gray skies and the semi-vacant, November-through-March landscapes that I favor also helped to achieve my formal goals.

My second approach to the photography (as seen in the "Topographies" section of the book) is more narrative in scope and style, siting the coaling towers within broader landscapes that contextualized their original placement and utility within the overall railroad environment. I've included several diptychs that fall into this category, offering a more panoramic perspective. These accompanying images also help situate the towers in the current timeframe, showing some rail yards still active, while others lie fallow or are entirely gone.

IN CONSIDERING THAT TIMEFRAME, I was witnessing what Walker Evans referred to as the "historical contemporary," a term suggestive of the dichtomy that often hovers between the past and the present in material culture. In this case the coaling towers reflect the past but also stand in the present. This notion then is foundational to my work, which I think of as a form of visual anthropology. The numerous photographic projects I've done over the years have often included older elements of our cultural landscape, done without nostalgic overlay, but with an acknowledgement that change is the one constant upon which we can depend. I document these changes—that can often have a multiplicity of meanings—to remind us of our origins, and the impact we have had in the making of our built environment. The coaling tower project reflects this attitiude and approach. Still in possession of a majestic presence and formal beauty, these brutalist-like structures speak to us of the arc from innovative use to industrial remnant.

Coaling Tower Specifications

Page	Location	Builder	Date	Tonnage
COVER	Gilman, IL	*	*	*
2	Aylmer, ON		1944	150
6	Augusta, MI	F-M	1923	500
9	Glenns Ferry, ID	F-M		500
15	Cushing, OK	USRA	1917	
19	Frankfort, IN	R&S	1937	700?
21	Irvington, KY	R&S		
23	Iaeger, WV	R&S	1956	400
24	Lake, Michigan		1929	250
25	Bluford, IL		1925-28	
28	Susquehanna, PA	R&S		
29	Susquehanna, PA	R&S		
31	Marion, OH			
33	Baldwin, MI	F-M	1936	300
34	New Buffalo, MI	R&S	1942	300
35	Prichard, WV	R&S	1926	2000
36	Pontiac, MI	Ogle	1929	300
37	Nelson, IL	R&W	1947	300
39	Sullivan, IN	R&W	1941	500
40	Carbondale, IL		1913?	
41	Gilman, IL			
43	Dalton, WI	F-M	1943	
44	Augusta, MI	F-M	1923	500
45	Council Bluffs, IA			
47	Lambert, MS			
48	Cushing, OK	USRA	1917	
49	Irvington, KY	R&S	1926	2000
50	Elk River Jct., WV	F-M		500-1000
51	Marceline, MO	F-M		800
52	Oakfield, ME	R&S	1933	
53	Derby, ME	R&S		
54	Central City, KY			
55	Central City, KY			
56	Lafayette, IN			
57	Ronceverte, WV	Ogle	1935	75

Page	Location	Builder	Date	Tonnage
58	Decatur, IL		1937	
59	Flomaton, AL**		1943	
60	Oneonta, NY			
61	Great Bend, KS	R&S	1928	300
62	Springfield, OH	Ogle		150-200
63	Clyman Jct., WI			
64	Frankfort, IN		1937	700?
65	N. Maine Jct., ME	R&S		200
66	Millinocket, ME	R&S		200
67	Bartlesville, OK	R&S	1926	200
69	Nelson, IL	R&W	1947	300
70	Adams, WI	R&S	1946	150
71	Adams, WI	R&S	1946	150
72	Freeport, IL	F-M		100-200
73	Monfort Jct., WI	F-M		150
74	Monfort Jct., WI	F-M		150
75	Monfort Jct., WI	F-M		150
76	DeKalb, IL	F-M	1927	500-1000
77	Lansing, MI	Ogle	1928-29	
78	Clarendon, MI	F-M	1929	150-300
79	Clarendon, MI	F-M	1929	150-300
80	Bluford, IL		1925-28	
81	Reevesville, IL	R&S	1927	
82	Chester, MA			
83	Chester, MA			
84	Montgomery, AL	R&S	1913	600
85	New Buffalo, MI	R&S	1921	150-250
86	Handley, WV	R&S	1919	500
87	Owensboro, KY	H		
88	Lebanon Jct. KY		1914	
89	Gilman, IL			
90	Dawson Springs, KY	F-M		150-300
91	Opelika, AL	F-M		150-300
92	Girard, OH	R&S	1922	1100
93	Girard, OH	R&S	1922	1100

Page	Location	Builder	Date	Tonnage
94	Akron Junction, OH	Ogle	1927	75-150
95	Michigan City, IN†	R&S	1924	250-500
97	Council Bluffs, IA			
98	Centrailia, IL			
99	Durand, MI	Ogle		300
100	Cowen, WV	R&S		300
101	Cowen, WV	R&S		300
102	Carbondale, IL		1913?	
103	Gilman, IL			
104	Hinton, WV	F-M	1930	800
105	Cane Fork, WV	Ogle	1935	50
106	Welch, WV			
107	Bluefield, WV	Ogle	1952	2000
108	Iaeger, WV	R&S	1956	400
109	Bluefield, WV	Ogle	1952	2000
111	Vicker, VA		1951	
112	New Haven, CT	R&S	1927	2400
113	Leadvale, TN	R&S	1925	1000
114	Clifton Forge, VA	F-M	1922	800
115	Macon, GA	Ogle	1927	600
116	Macon, GA	Ogle	1927	600
117	Macon, GA	Ogle	1927	600
118	Social Circle, GA**			
119	Camak, GA			
121	Camak, GA			
122	Washago, ON		1936	150
123	Aylmer, ON		1944	150
124	Hornpayne, ON			100
125	Foleyet, ON		1911-1915	100
126	Ludington, MI	F-M	c1939-1942	500
127	South River, ON			100
128	Beckley, WV	Ogle		300
129	Beckley, WV	Ogle		300
130	Lexington, KY	Ogle		300
131	Balcony Falls, VA	Ogle	1942	300

* While every effort has been taken to insure that the information presented above is accurate, we also acknowledge, despite consulting numerous sources in print and on-line, that there were sometimes conflicting construction dates, names of builders, and tonnage ratings. Where no information was available the spaces have been left intentionally blank.

† The Michigan City coaling tower, as of this writing, is slated for demolition in September of 2025.

Three of the coaling towers photographed were once co-joined: Dawson Springs, Kentucky (see page 204); Carbondale, Illinois and Gilman, Illinois (see pages 102-103).

Similarly, New Buffalo, Michigan, had two separate coaling towers in close proximity to one another but not co-joined (see pages 34 and 85).

** Denotes that the coaling tower has been demolished.

Builders designations

WMB Ballard Construction Company
F-M Fairbanks-Morse
H Howlett Construction Company
Ogle Ogle Construction Company
R&S Roberts & Schaefer
R&W Ross & White
USRA United States Railroad Administration

Page	Location	Builder	Date	Tonnage
132	Charlottesville, VA	Ogle	1942	300
133	West Hamlin, WV	Ogle	1942	300
134	Newport News, VA	R&S	1939	300
135	Newport News, VA	R&S	1939	300
137	Wilmington, DE	R&S	1919	1200
138	Toledo, OH**	R&S		
139	Red Bank, PA	Ogle		
140	Akron Jct., OH	Ogle	1927	75-150
141	DeKalb, IL	F-M	1927	500-1000
142	New Buffalo, MI	R&S	1942	300
143	Decatur, IL		1937	
144	Reevesville, IL	R&S	1927	
145	Bluford, IL		1925-28	
146	Freeport, IL	F-M		100-200
147	Detroit, MI			
148	Malone, NY			
149	Gladstone, VA		1922	300
150	Ashland, WI	Ogle	1944	150
151	Escabana, MI	Ogle		150
152	Solvay, NY	WMB		
153	Salamanca, NY**		1918	
154	Girard, OH	R&S	1922	1100
154	Gilman, IL			
154	Coxton, PA			
154	Sullivan, IN	R&W	1941	500
155	Millinocket, ME	R&S		200
155	Cowen, WV	R&S		300
155	Montgomery, AL	R&S	1913	600
155	Irvington, KY	R&S	1926	2000
156	Raymond, GA	F-M	1926	150
157	Chaska, TN			
158	Newnan, GA			
159	Paris, TN	R&S		250
161	Dawson Springs, KY	F-M		150-300
162	Union Springs, AL	F-M	1925	25 or 40

Page	Location	Builder	Date	Tonnage
163	Muskogee, OK		1913	
164	Thurmond, WV	F-M	1922	500
166	Thurmond, WV	F-M	1922	500
167	Bluefield, WV	Ogle	1952	2000
168-169	West Seneca, NY			
170-171	Girard, OH	R&S	1922	1100
172-173	Chester, MA			
174-175	Monfort Jct., WI	F-M		150
176-177	Glenns Ferry, ID	F-M		500
178-179	West Seneca, NY			
180-181	N. Maine Jct., ME	R&S		200
182-183	Handley, WV	R&S	1919	500
184	Chester, MA			
185	Aylmer, ON		1944	150
186-187	Oneonta, NY			
189	Balcony Falls, VA	Ogle	1942	300
190-191	Akron Junction, OH	Ogle	1927	75-150
192-193	Gilman, IL			
194-195	Carbondale, IL		1913?	
196-197	Lees, MD		1940s?	
198-199	Coxton, PA			
200	Irvington, KY	R&S	1926	2000
201	Owensburg, KY	H		
202	Cane Fork, WV	Ogle	1935	50
203	Cane Fork, WV	Ogle	1935	50
204	Dawson Springs, KY	F-M		150-300
205	Girard, OH	R&S	1922	1100
206	Bluefield, WV	Ogle	1952	2000
207	Cushing, OK	USRA	1917	
208-209	Michigan City, IN†	R&S	1924	250-500
210-211	Clyman Jct., WI			
212-213	Frankfort, IN	R&S	1937	700?
217	McComb, MS			
217	Lynchburg, VA			

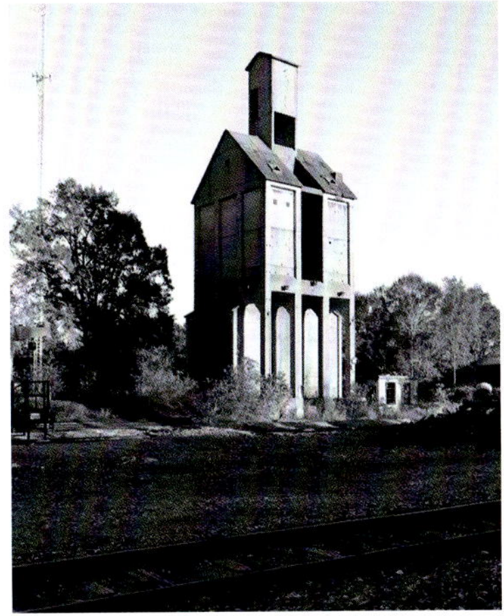

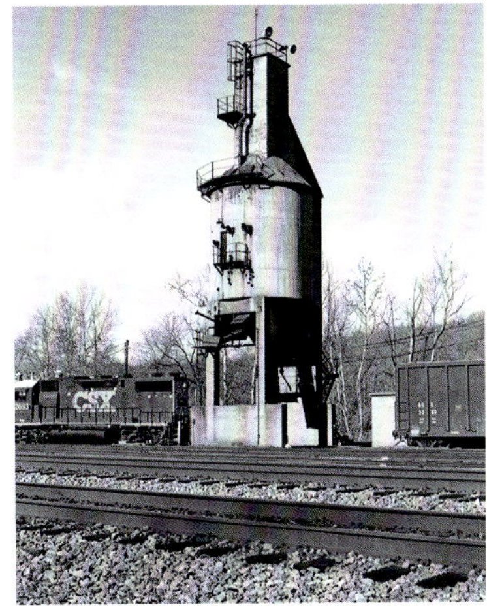

McComb, Mississippi
Lynchburg, Virginia

List of Coaling Towers

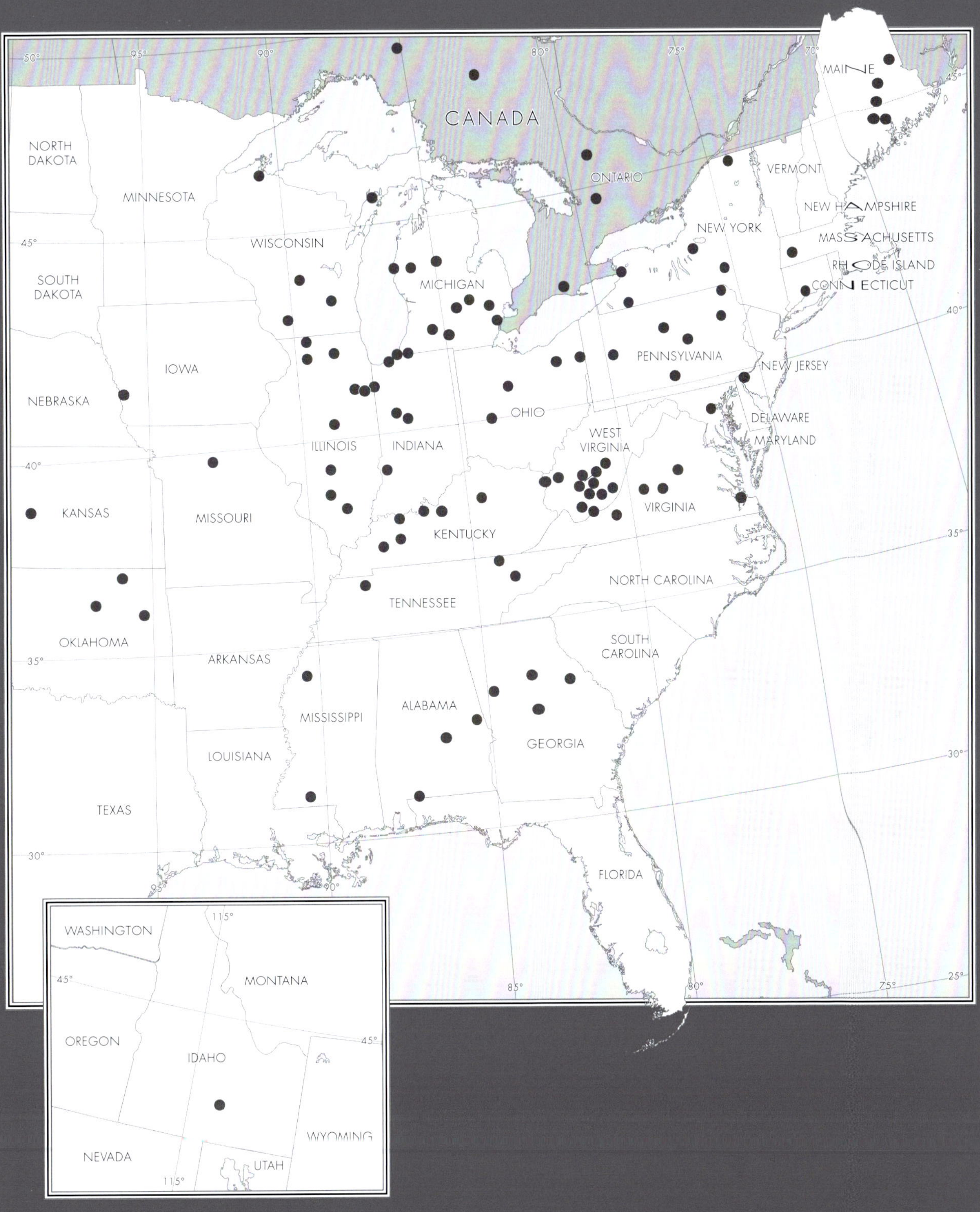

CANADA
ONTARIO
NORTH DAKOTA
MINNESOTA
WISCONSIN
SOUTH DAKOTA
MICHIGAN
IOWA
NEBRASKA
ILLINOIS
INDIANA
OHIO
PENNSYLVANIA
NEW YORK
VERMONT
NEW HAMPSHIRE
MAINE
MASSACHUSETTS
RHODE ISLAND
CONNECTICUT
NEW JERSEY
DELAWARE
MARYLAND
WEST VIRGINIA
VIRGINIA
KANSAS
MISSOURI
KENTUCKY
NORTH CAROLINA
TENNESSEE
OKLAHOMA
ARKANSAS
SOUTH CAROLINA
MISSISSIPPI
ALABAMA
GEORGIA
LOUISIANA
TEXAS
FLORIDA
WASHINGTON
MONTANA
OREGON
IDAHO
WYOMING
NEVADA
UTAH